PEOPLE PHOTOGRAPHY

Introduction by **Philip Smith**

The photographers featured in this volume are mainly concerned with the photography of people. In various degrees, all the photographers see themselves in some way connected with film. Some liken themselves to directors or producers, others refer to their particular assignments as "scenes" and models as "actors and actresses." Some aspire to eventually move on to moving pictures while others have left the world of film for still photography.

These cinematic references are not without validity. The work of the photographer is not that far removed from the cinematographer. A scene must be staged or a location found, models cast, a story told and of course action, lights, camera. Most critical in the making of these images is the role of the photographer as director. He must set the scene and prepare the characters for their role.

Knowing how to talk to a model, how to work with a model and when to press the shutter requires a personal and stylistic vision as well as psychological insight. Of the photographers profiled here, each has his own distinct approach. Rob Goldman, for example, practically hypnotizes his models into feeling and being the character required. At the other end of the spectrum Robert Whitman tends to just let his models "be."

These two methods produce very different types of work. Goldman's photographs are about feeling good and high energy living, while Whitman explores close up portraiture. Both however, appear to be out-takes from film. Goldman from an early fifties black and white love story and Whitman from a sixties French film starring Jean Paul Belmondo. Clearly, there is no one school of people photography.

Story telling is a strong priority with these photographers. But unlike film, where one has 120 minutes to develop the plot and characters, photographers have just one frame. With this one shot a photographer has to tell it all. The challenge brings to mind Haiku poetry with its content-rich brevity.

It is knowing the exact moment when the model's face and eyes and body and posture are saying everything that makes a great photographer. Ask any photographer in this book and he or she will tell you "I pretty much know when I have the shot." For some, this is an instinct they are born with and for others it is a skill that comes with time and experience. It is this moment that conveys the total story.

continued on page 16

BARD Martin started out life as the son of a well-known portrait photographer, and he has chosen to follow in his father's footsteps. He brings a Masters Degree in Film and a director's eye to his print work. This combination of backgrounds results often in work that strongly resembles the best black and white films of the forties and fifties, but he is happy to tell photographic stories about any time or place.

More often than not, Martin's work is in black and white. "I go after a mood, and more than that. Color tends to be about sensation, where black and white perhaps adds an element of the intellect. Until recently black and white seemed to be a dying art, but there's a revival of interest now. It's difficult to find people who can print to my standards, and I usually wind up making the final print."

Martin's studio is often booked for individual or group portraiture. In his photographs he wants emotion and personality to emerge. "I'm looking for a moment in time, not a pose. Or you could put it this way: I want to take pictures of people who don't look like people having their pictures taken."

Martin says that he tends to get hired "to evoke a feeling. I work best with a flexible art director who knows exactly what his or her destination is, but is happy to explore interesting back roads in order to get there."

A case in point is a recent shot done to portray "Lucky Luciano" in an ad for the Hearst Corporation. The challenge was to illustrate an incident from a Sidney Sheldon novel in which Lucky Luciano confronts a boy through the window of his car. The art director had commissioned a tight sketch of the scene, which made little allowance for the laws of optical physics, and it came to serve mainly as a starting point.

Martin rented a 1937 Cadillac which was squeezed into a small space rented in a midtown Manhattan parking garage. The most difficult aspect of the shot was lighting the Lucky Luciano actor and the boy, as well as the boy's reflection in the car window. Martin front-lit the boy with a point source electronic flash to simulate the effect of direct sunlight. A roll of white seamless paper strategically placed in back of the boy served both to evoke a clear sky and to bounce wide reflections into the shiny black surfaces of the car. The mask-like effect around the boy's eyes in the reflection was a happy accident of light, which both photographer and art director immediately recognized would add a final element of drama to the photograph.

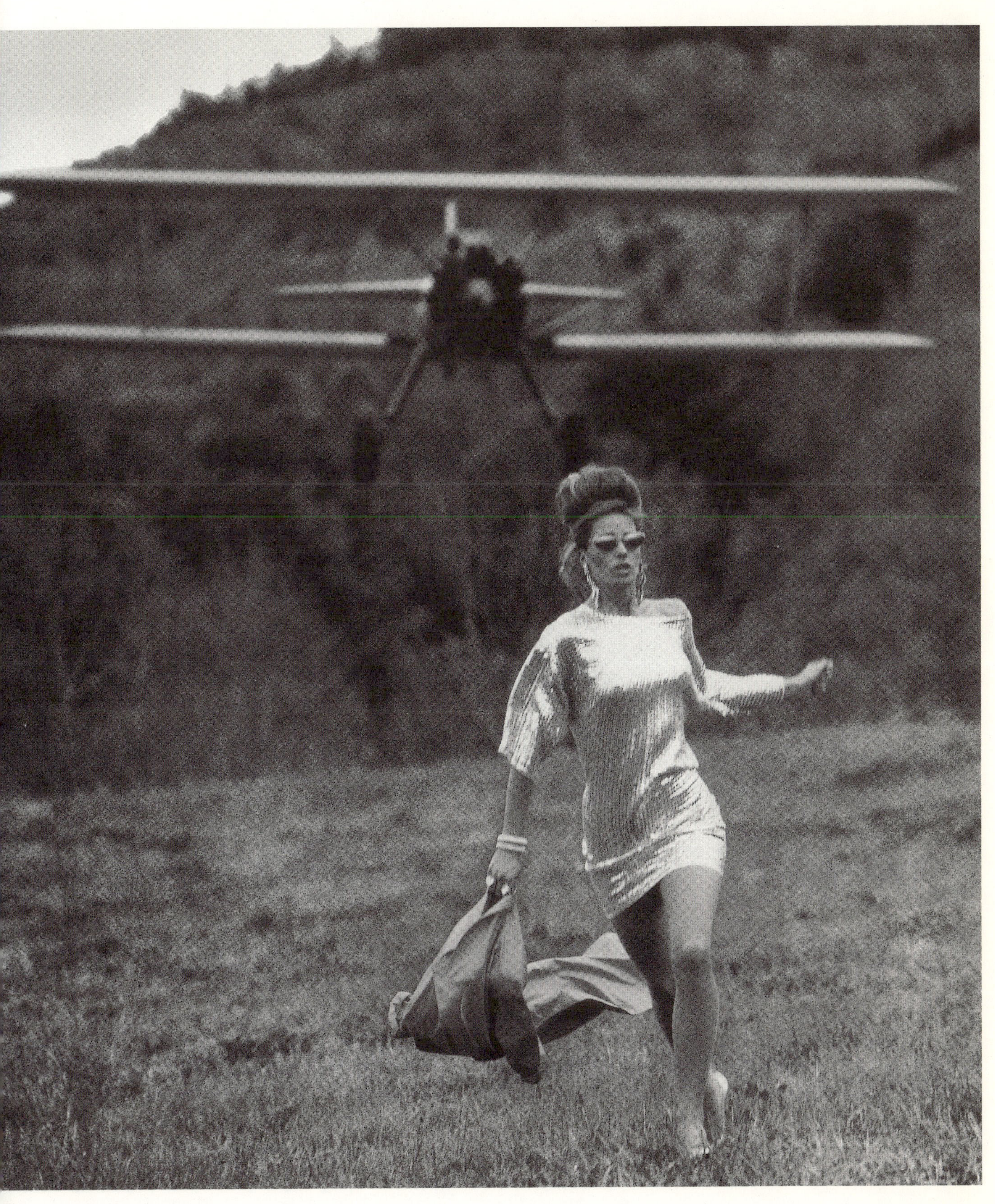

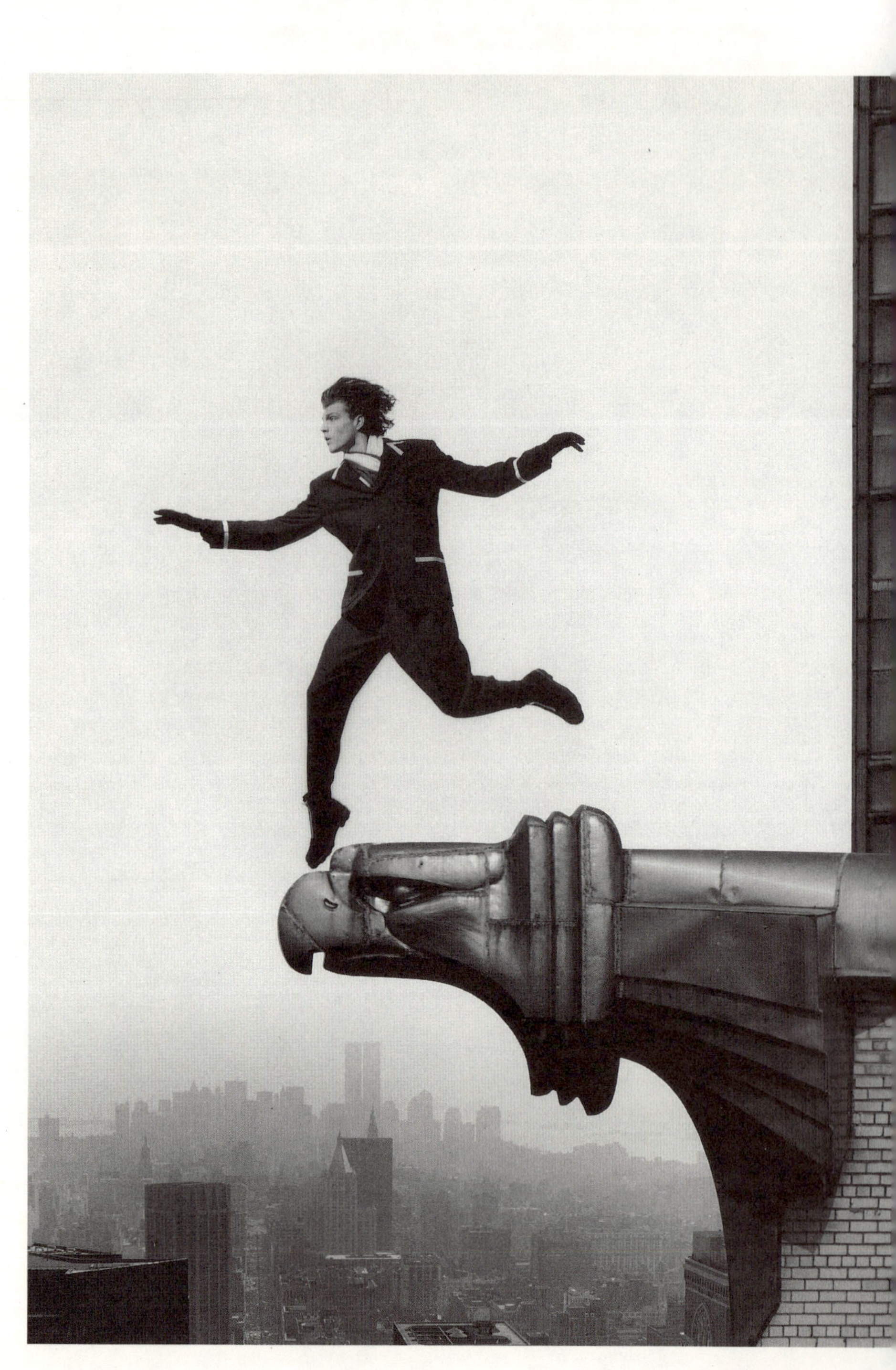

MARTIN

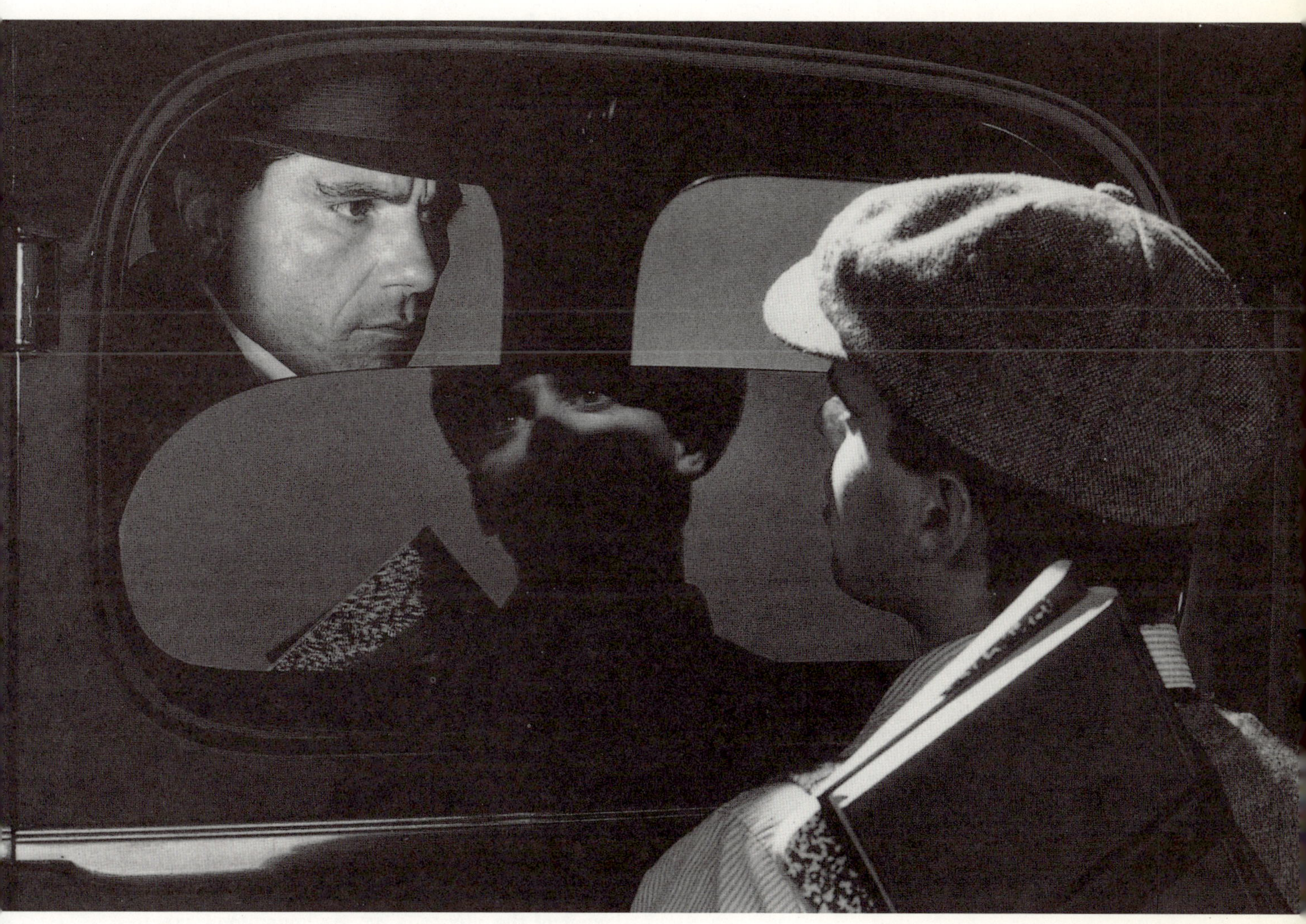

Whether it is a collection of stroboscopic stills strung together to create a narrative or a single powerful image of a girl running away from a plane, a strong sense of cinema pervades Lee Page's work. Page produces a sizeable amount of work that includes fashion and advertising images for clients such as American Express, Canon and Atlantic Records.

As is industry practice, clients come to Page with open-ended problems and tight solutions to be shot. Recently, an art director called from Grey Advertising on behalf of their client Canon. They had just released a new auto-focus camera and needed a visually arresting campaign to announce its introduction.

What was unusual about the assignment was the creative director asked Page to make a list of photographs he had always wanted to shoot. After reviewing Page's initial list, the creative director asked him to clarify and enhance several of the ideas. Page's first choice went something like "girl running toward camera/airplane chasing her/a suspenseful James Bond feeling." The concept brings to mind classic Hitchcock.

The client was after a highly dramatic image that could only be captured with an auto-focus camera. They liked the plane concept immediately. Producing it, however, was not unlike filming a small feature with stylists, hair & makeup, assistants, agency people, model, camera crew and a pilot.

Finding a model to run away from a plane in hot pursuit was not easy. "A lot of models didn't want the job. The woman who accepted really got into it. She said that it sure beats standing around the studio in front of a roll of seamless." Next, Page called around looking for a pilot with an old plane who wanted to make some extra money. He found one in Vermont.

Four days before the shoot, Page headed up to Vermont for pre-production. "I don't like last minute situations. I like to have as much pre-production with the client as possible." The pilot was shown a layout of the proposed ad. He understood exactly how and when to fly during the shooting. "I gave the model directions and let her act it out. She really took the theme and ran with it."

Though the forecast for the weekend was sunny, the weather turned just as the shoot began. "We worked around the threatening weather as best as possible." The ad was shot in 35mm with Kodak Ektachrome and required between 20 and 25 takes.

LEE PAGE

James Porto combines multiple photographs to create one perfect image that stretches our expectations of reality. "What I do is extremely technical, yet I want it to look very straight forward—as if it were a regular photograph." There is always the feeling of the unreal about James Porto's work.

JAMES PORTO

"Clients come to me for radical imagery. I don't want to produce a photograph that I've seen a million times before." His recent assignments include work for AT&T, Sony, Seagram's and Charivari. "Rarely do I shoot straight photography. The majority of my work requires the combination of many photographs to create the effect that I'm after. I shoot every element I can for the client's photograph and then add from my file whatever is necessary."

In his studio Porto keeps on file thousands of photographs categorized under headings such as landscape, people, cities etc. Without the aid of computer or microfilm, Porto mentally remembers them. "When a client comes with a problem I can recall what's in my files and help make creative decisions. I like to get in on the conceptual stage early on because the art director does not always know what I'm capable of."

One of Porto's recent photographs that had the New York photography community talking was his "on the edge" series for the Charivari clothing stores. Debate raged on for weeks whether it was an actual photograph, computer generated or a composite. The photograph illustrated here is from that campaign. It started when art director Rocco Campanelli called in Porto's book. Based on the work he saw he gave Porto a sketch that featured a man perched on the edge of the Chrysler Building's art deco eagle. Porto was inspired by working with Campanelli and called him "a great art director."

To create the image, Porto shot a number of locations in 35mm to create a believable but not realistic setting. First, he shot a telephoto of the Eagle and the metal edge of the building. Next, from the Pan Am Building with a wide angle he photographed downtown New York. Back at the studio the model was posed against white seamless and shot in 2 1/4 format. All of these images were then pin registered to create a multiple, sepia-toned print.

One of the technical problems the print posed was getting the various perspectives to match up. "I like the simplicity of the telephoto foreground combined with the wide angle background. You would never see any city-scape this way, but the picture makes it look possible. This particular image was very satisfying to create."

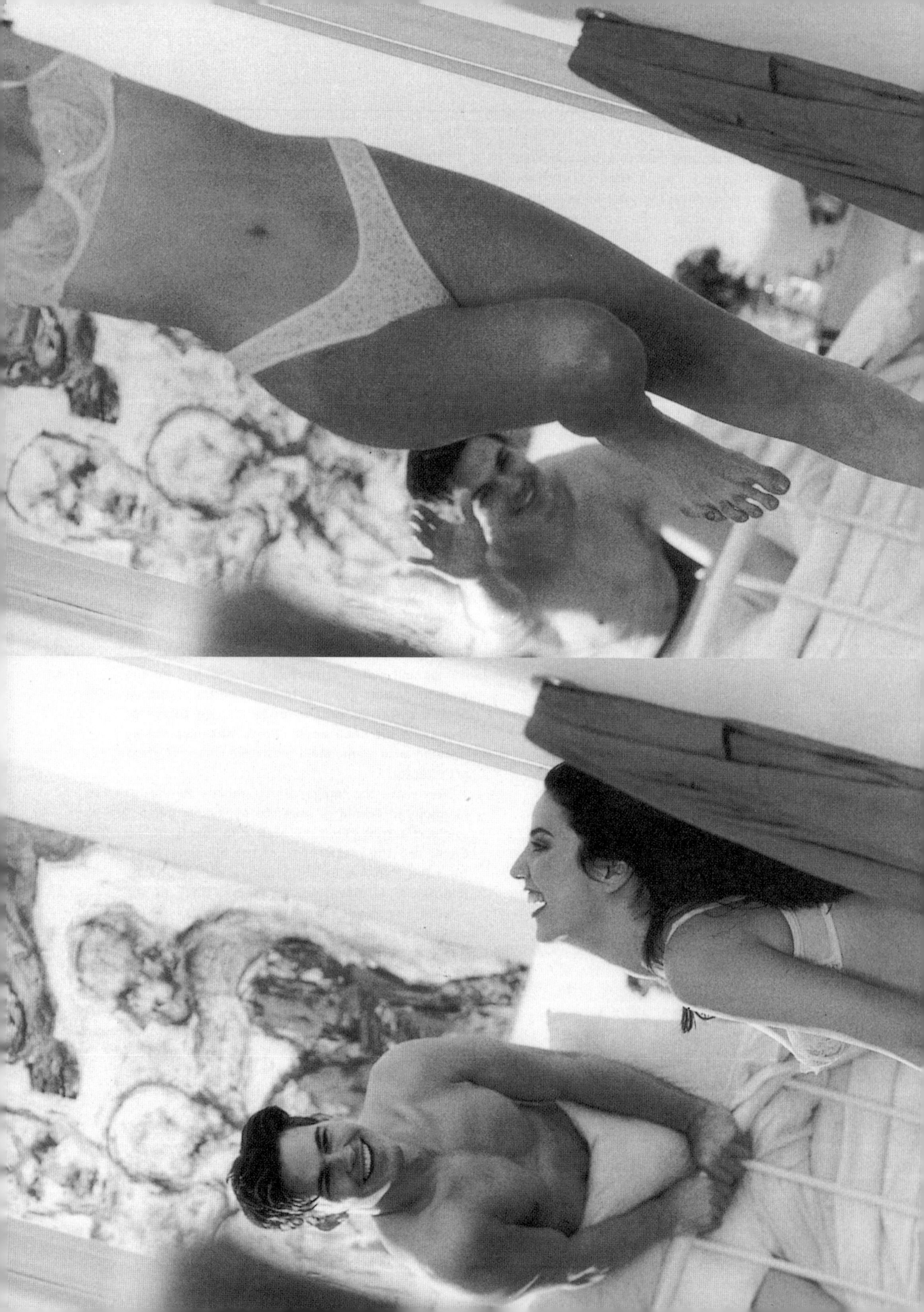

Looking at Rob Goldman's new photographs is like listening to the music of jazz trumpeter Chet Baker. Sweet, innocent, sexy and fun are the words and moods that come to mind. The photography is seemingly from another time when life and love were simple. Goldman is at his best when shooting couples. So many of his photographs are about being in love.

Goldman began shooting couples when a rep noticed that these were the strongest photographs in his book. "I had a knack for shooting couples, and the market needed it. I see life as a movie and create it through my photography. I live my fantasies through my work." Goldman sees himself as both a producer and director. "Sometimes I find the producing aspect of a shoot draining, so I hire someone else to deal with getting everything organized."

His directorial skills seem to bring out the best in his models. "A lot of my models are also actors and actresses, which helps a great deal. I can usually look at someone's book and know whether or not it's going to work; not just in terms of their looks, but in how they will react emotionally during the shoot. I never say 'act natural', which I think is a contradiction. Sometimes I tell them that they have been in this situation before, and they know what it feels like. Once they feel the scene, they become the characters, and their faces and bodies take over. I need soul in my models, not just a beautiful face."

For his page in New York Gold, Goldman wanted to do something with lingerie. "I wanted to shoot lingerie not from the point of view of being sexy or romantic, but about being fun." As with all his couples, Goldman has to get the models to "become friends" in order for the shoot to work. Otherwise the photograph "looks fake or acted."

"The shot was a real situation. They were in bed wrestling around. I had to get her full of energy, so that she would run out the door wanting him to chase her. I got them to the point where it was totally spontaneous." Like most of his photographs, Goldman shot with the camera tilted at a diagonal. "I like diagonal lines. Everday things in life are monotonously vertical. Diagonals give the photograph real dynamics."

The "scene" took about three hours and was shot in 35mm with Tri-X. The color print was created from a black and white negative. "This gives a real warmth to the photograph; like life at sunset."

ROB GOLDMAN

TOM ARMA

Tom Arma loves his kids. "People find kids difficult, I find them refreshing." Most of his work is photographing children for firms such as Proctor & Gamble, Tylenol, Motts, Crest and Johnson & Johnson. His editorial work appears in Time, Money and Victoria magazines.

Several years ago Ladies Home Journal asked Arma to do a special Christmas cover using children. This began an annual tradition, and the covers in his portfolio always received a strong response. From that initial assignment, Arma found his particular niche in the market.

A lot of photographers say no when asked to photograph kids for clients. "I have a lot of patience and never show my displeasure with the models. You get a lot from kids. They're not some jaded model who has smiled a million times before. Kids are super real when they smile. They are children first and models second. The kids I work with think they're just here to have fun. They don't realize they are working."

Arma has his rep and his assistant always on the lookout for great kids. "I have a house on Long Island, and I'm always going up to mothers to talk about their kids." For most of his shoots, Arma holds an open casting. He always produces a spec sheet for the parents as to the type of kid he's looking for and what the shoot is about.

Tylenol asked Arma to produce a calendar of kids based on movie stills from the thirties and forties. The celebrities to be featured included Humphrey Bogart, Charlie Chaplin and Carmen Miranda. For the Miranda shot, there was an open casting for a three-year-old Hispanic girl. One mother, brought her little girl to the casting all dressed up as Carmen Miranda in a special costume she had created.

After a Polaroid test, she was approved by the client. "This was her first shoot, and she was just delightful. She giggled the whole time. It is very hard to get a three year old to stay in that position. She was very comfortable in her costume." Arma lit a palm tree to cast some background shadows, while using bare bulb strobes to create strong highlights on the face. The lighting was intended to recreate the look of a thirties photograph. The piece was shot 2 1/4 in black and white and printed on color paper to produce a sepia-toned appearance.

The calendar was spotted by a European company that has since commissioned Arma to produce posters of kids as celebrities. The list includes Marilyn Monroe and James Dean. Arma is looking forward to the project. "After all," he says, "the kids trust me."

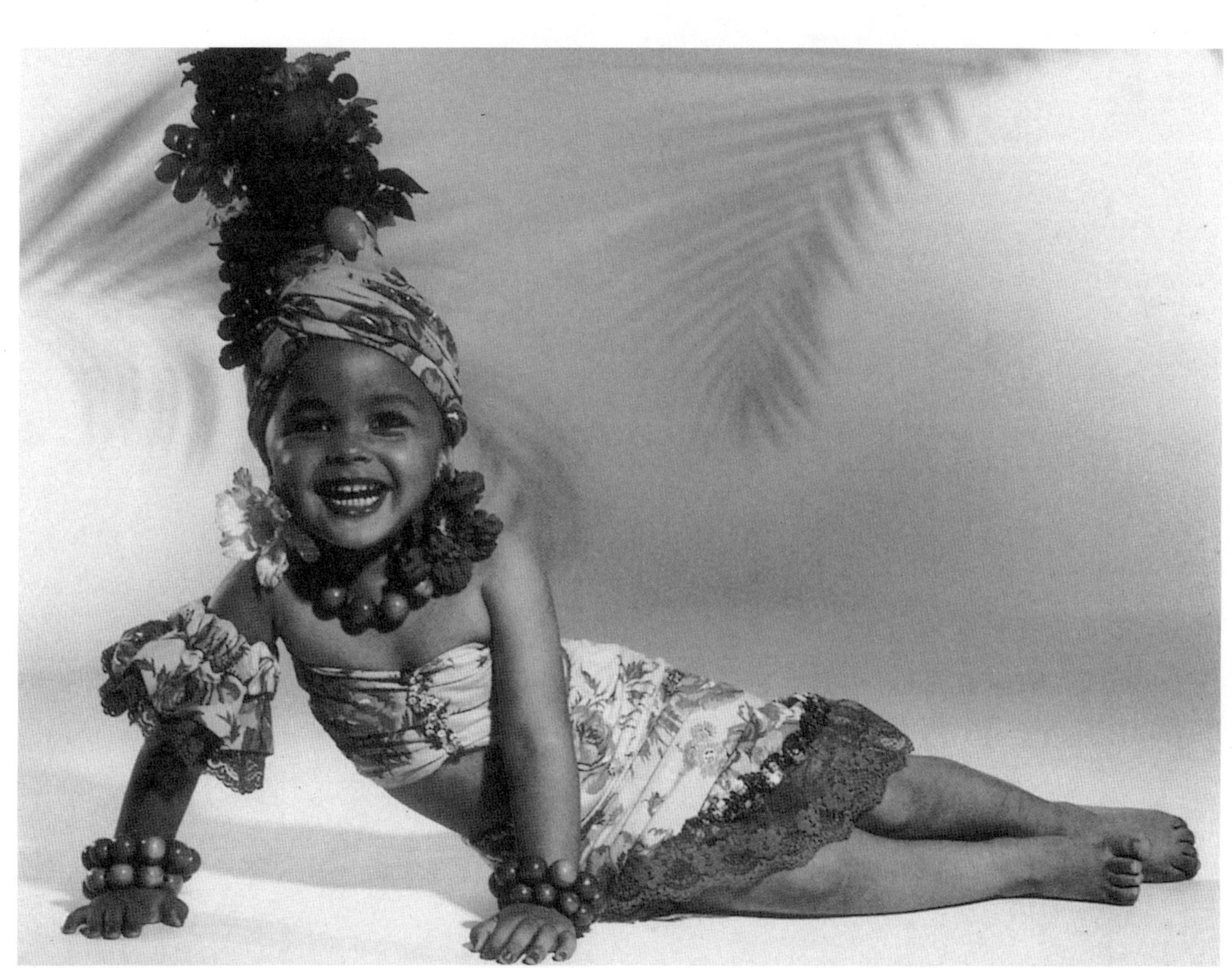

ROBERT WHITMAN

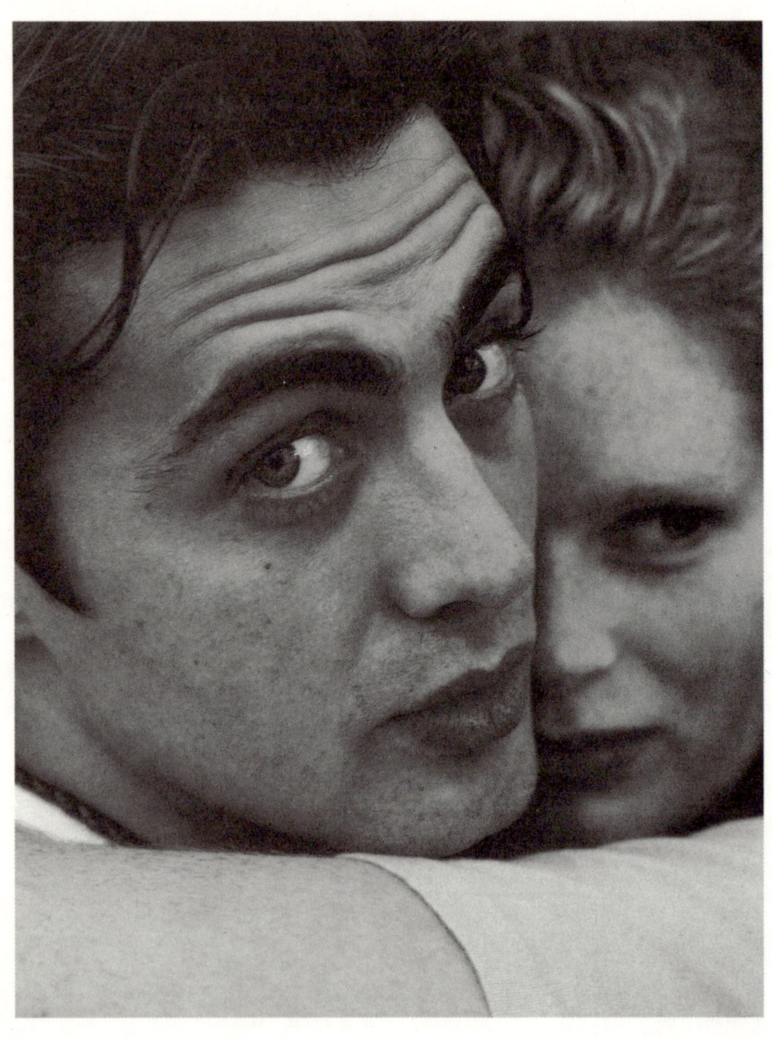

Three years ago Robert Whitman moved to New York from Minneapolis.

He had developed a portfolio of work that included some interesting tightly-cropped imagery. As he made the rounds, his close-ups received the strongest response. "My work began to naturally evolve in this direction. I was pleased, because they were the photographs that were the most satisfying to produce."

For Whitman, New York Gold has been a tremendous source of clients. "I get a lot of calls for my book based on my ads." Advertising accounts for most of his work. Recent clients include a catalog for La Costa Spa and Panasonic. His strongest accounts are the various fashion lifestyle catalogs. "Clients come to me for the humanness of my photographs. They are very real."

His favorite clients are those that just give him a green light to shoot with a loose concept. "A lot of time with advertising, the client has been presold on the concept, and you have to work with those parameters. But you can always go beyond the basic idea and enhance it, bring it to another level. In most of my jobs, I can do what I need to do to produce good pictures."

Whether it is people or product he's shooting, Whitman gets in real close to the subject. "My work is very aggressive, graphic and tight. Whether I'm shooting a woman's watch or her face, I'm right in there." Other photographers have wondered whether there is a lot of darkroom cropping in Whitman's pictures. "I just shoot what I see, I don't crop the print."

Most of Whitman's work is done on location. For a Dayton Hudson department store catalog, he worked with a young couple in a park in New York to create a lifestyle mood shot. "I moved in real tight and they looked so great together. What I liked was him against her, the black hair against the red. I shot the piece with a 135 Nikon lens in 35mm."

Whitman has somewhat of a natural approach when it comes to working with models. "I try not to direct. The best shots are when the models are not paying attention. It's when they relax that you get the perfect shot. I want to catch them in the things they are doing. If I see something that I like, I'll make a suggestion to try and fine tune the shot. But otherwise I just let them do what they're doing."

Based in London, Desmond Burdon has become well known for his evocative black-and-white photographs. Clients like Marlboro, BBC, Eastman Kodak and Johnson & Johnson hire Burdon for his work that often recalls another era. Recently, Burdon has begun marketing his talent in the United States through his rep Susan Miller and with pages in New York Gold.

"I've always gotten clients by showing my best work in my promotional ads and in my portfolio. I see no problem shooting in England for an American client or in America for an English client. People in New York think nothing of hiring a photographer from the West Coast for a shoot. England is just as close to New York as California."

Clients find that Burdon is a unique problem solver. Burdon has an unusual range of back-up services that includes expert animal handlers, set builders, model makers and background painters. A great deal of this talent comes from the British cinema. In addition, Burdon has a special gift for black and white film. "For me color is just the bare facts, but black-and-white is a very dramatic medium with great character and atmosphere. You can read so much more into it."

His campaign for British Coal is a good example of the technique and details that go into one of Burdon's photographs. The agency wanted a 1930's aristocratic living room at Christmas time with a warm fire that would highlight the client's new smokeless coal product. "Basically, I was asked to bring this concept to life."

As with most of his work, Burdon had a complete set built in his studio. "I knew that if we had to find a location, it would cost about the same amount of money. But more importantly, a set gives me total control. I don't have to leave a location by a certain time. I also have more time to light the shot." Over a two-day period, his stylist organized all the props for the shoot.

"People think I'm a little backwards because I use tungsten lighting. But tungsten is the lighting used in the cinema from the thirties. For me lighting is the real fun of photography. I know the lighting is correct when everything looks natural and sparkling. I think lighting tells a large part of the story in the photograph."

Burdon's actual photographic technique is a somewhat elaborate process. The shot is first done in 4x5 black-and-white sheet film. A black-and-white print is made. Burdon then carefully lights the print with colored filters and rephotographs it onto 11x14 color film. This gives the final photograph a tinted quality. The result is pure enchantment.

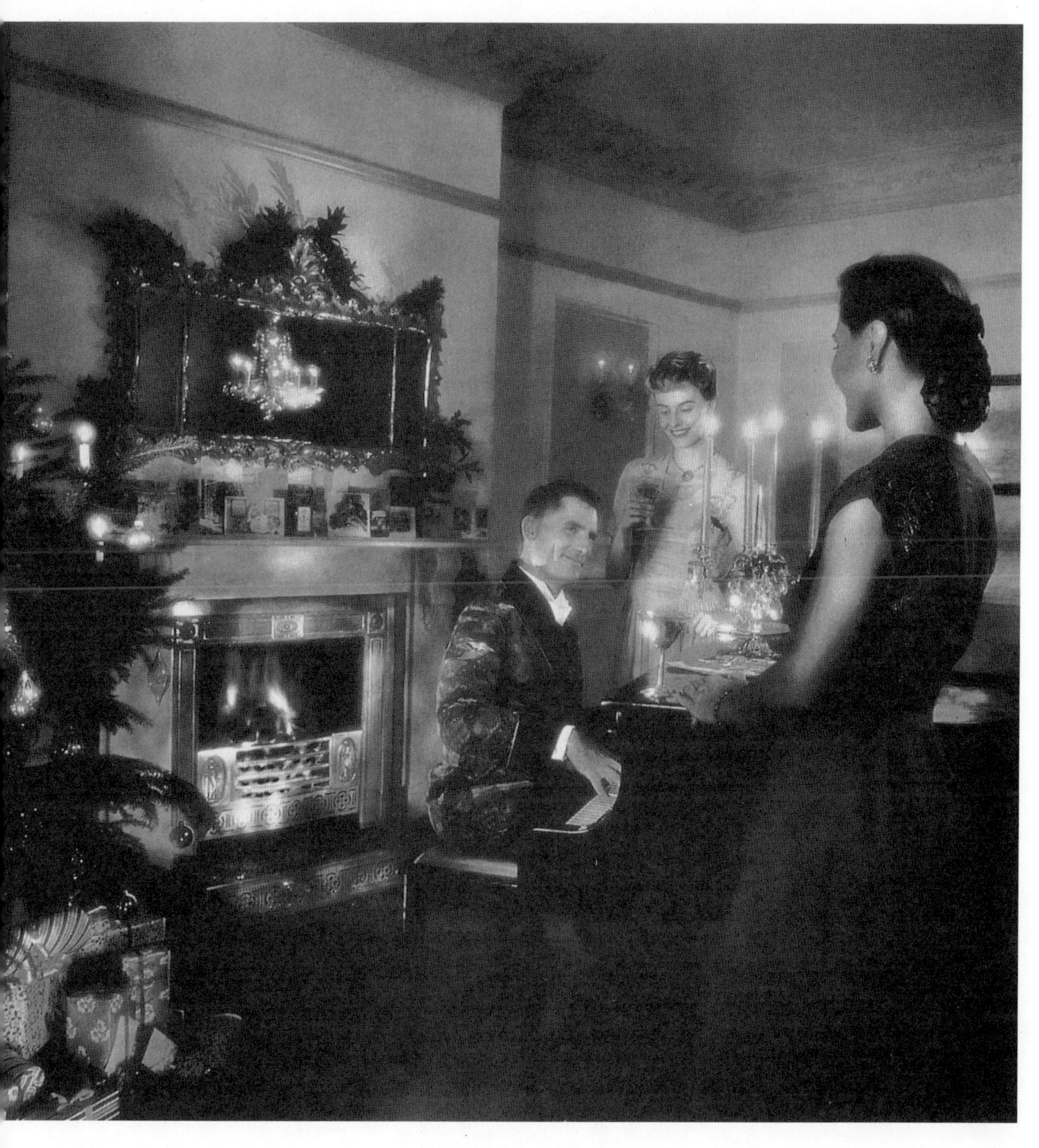

DESMOND BURDON

For the photograph to really work it must be psychologically evocative. In whatever way he accomplished it, this must be one of the photographer's most critical skills. To convey and convince the model that she is someone else and that something is happening. Whether it is spring and romance in the air, sheer beauty or provacative mystery, the model has to convince you that she is experiencing that emotion.

An important direction that has been building for the past several years is the increasing use of black and white. For those working in black and white, the medium offers strong ties to the great films of the thirties. Many photographers disavow contemporary lighting techniques, such as strobe, and use tungsten exclusively. Photographer Desmond Burdon notes that "people think I'm a little backwards, because I use tungsten lighting. But tungsten was the lighting used in the cinema of the thirties."

Those working in this medium find it less factual than color and more thoughtful. Photographer Bard Martin feels that his work in black and white has a strong appeal to the intellect. Interestingly, many of the photographers transcend the limitation of pure black and white work. Using various techniques they add a bit of coloration to the image that makes it appear from another time.

Desmond Burdon lights his black and white prints with colored filters and rephotographs them onto color film.The result is something apparently, but not quite, from the thirties. Rob Goldman shoots in black and white and prints on color paper. This process imparts a warm, hazy sensation to his photographs. After Jim Porto finishes his darkroom wizardry, his photographs are often sepia toned. All of these techniques are meant to enhance the image and remove it from the immediacy of everyday life.

Color, of course, has instantaneous reference to the film of today. You can easily envision any number of the images reproduced here as a clip pulled from the latest release. Film and photography continuously inspire and cross reference each other. The lifestyle photograph of today becomes tomorrow's "Pretty Woman."

We have chosen seven photographers to highlight some of the philosophical and practical techniques in Conceptual People Photography. Whether it is Lee Page recreating classic Hitchcock or James Porto producing special effects with composite images, each photographer defines photography in a slightly unique way. They openly discuss their thoughts on models, on the business and how they pursue their particular style. For them, the human body is forever fascinating.

While each photograph here carries the unique stamp of its creator, it also serves as a document of its time. Whether in color or black and white, the images collected here could only be made in our era. Every detail is revealing—the faces, the clothing, the shape of the bodies, the moods, the lighting. Unquestionably, these are photographs of lifestyles today.

Just as one refers to photo yearbooks from another decade, imagine looking at these photographs 50 years from now. As a time capsule, they will unquestionably appear to be circa 1990. Certainly there will be references to other eras like the thirties or the fifites. But these photographs will never lose the imprint of their time code that states made in 1990.

In short, the photographs speak of the conflicts and the invention that mark our time. Romantic introspection fused with raw physicality, traditional values poised along with aggressive experimentation, a glance at the future and a long sentimental gaze to the past. Young and old, present and past. Most of all these images speak of being alive at the end of the great American century.

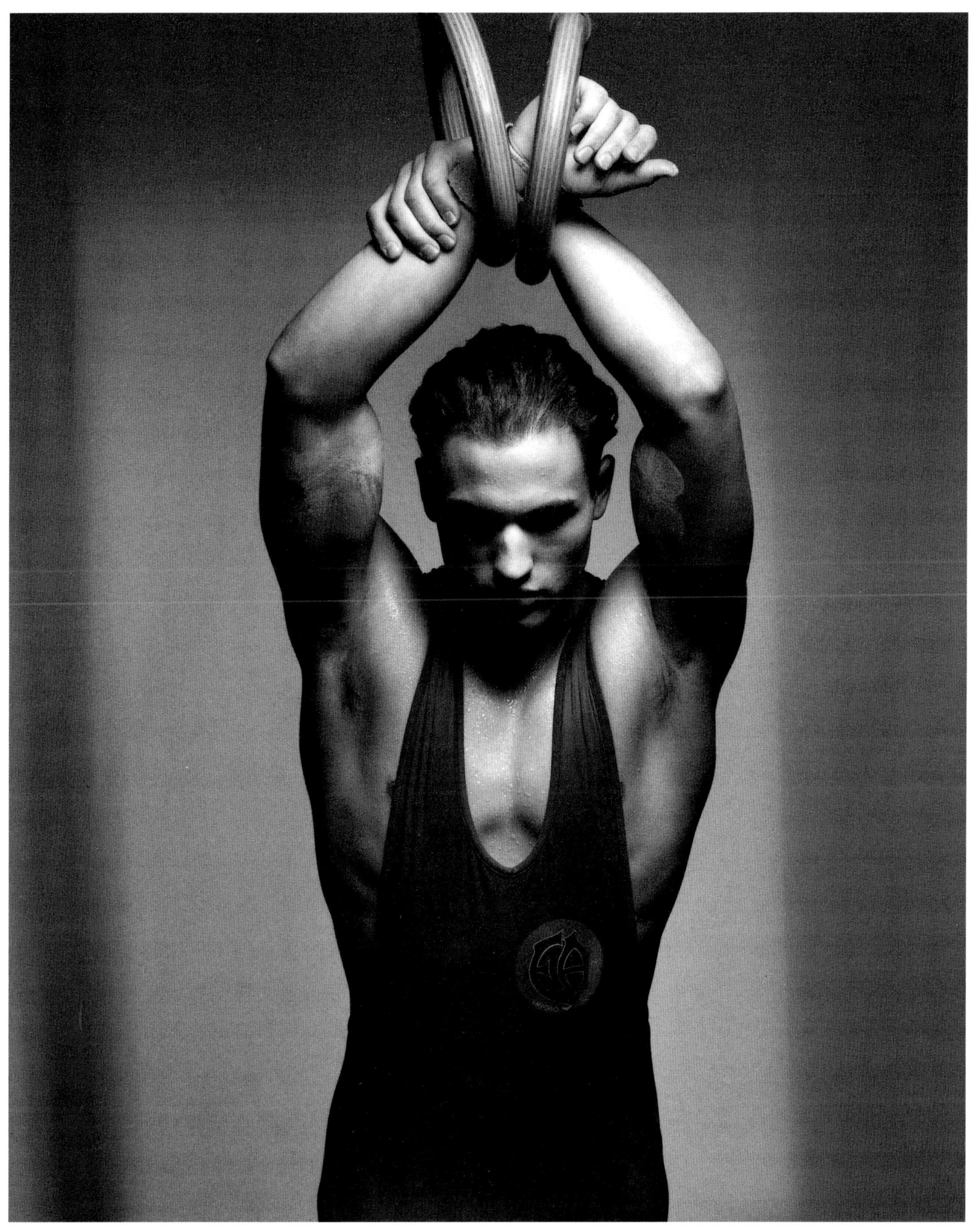

VOLKMANN

REPRESENTED BY: LIZ-LI 212-889-7067

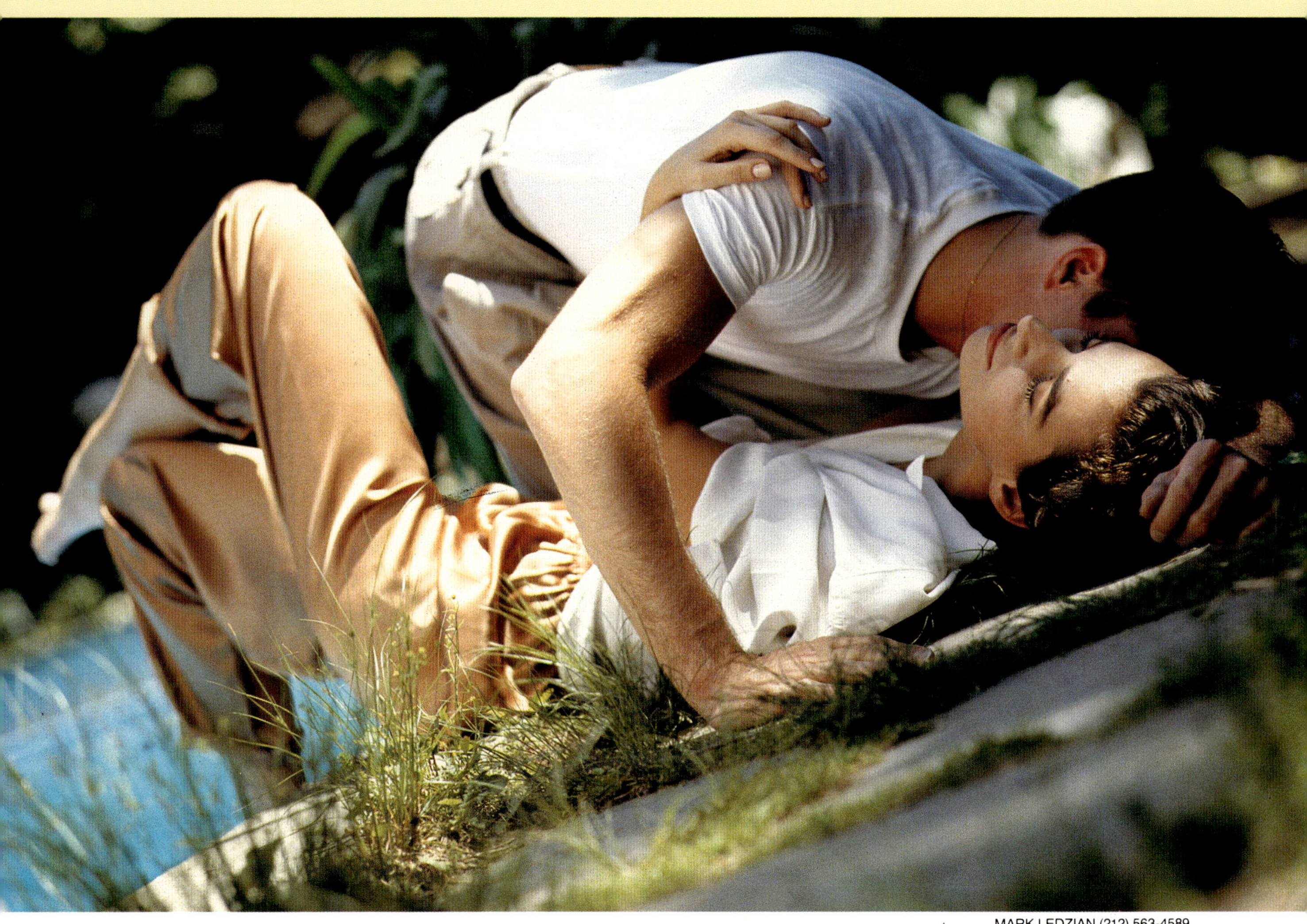

MARK LEDZIAN (212) 563-4589

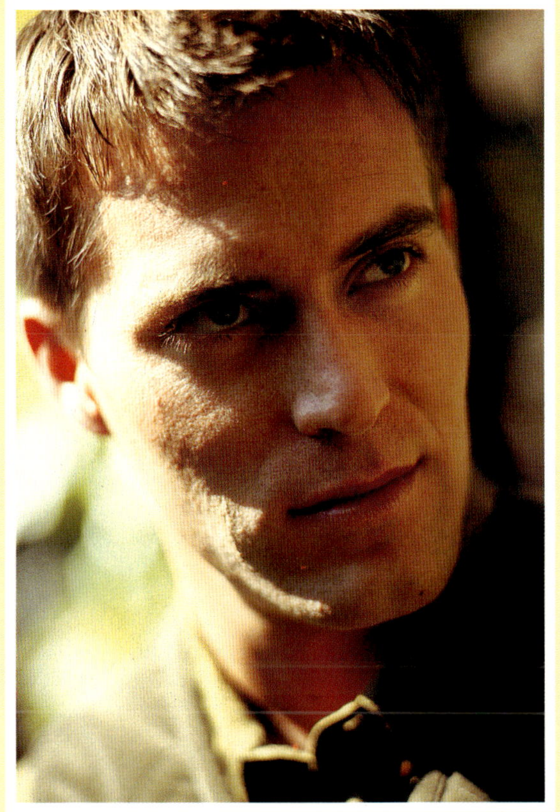

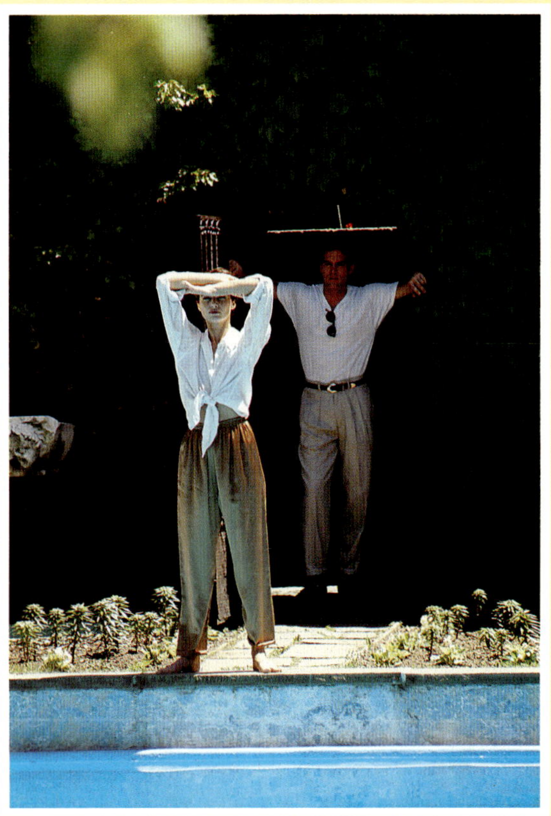

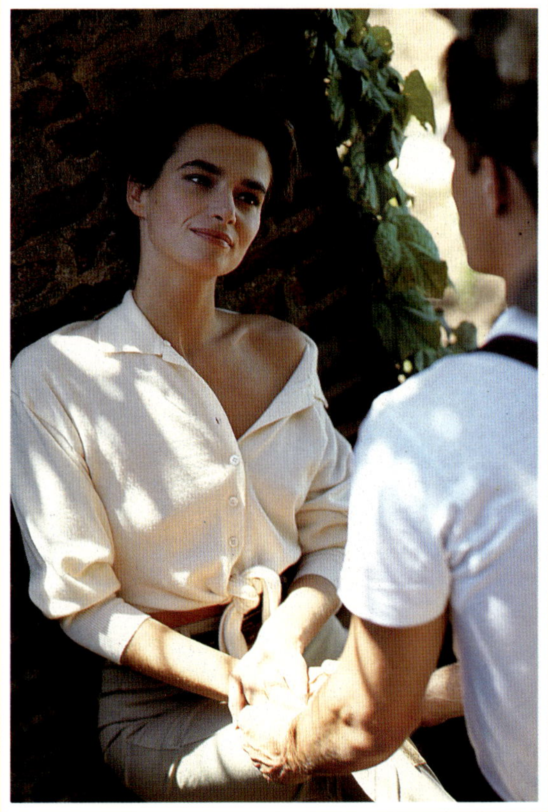

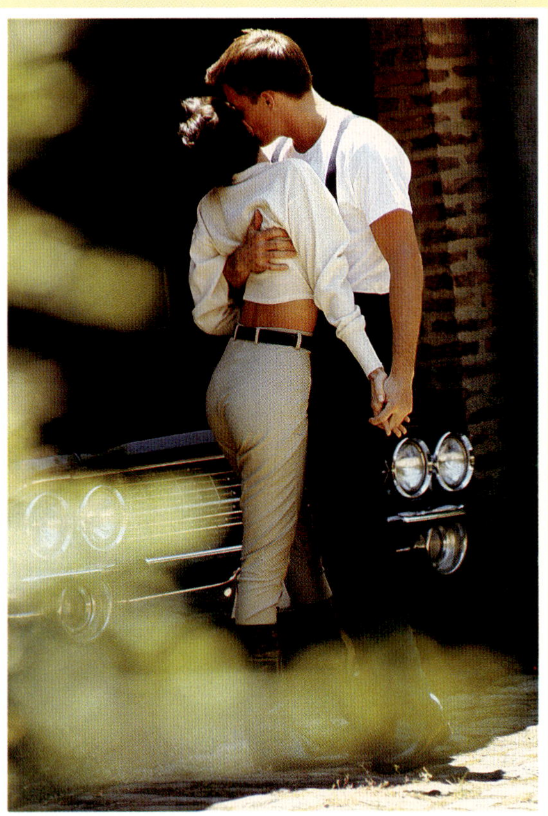

Mark Ledzian Photography

245 West 29th Street, New York, N.Y. 10001 (212) 563-4589; Represented By Katie Daley (212) 465-2420

Film/Print

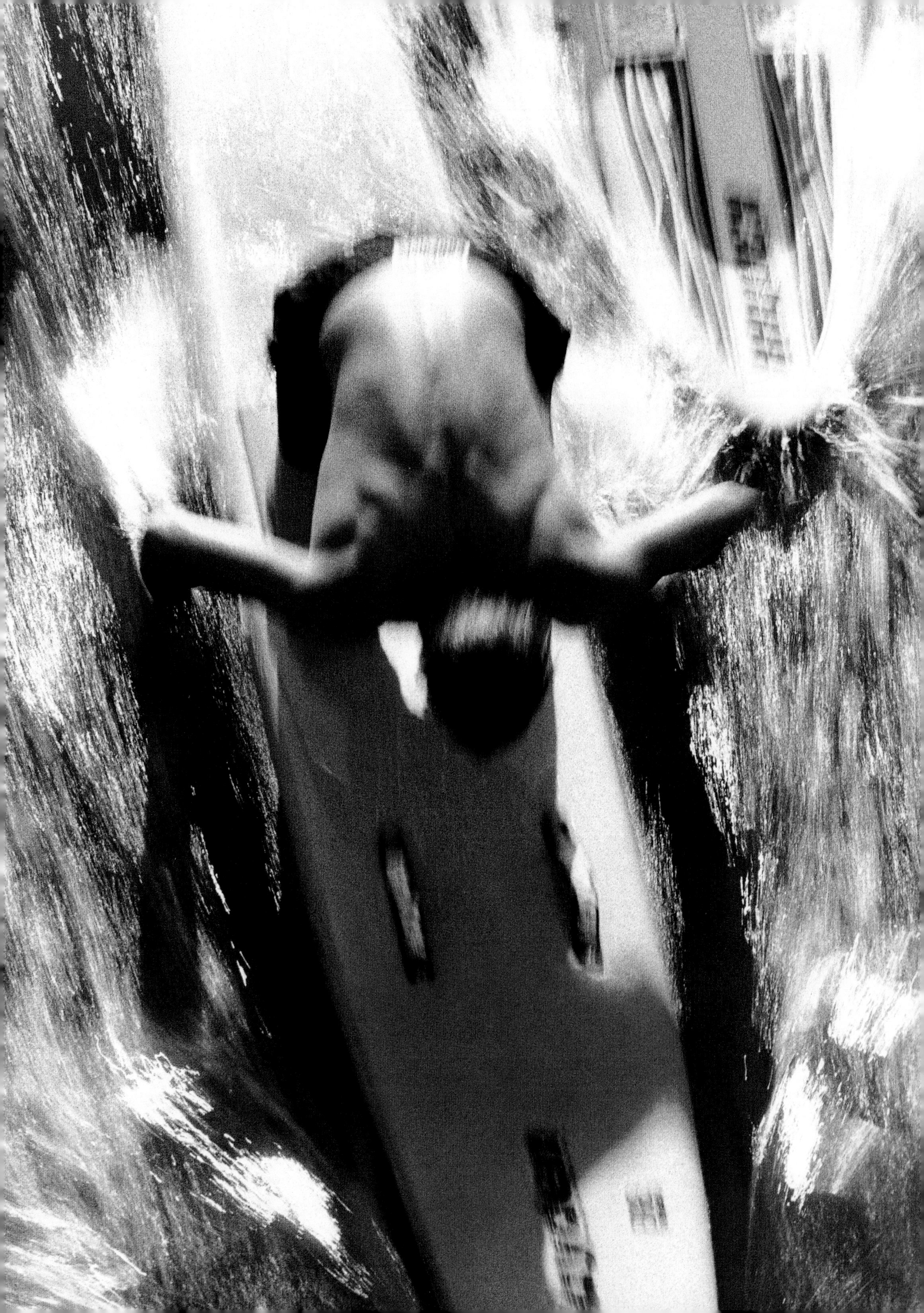

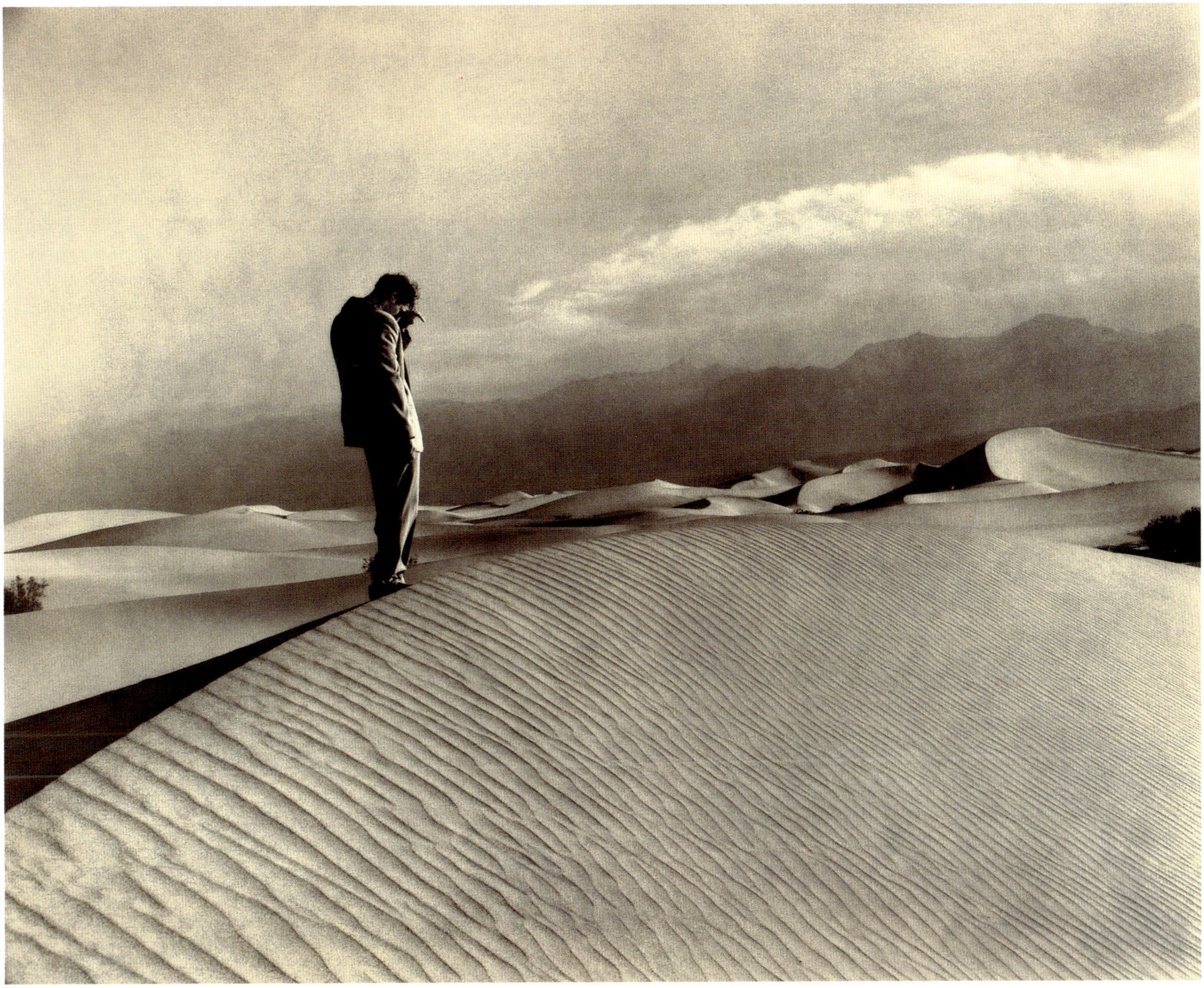

MARK HANAUER

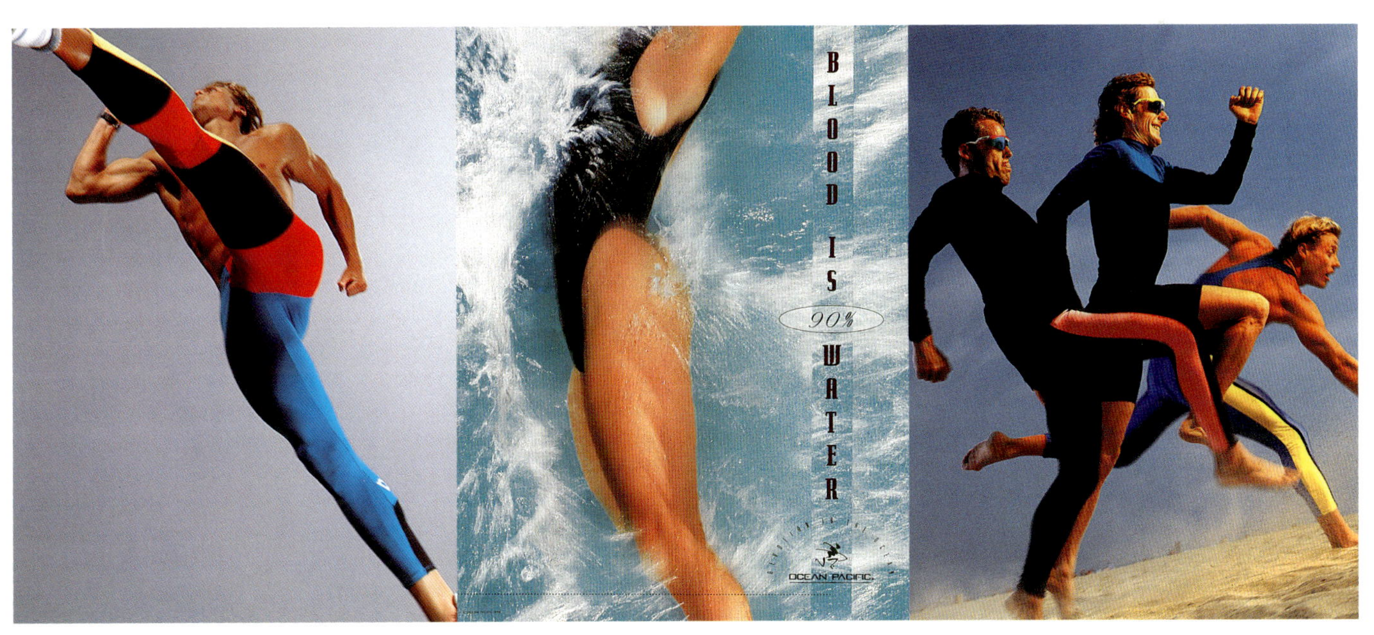

213 462·2421

REPRESENTED IN NEW YORK BY BARBARA UMLAS & ASSOC. 212 534·4008

REPRESENTED IN LOS ANGELES BY ONYX 213 965·0899

DENNIS CHALKIN

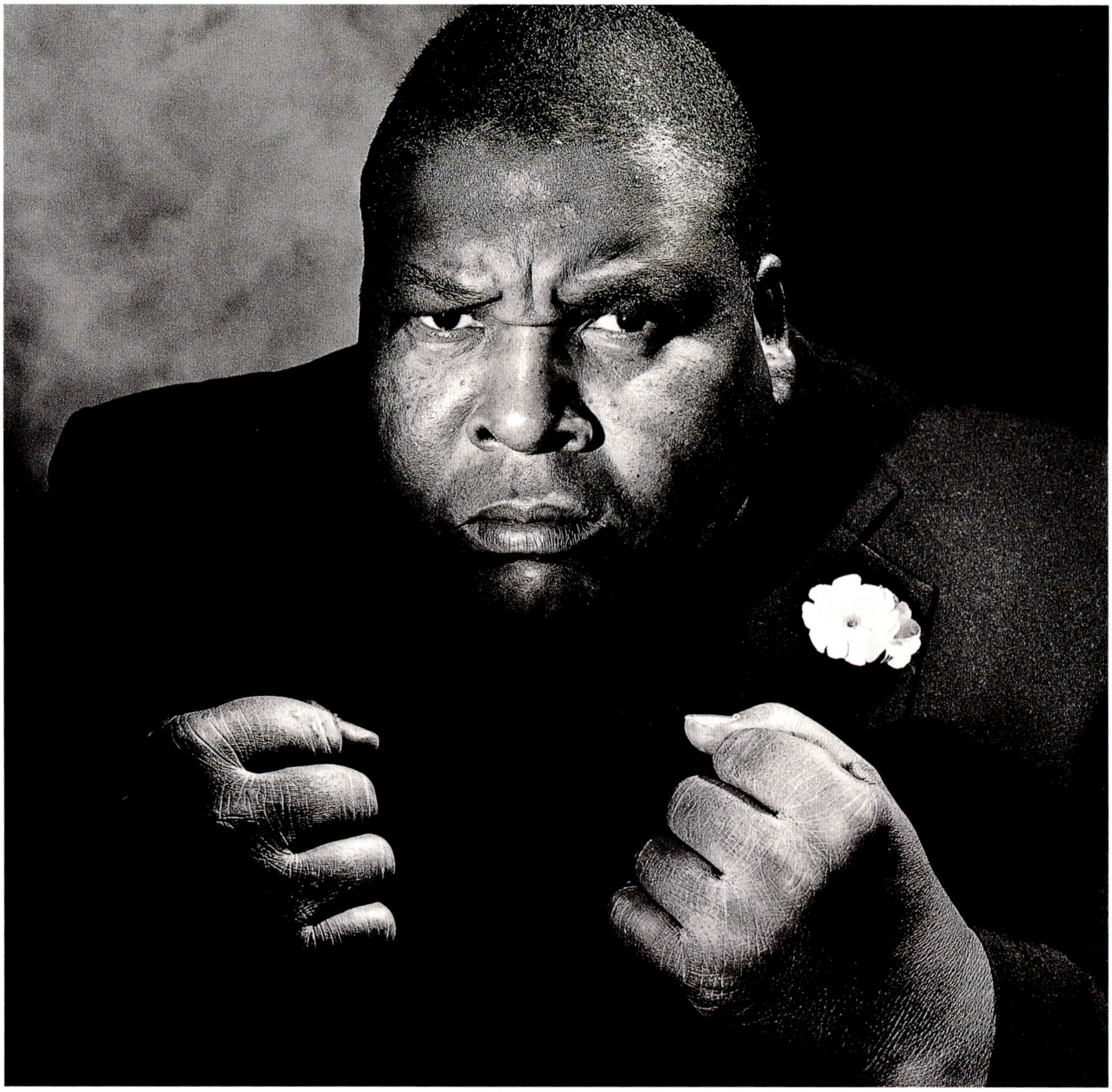

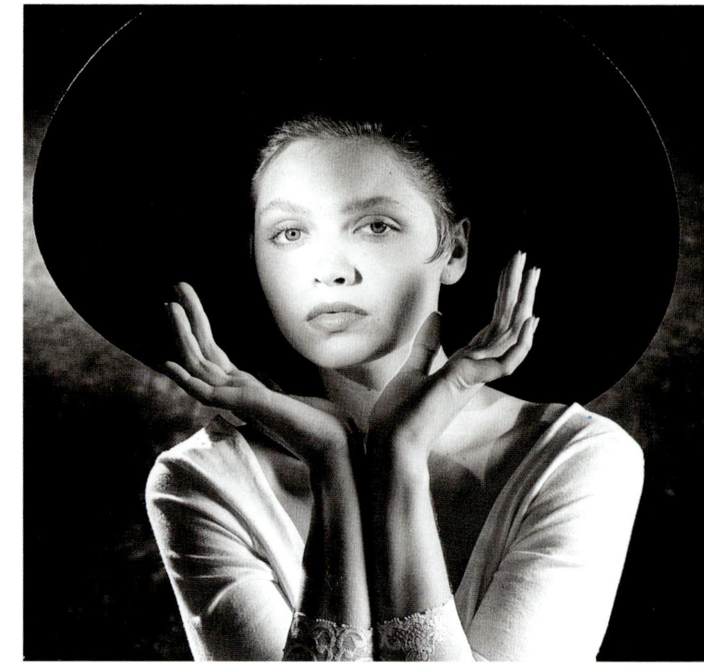

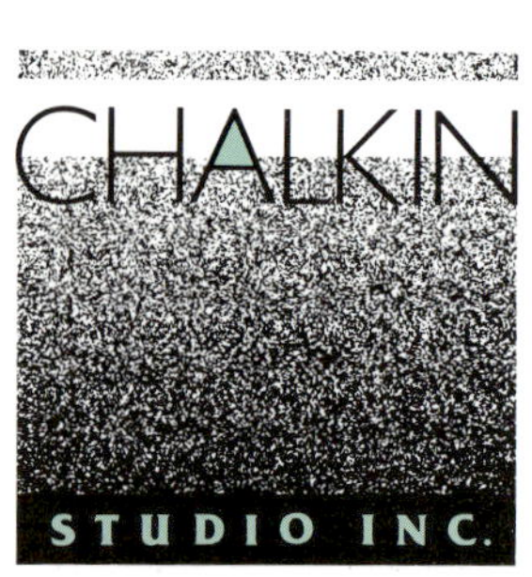

212-929-1036, 5 EAST 16TH STREET, NYC 10003, REPRESENTED BY BARBARA UMLAS ASSOCIATES, 212-534-4008

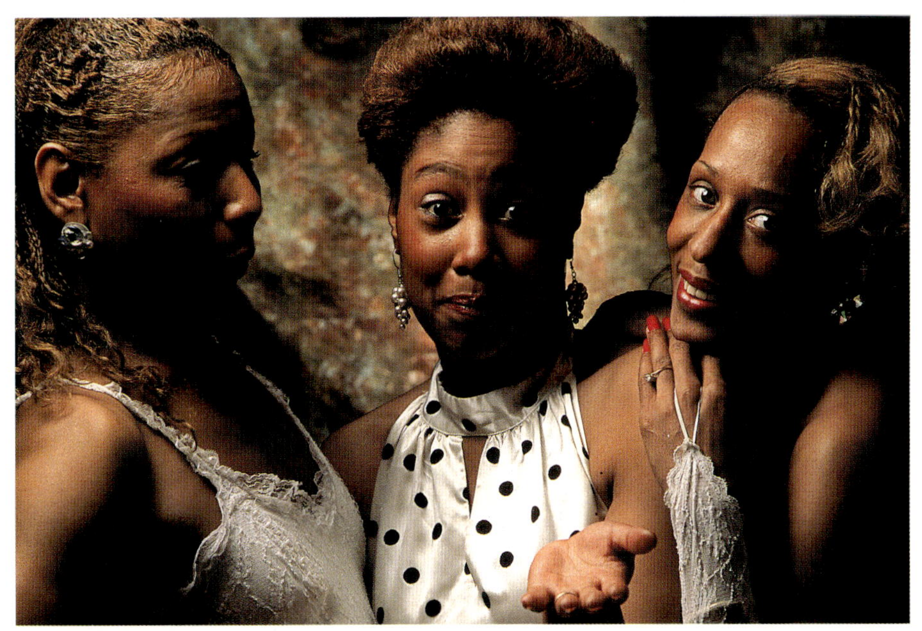

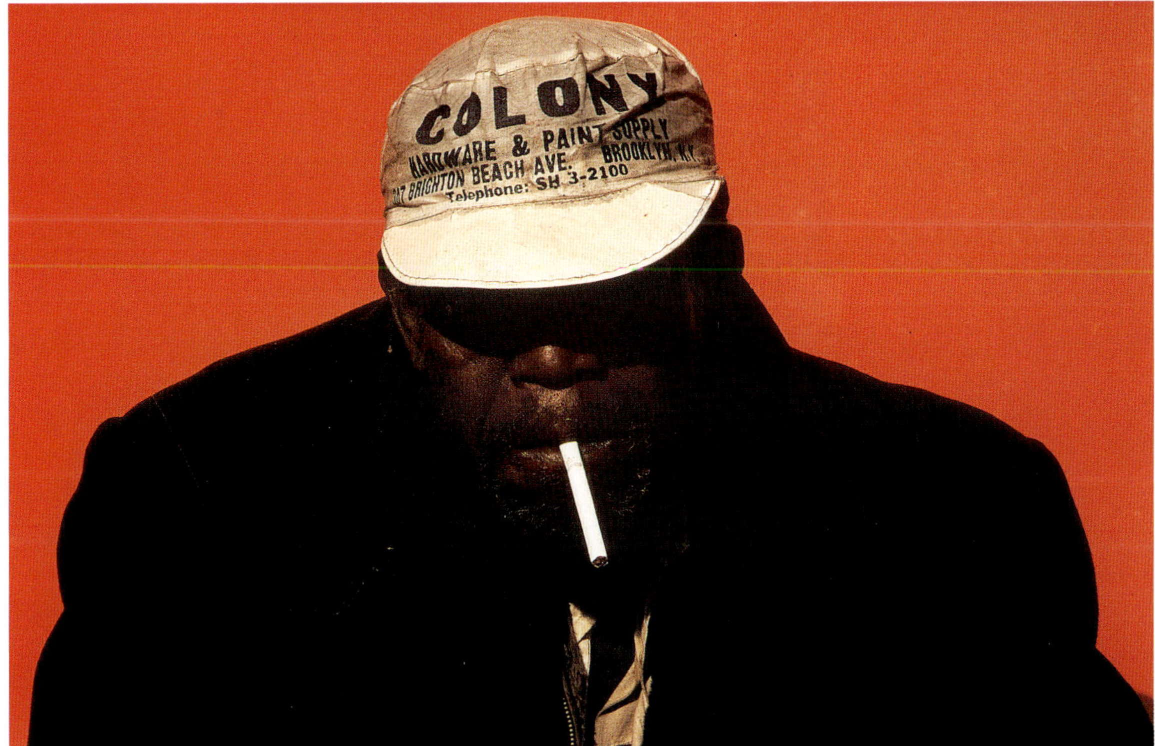

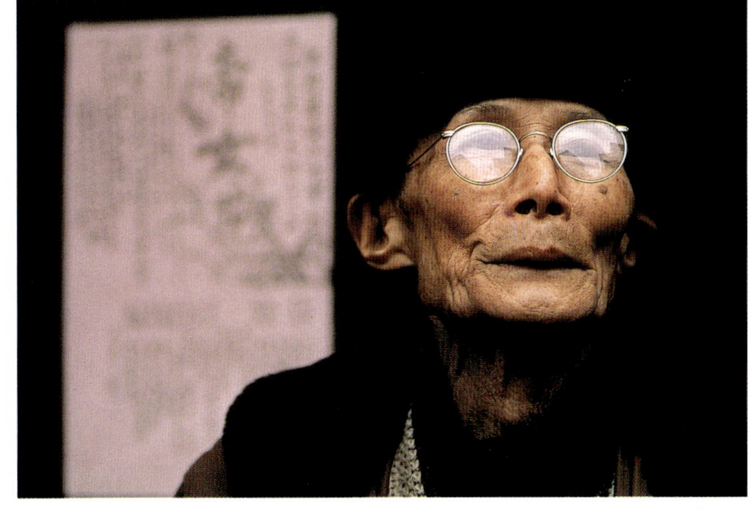

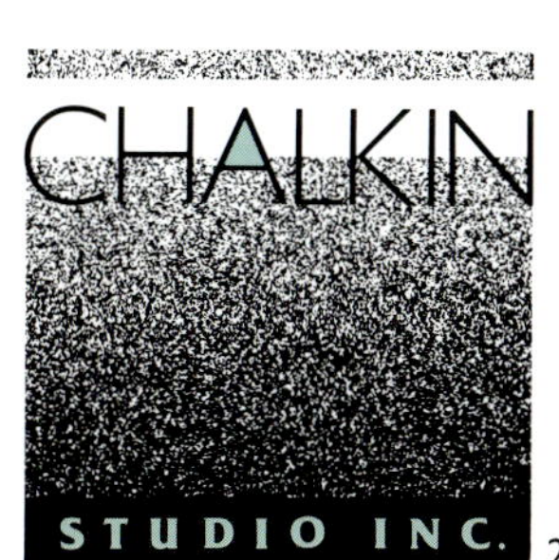

212-929-1036, 5 EAST 16TH STREET, NYC 10003, REPRESENTED BY BARBARA UMLAS ASSOCIATES, 212-534-4008

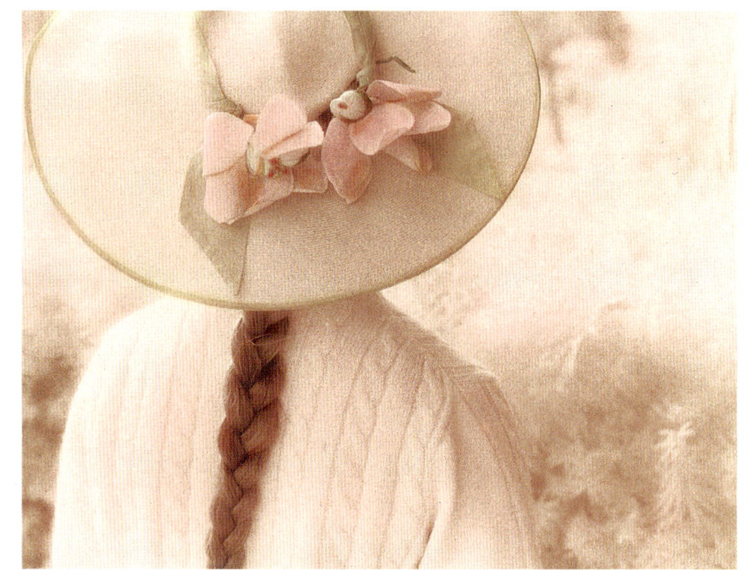

MARCIA LIPPMAN

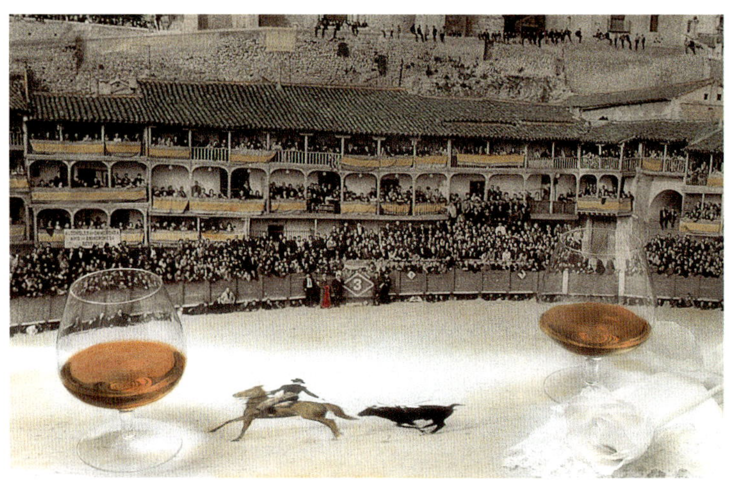

220 EAST 63RD STREET NYC 10021 (212) 832-0321

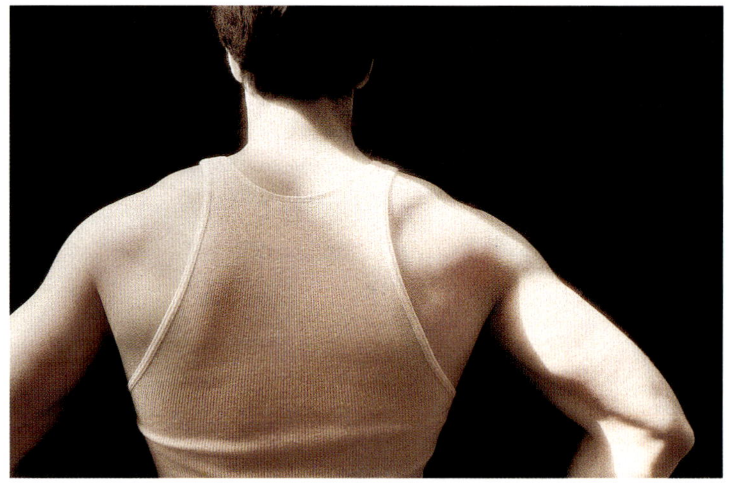

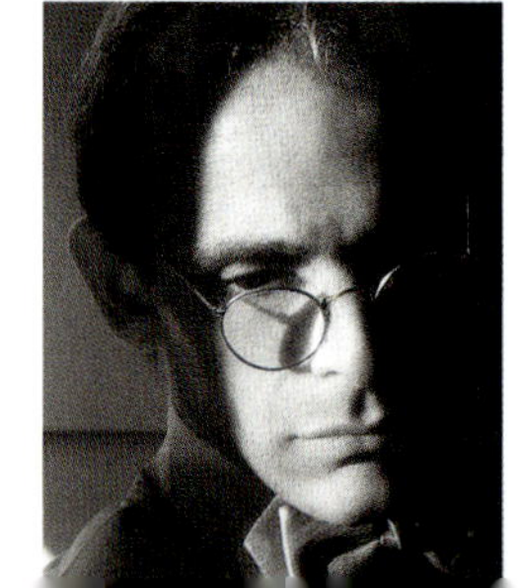

LEON LECASH

TWO HUNDRED AND EIGHTY FOUR FIFTH AVENUE/NEW YORK CITY/ONE ZERO ZERO ZERO ONE

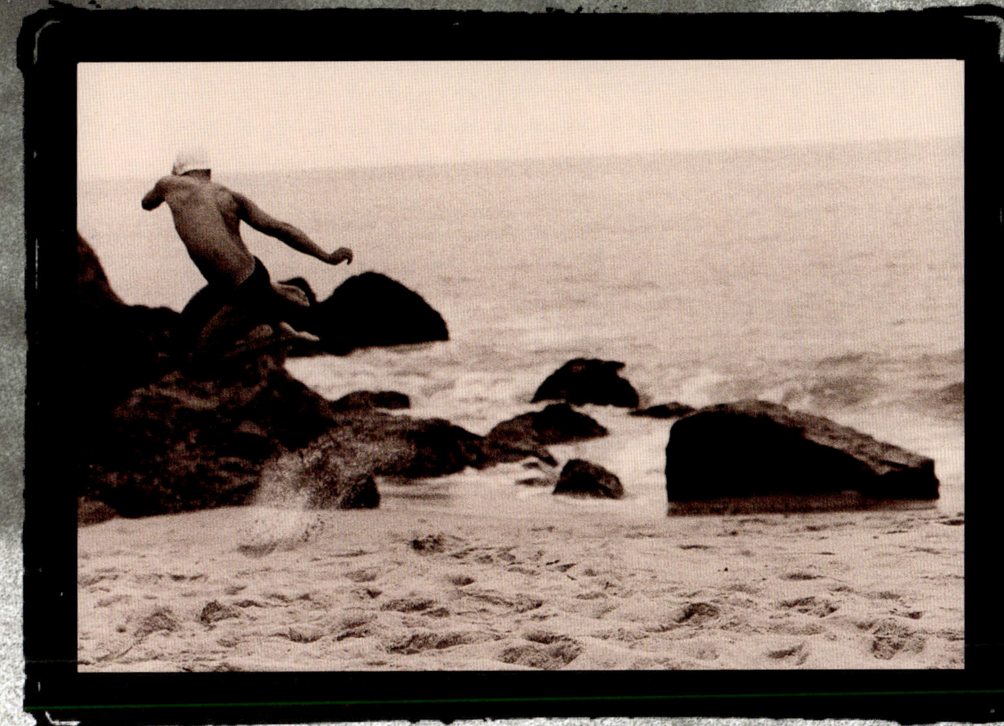

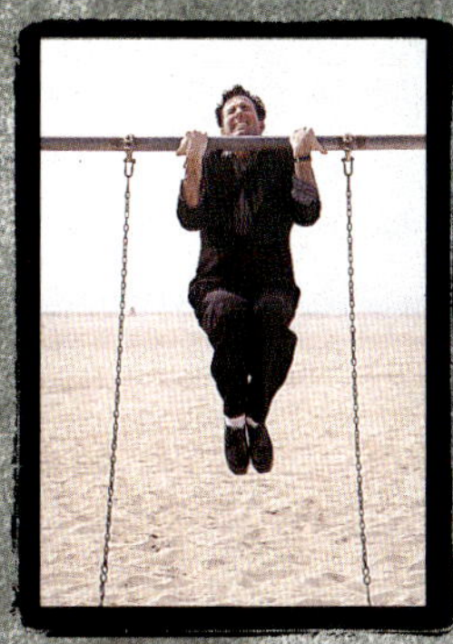

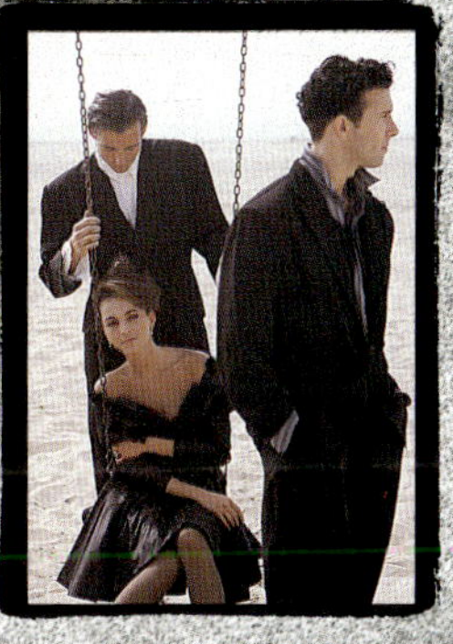

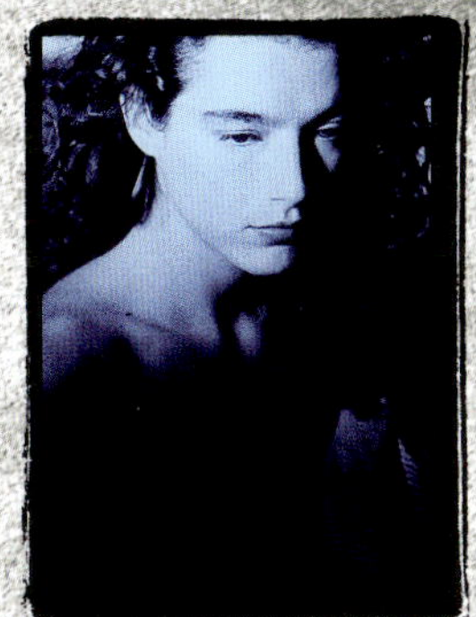

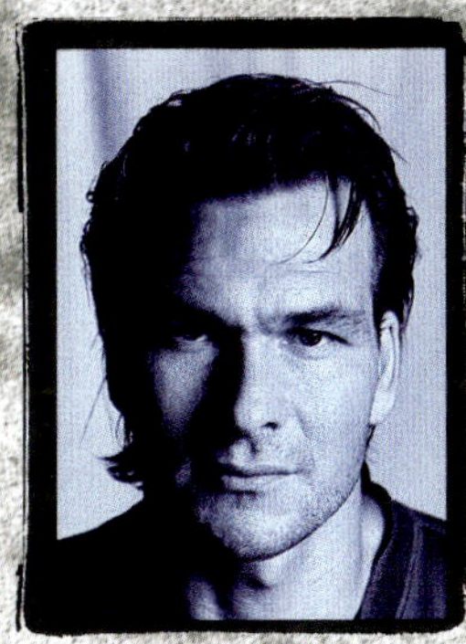

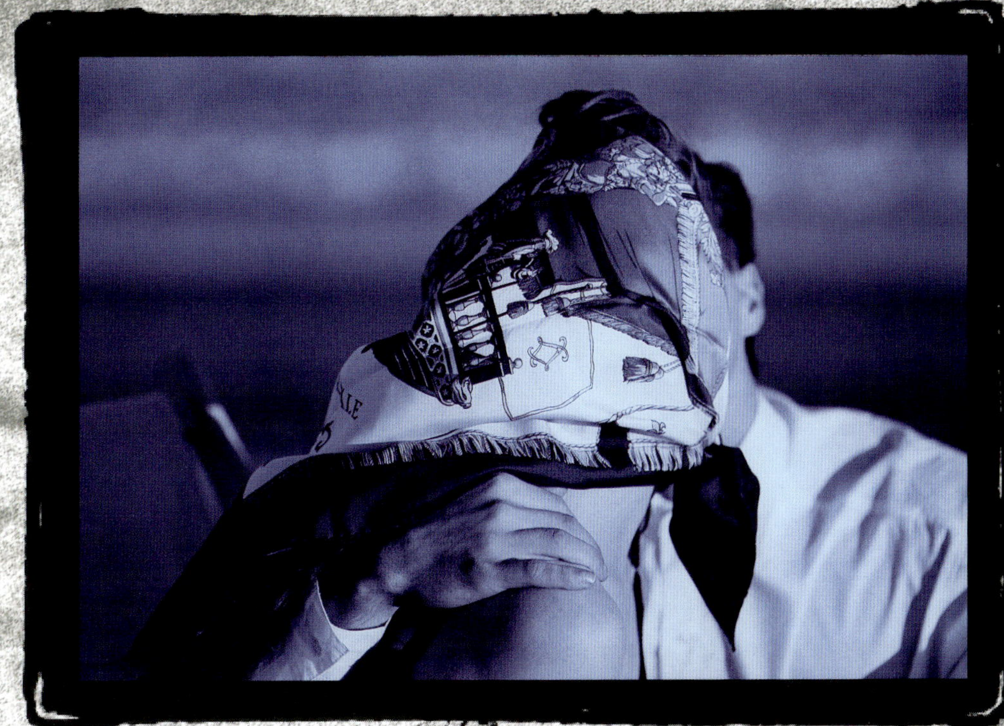

212-967-0827

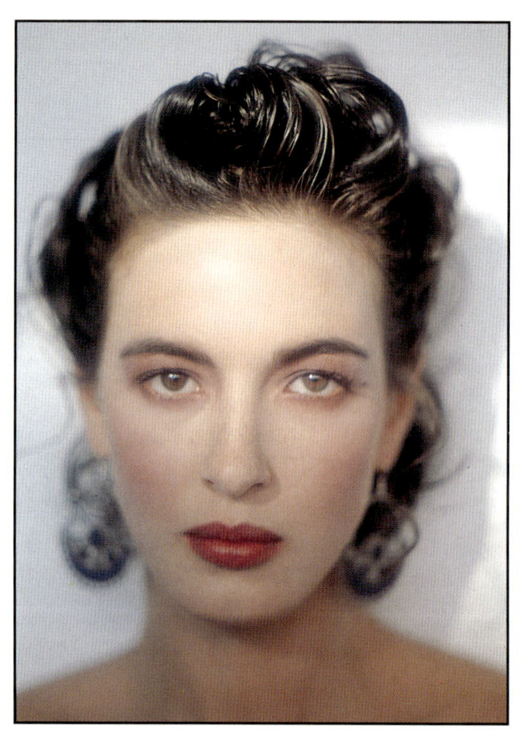

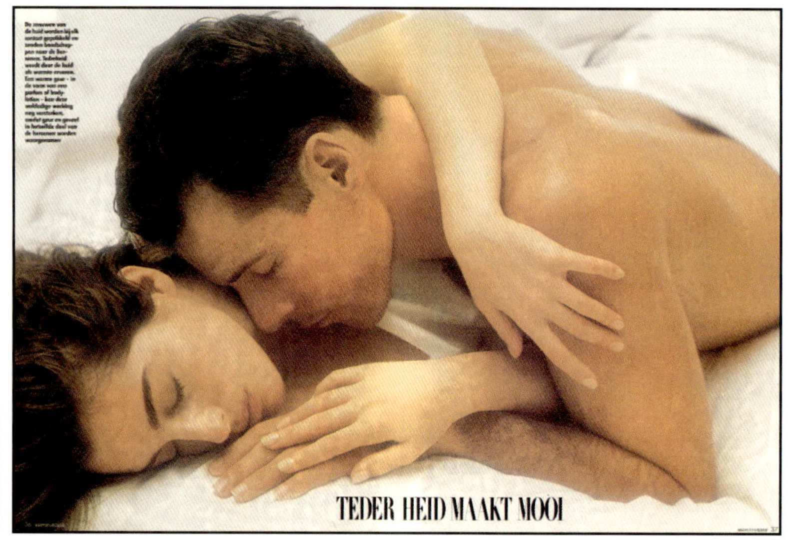

German Bazaar

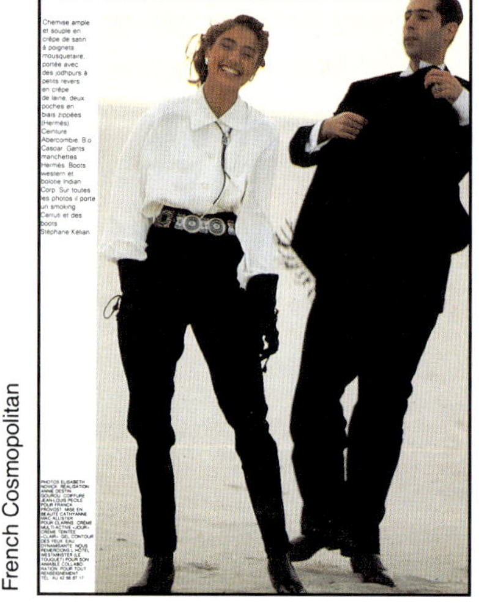

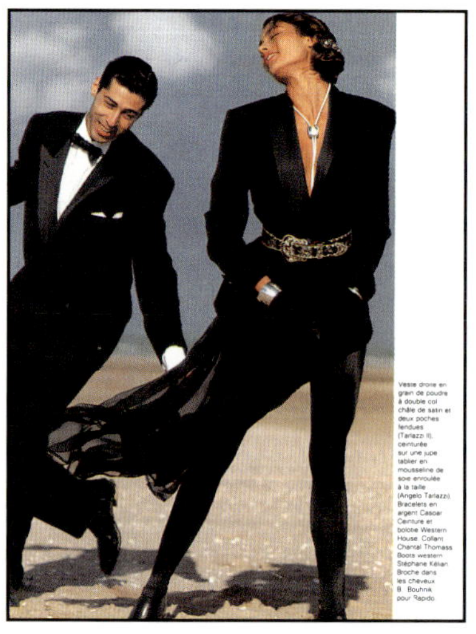

French Cosmopolitan

ELISABETH NOVICK

represented by Jean Gabriel Kauss • 212 370-4300 • FAX 949-7483

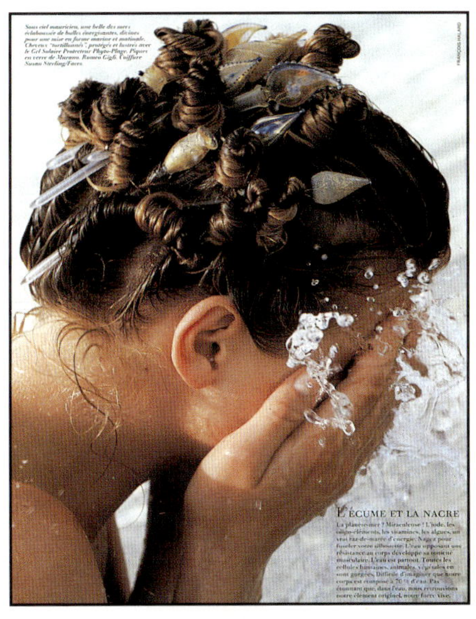

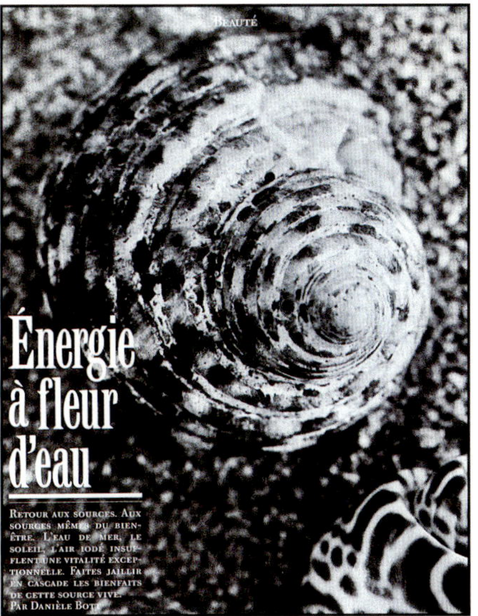

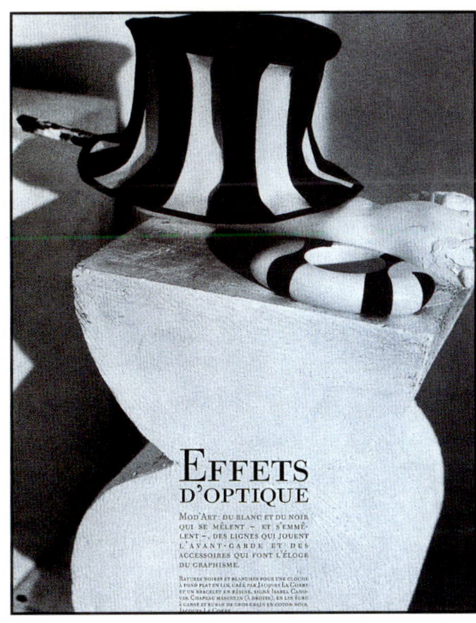

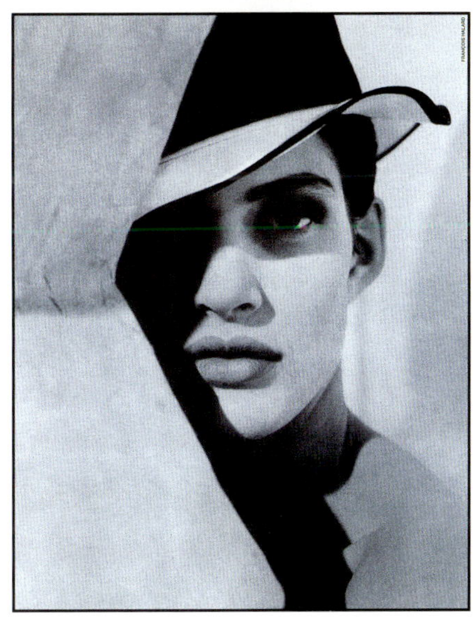

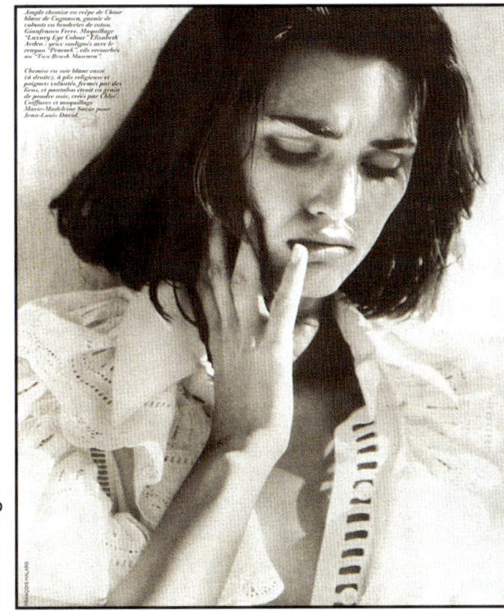

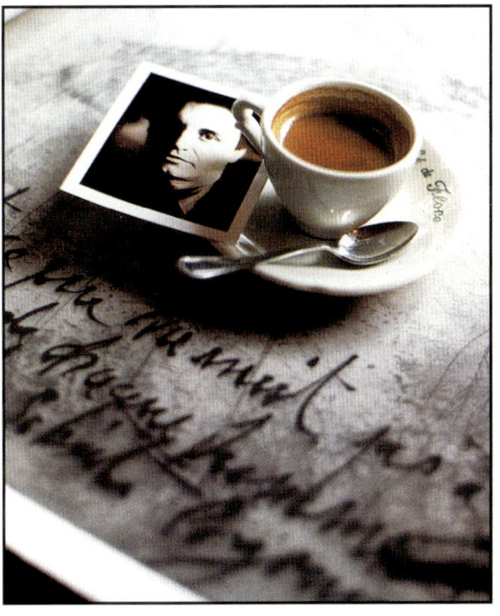

French Vogue

FRANÇOIS HALARD

represented by Jean Gabriel Kauss • 212 370-4300 • FAX 949-7483

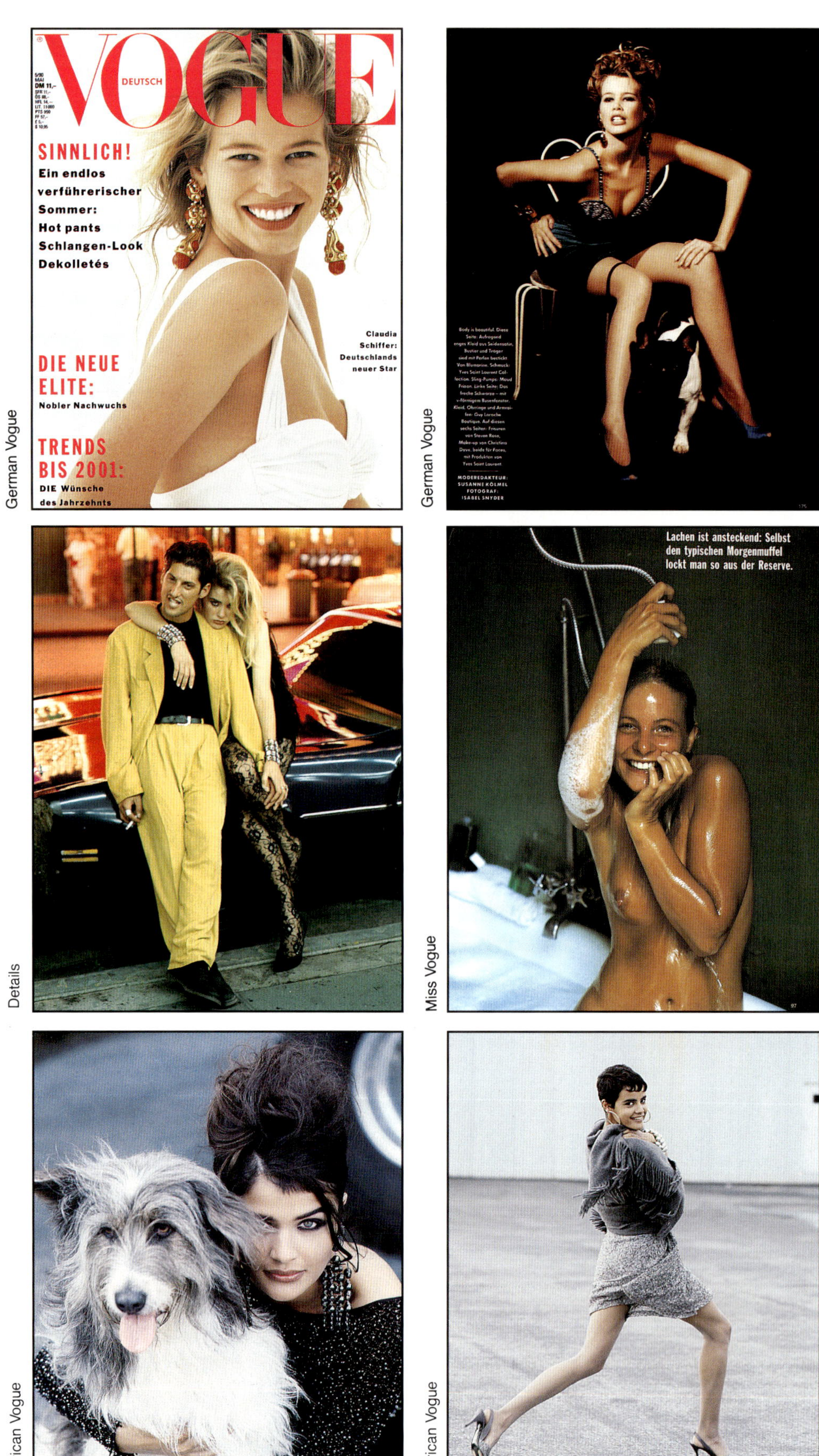

ISABEL SNYDER

represented by Jean Gabriel Kauss • 212 370-4300 • FAX 949-7483

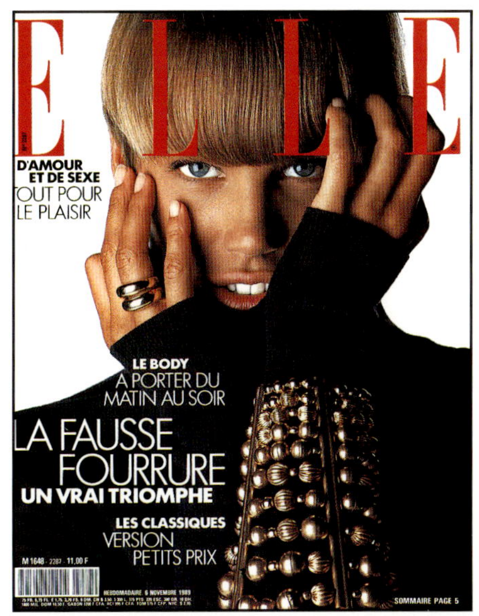

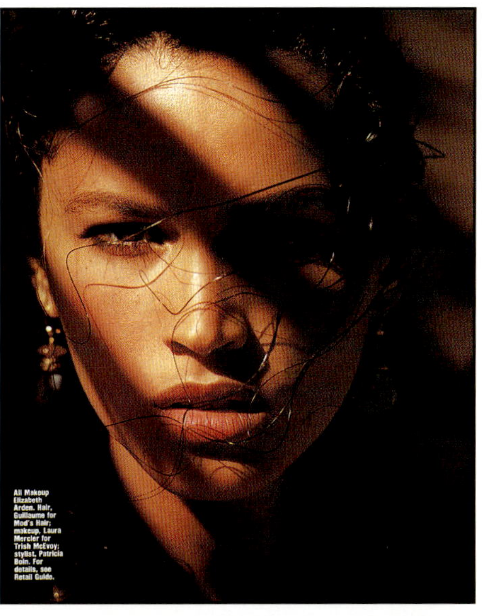

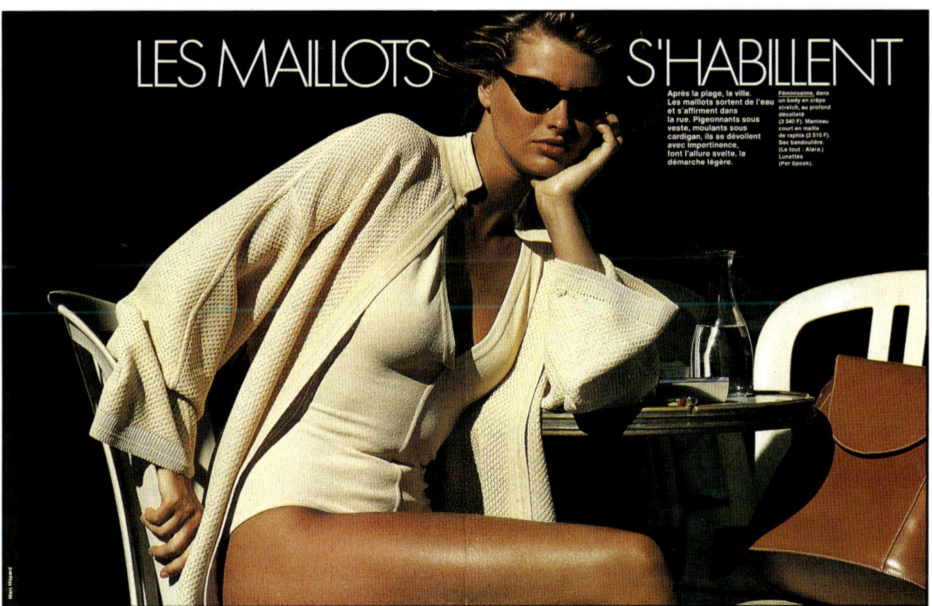

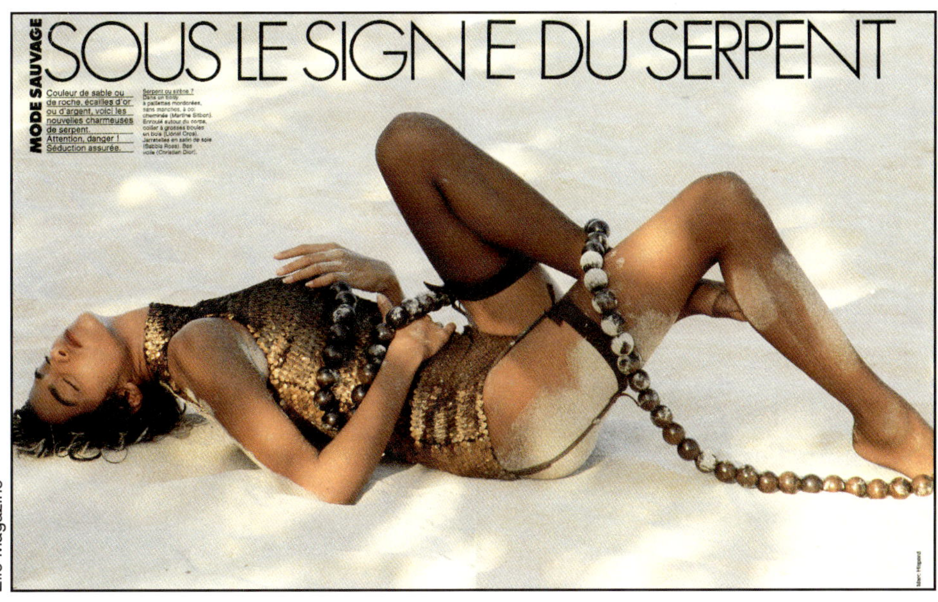

Elle Magazine

MARC HISPARD

represented by Jean Gabriel Kauss • 212 370-4300 • FAX 949-7483

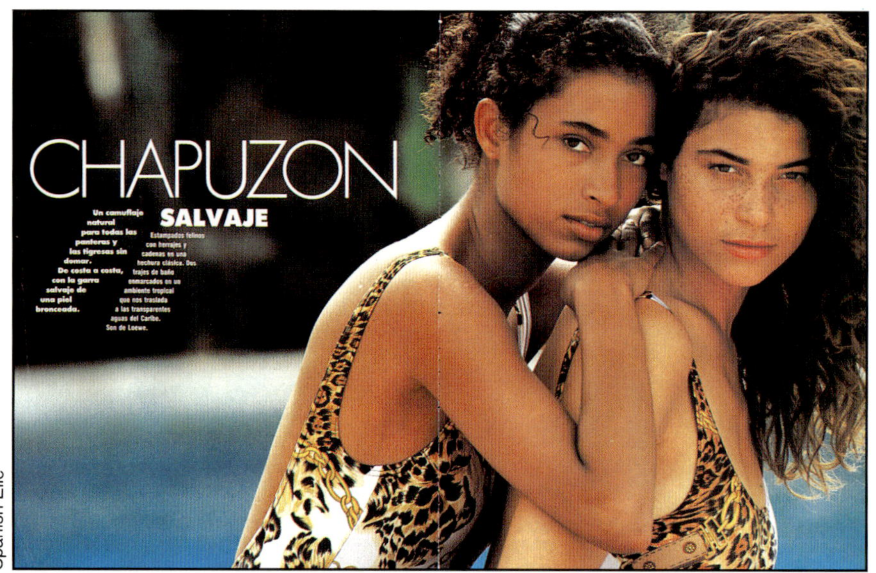

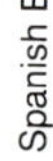
Spanish Elle

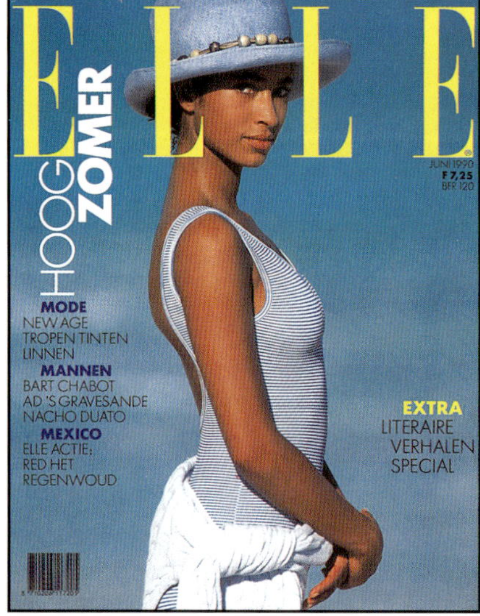

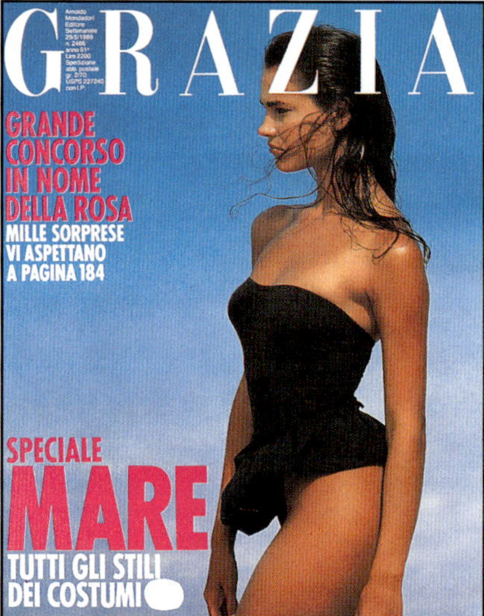

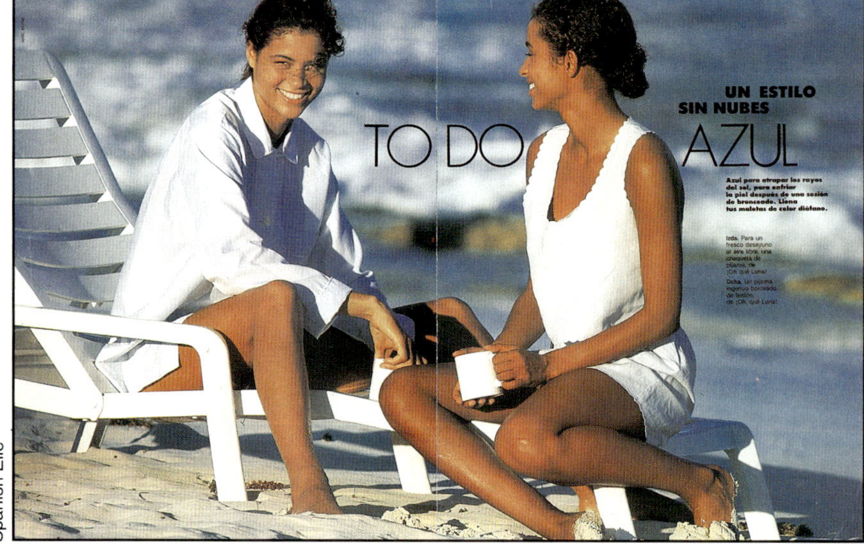

Spanish Elle

MARC KAYNE

represented by Jean Gabriel Kauss • 212 370-4300 • FAX 949-7483

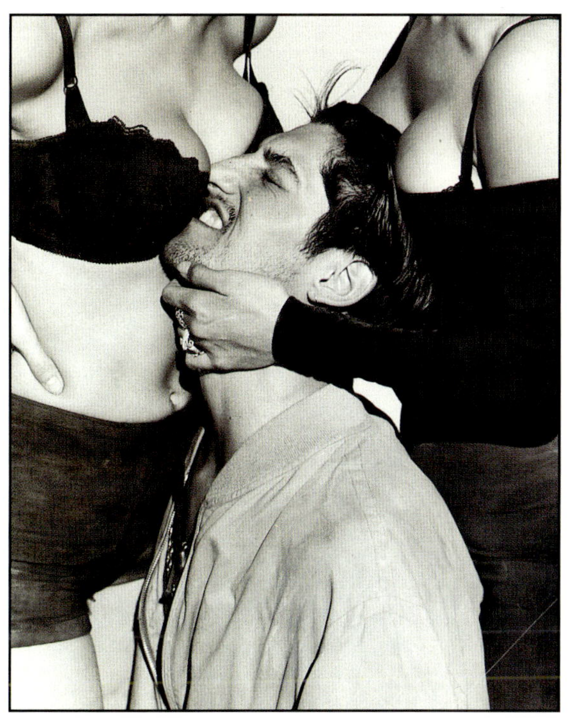

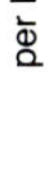

per Lui

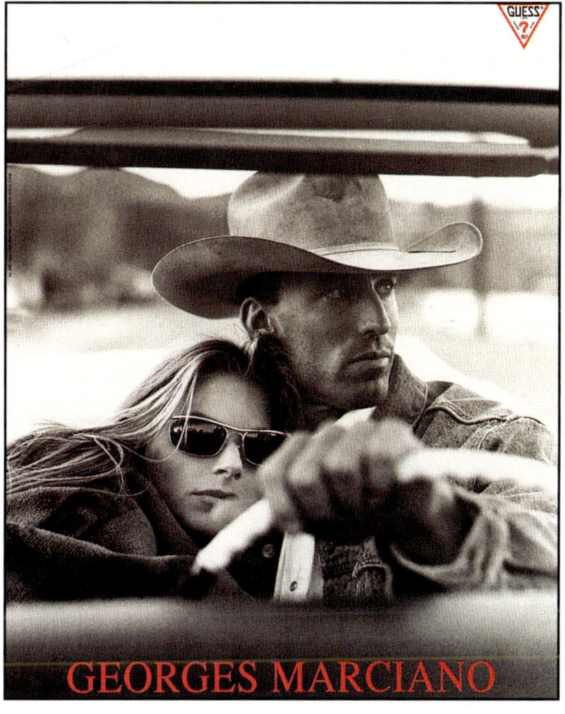

Guess Jeans

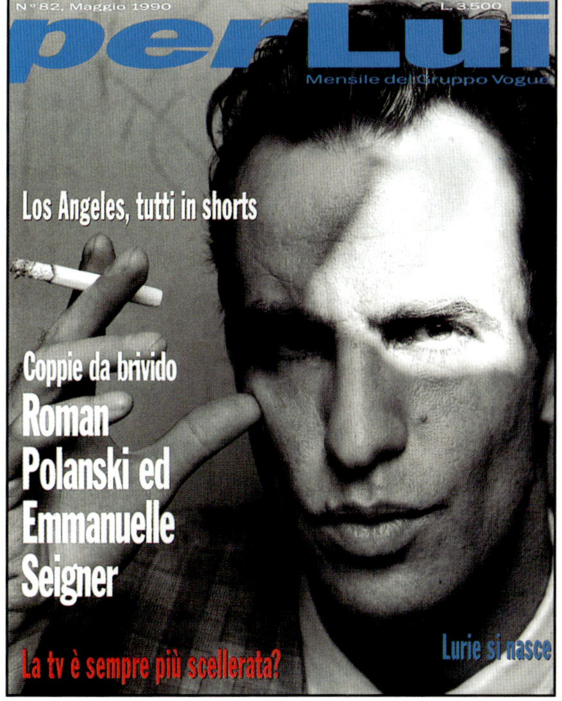

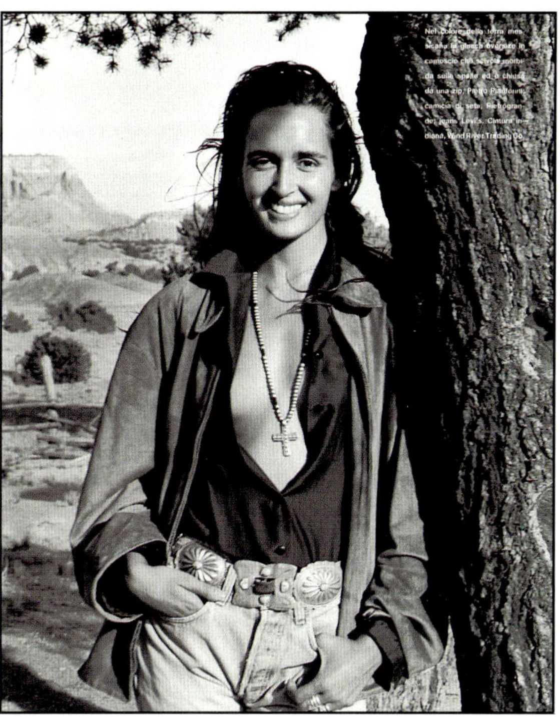

LANCE STAEDLER

represented by Jean Gabriel Kauss • 212 370-4300 • FAX 949-7483

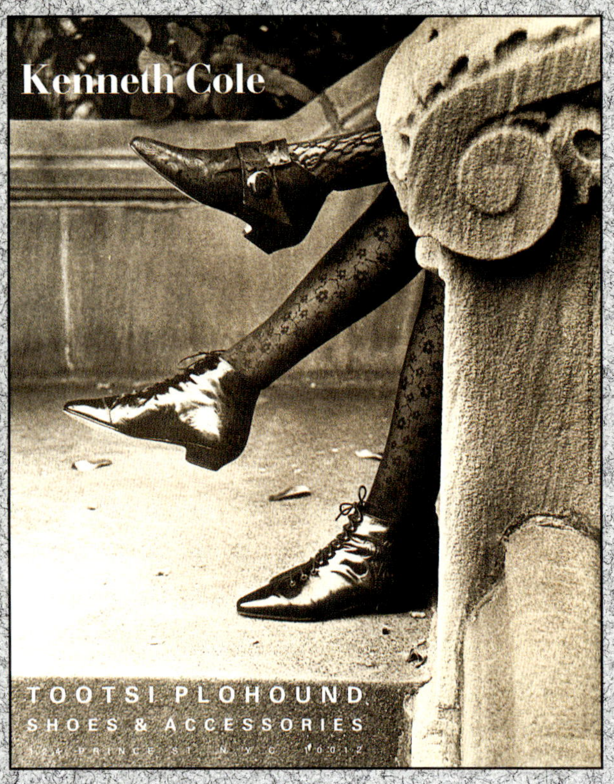

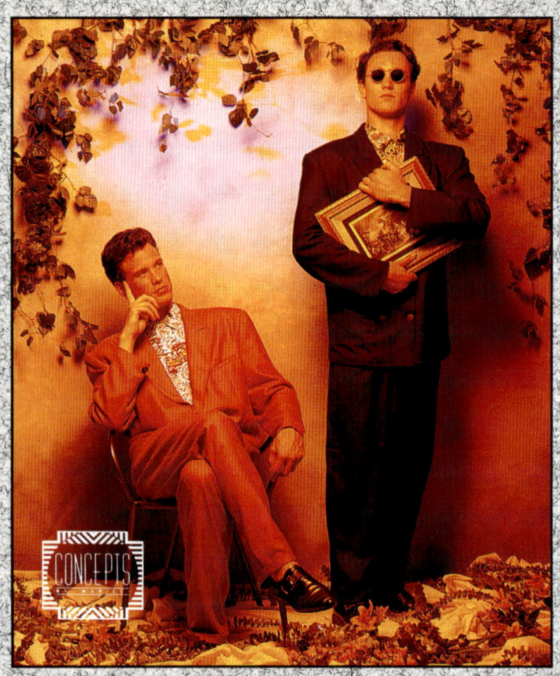

JAMES STILES

PHOTOGRAPHY

212 • 627 • 1766

413-15 WEST 14th ST.
NEW YORK • NEW YORK 10014

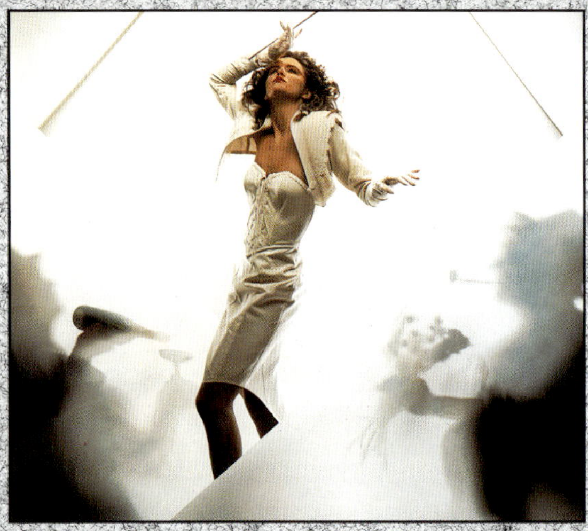

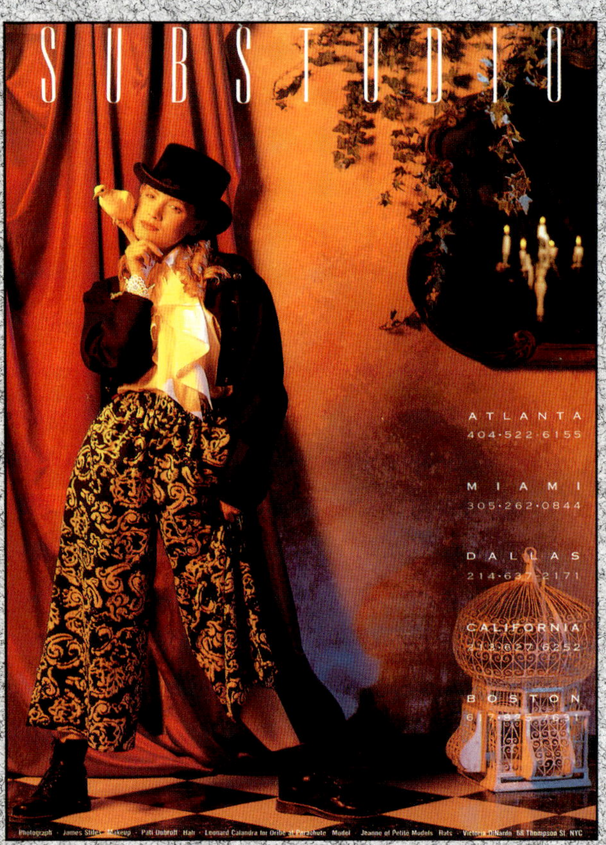

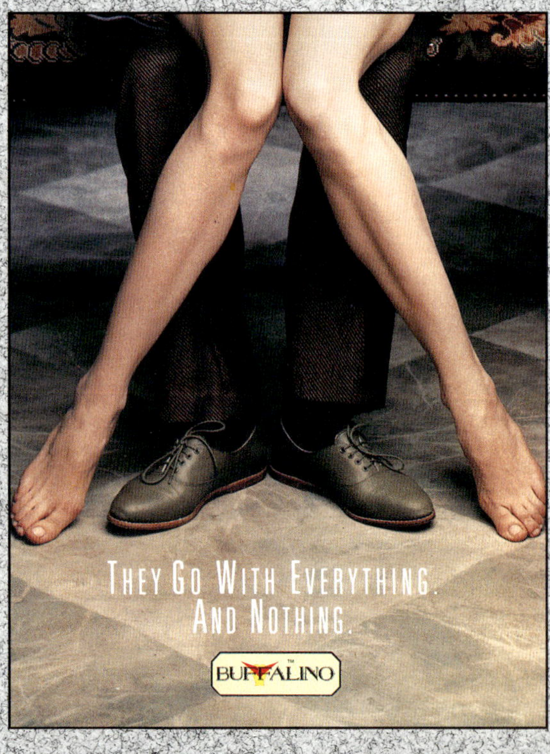

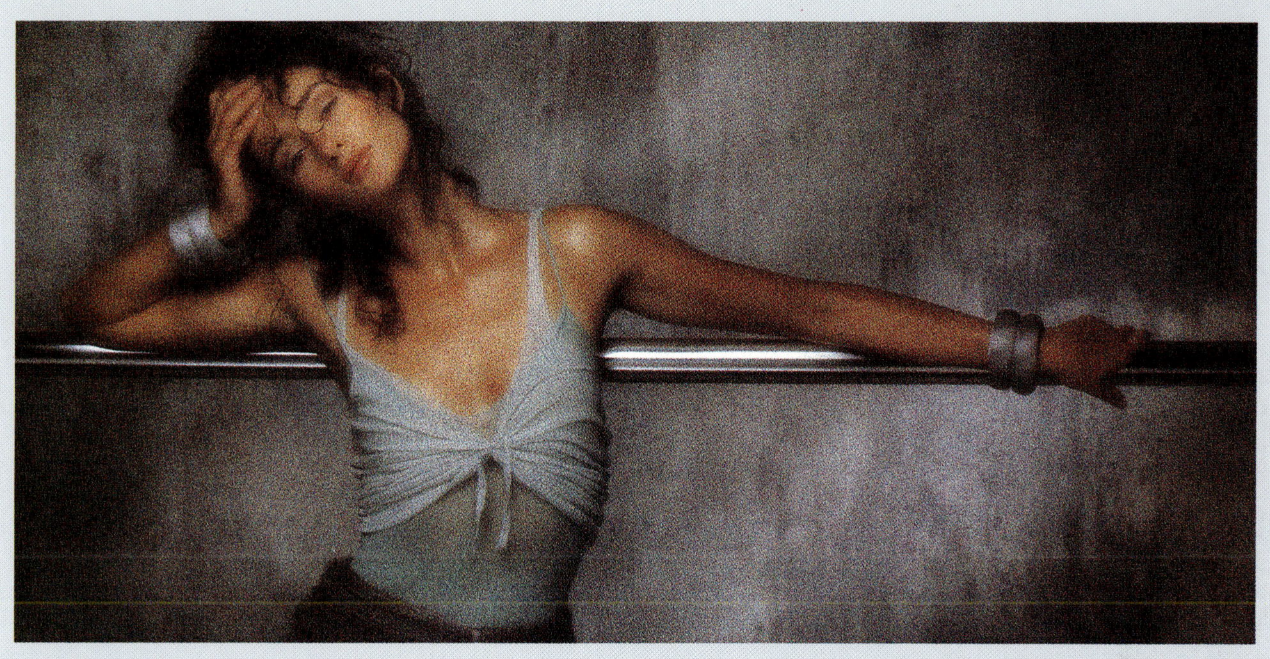

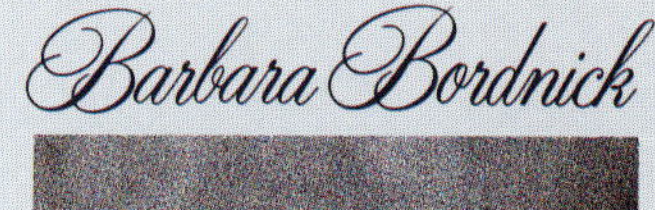

THIRTY-NINE EAST NINETEENTH STREET, NEW YORK NY, 212 533 1180

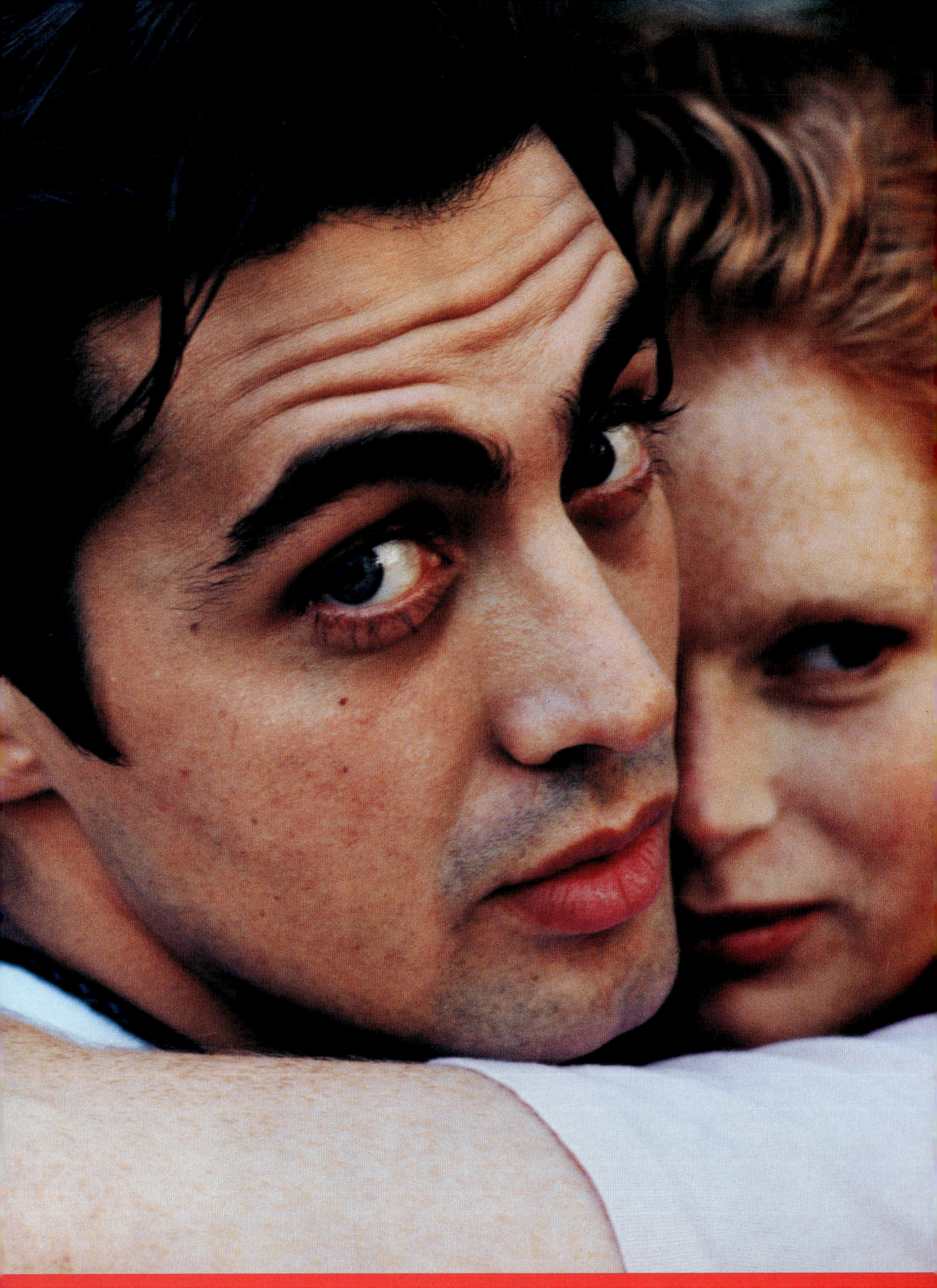

ROBERT WHITMAN PHOTOGRAPHY 1181 BROADWAY NYC 10001 212.213.661

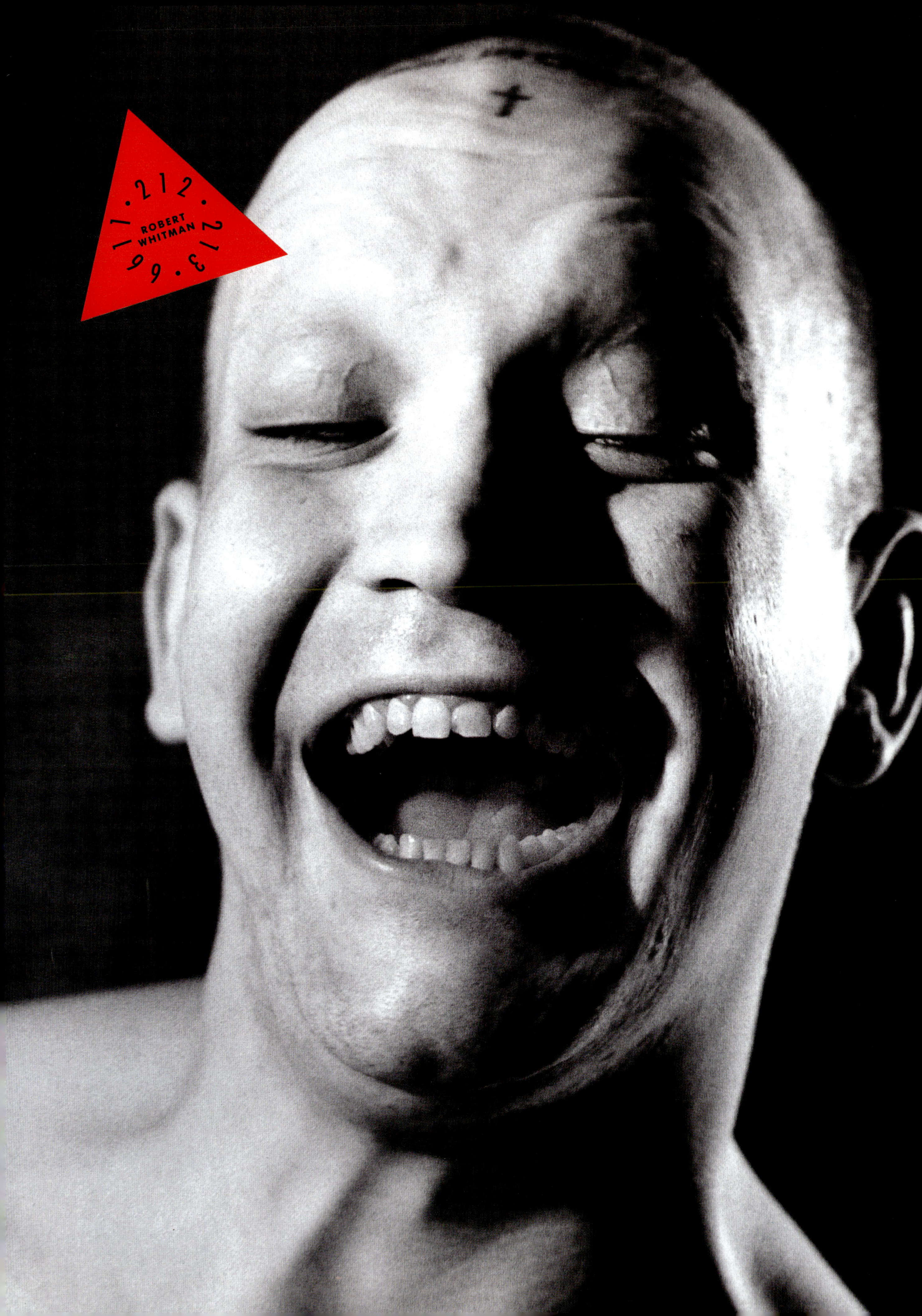
ROBERT
WHITMAN

C H U C K

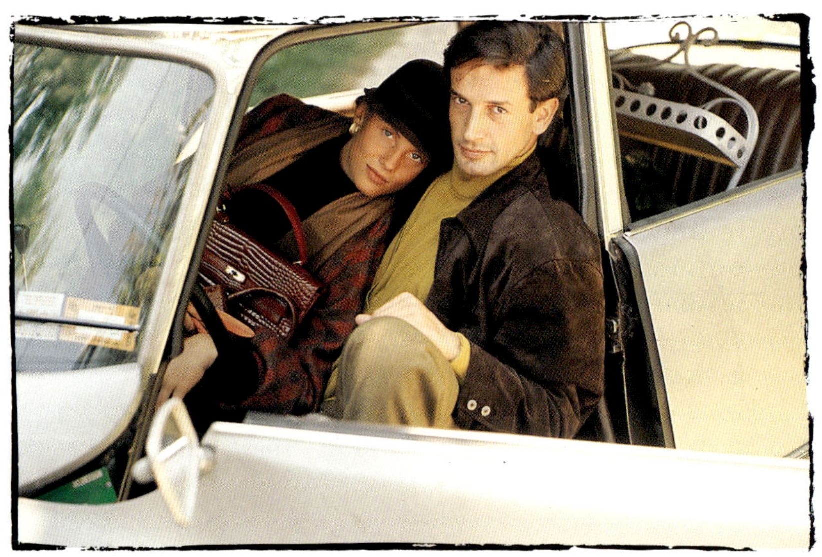

Alone Together

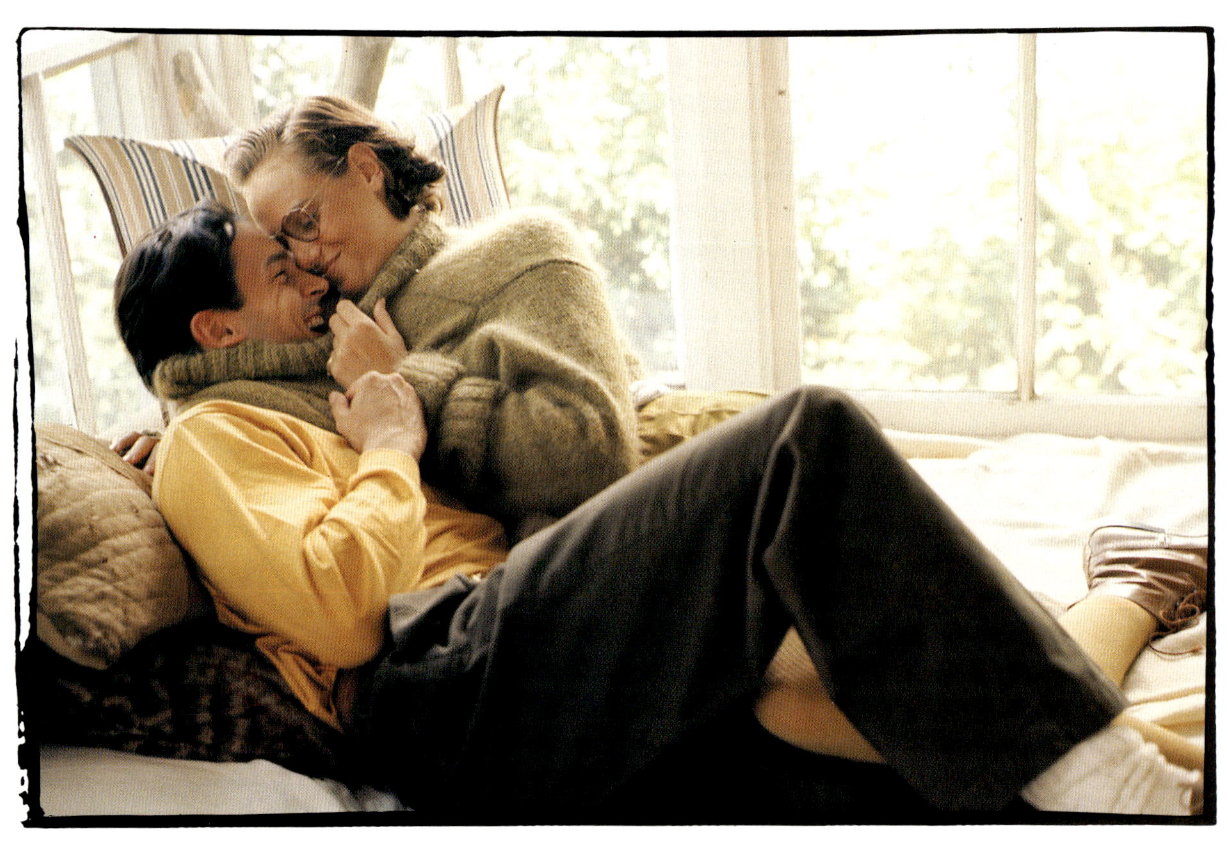

1630 • YORK • AVE • NYC

B A K E R

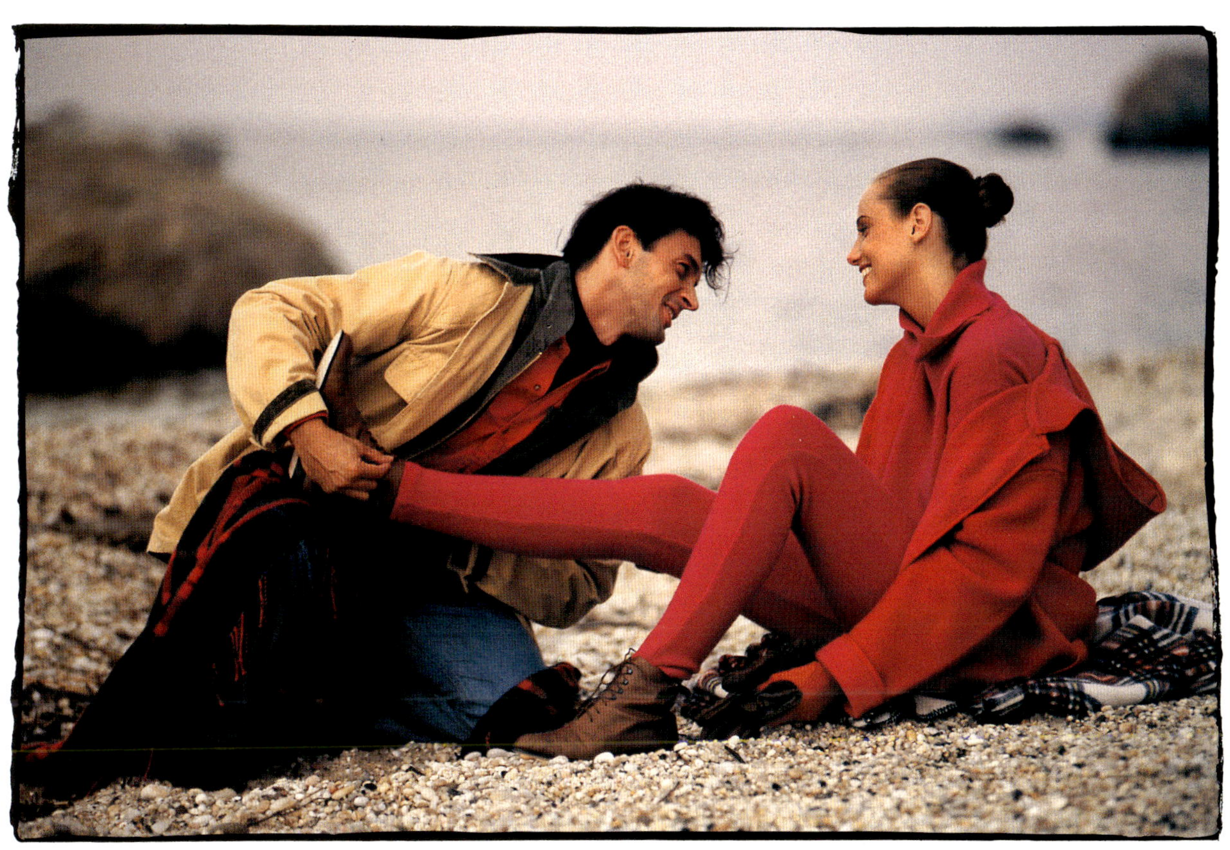

Sept. 24, 1989 for N.Y. Magazine

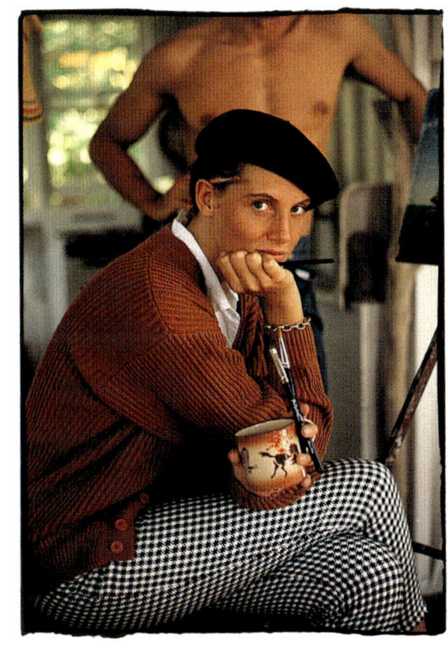

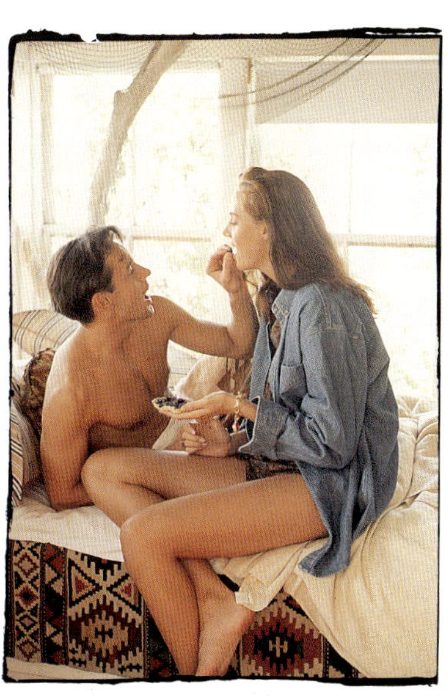

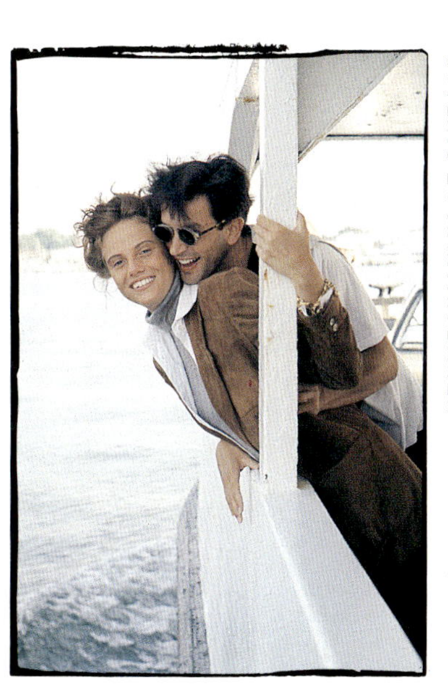

STYLING BY MARTHA BAKER

2 1 2 • 5 1 7 • 9 0 6 0

Maureen Lambray New York City (212) 879-3960

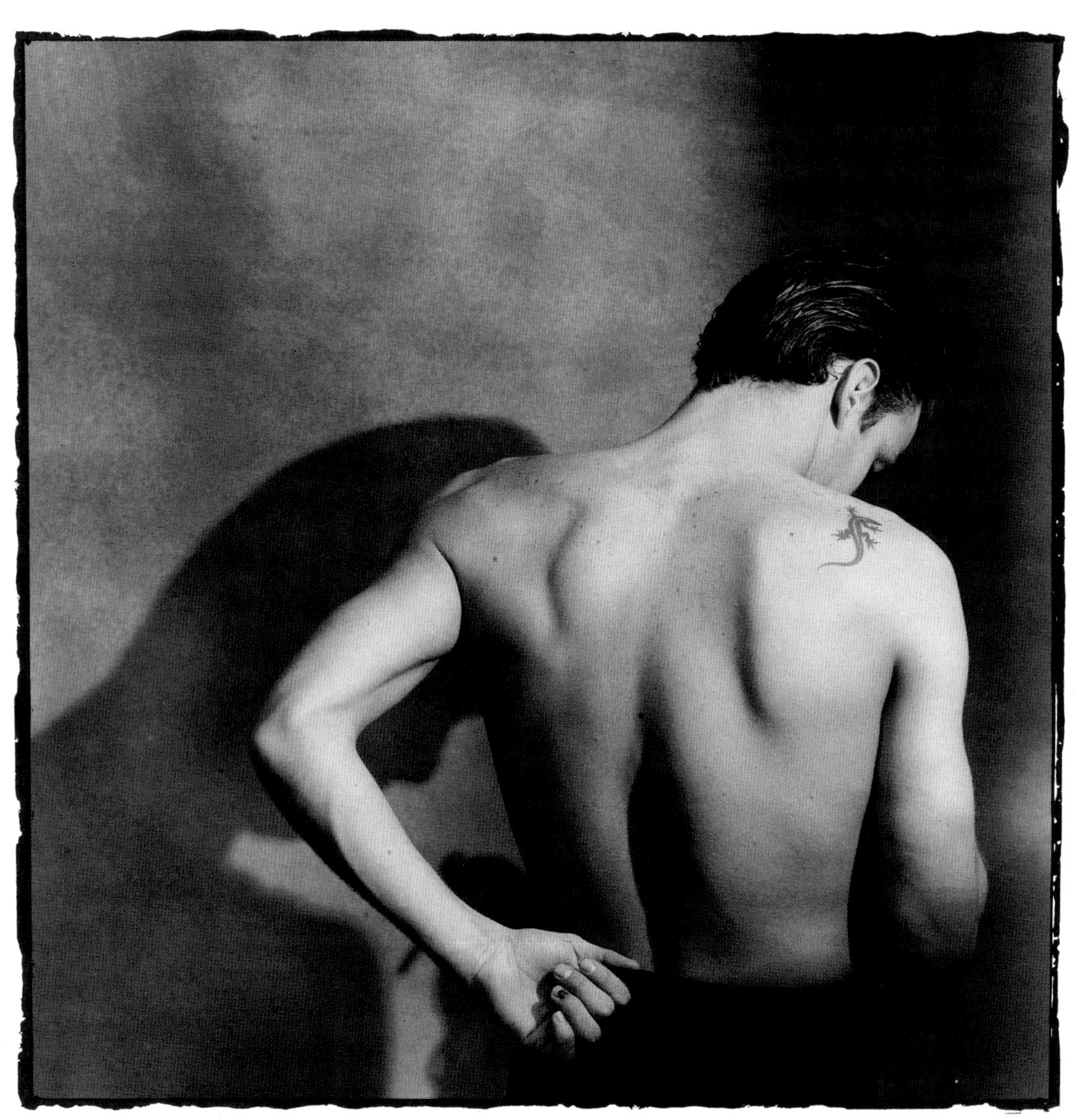

Emanuel, New York City, 1990

Maureen Lambray New York City (212)879-3960

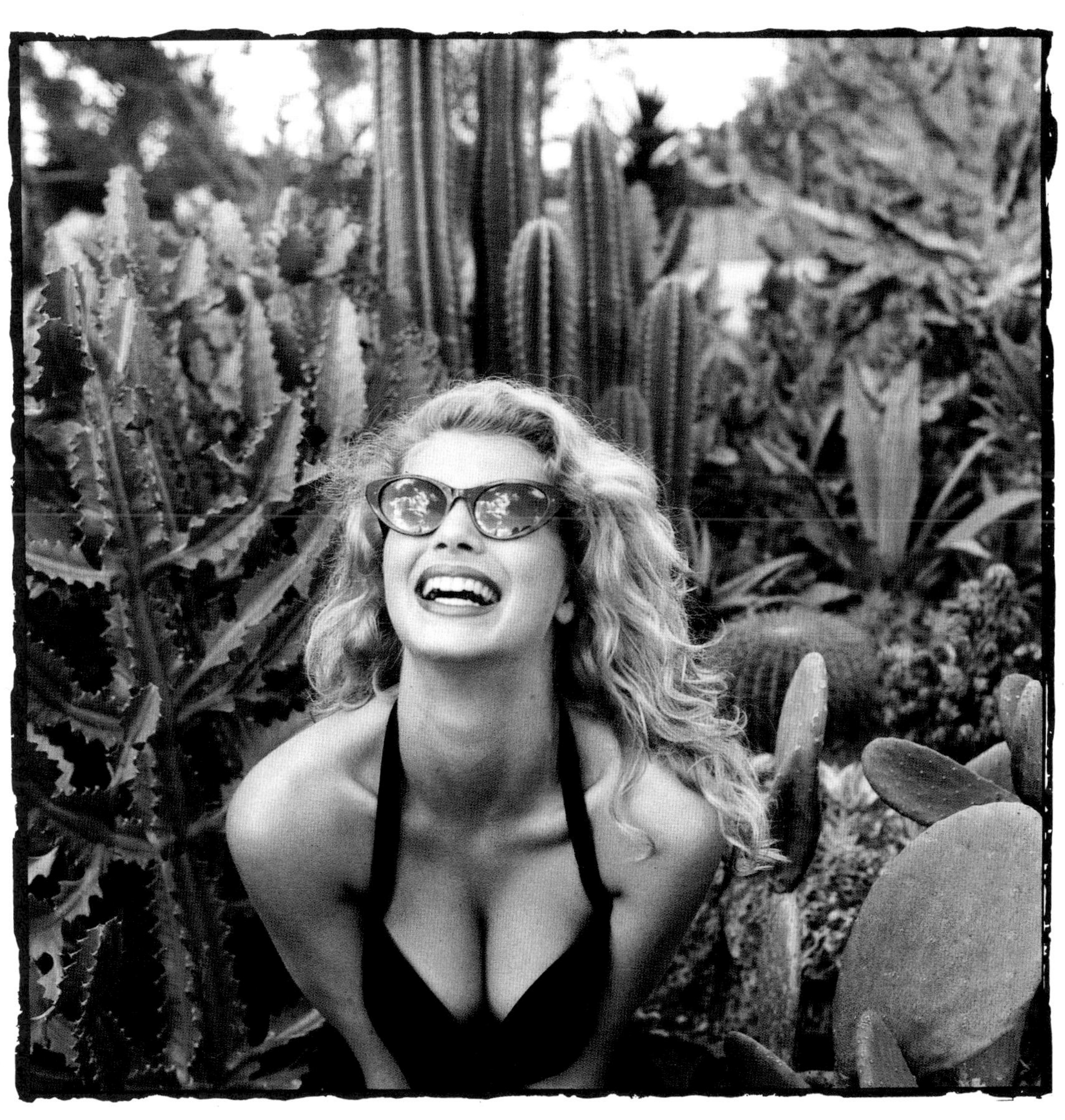

Amber, Miami Beach, Florida, 1988

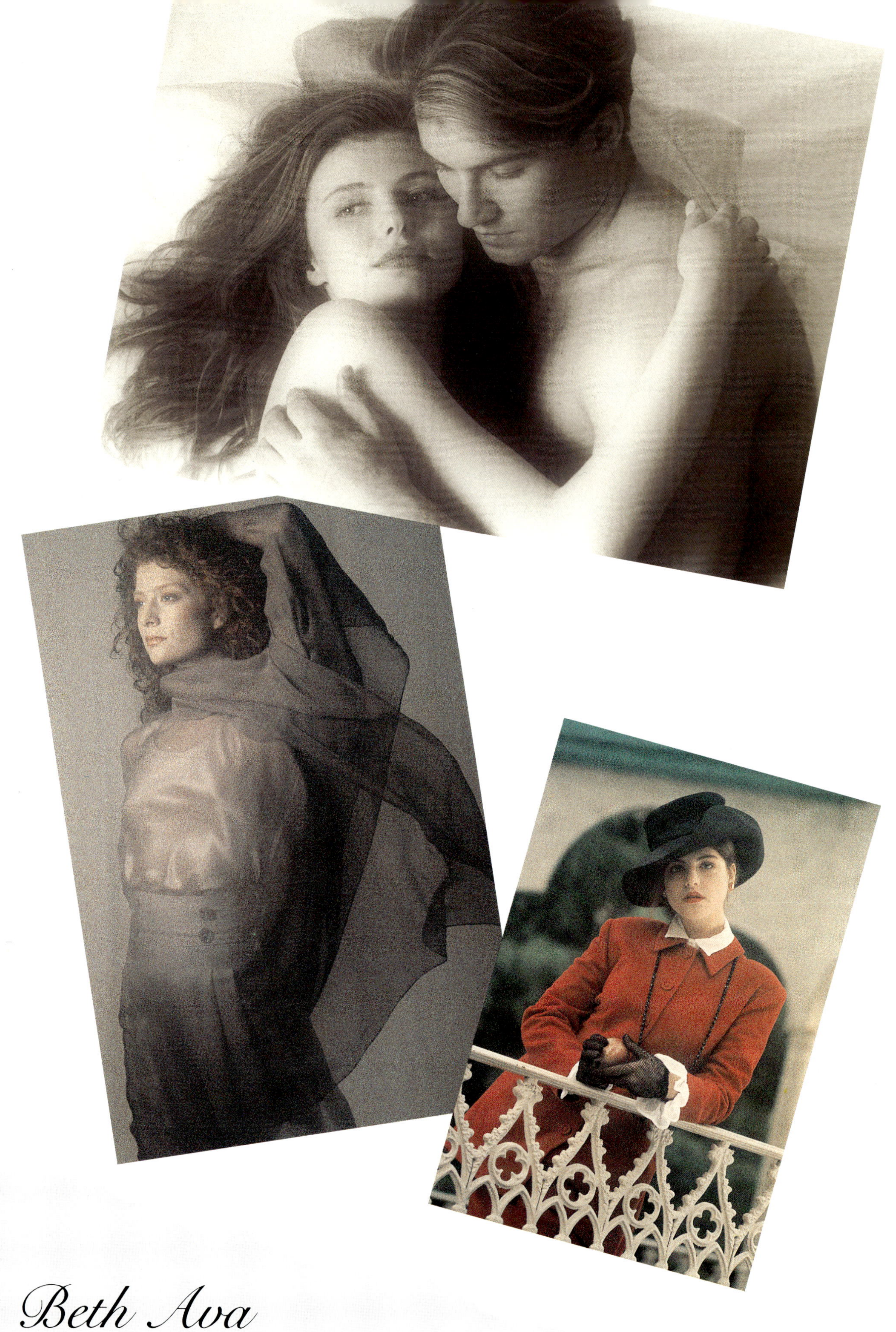

Beth Ava

Photography 87 Franklin Street New York N.Y. 10013 212 · 966 · 4407

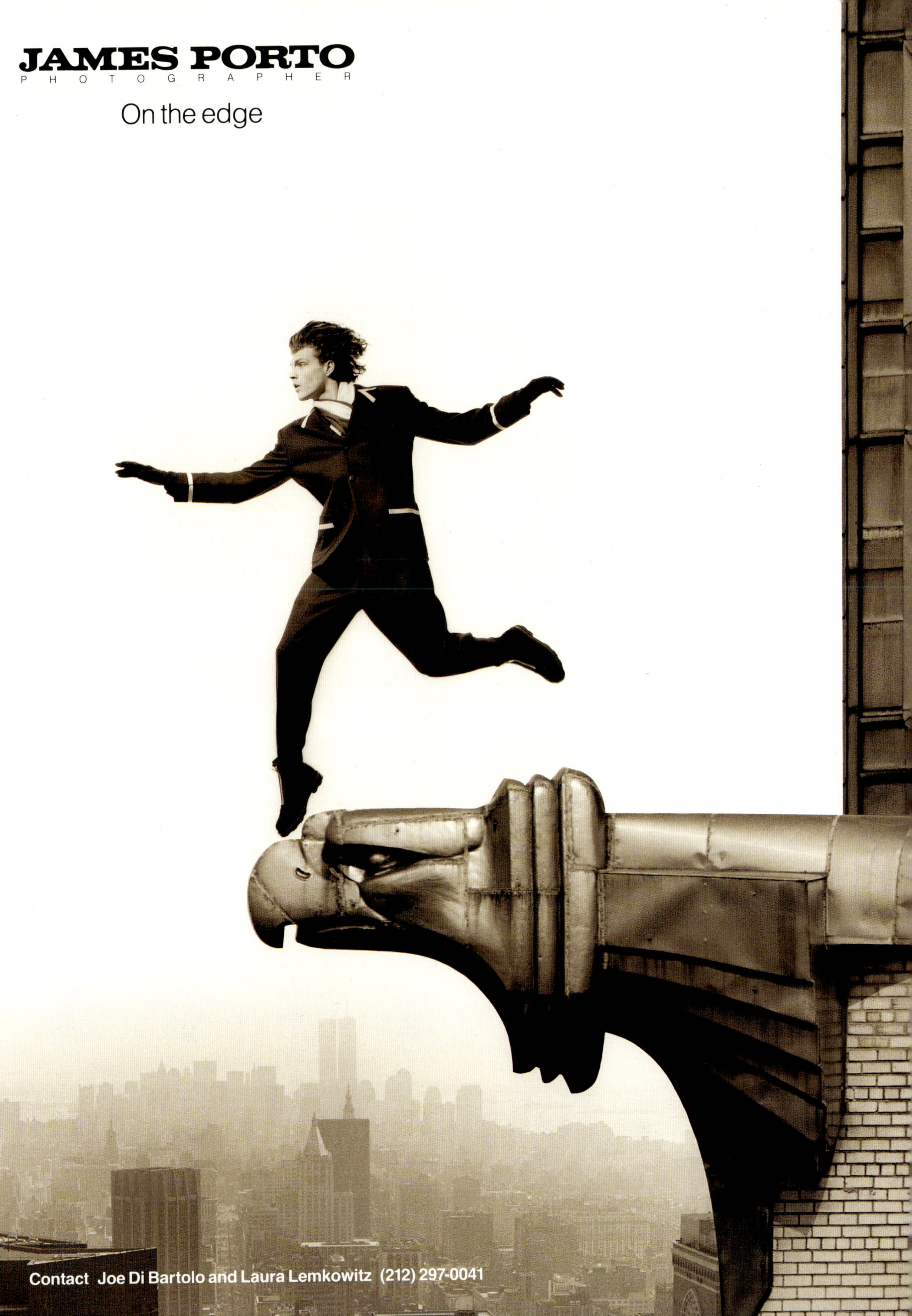
JAMES PORTO
PHOTOGRAPHER
On the edge
Contact Joe Di Bartolo and Laura Lemkowitz (212) 297-0041

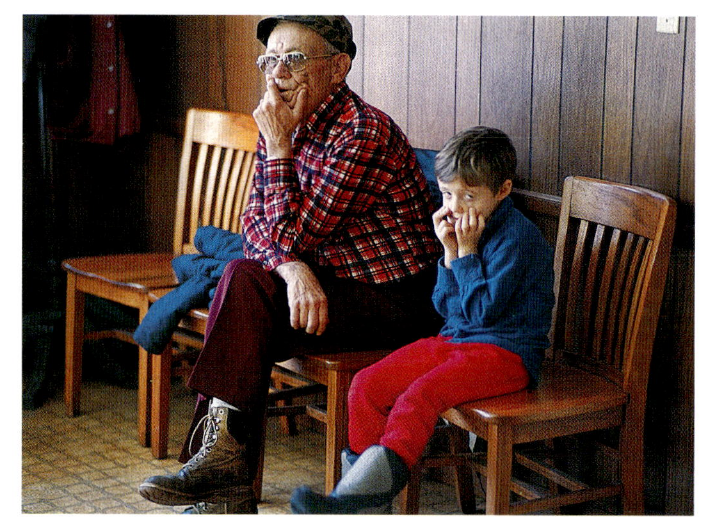

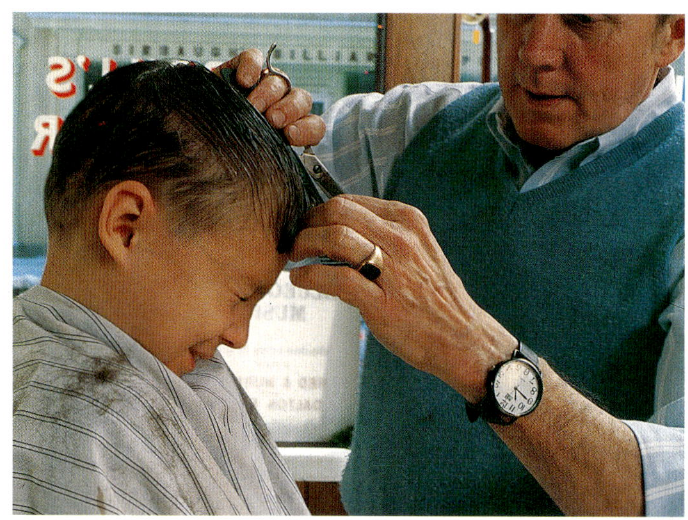

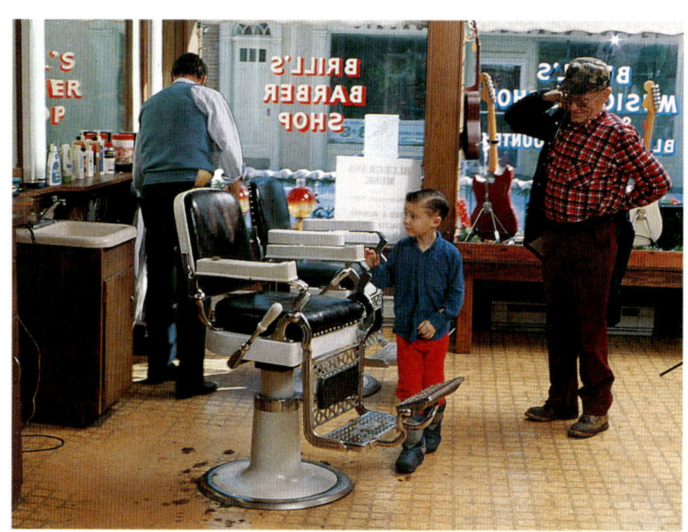

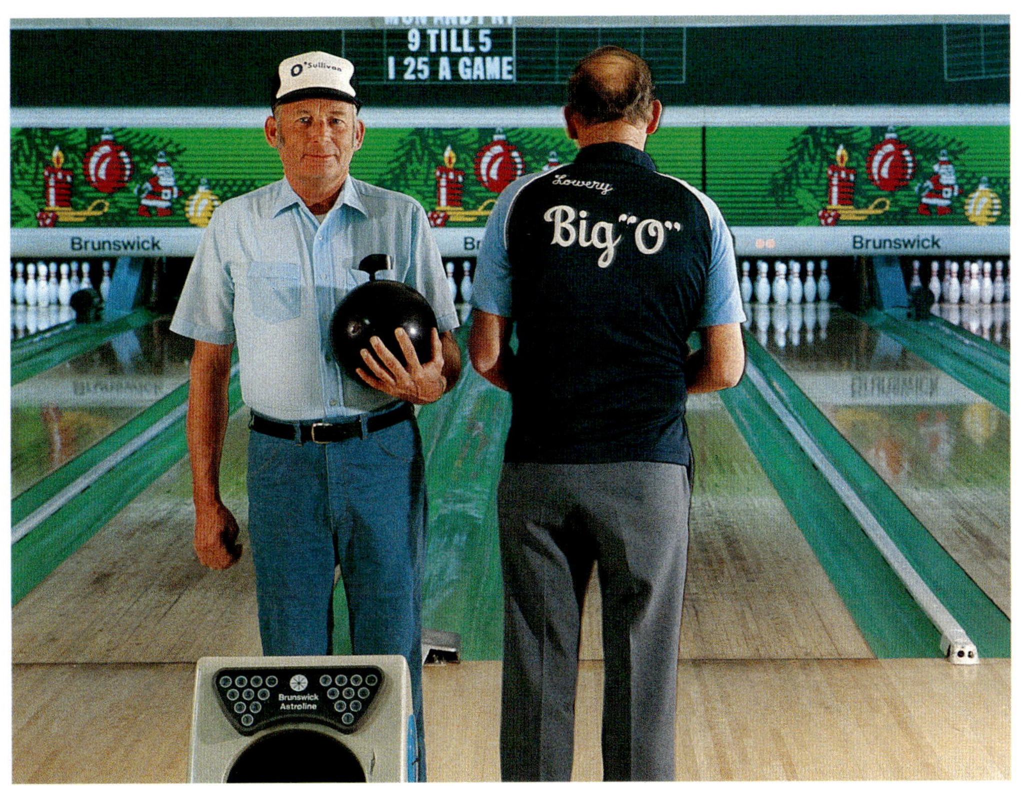

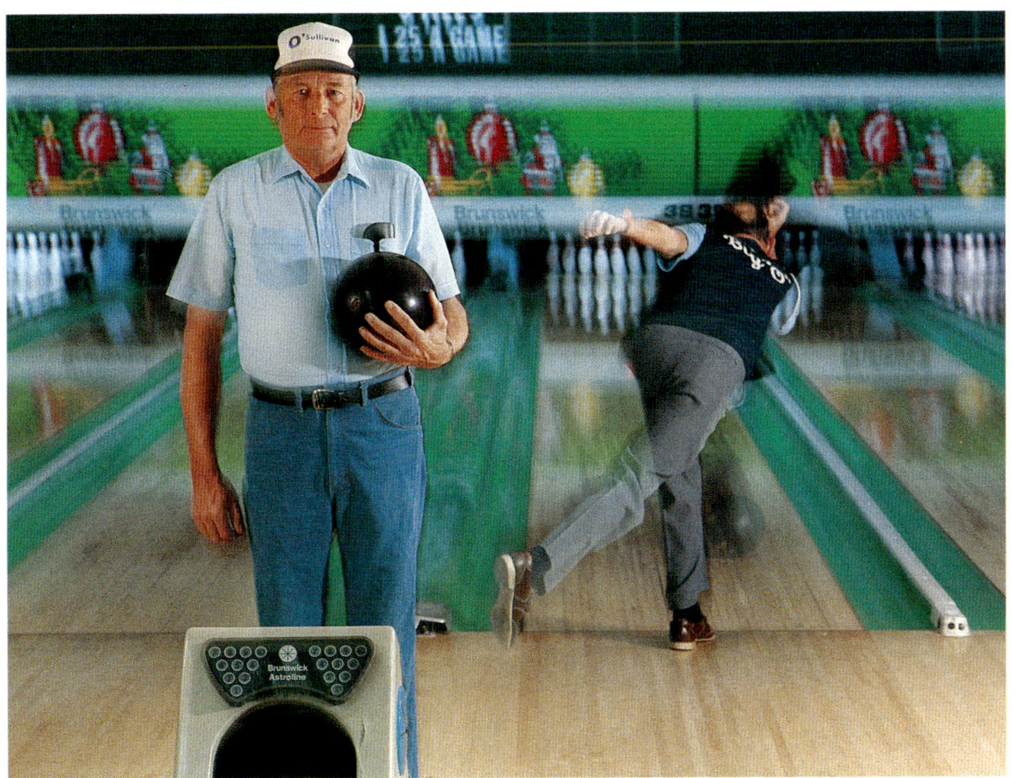

DAVID KATZENSTEIN

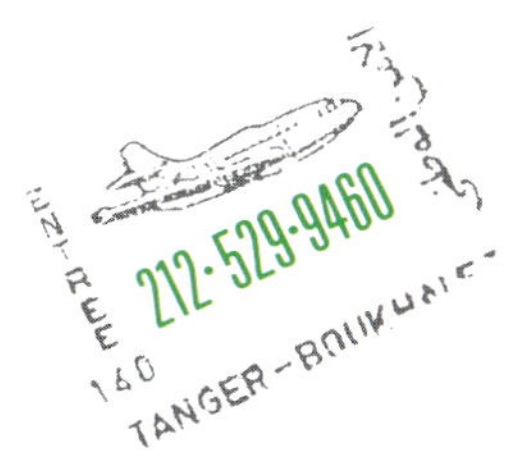

REPRESENTED BY
DOROTHEA SCHER 212·689·7273

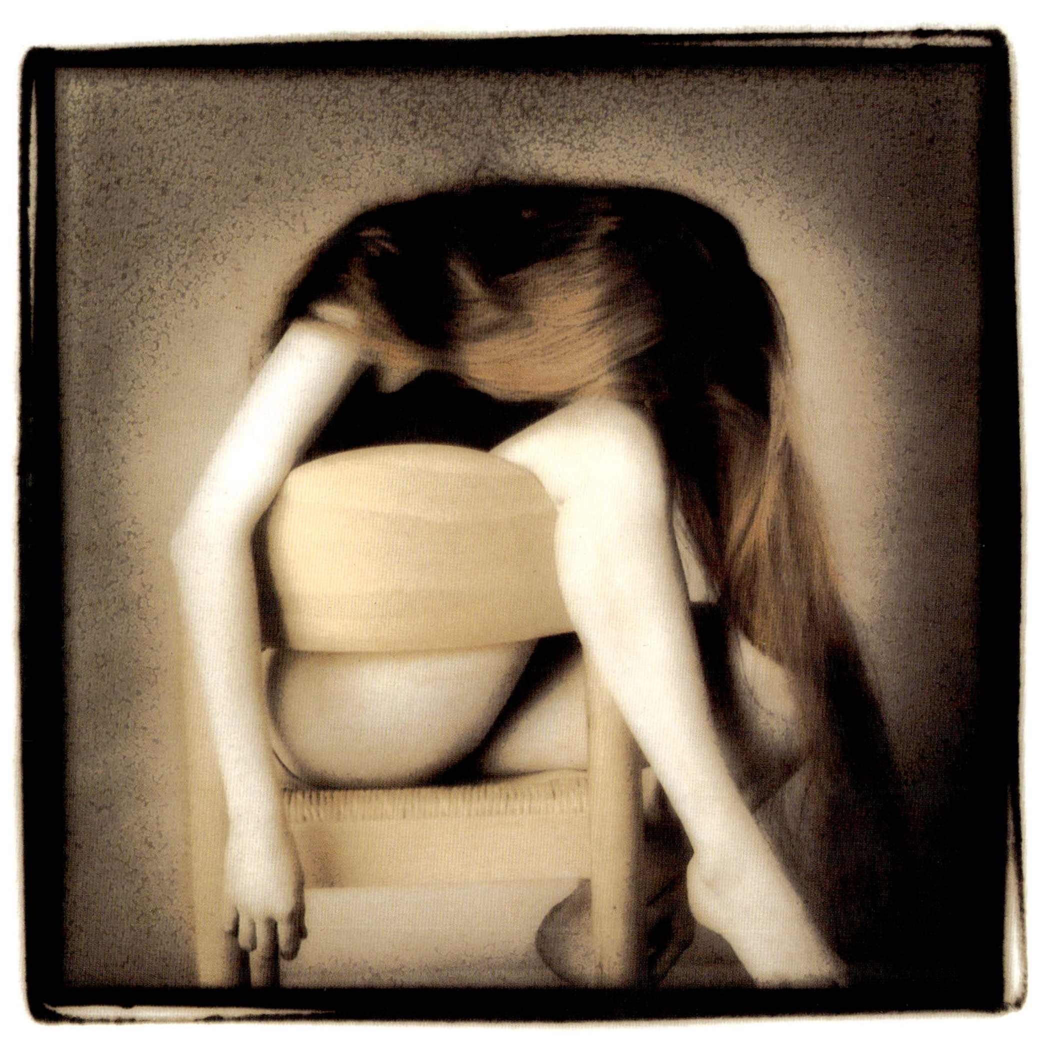

Studio: 212-529-4300 Fax: 212-529-4332

JIM GALANTE STUDIO

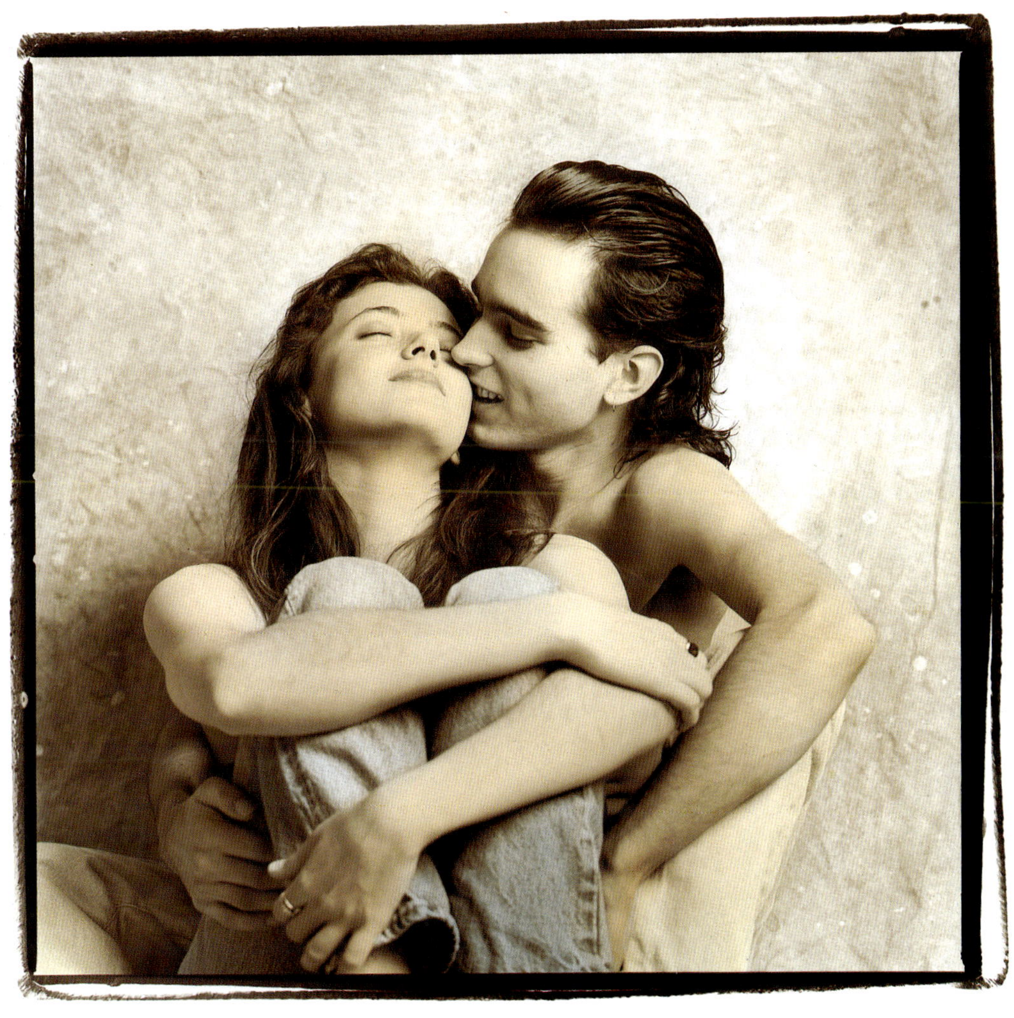

Represented by Randy Cole 212-679-5933

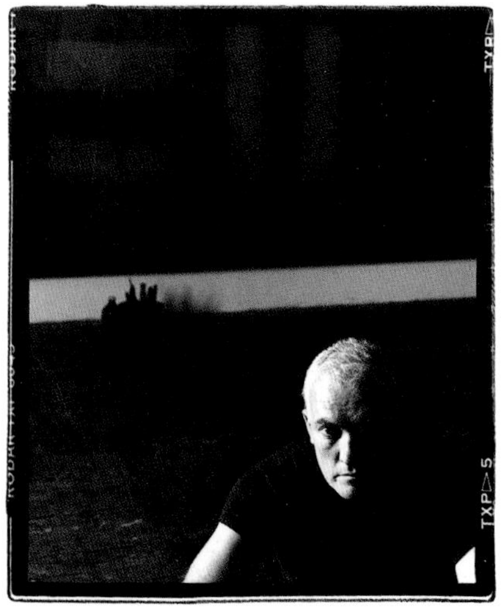

Sean Scully
PAINTER

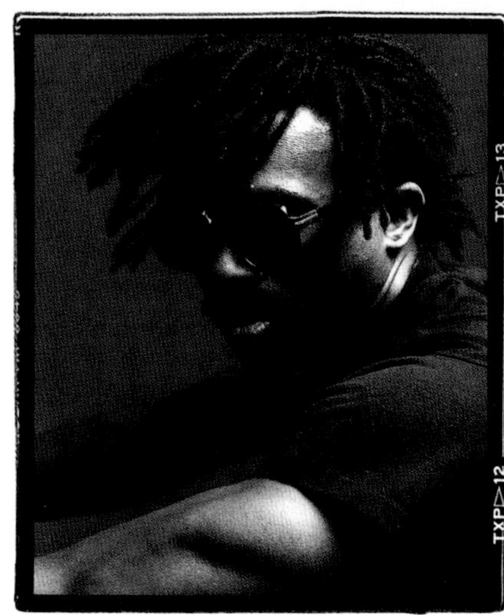

Craigwood Phillips
ILLUSTRATOR

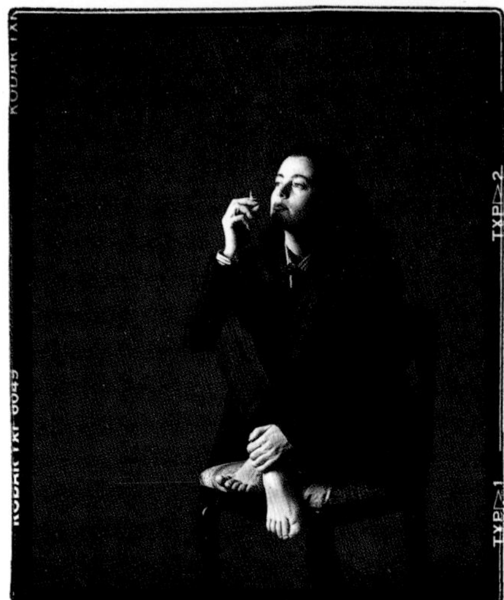

Maura McEvoy
STYLIST

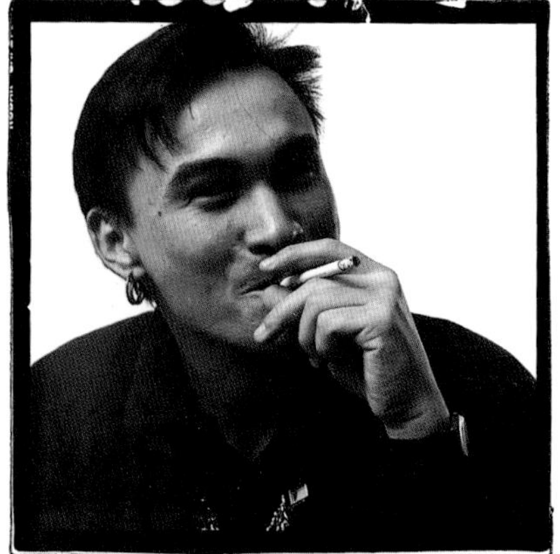

Sammy Rialto
FORTUNETELLER

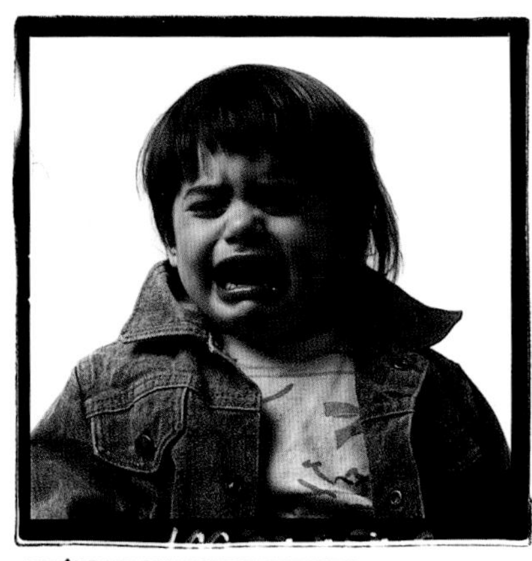

Jarrett Anabel
ACTRESS

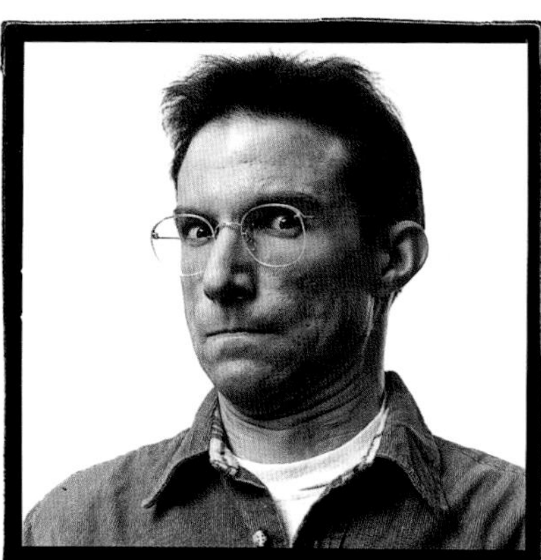

J. Ross Baughman
PHOTOJOURNALIST

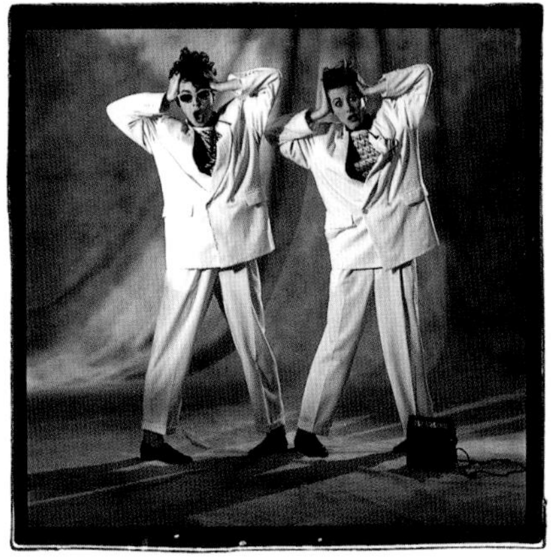

Doreen and Midge
EXISTENTIAL THINKERS

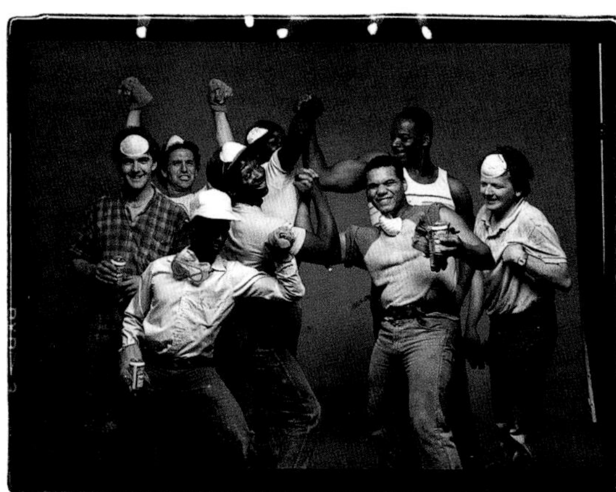

Sal and the Boys
DECONSTRUCTIVISTS

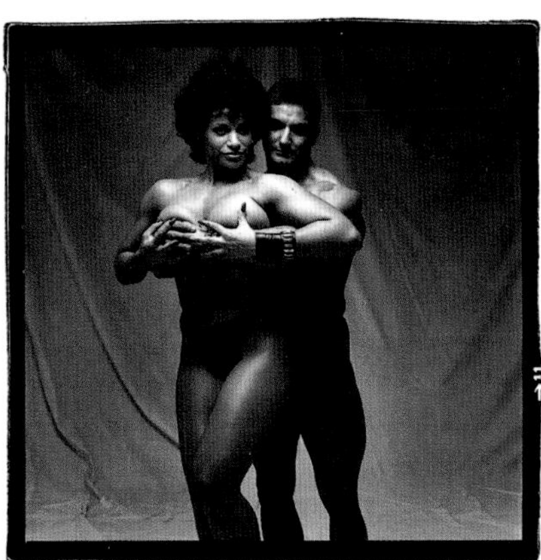

Mike Alatof
BODY BUILDER

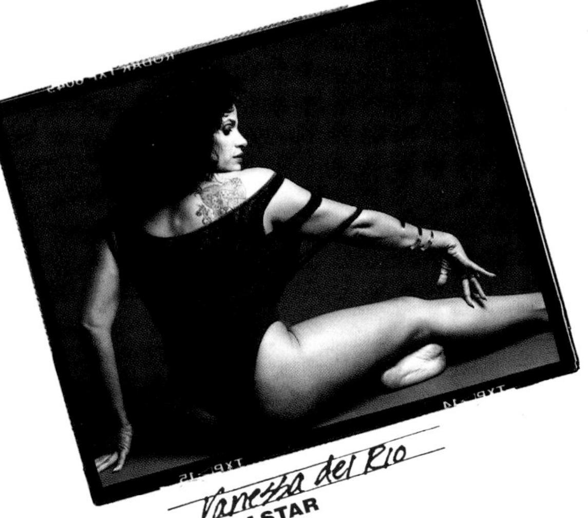

Vanessa del Rio
FILM STAR

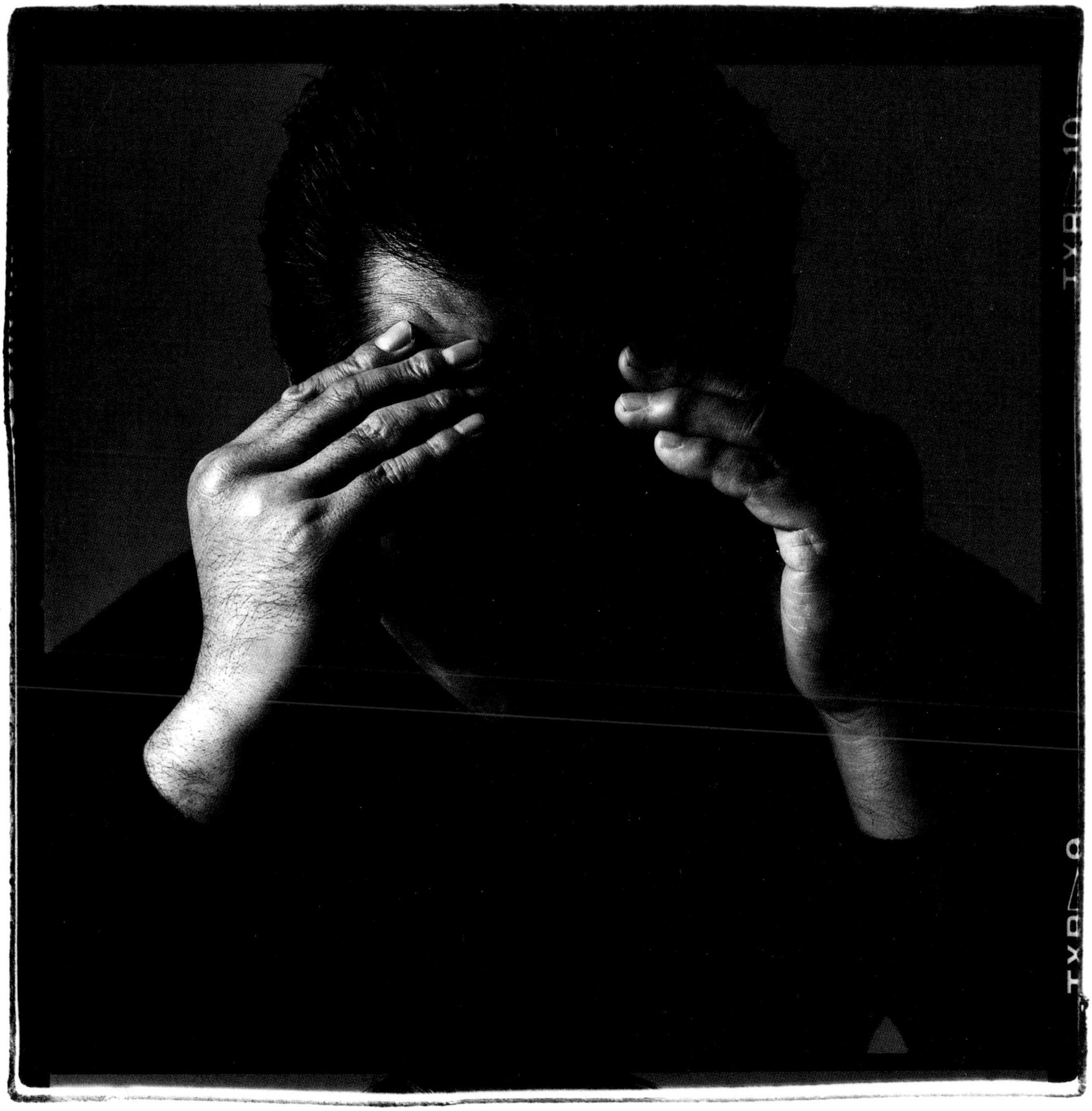

DESIGN *Susan Hunter*

Tadashi Nakamura
GRAND MASTER KARATE

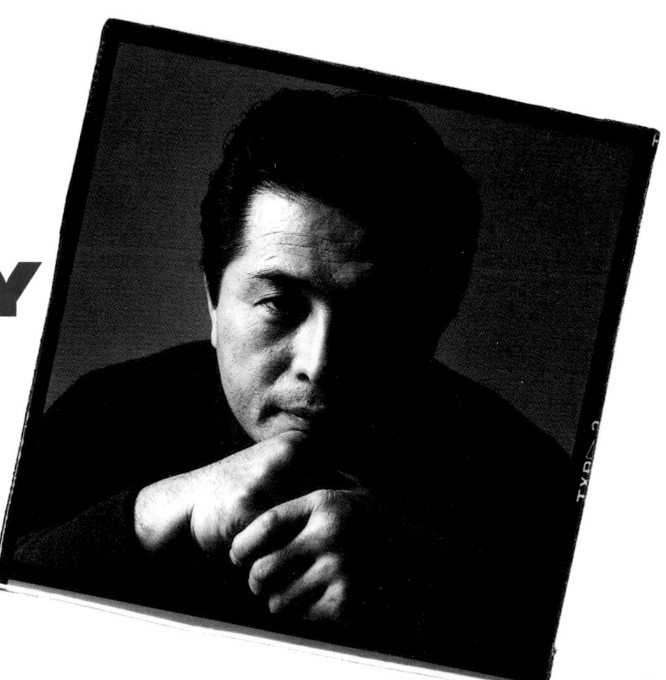

JOHN GREGORY

Portraits

REPRESENTED BY DALE DAVIS AND HARRIS SPYLIOS
(212) 581·5766 FAX (212) 956·8789

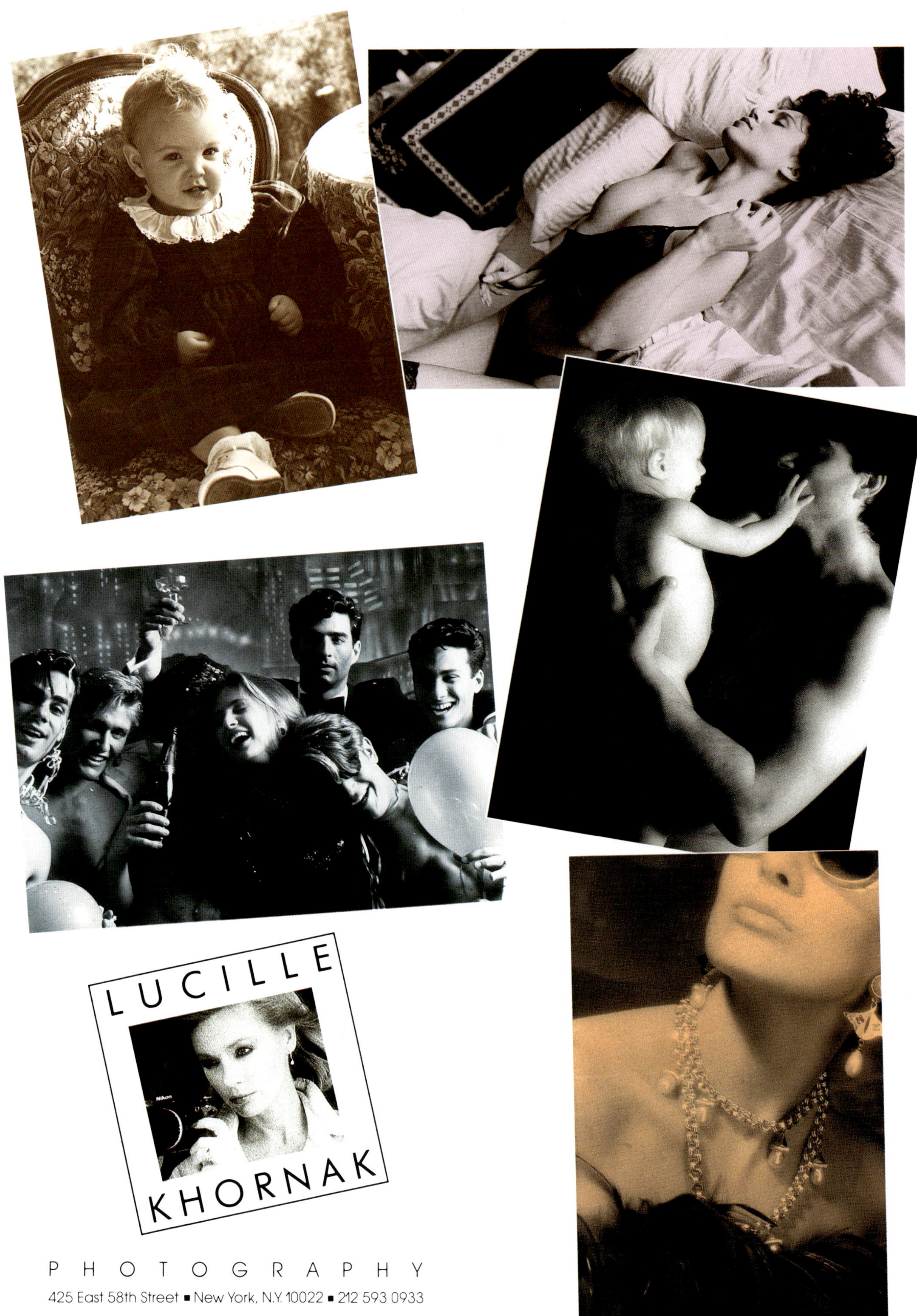
LUCILLE
KHORNAK
PHOTOGRAPHY
425 East 58th Street ■ New York, N.Y. 10022 ■ 212 593 0933

Jan Cobb Photography Ltd.

Represented

by

Gary Lerman

(212) 683-5777

Fax: 779-3697

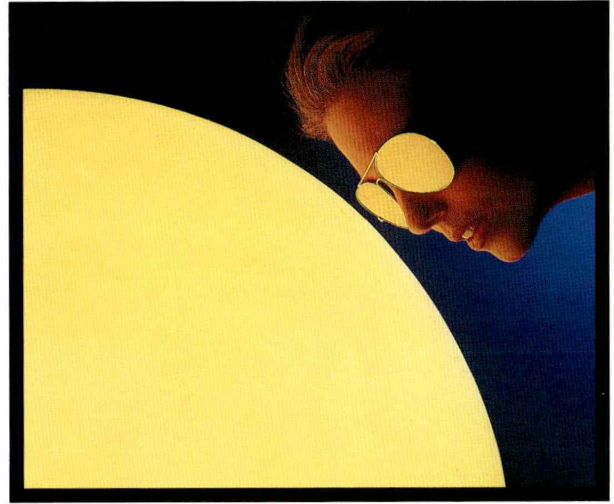

Color

☆

☎

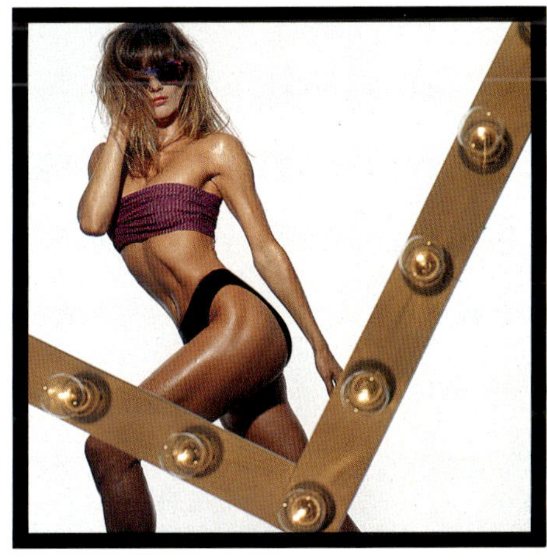

Studio:

5 West 19

NYC 10011

(212) 255-1400

Fax: 627-1962

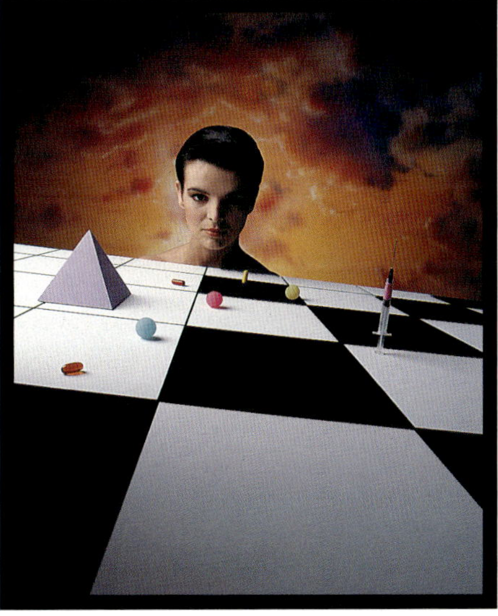

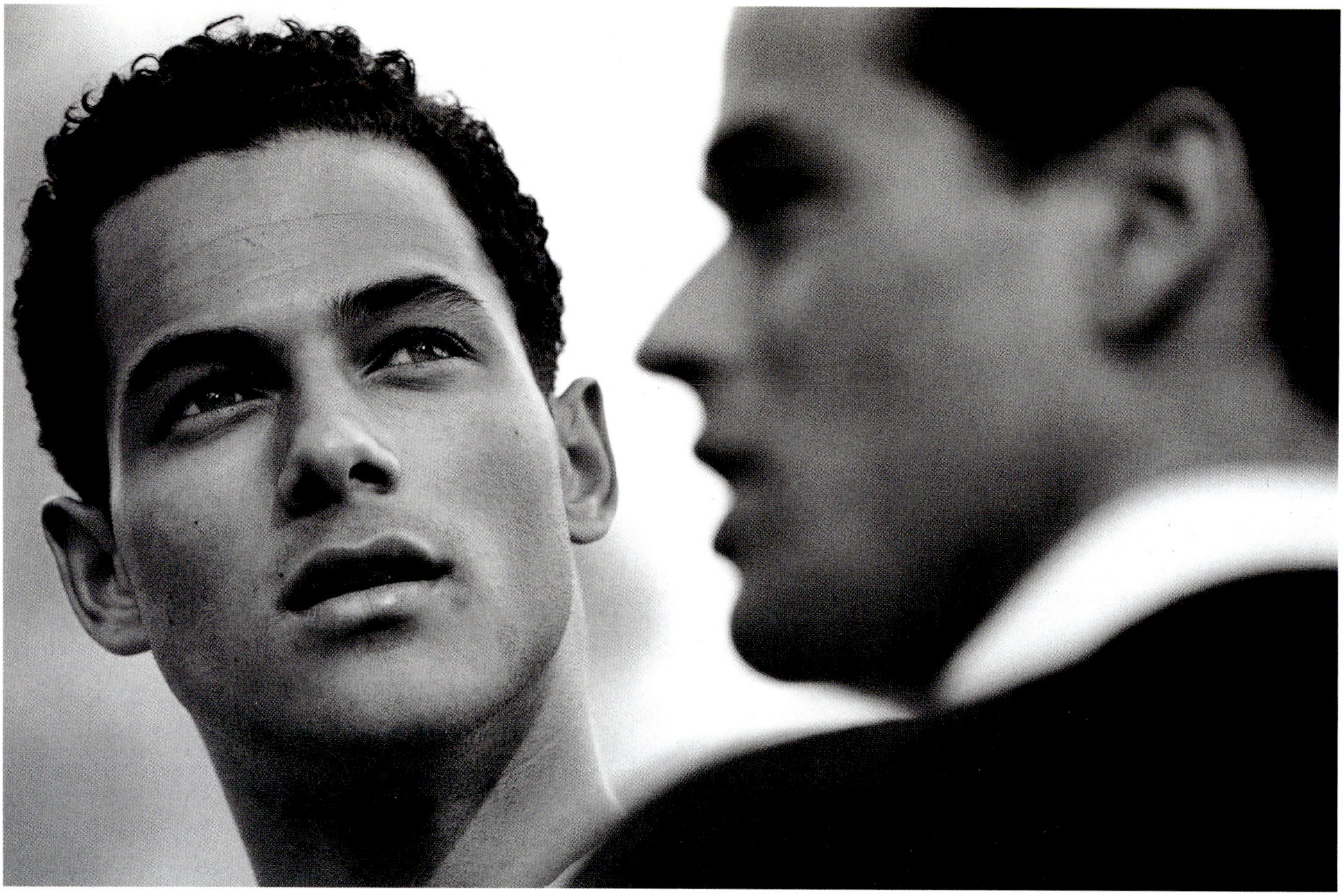

B A R D   M A R T I N

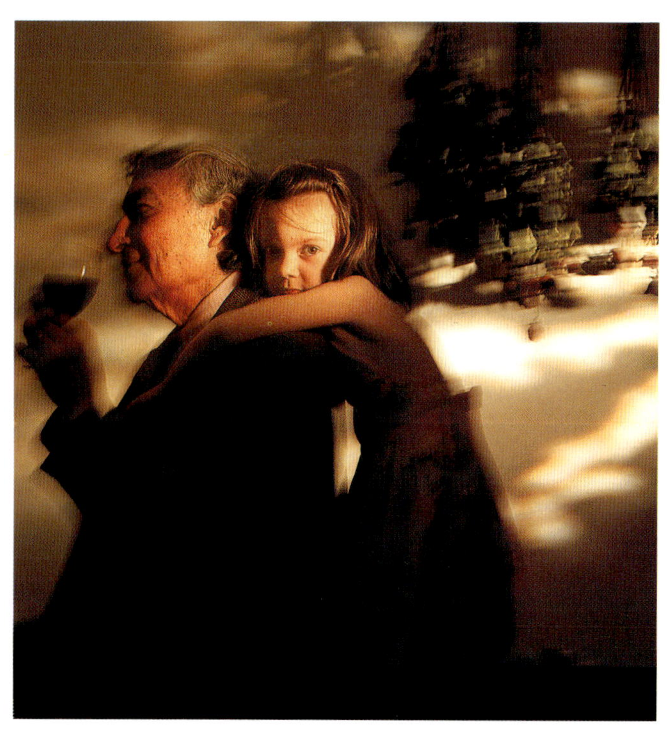

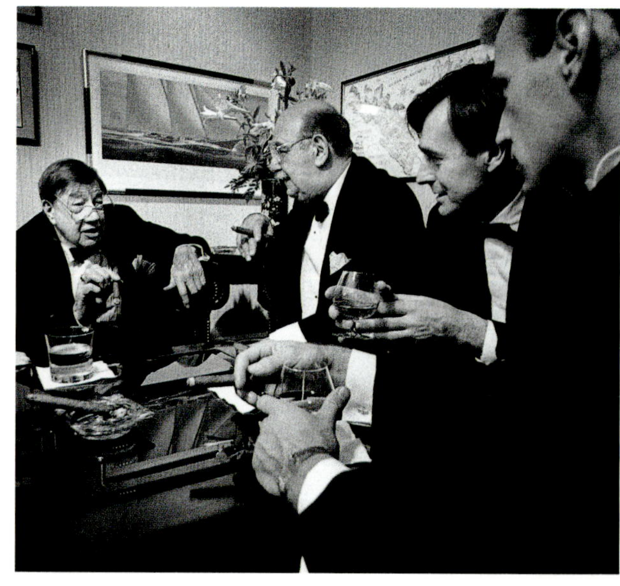

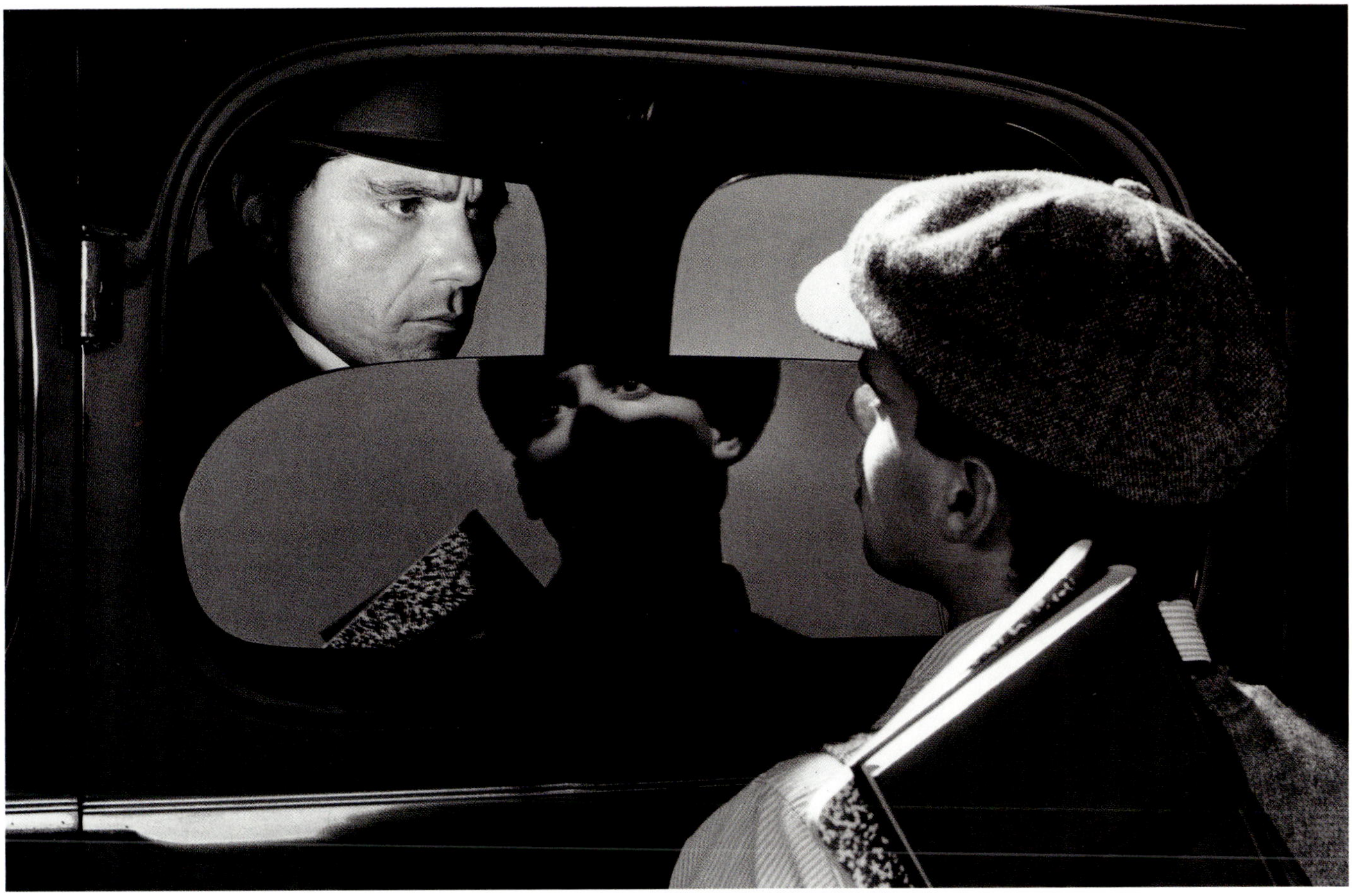

"Lucky Luciano" for the Hearst Corp; Jordan McGrath Case & Taylor; Anne Sullivan, A.D.

212 929 6712

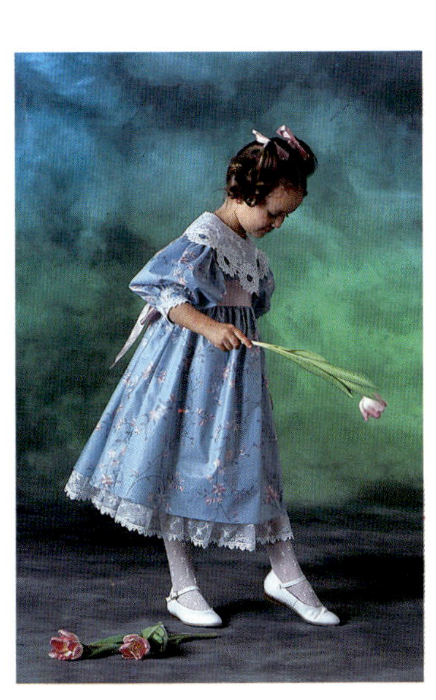

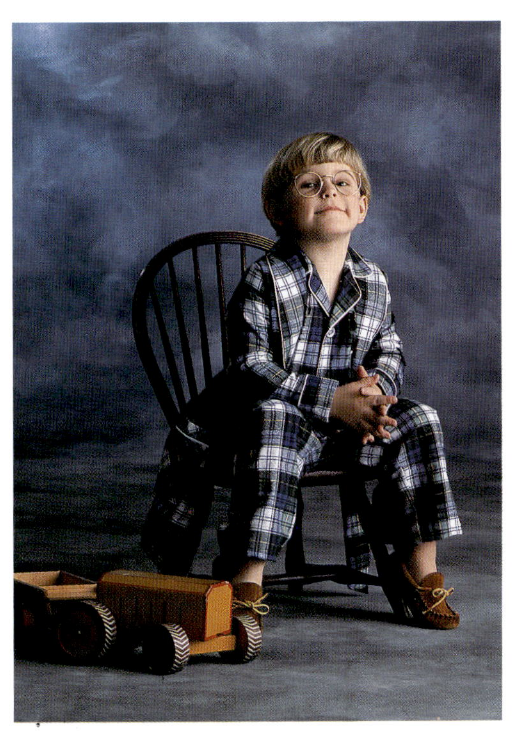

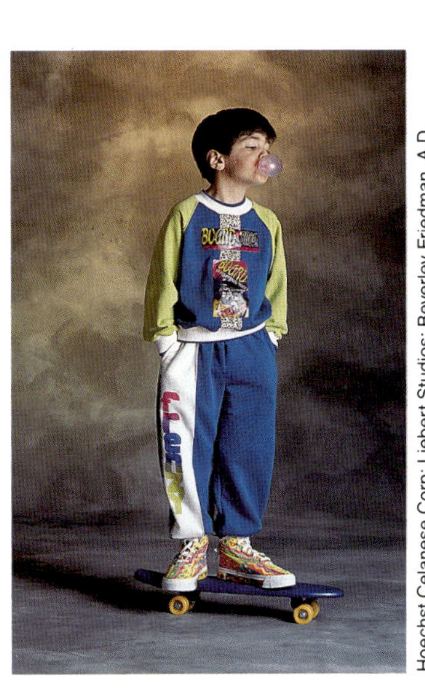

Hoechst Celanese Corp; Liebert Studios; Beverley Friedman, A.D.

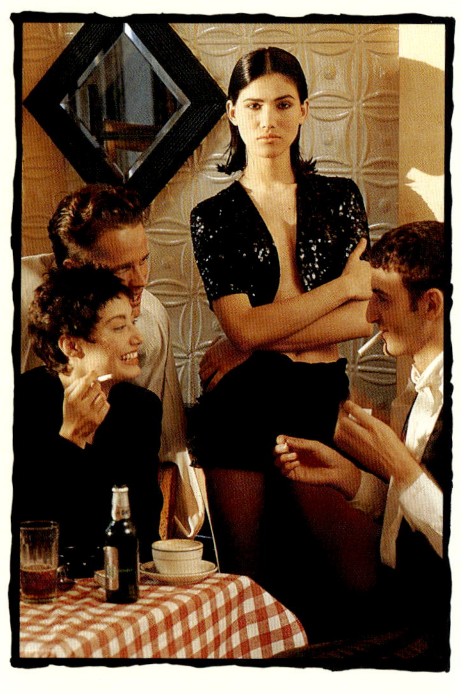
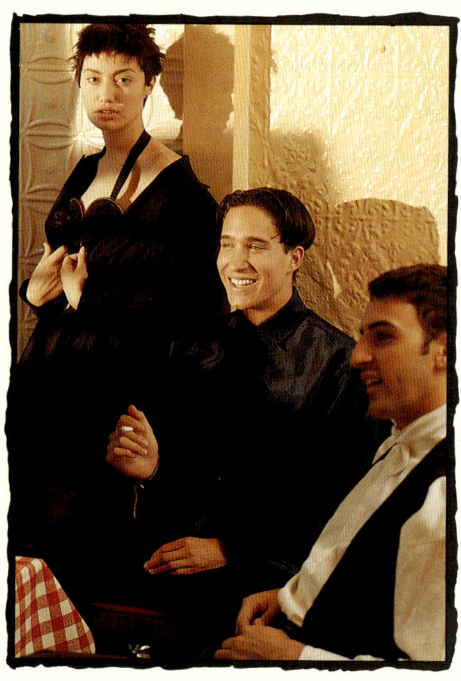
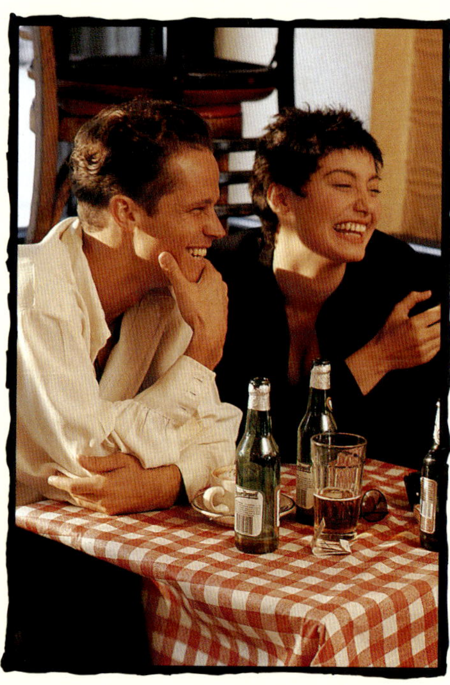
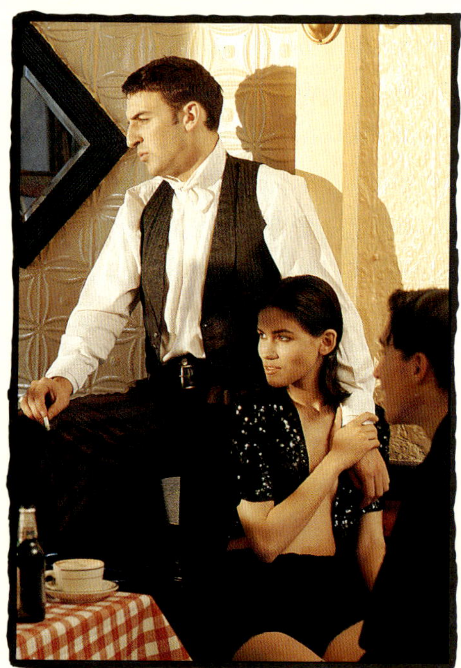
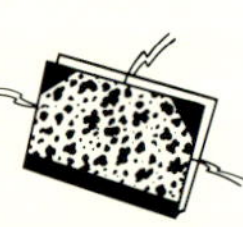

represented by marge casey & assoc

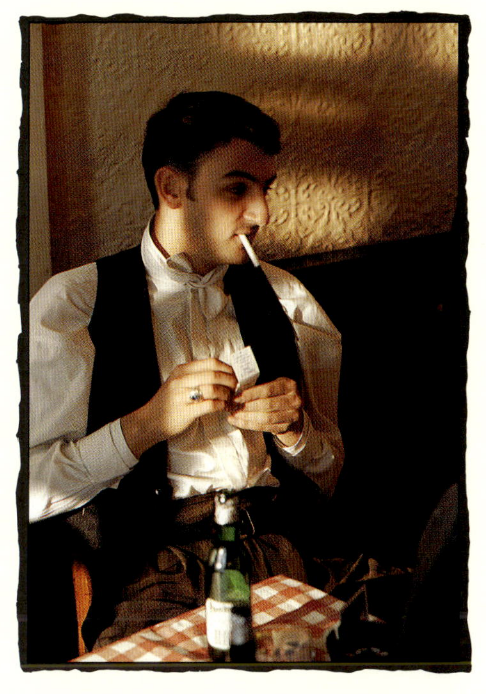

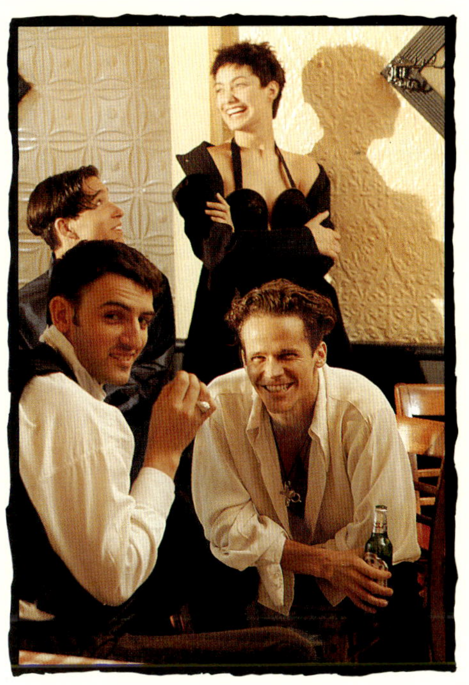

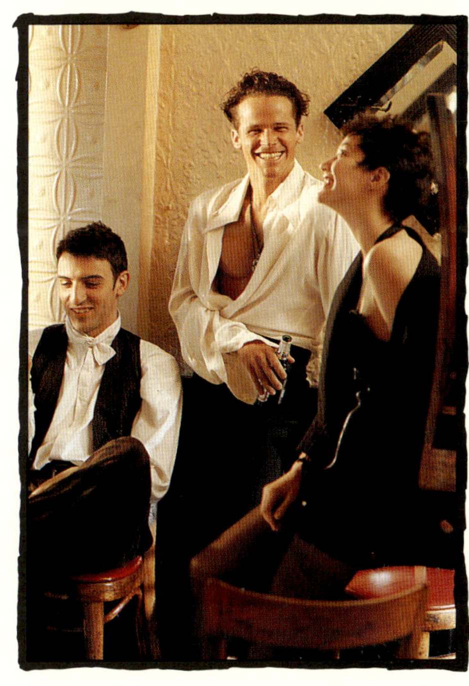

helen norman ltd

photographer

245 east 63rd st # 201 nyc phone 212.486.9575

TOMEK & ERYK
represented by
MARZENA
TEL (212) 772-2522
FAX (212) 249-6917

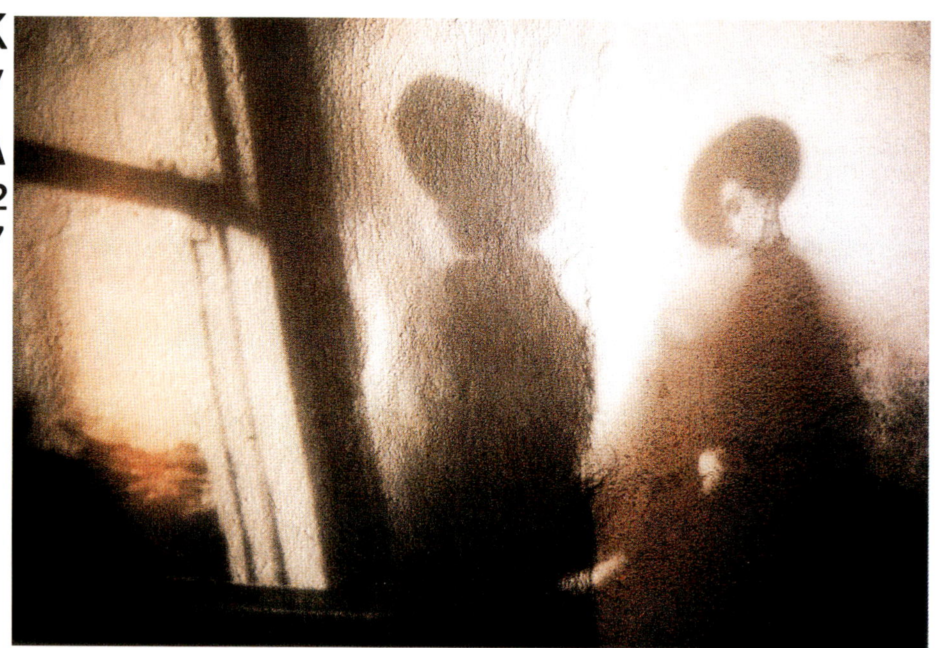

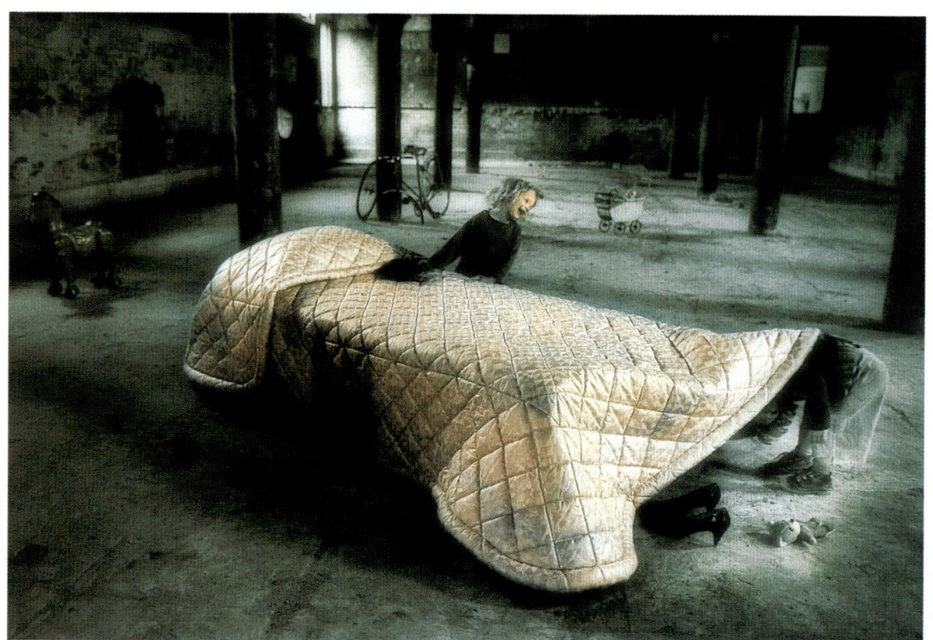

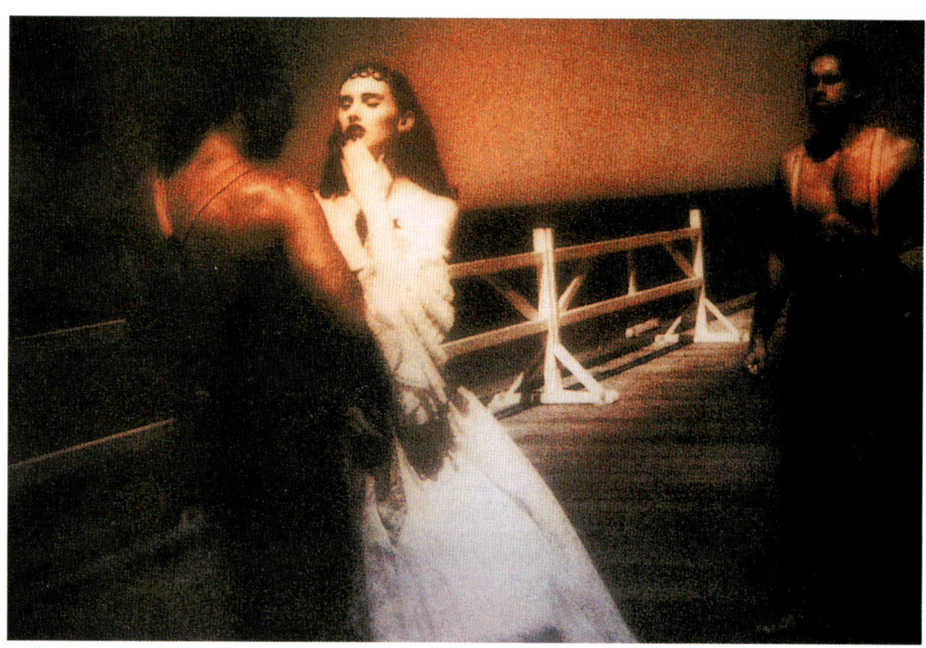

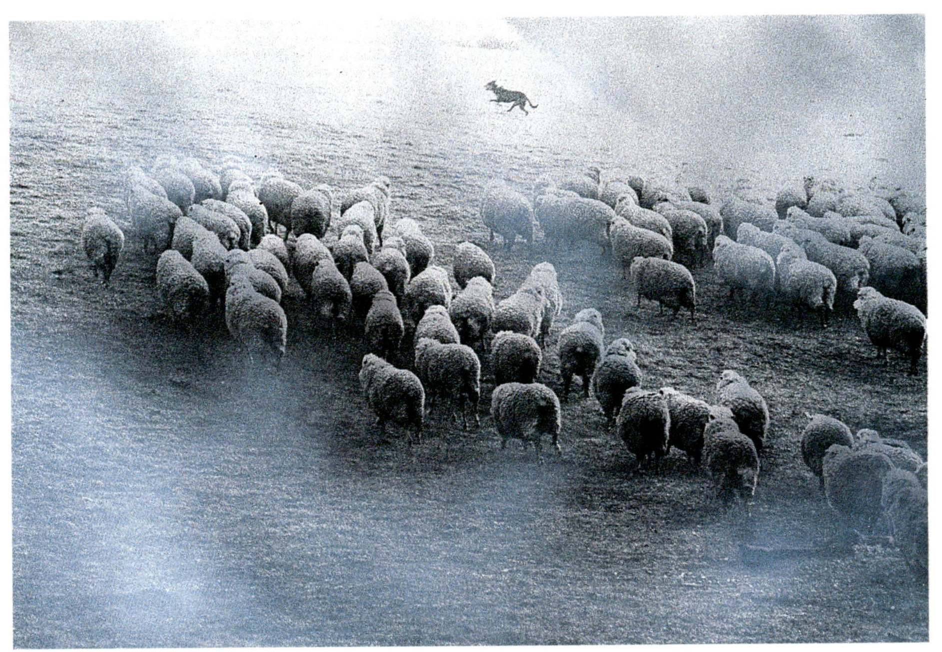

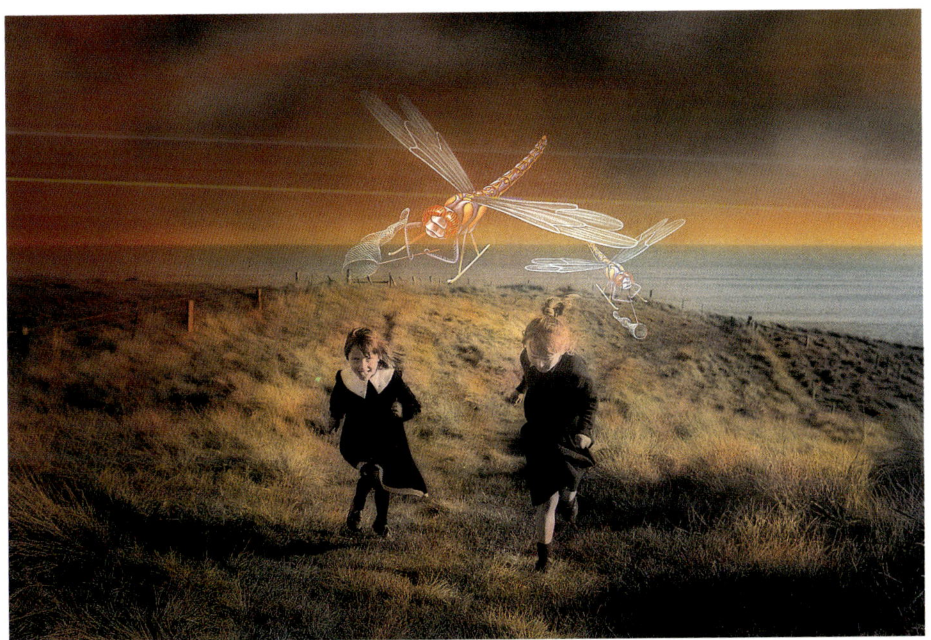

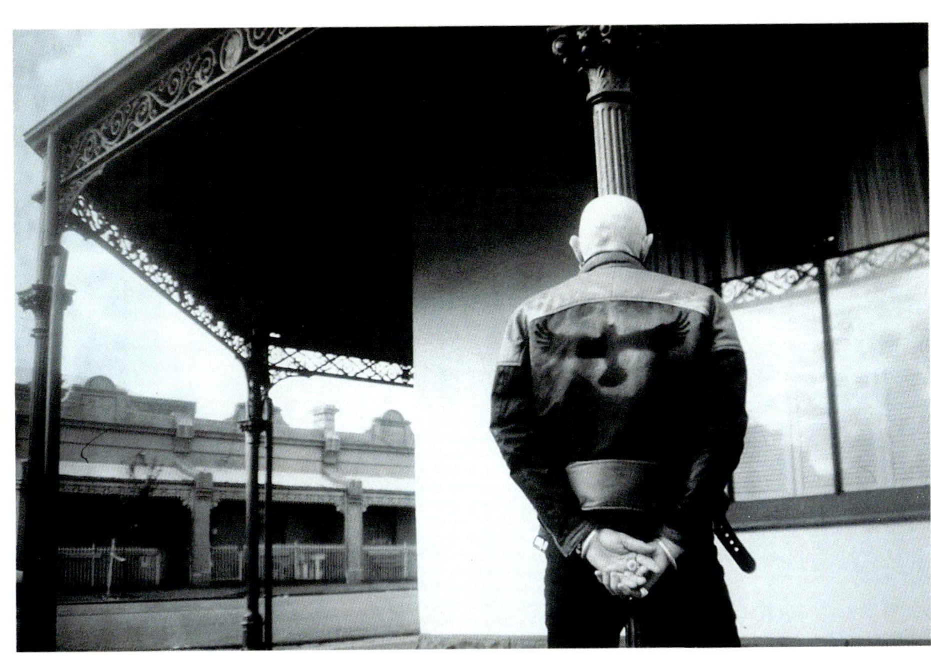

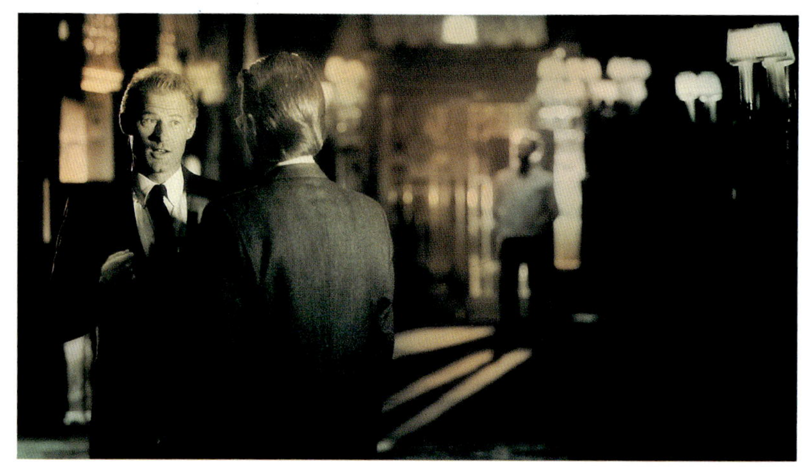

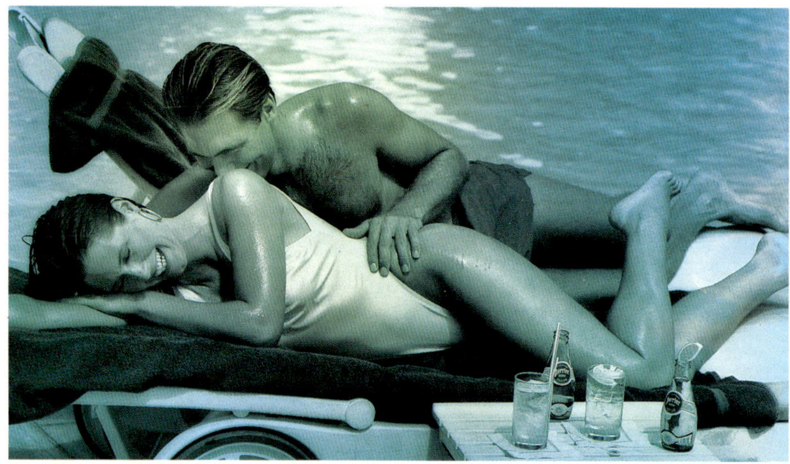

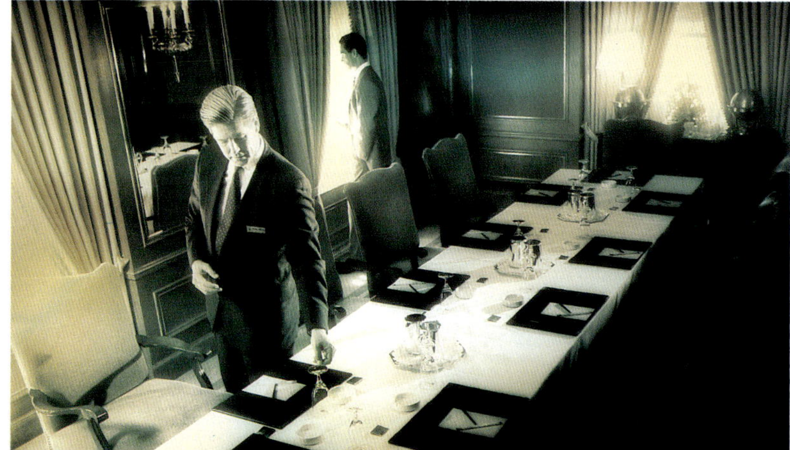

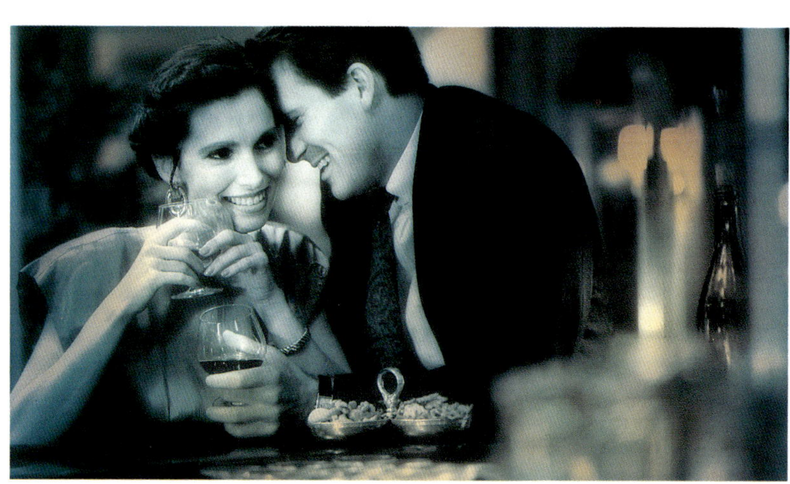

GELSOBELLO

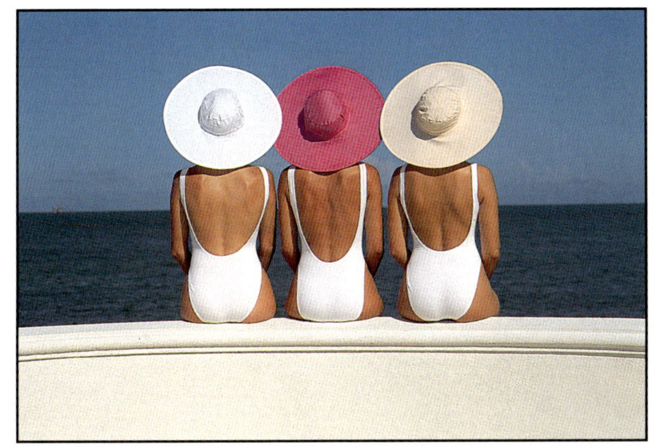

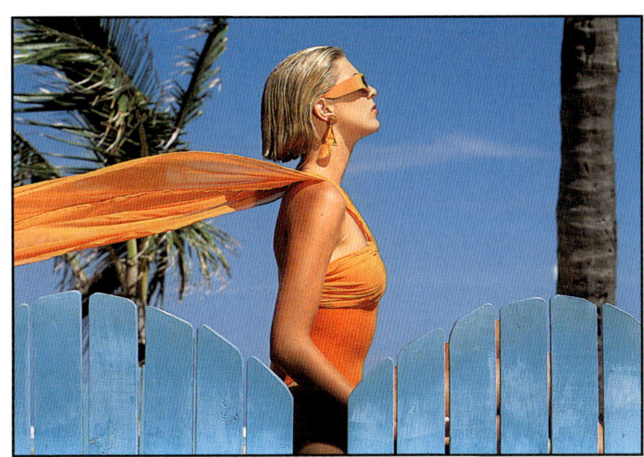

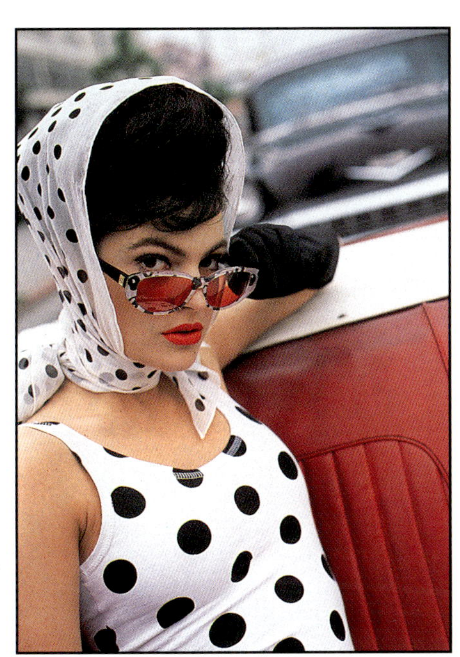

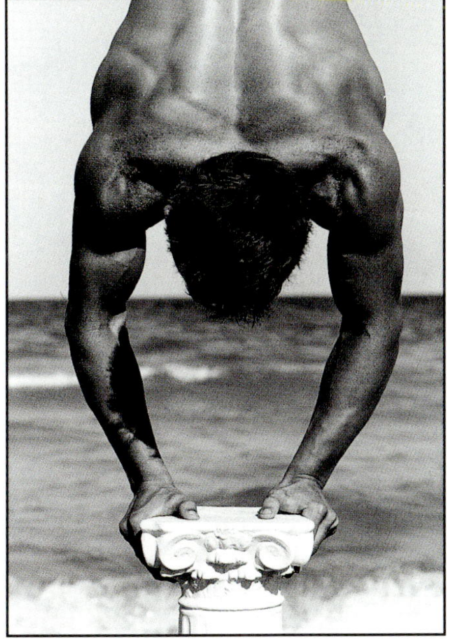

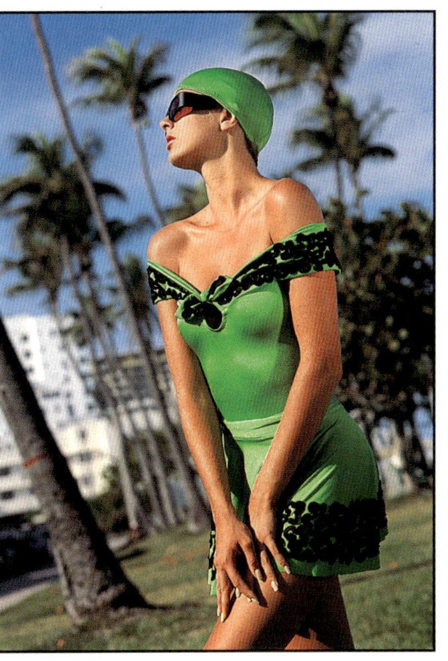

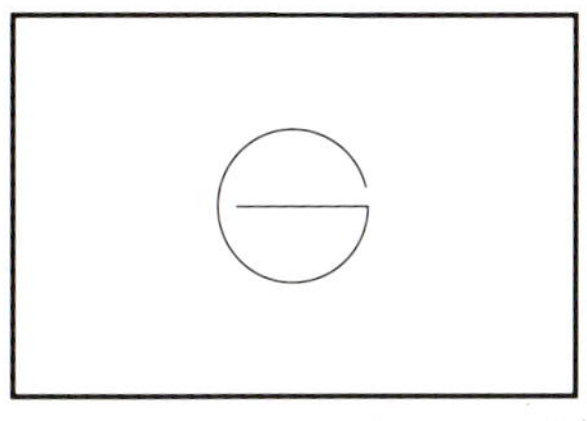

PAUL GELSOBELLO

245 WEST 29TH STREET • STUDIO 1200 • NEW YORK, NEW YORK 10001 • (212) 947-0317

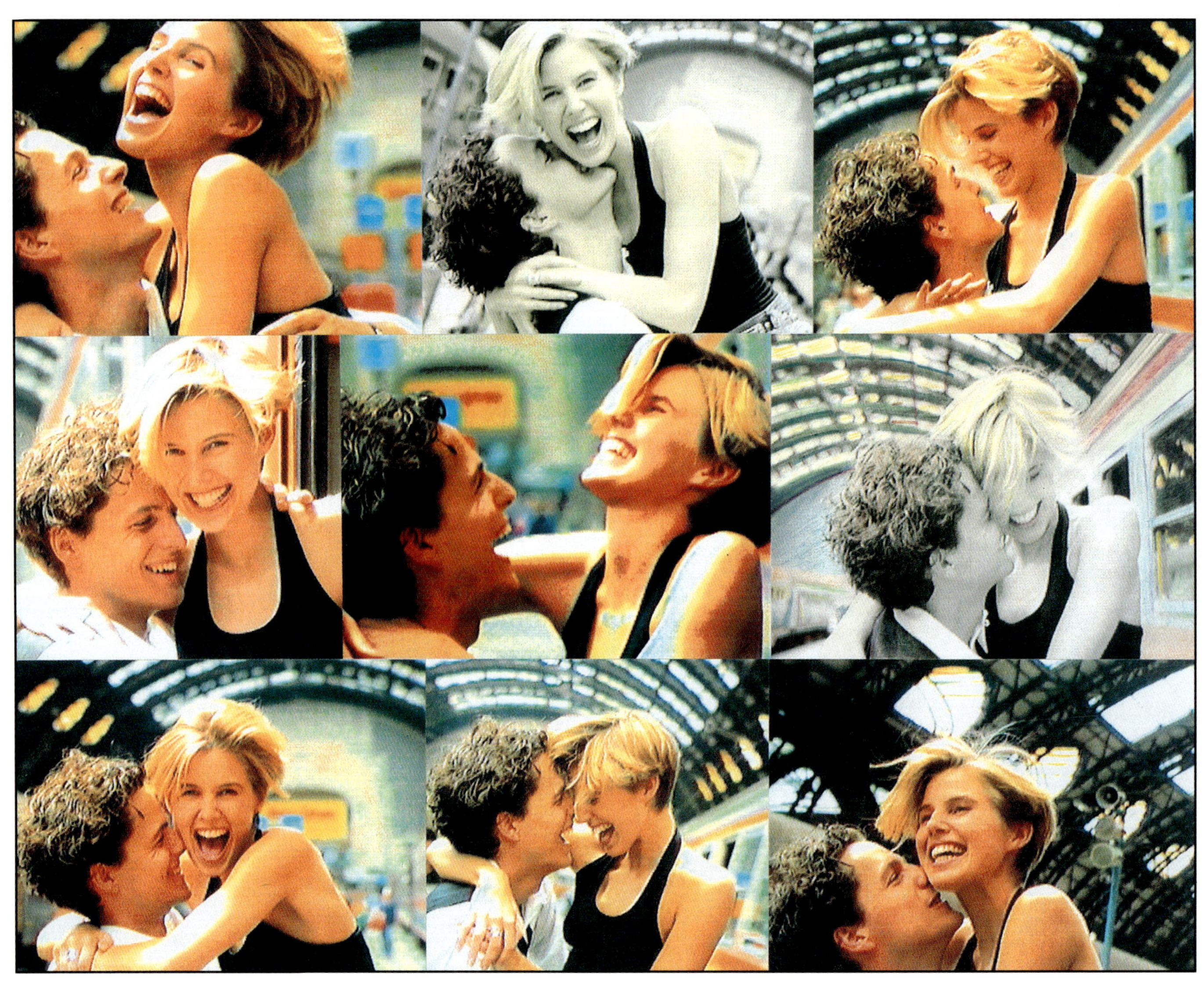

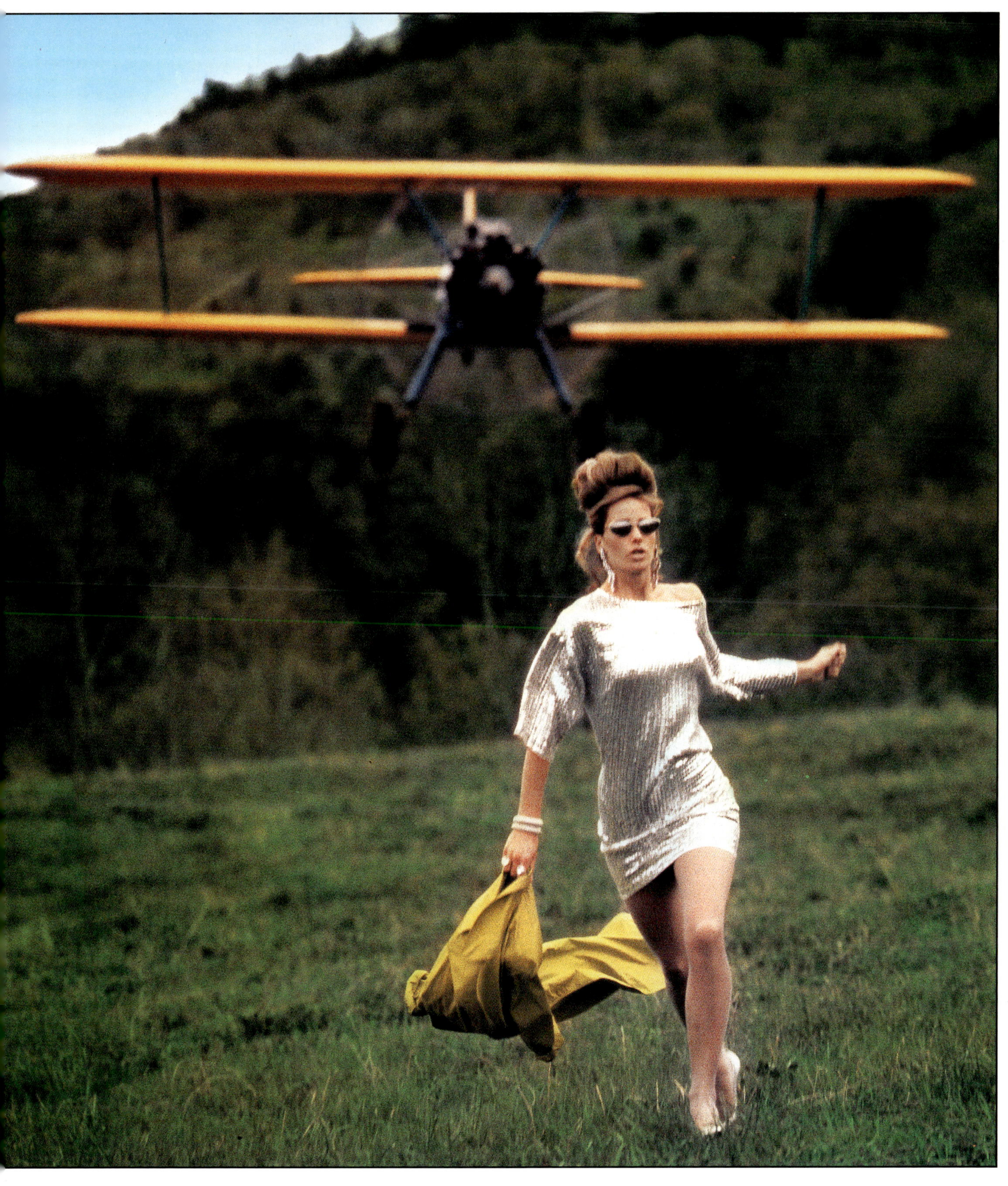

LEE PAGE

310 EAST 46TH STREET NEW YORK, NEW YORK 10017 212-286-9159

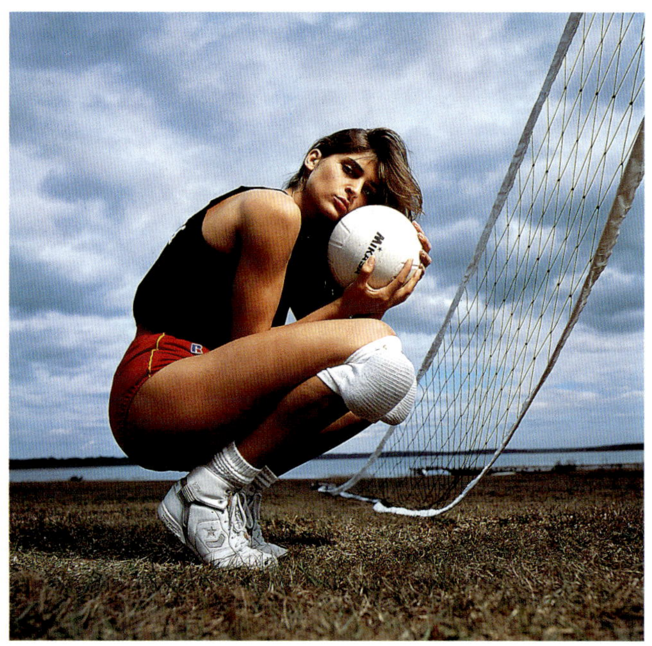

EJ Camp

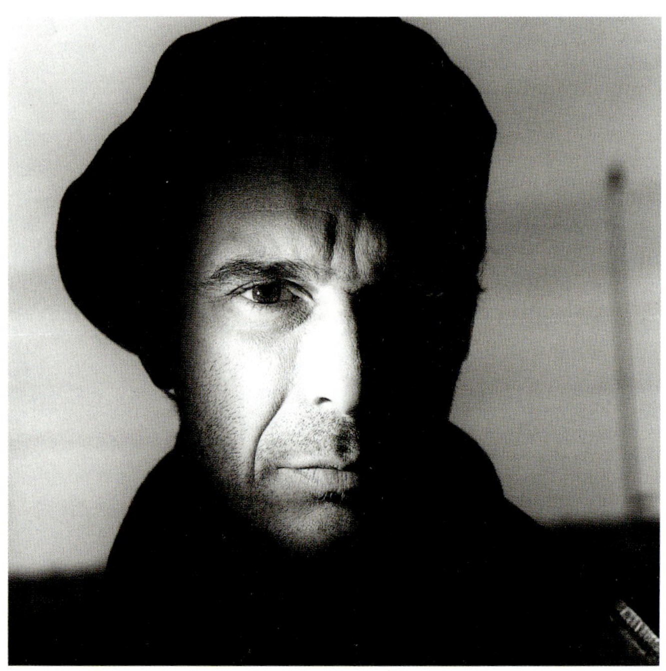

Frank W. Ockenfels 3

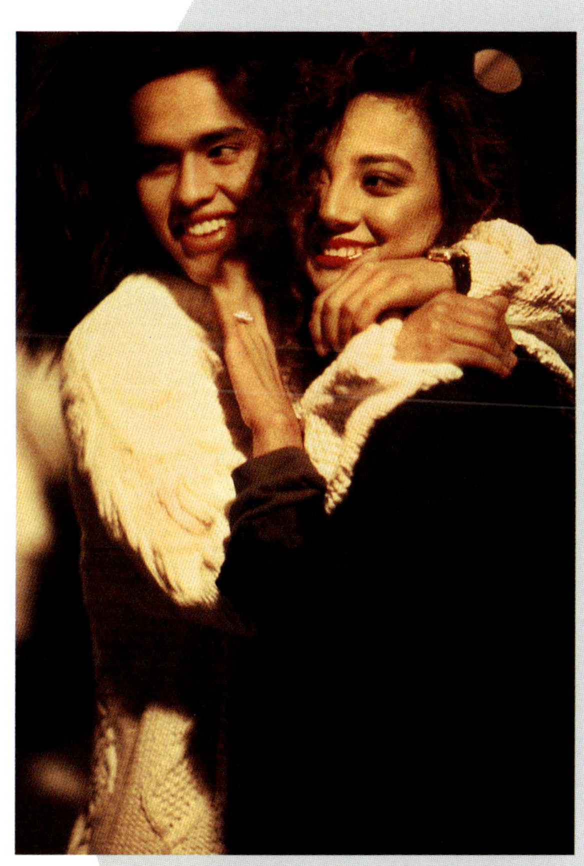

Catanzaro & Mahdessian

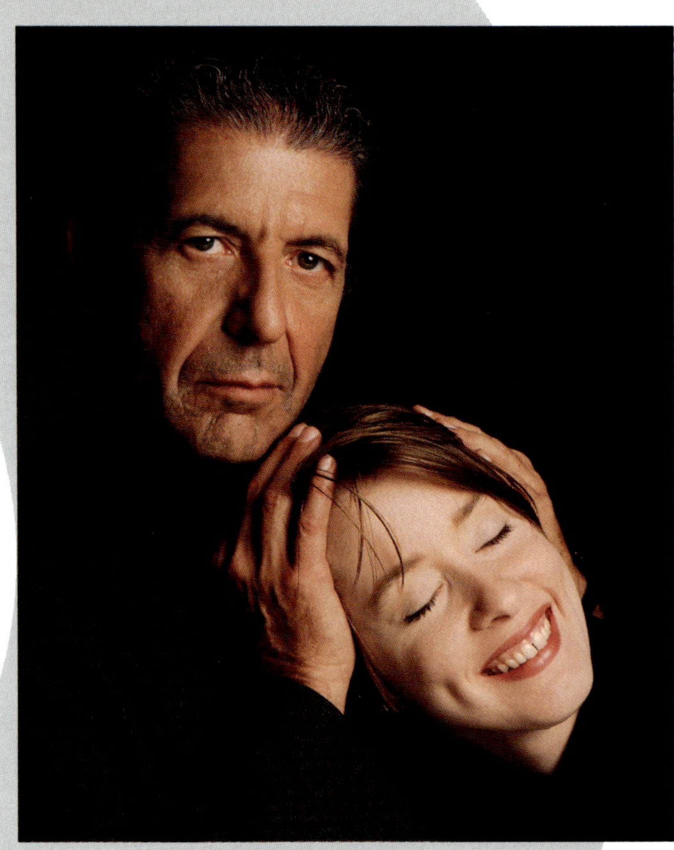

Deborah Feingold

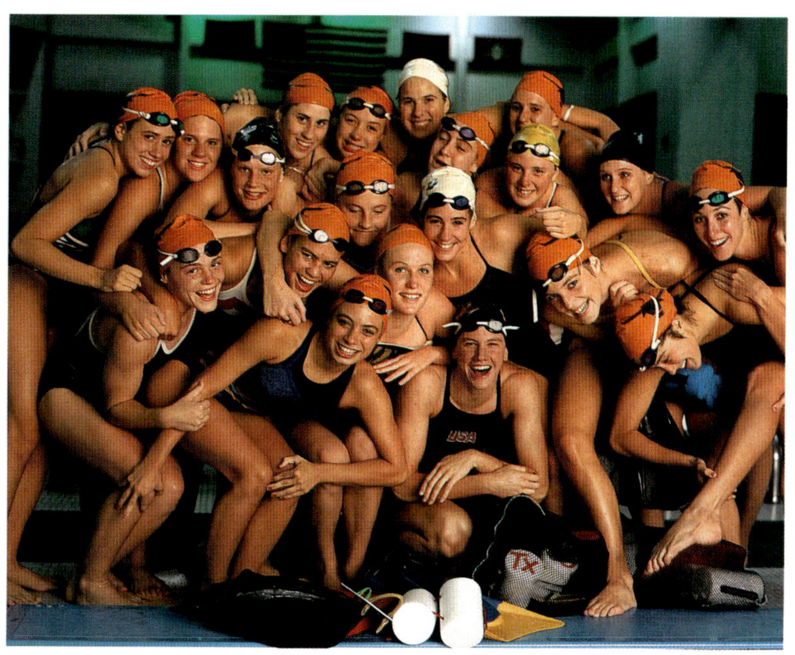

George Lange

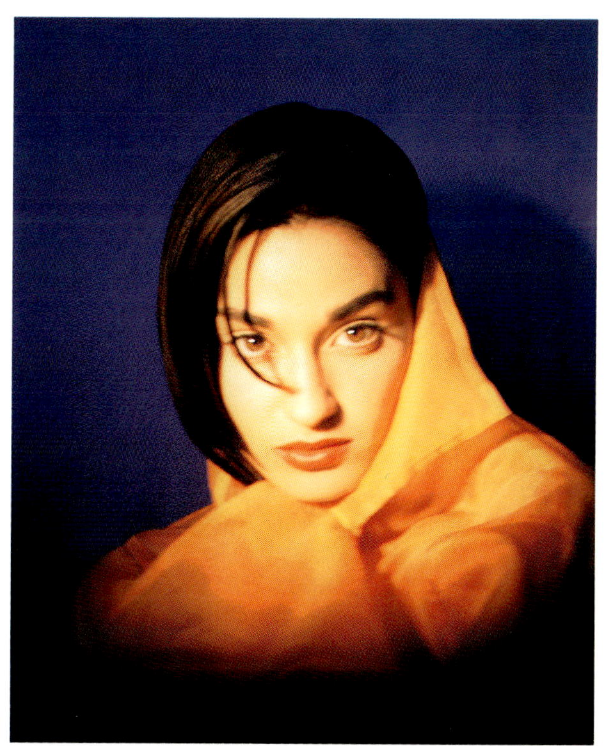

Diego Uchitel

IAN GRAY

212-557-8625

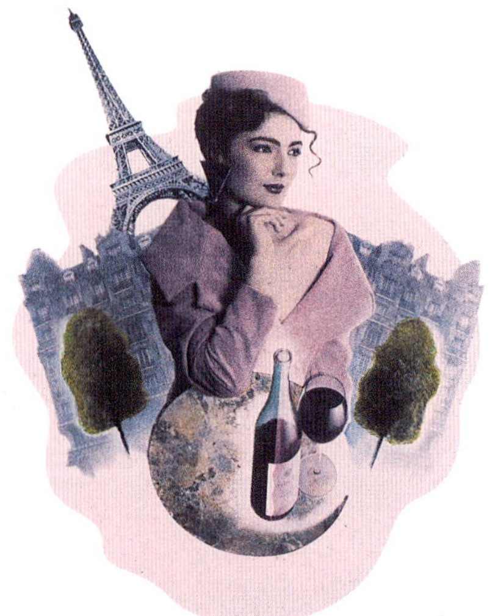

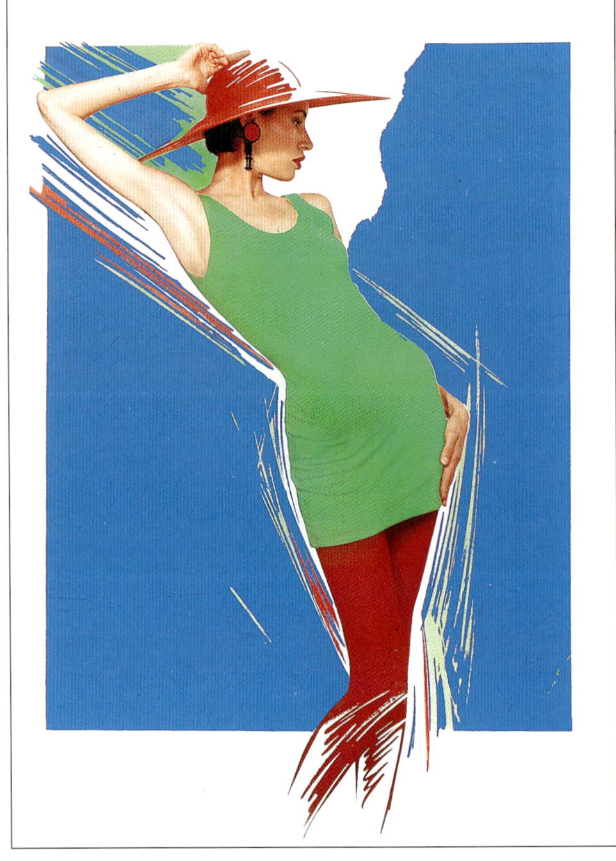

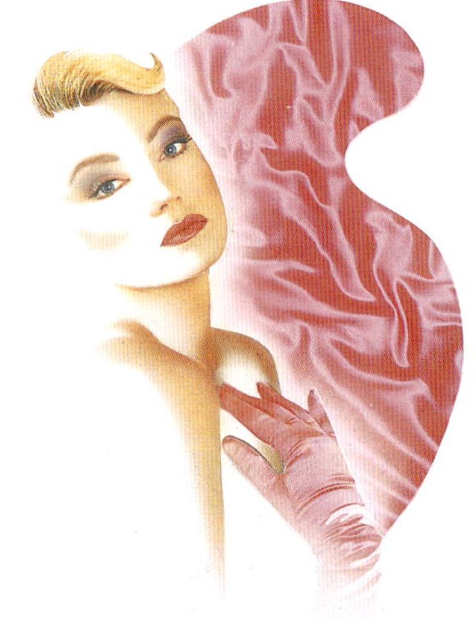

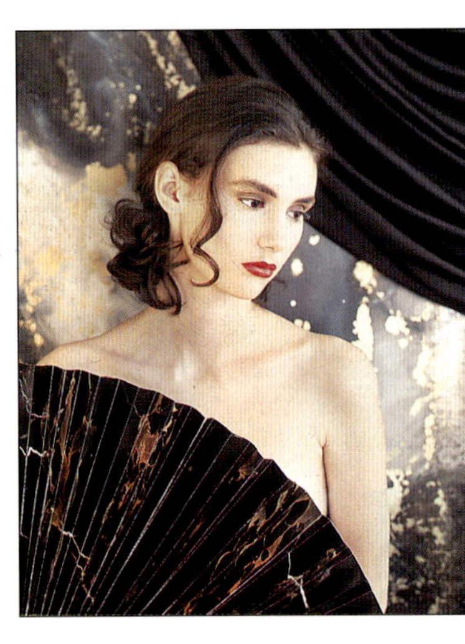

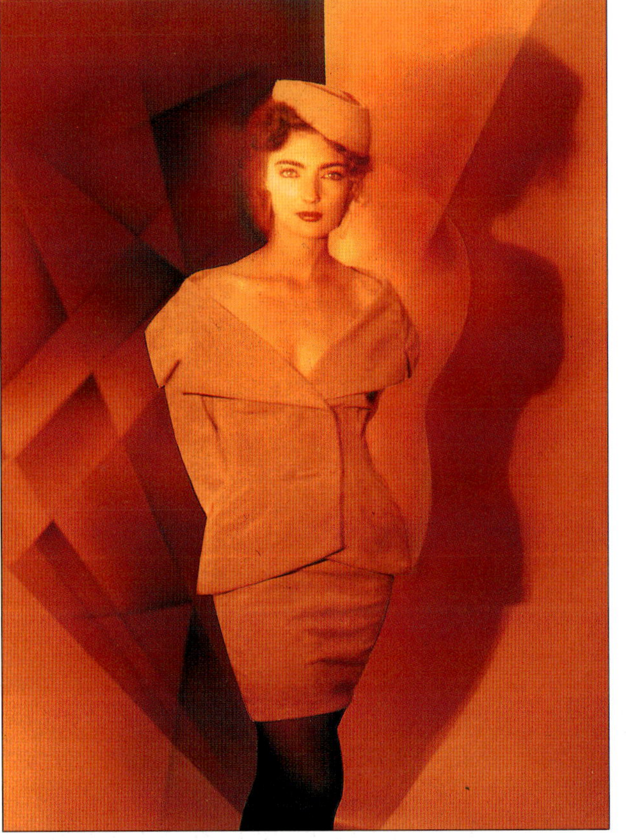

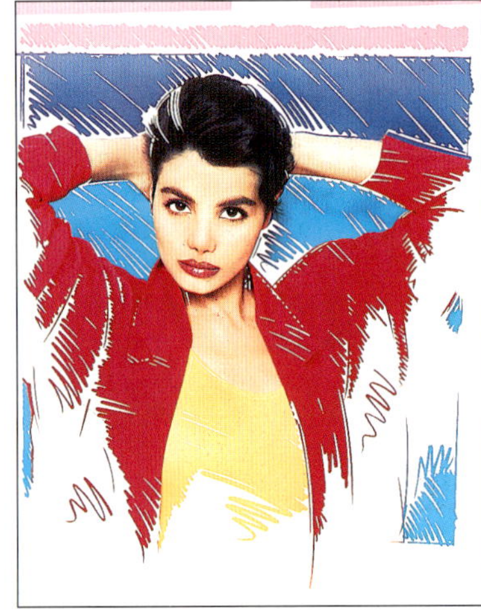

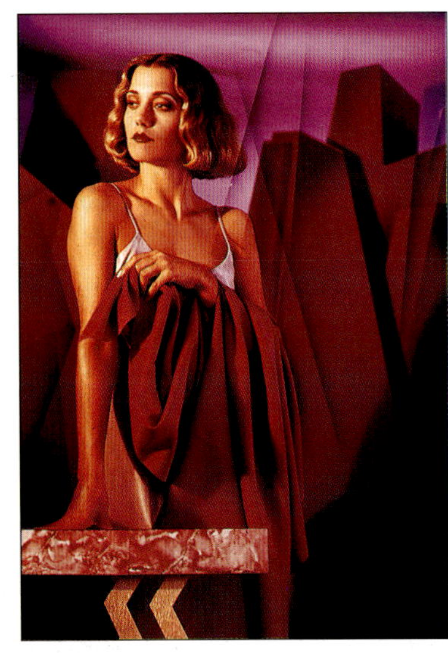

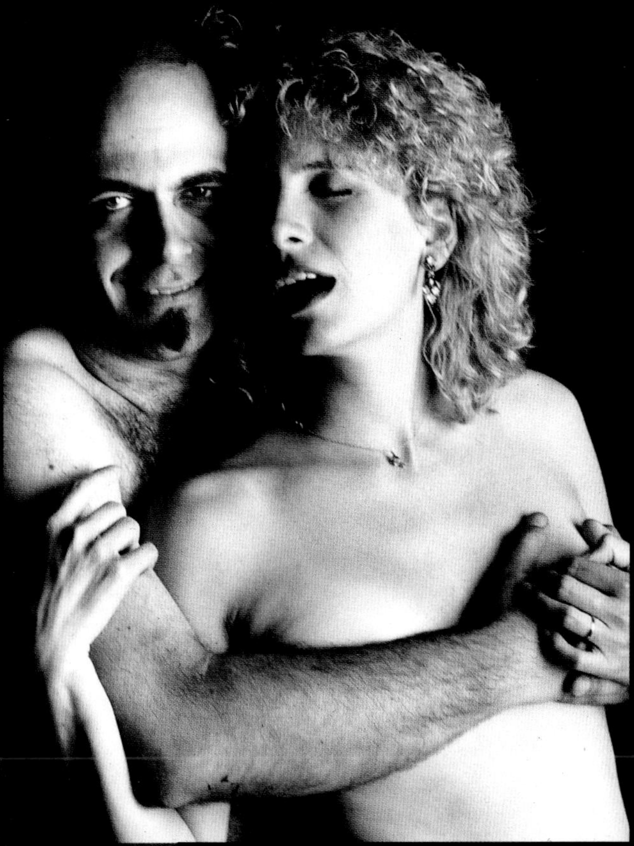

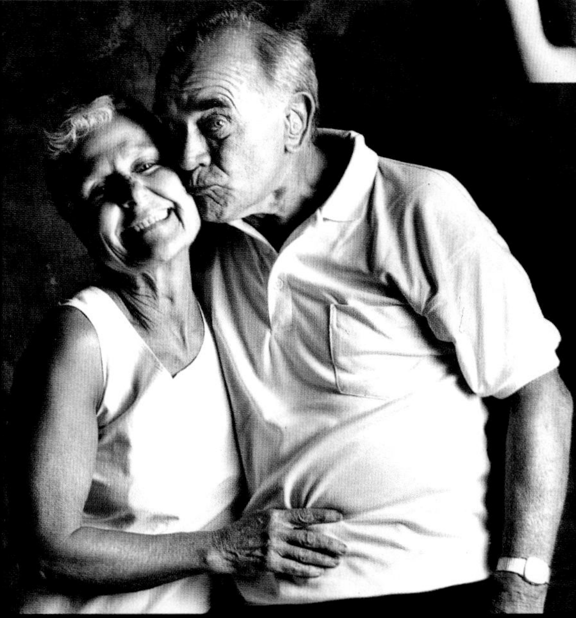

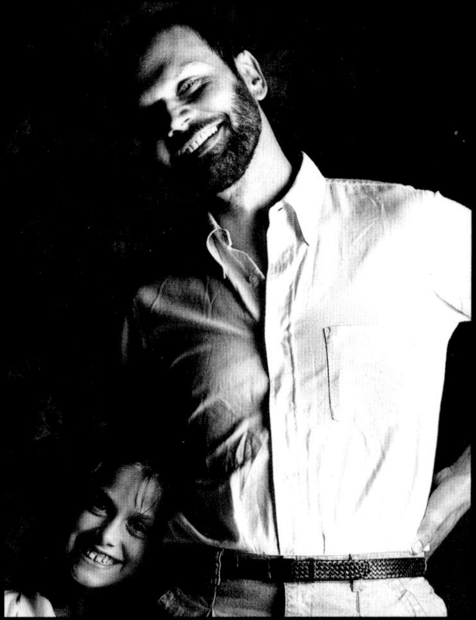

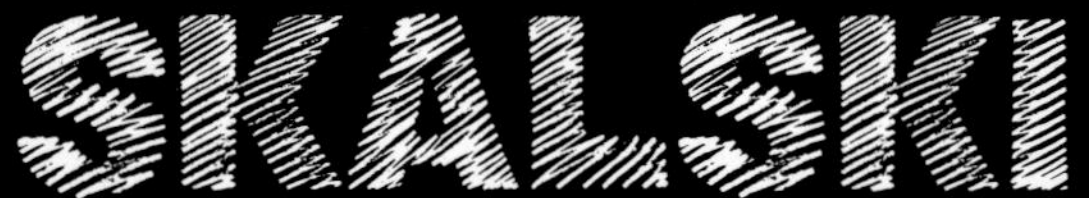

KEN SKALSKI · PHOTOGRAPHY 873 BROADWAY N.Y. N.Y. 10003 212·777·6207

REPRESENTED BY JOYCE PLUCK

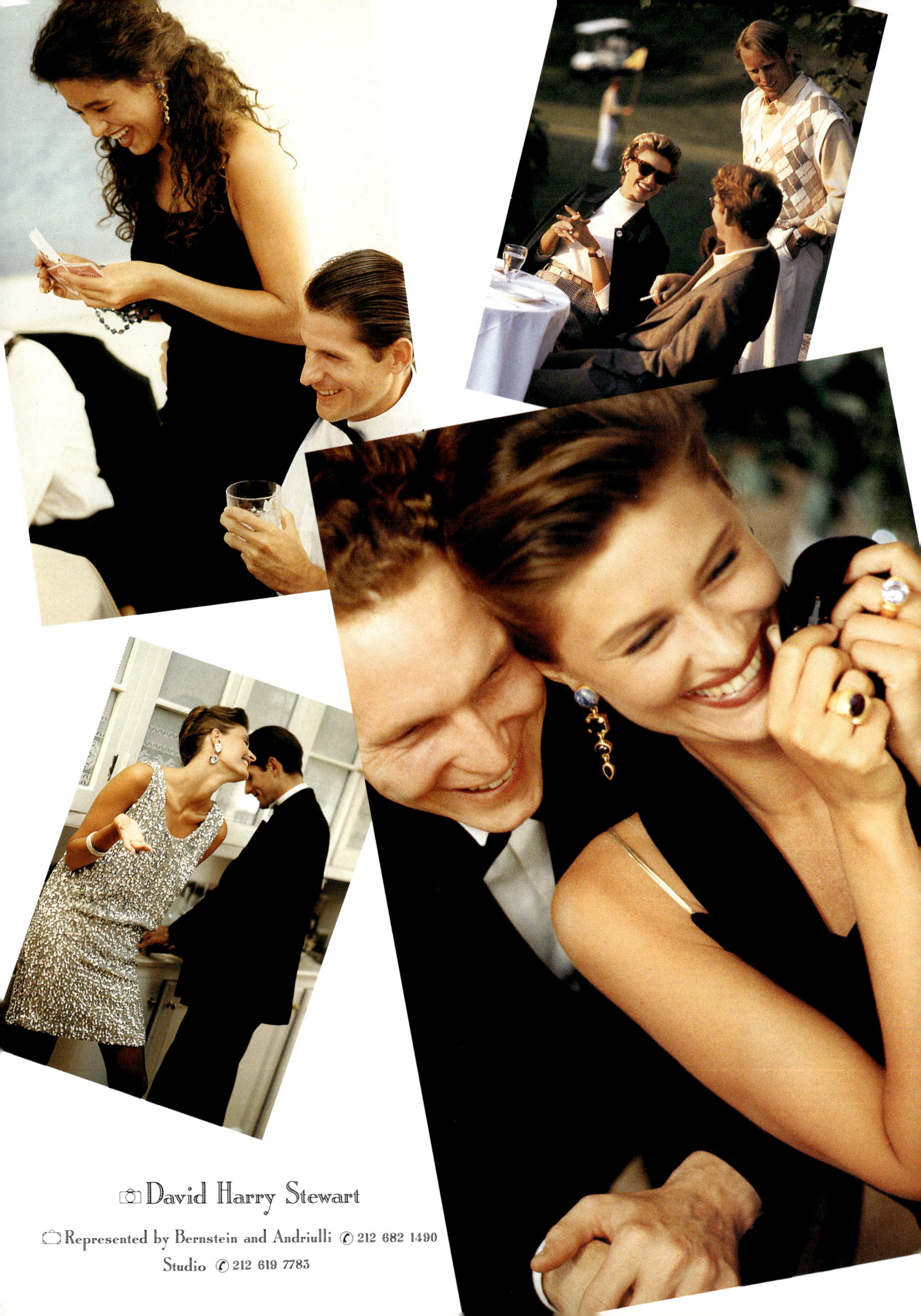
David Harry Stewart
Represented by Bernstein and Andriulli 212 682 1490
Studio 212 619 7783

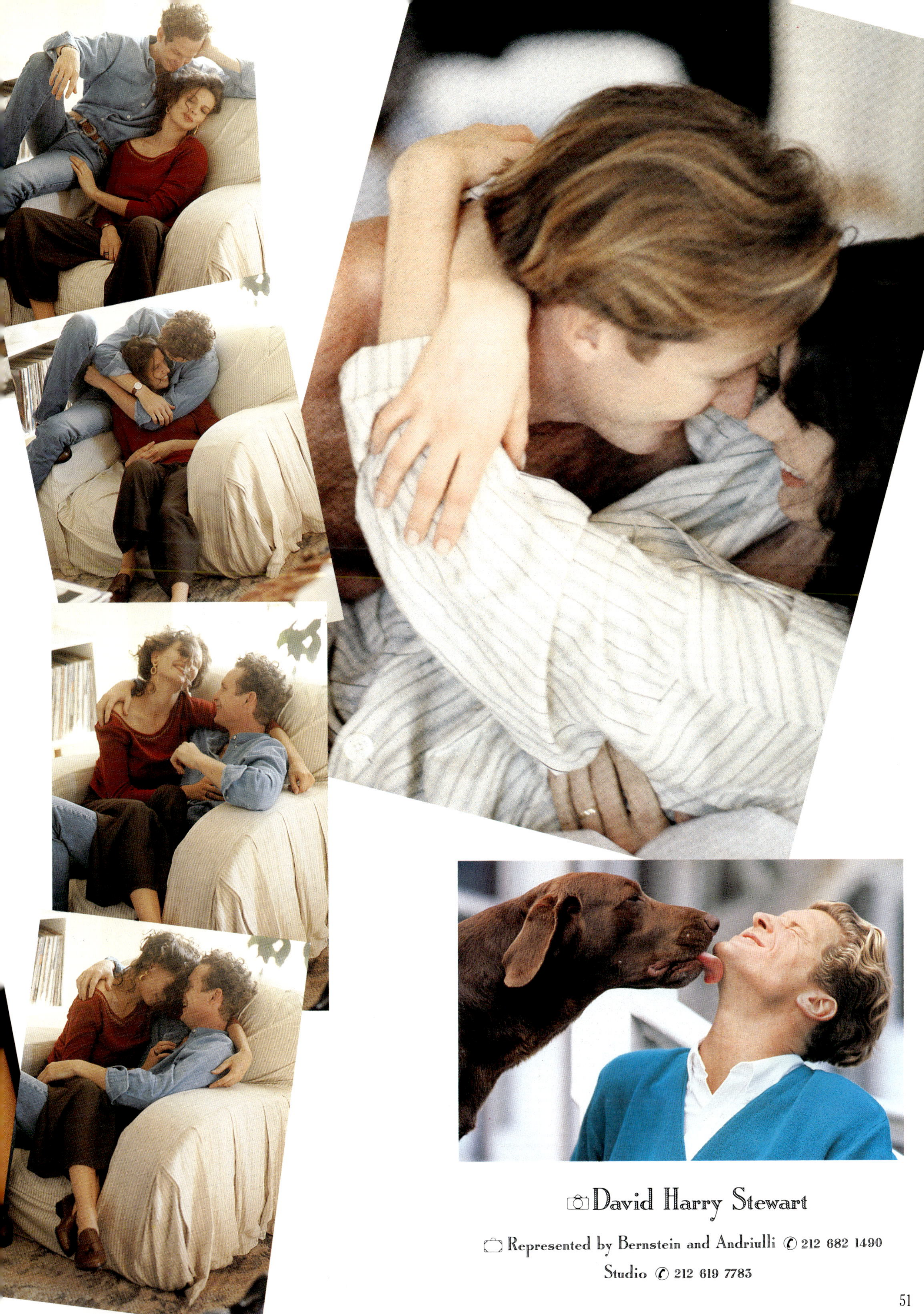

David Harry Stewart

Represented by Bernstein and Andriulli ✆ 212 682 1490
Studio ✆ 212 619 7783

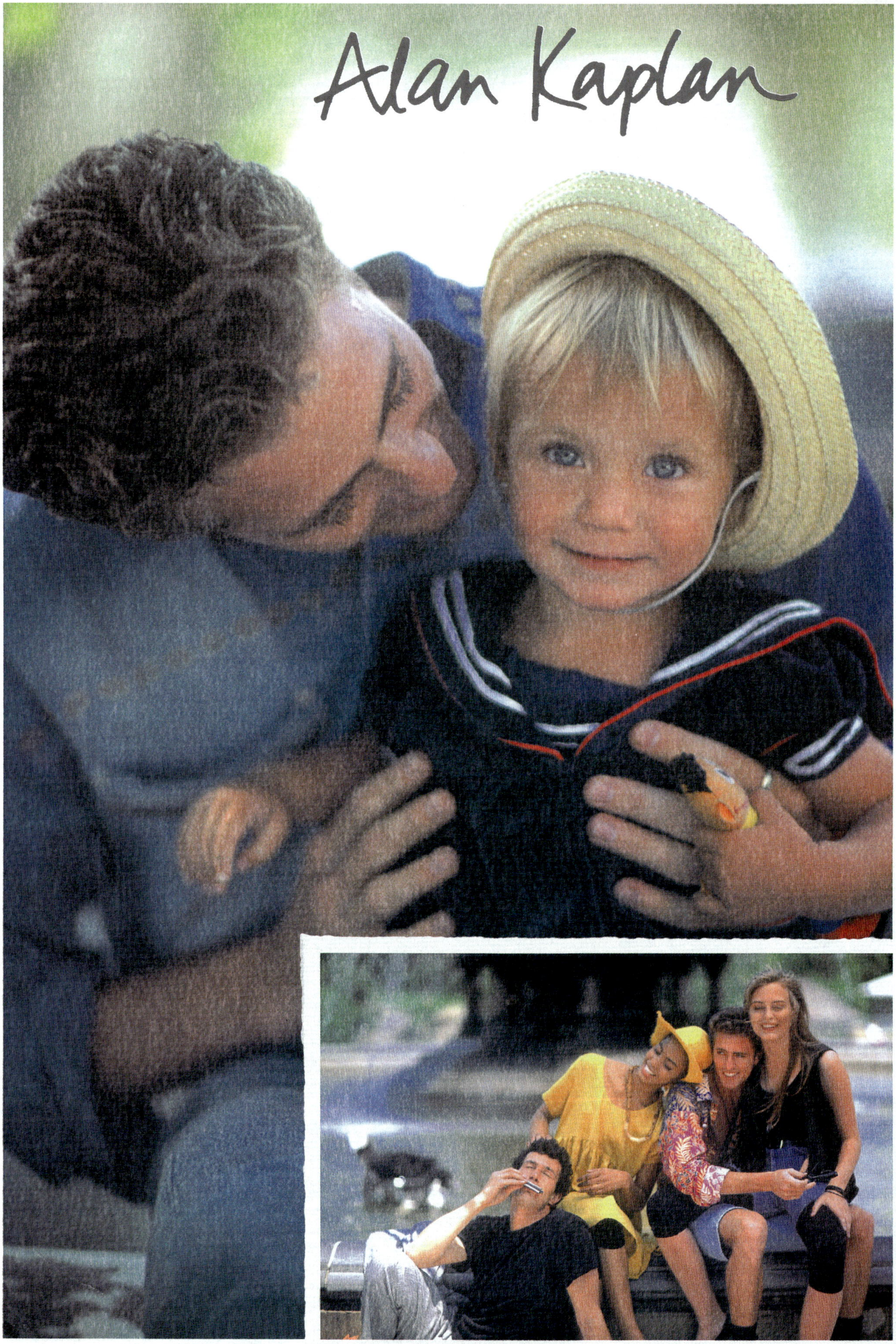

Alan Kaplan

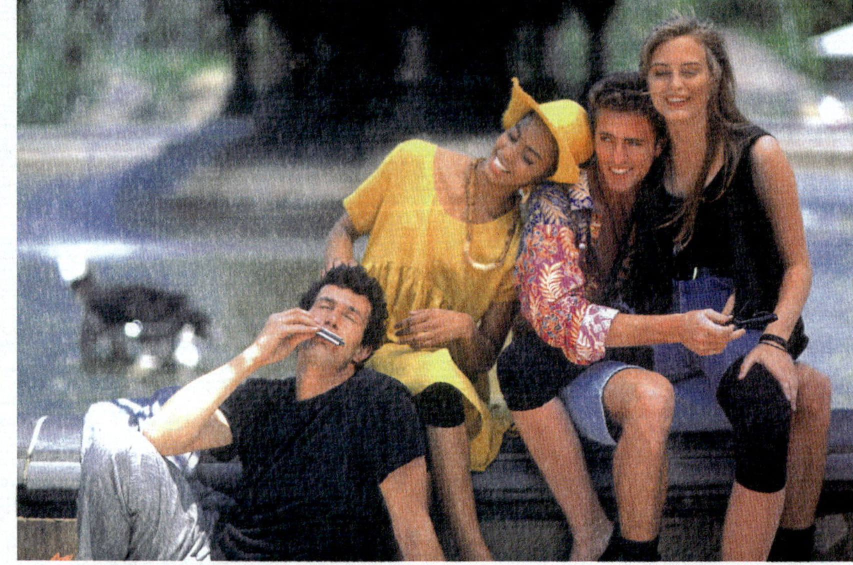

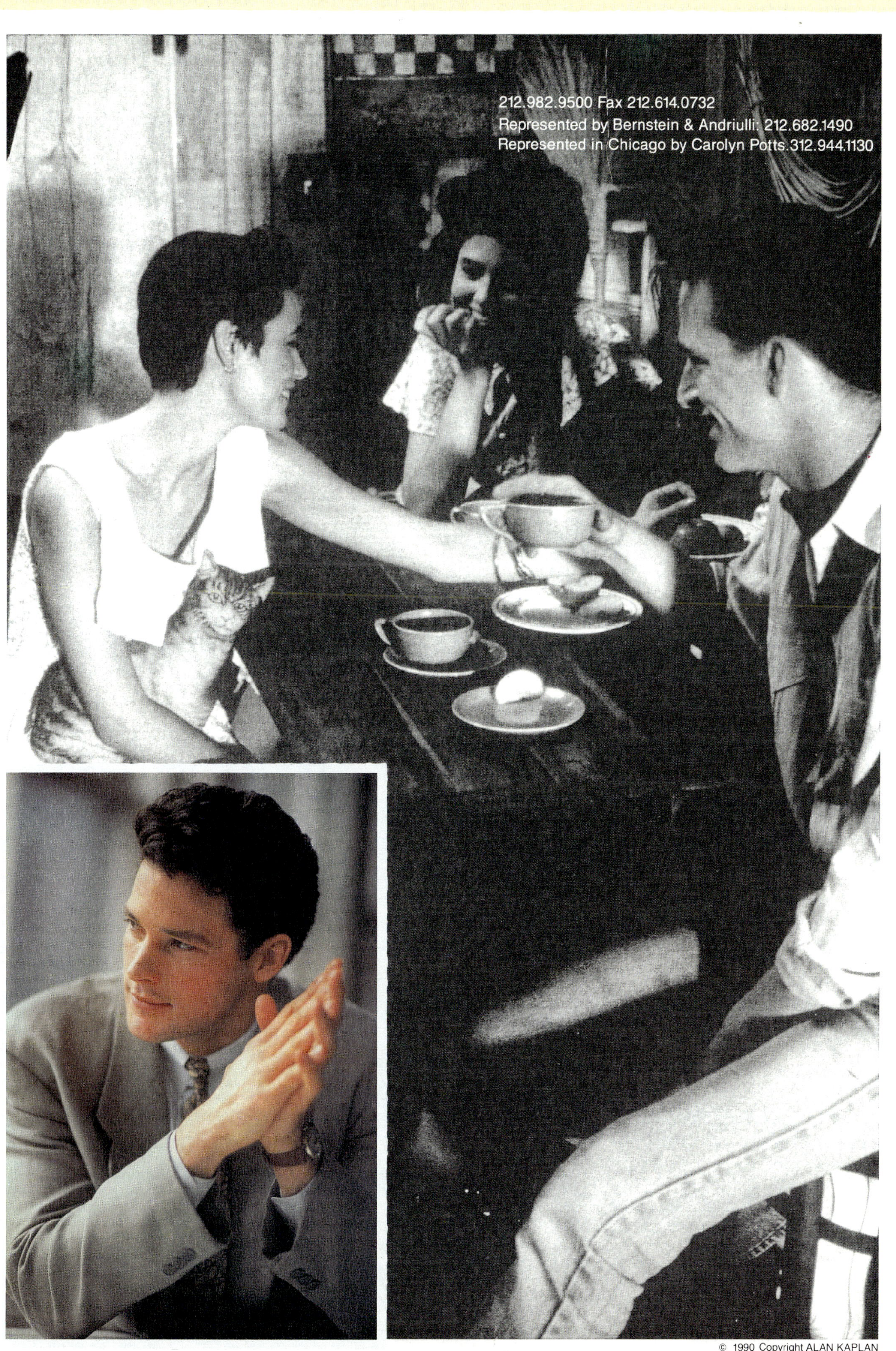
212.982.9500 Fax 212.614.0732
Represented by Bernstein & Andriulli: 212.682.1490
Represented in Chicago by Carolyn Potts.312.944.1130

Represented by
Bernstein & Andriulli Inc
60 East 42nd Street
New York, New York 10165
tel 212 682 1490
fax 212 286 1890

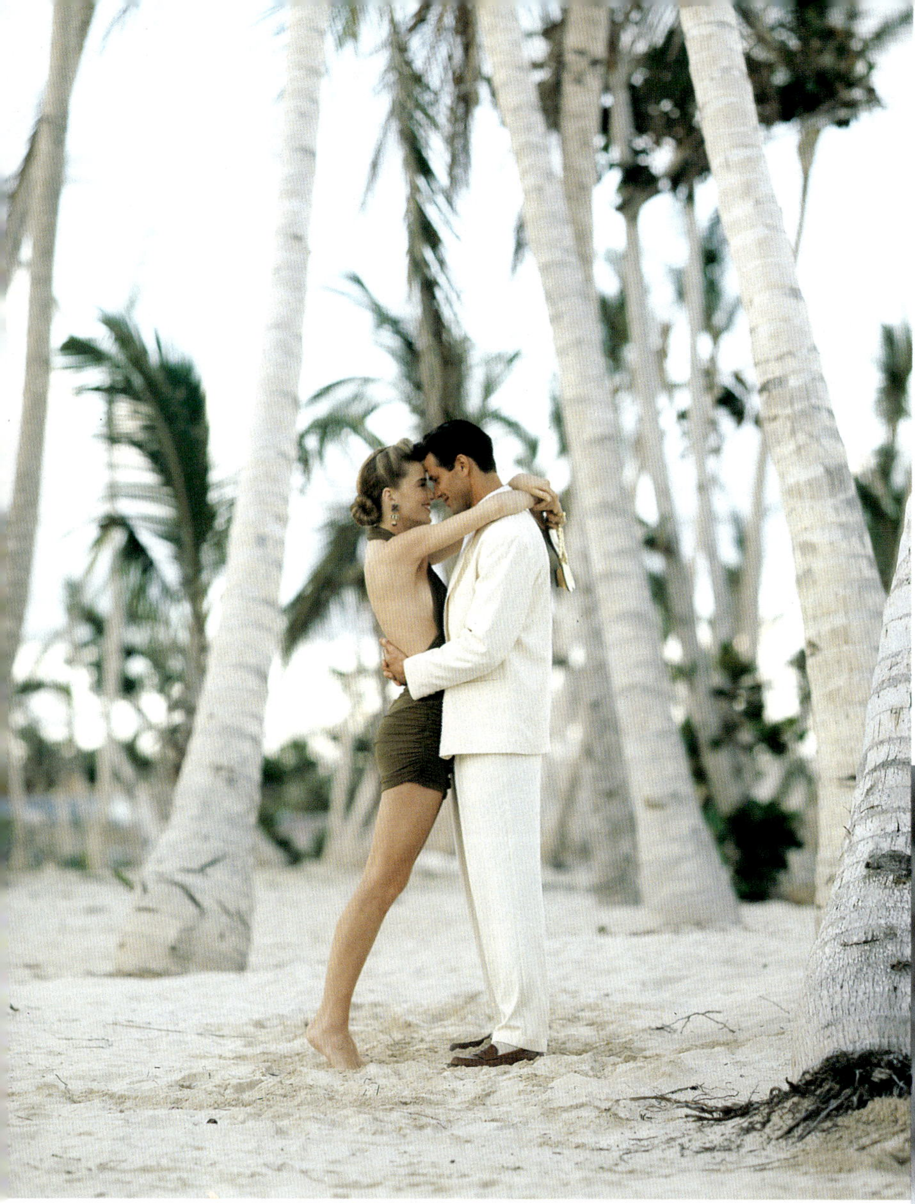

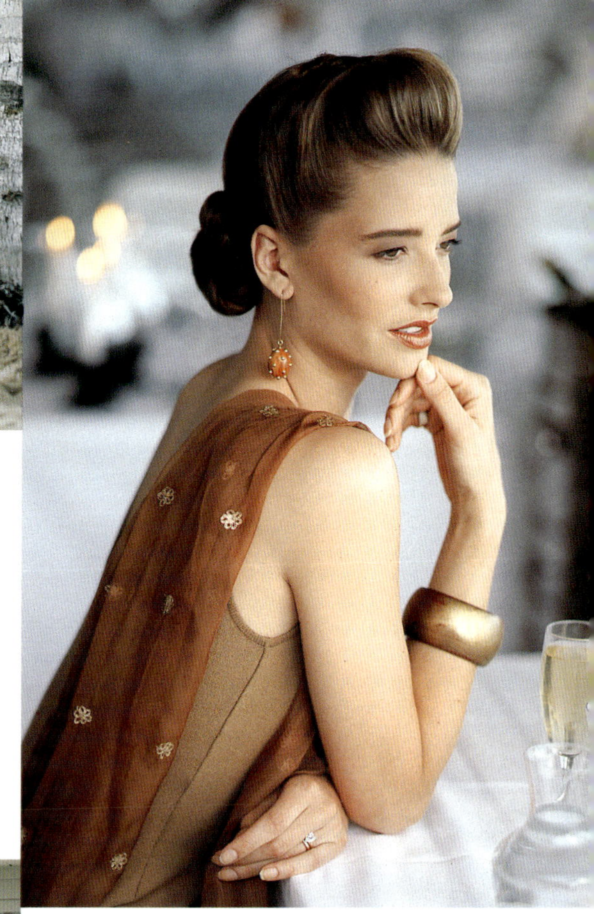

RICHARD
WARREN

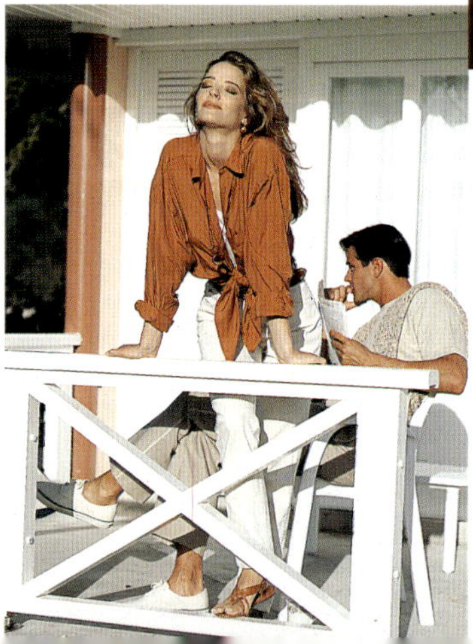

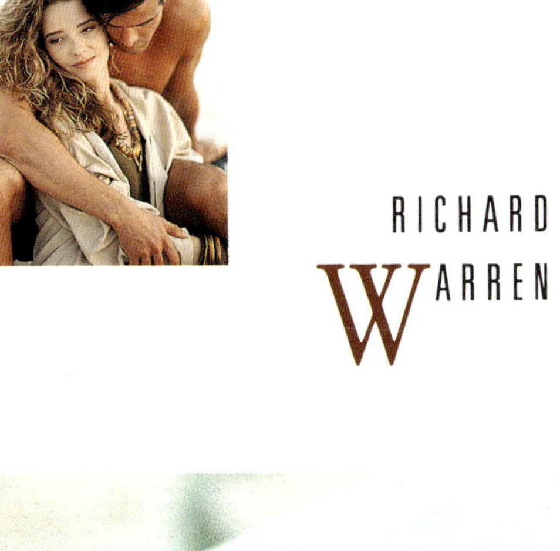

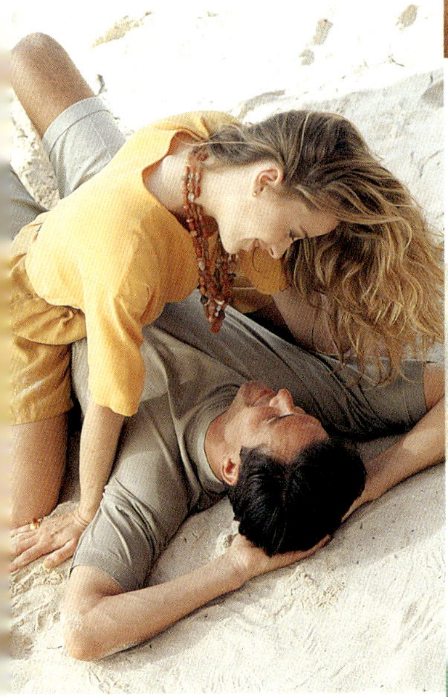

RICHARD

WARREN

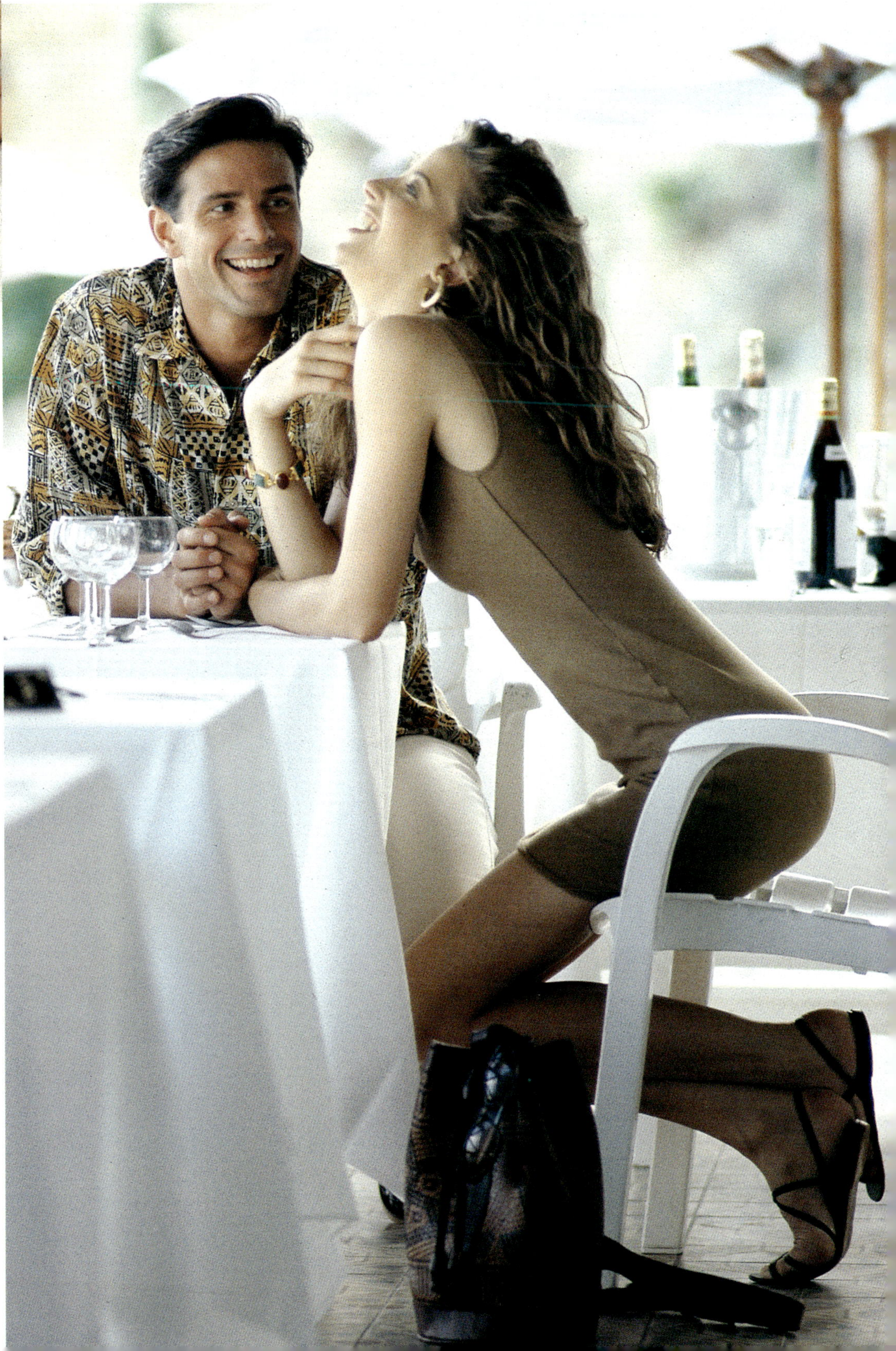

Represented by

Bernstein & Andriulli Inc

60 East 42nd Street

New York, New York 10165

tel 212 682 1490

fax 212 286 1890

ELLEN DENUTO

PHOTOGRAPHY

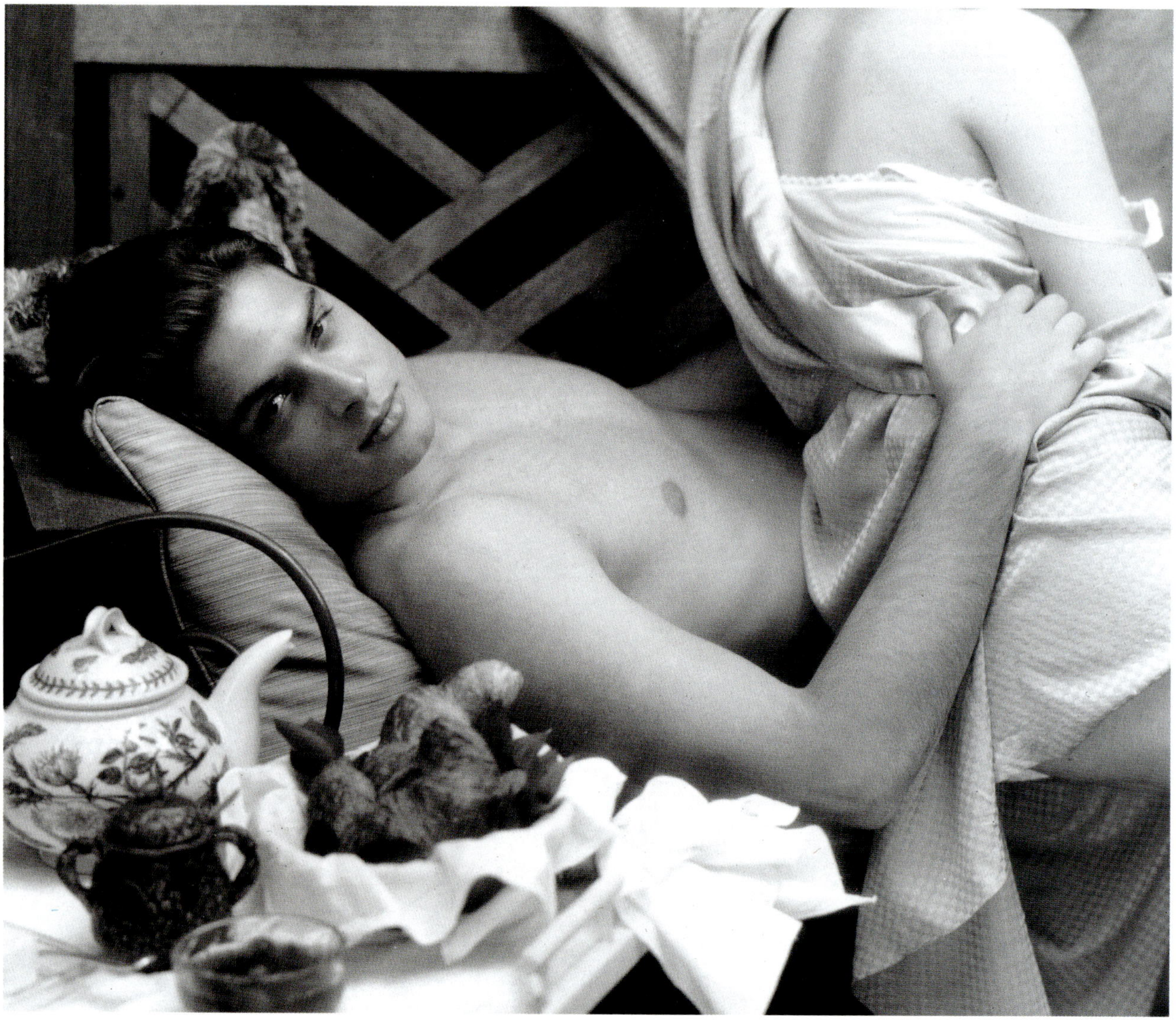

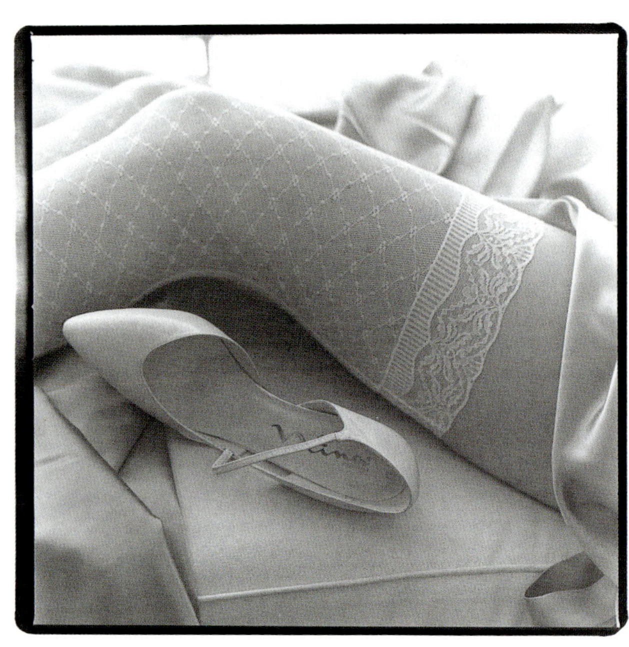

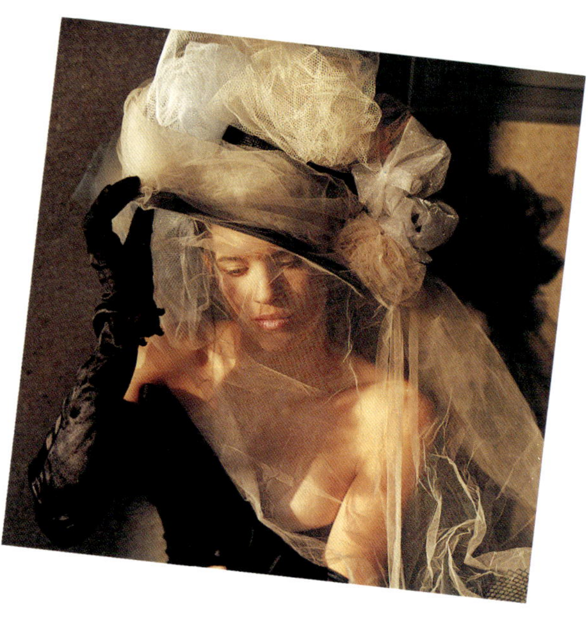

24 Mill Street • Suite 203 • Paterson, New Jersey 07501 • 201 881 0614

BILL WESTHEIMER
212-431-6360

PHOTO**GRAMS**:ILLUSTRATE

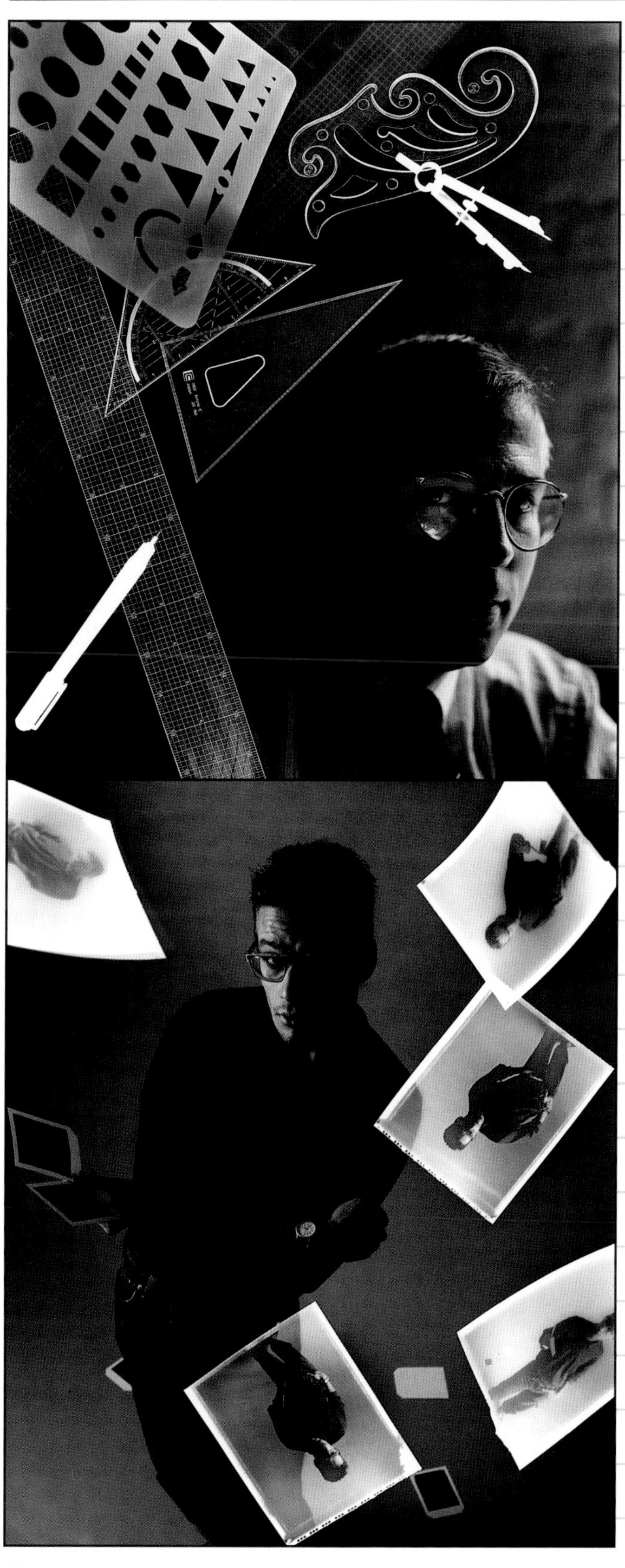

PHOTO**GRAMS**:ILLUSTRATE

BILL WESTHEIMER
212-431-6360

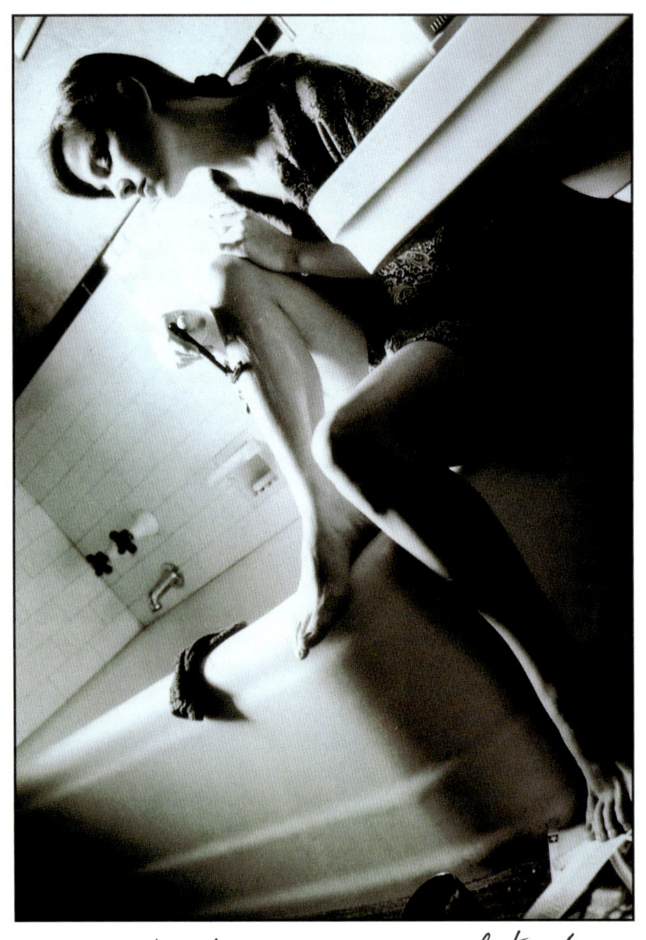

J. W. Thompson . personal touch

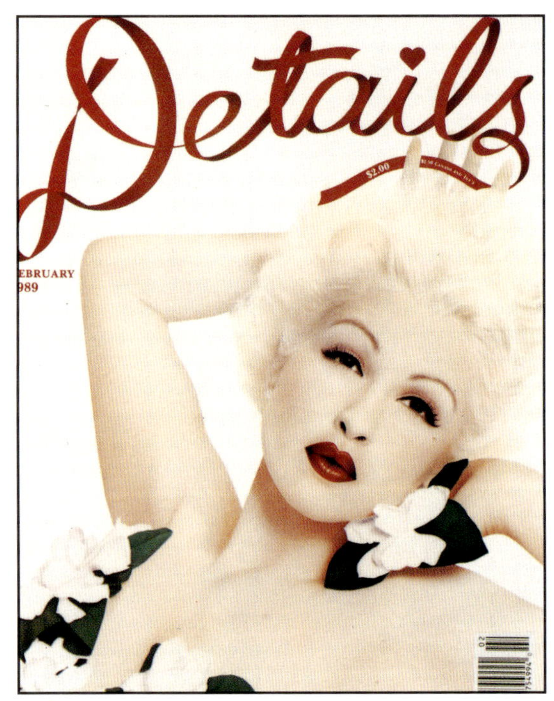

details

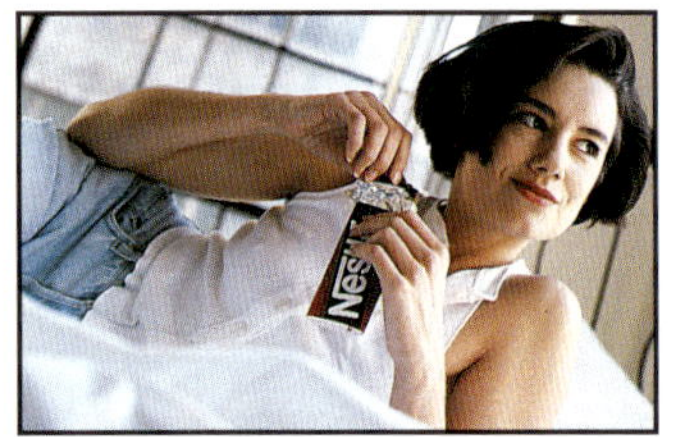

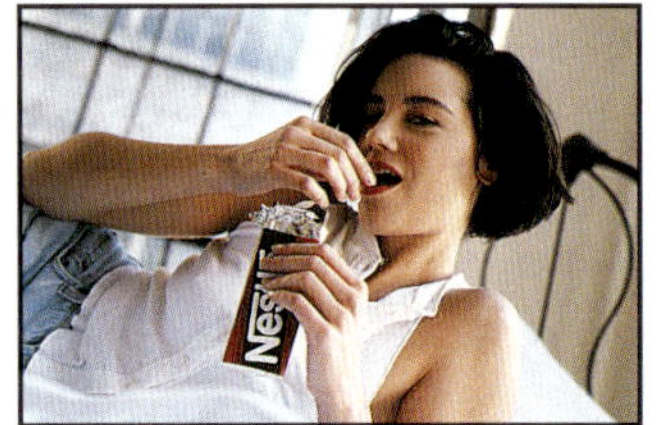

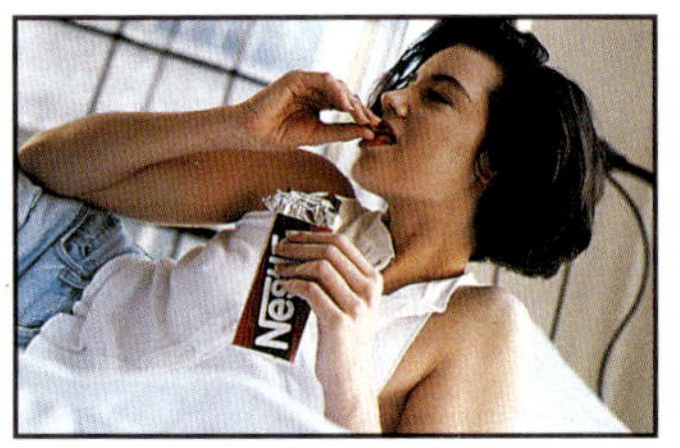

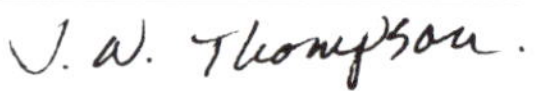

J. W. Thompson . Nestle's chocolate

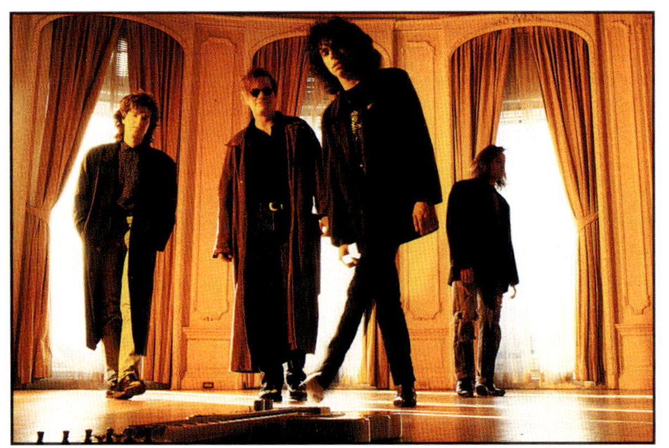

SBK records . the red house

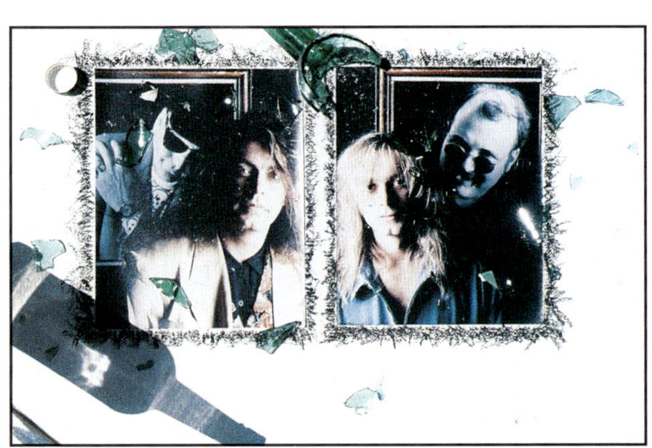

CBS records . cheap trick

Caroline Greyshock . represented by Janice Moses . 212 . 779 . 7929

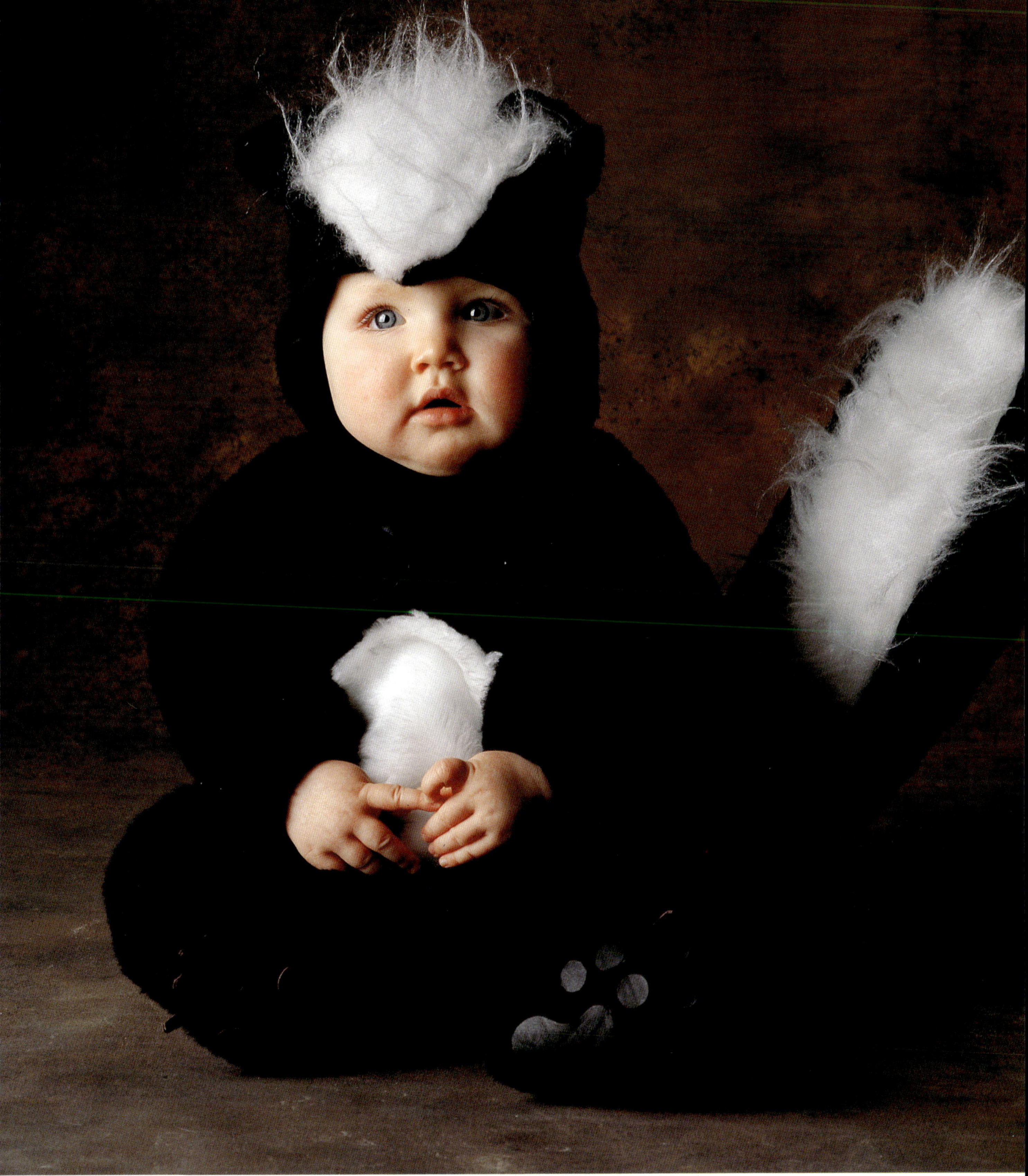

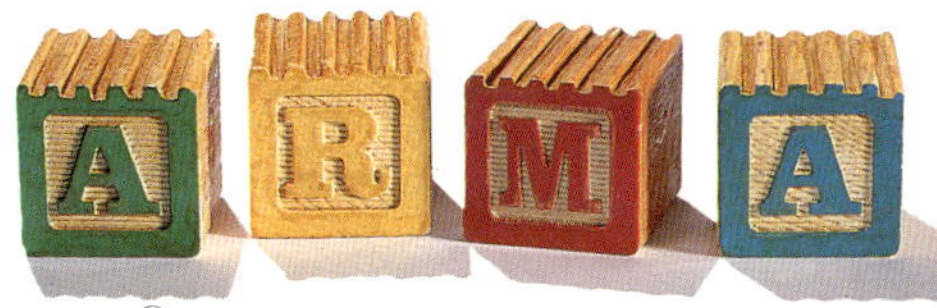
A
R
M
A

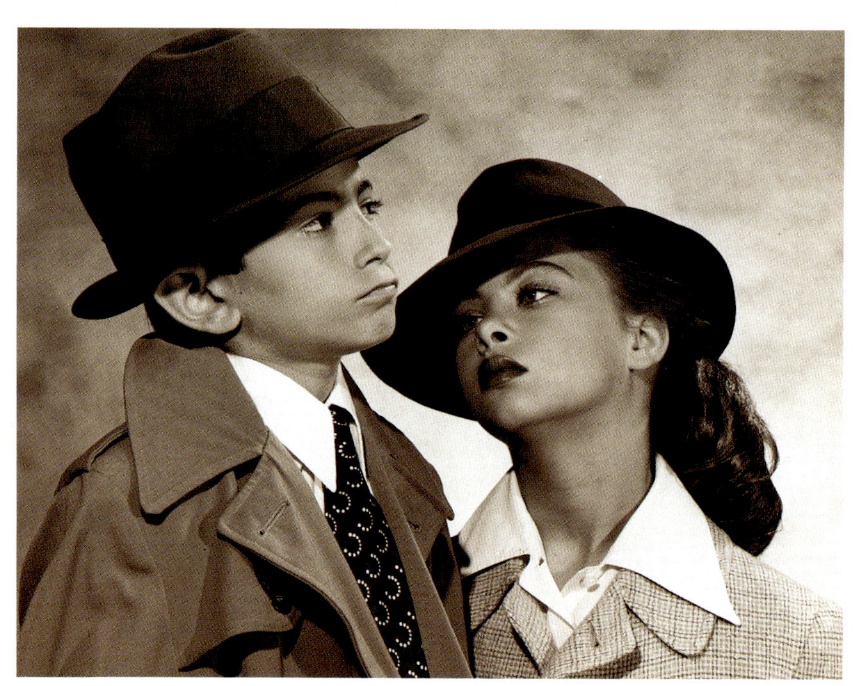

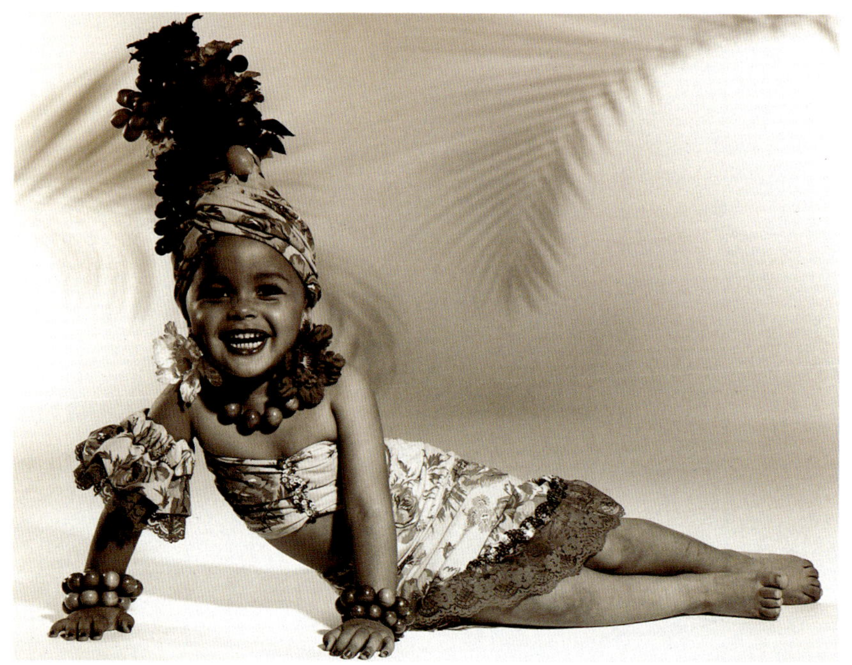

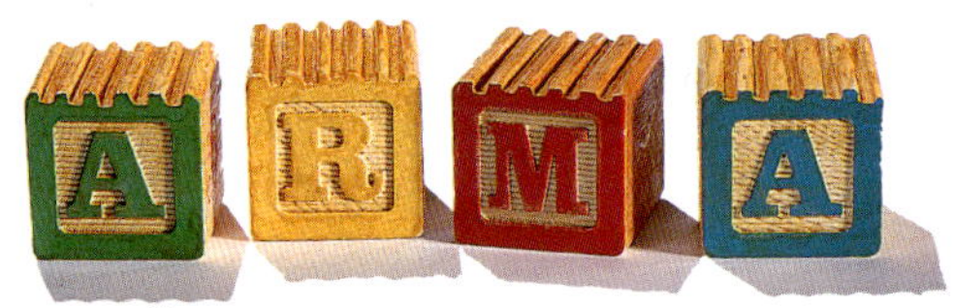

Tom Arma Studio, 38 West 26th Street, New York, NY 10010
Represented by Adrienne Rubin, 212·243·7904

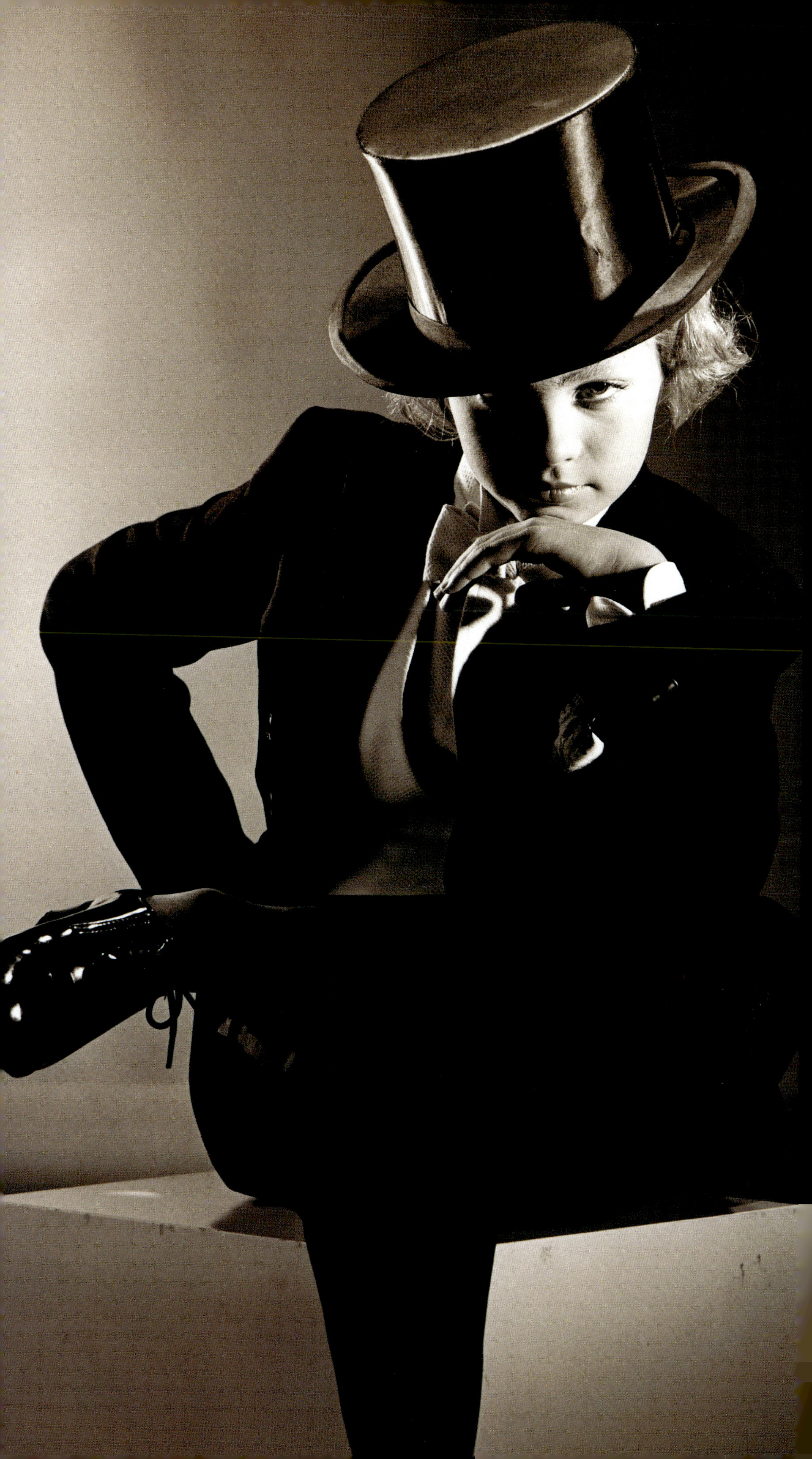

Jeanne Strongin

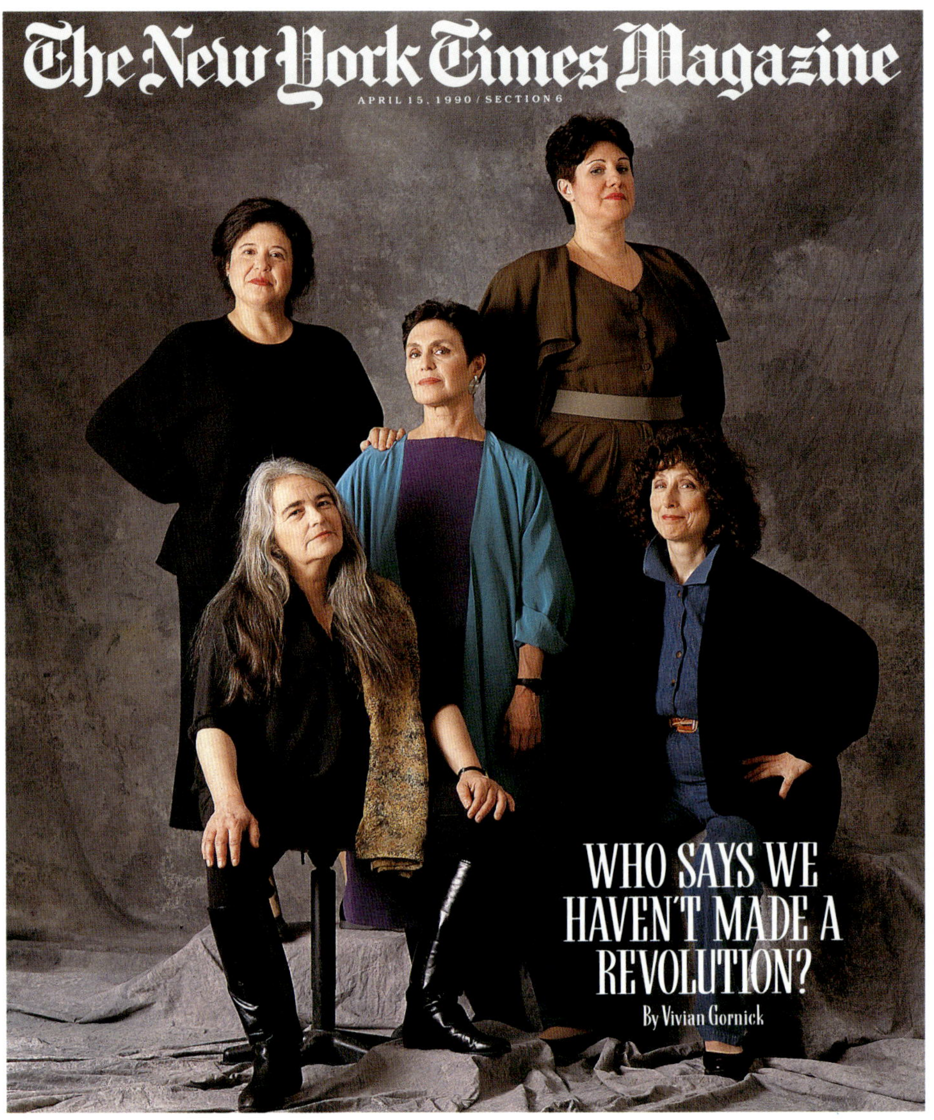

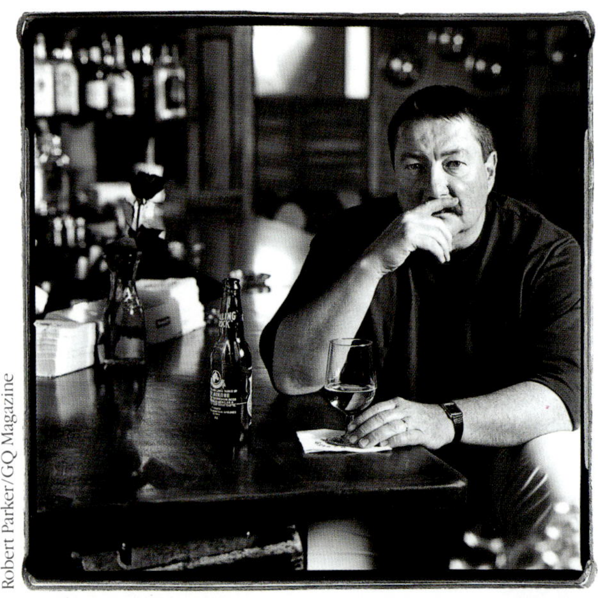
Robert Parker/GQ Magazine

61 IRVING PLACE
NEW YORK, NY 10003
212·473·3718

61 IRVING PLACE
NEW YORK, NY 10003
212·473·3718

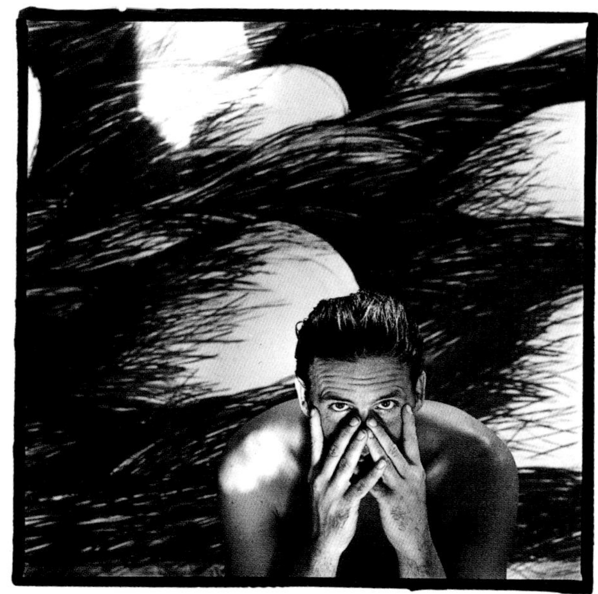

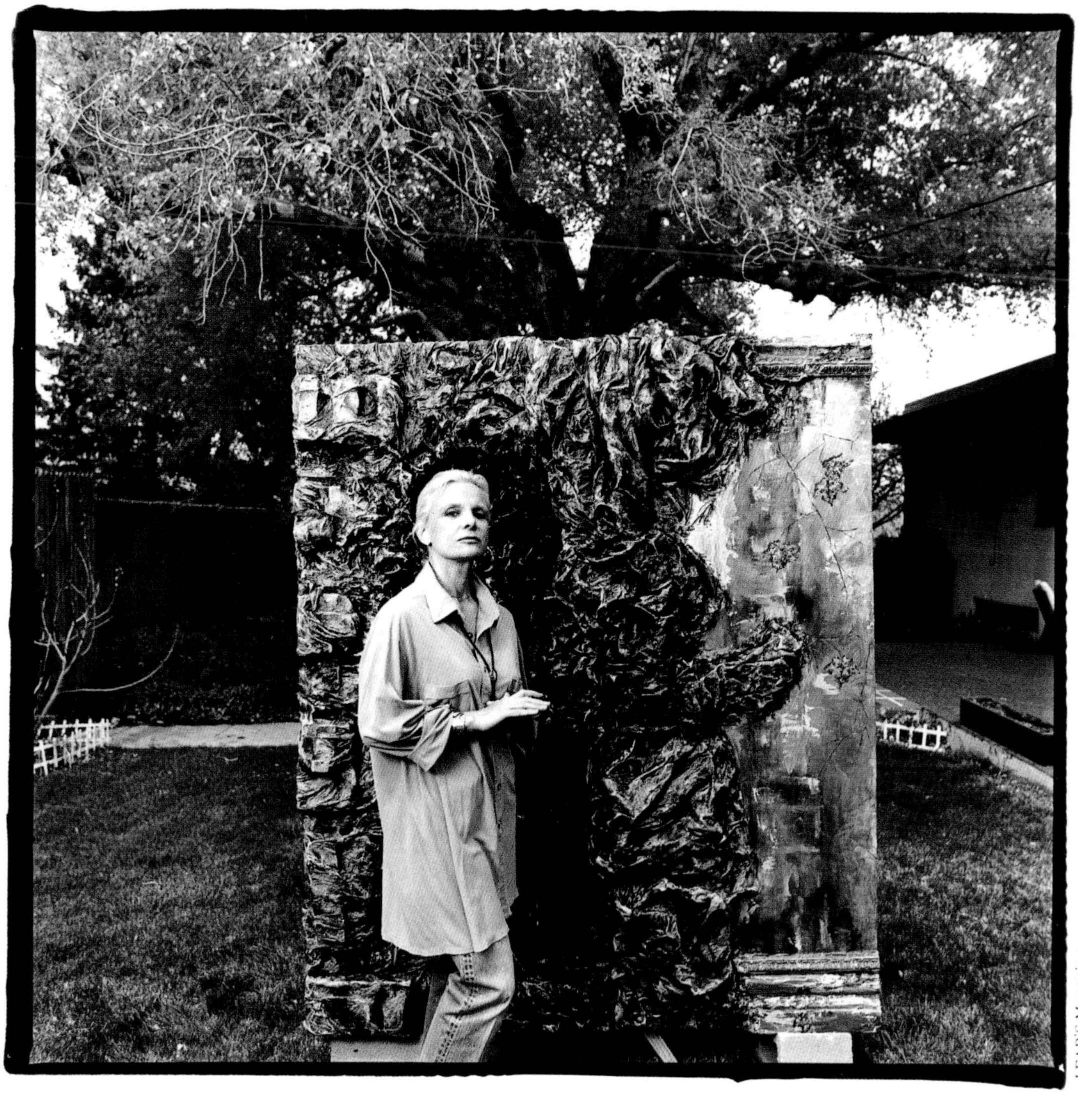

LEAR'S Magazine

Jeanne Strongin

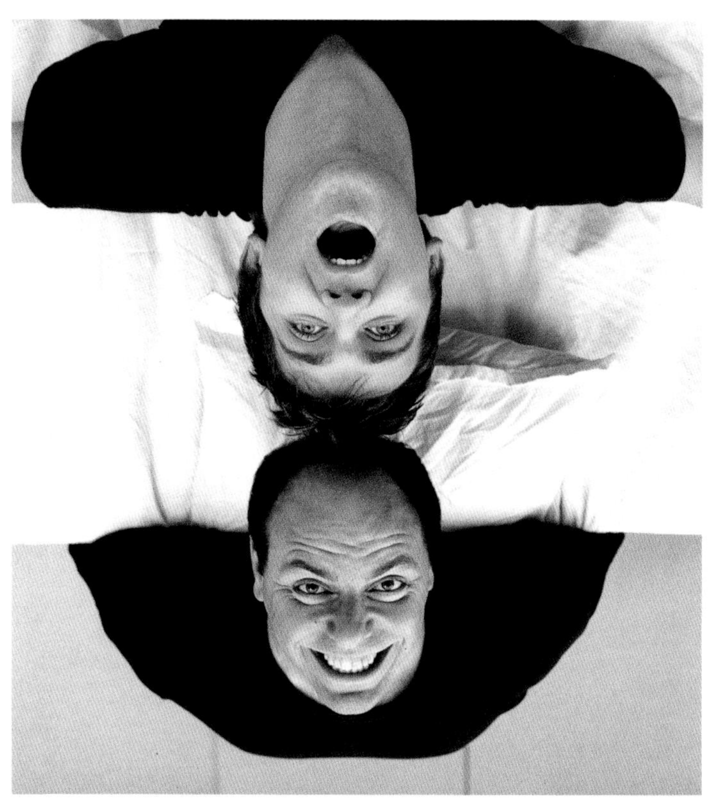

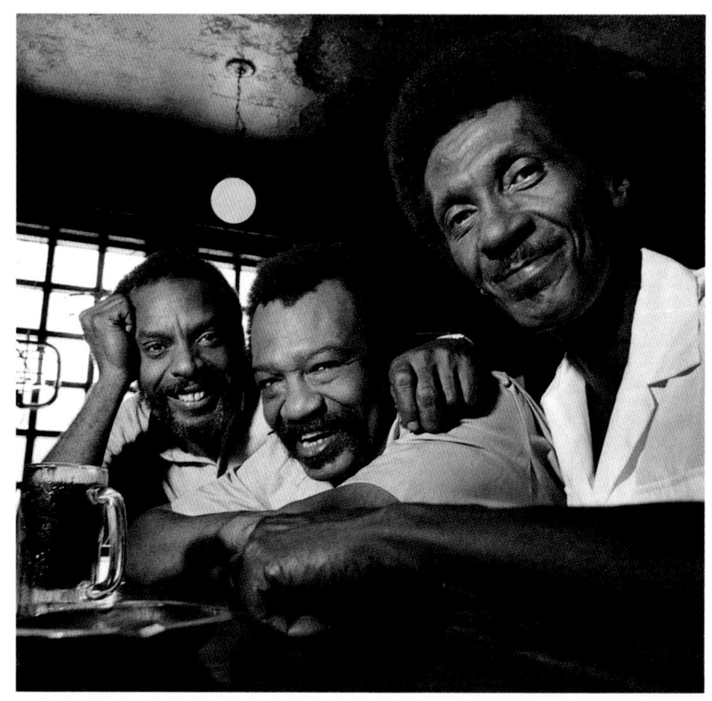

SHONNA VALESKA

140 EAST 28 STREET NEW YORK NY 10016 (212) 683-4448

CHRIS CALLIS

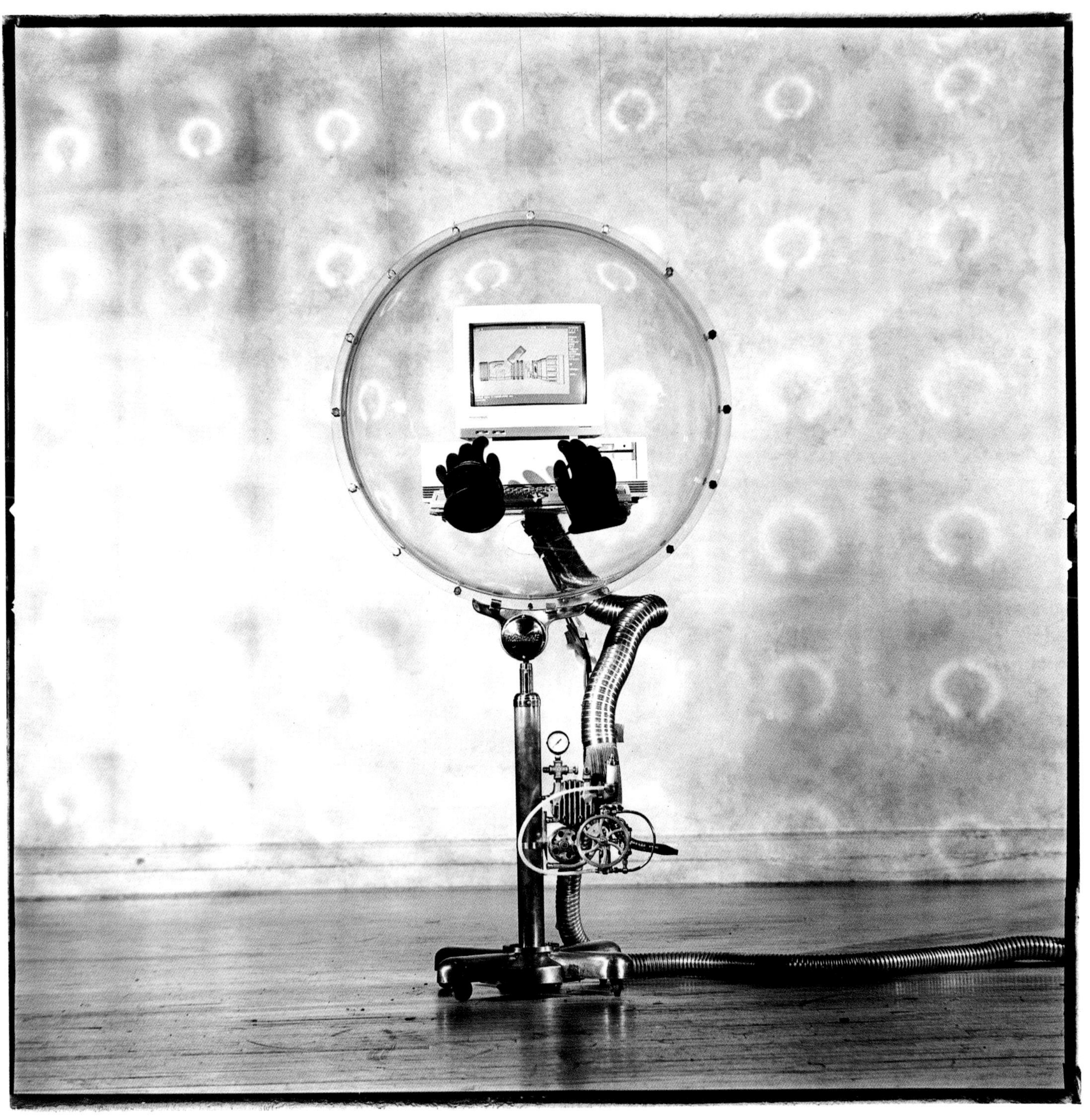

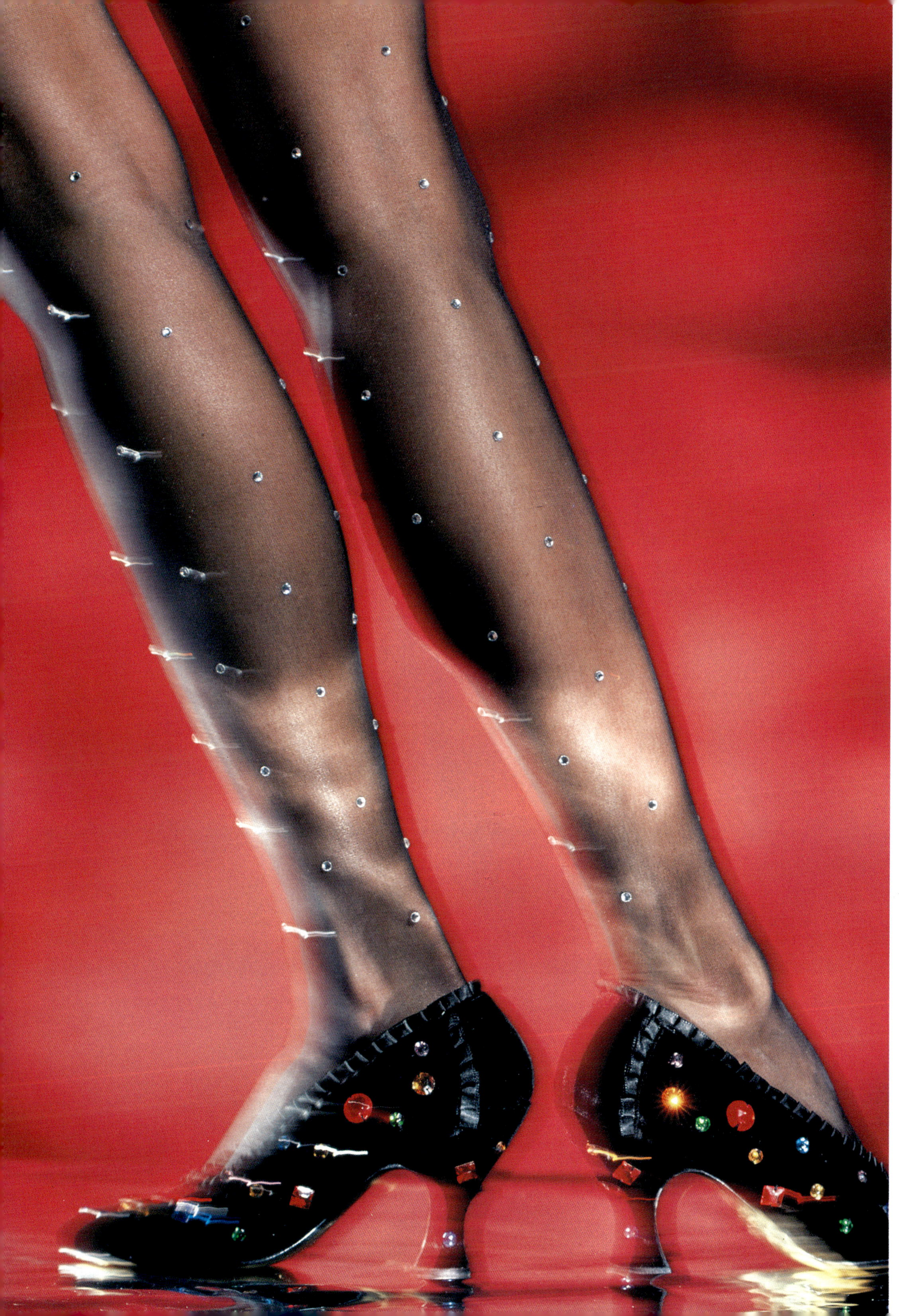

CHRIS CALLIS (212) 243-0231

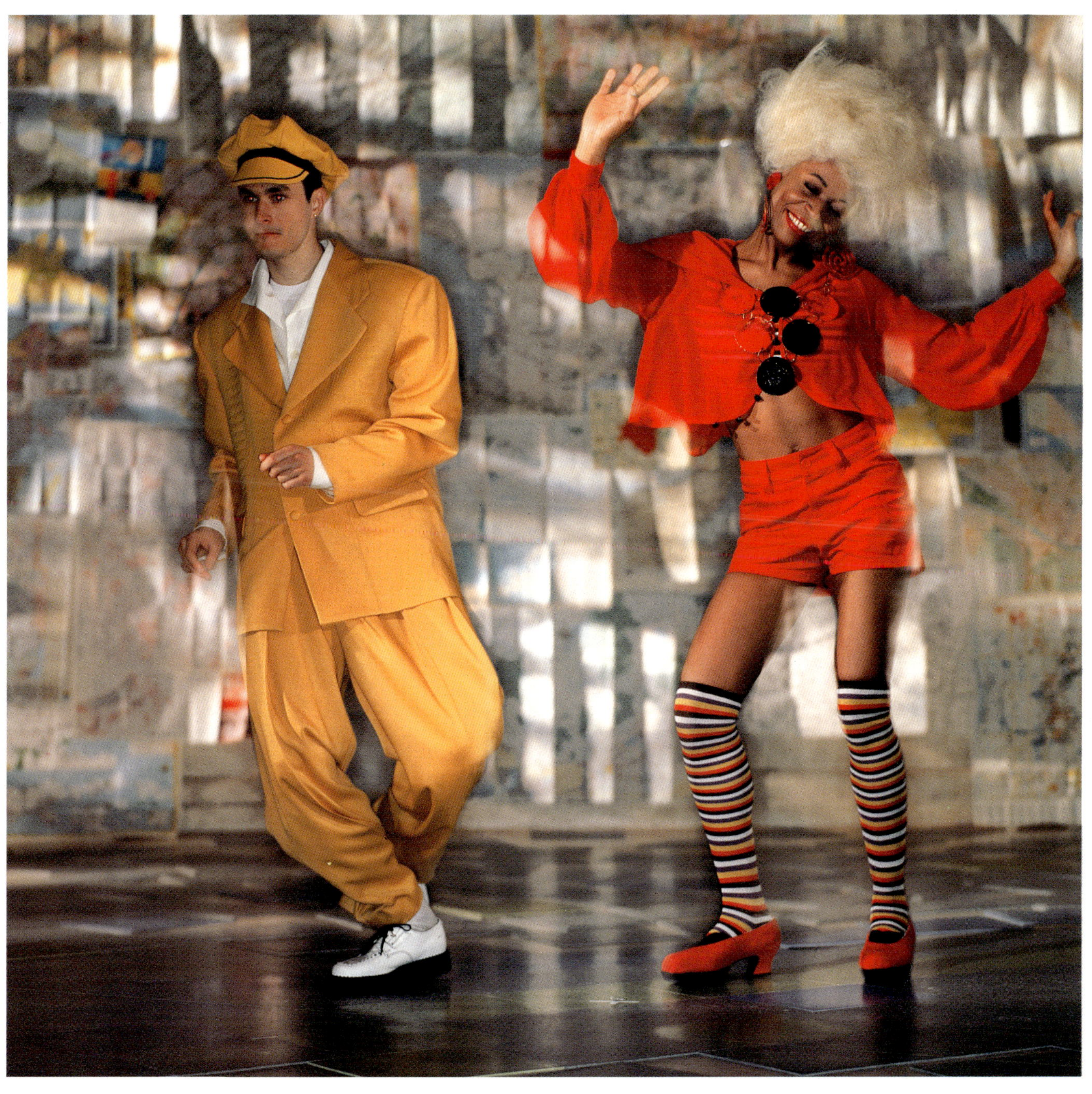

CHRIS CALLIS

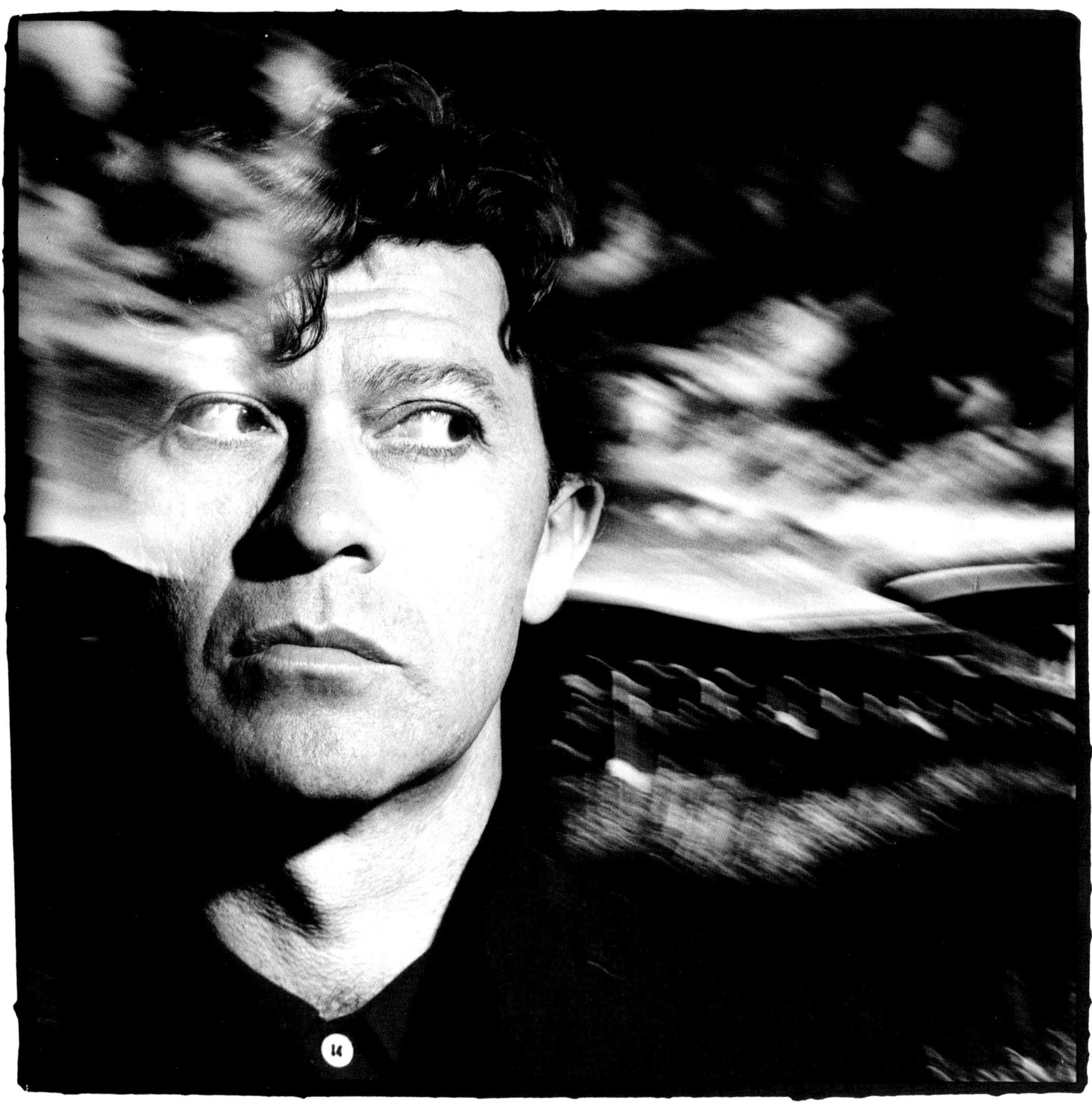

(212) 243-0231

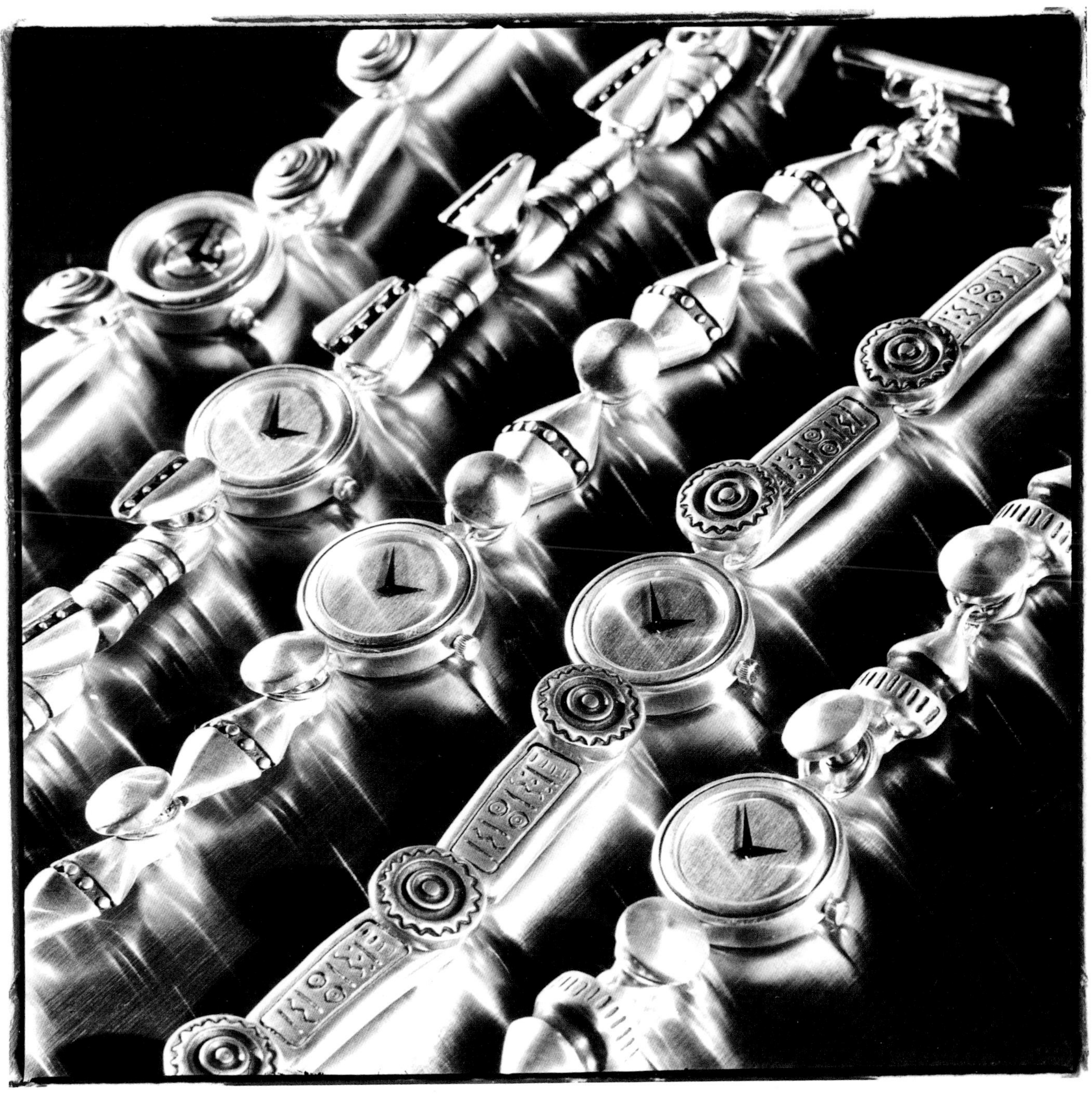

CHRIS CALLIS (212) 243-0231

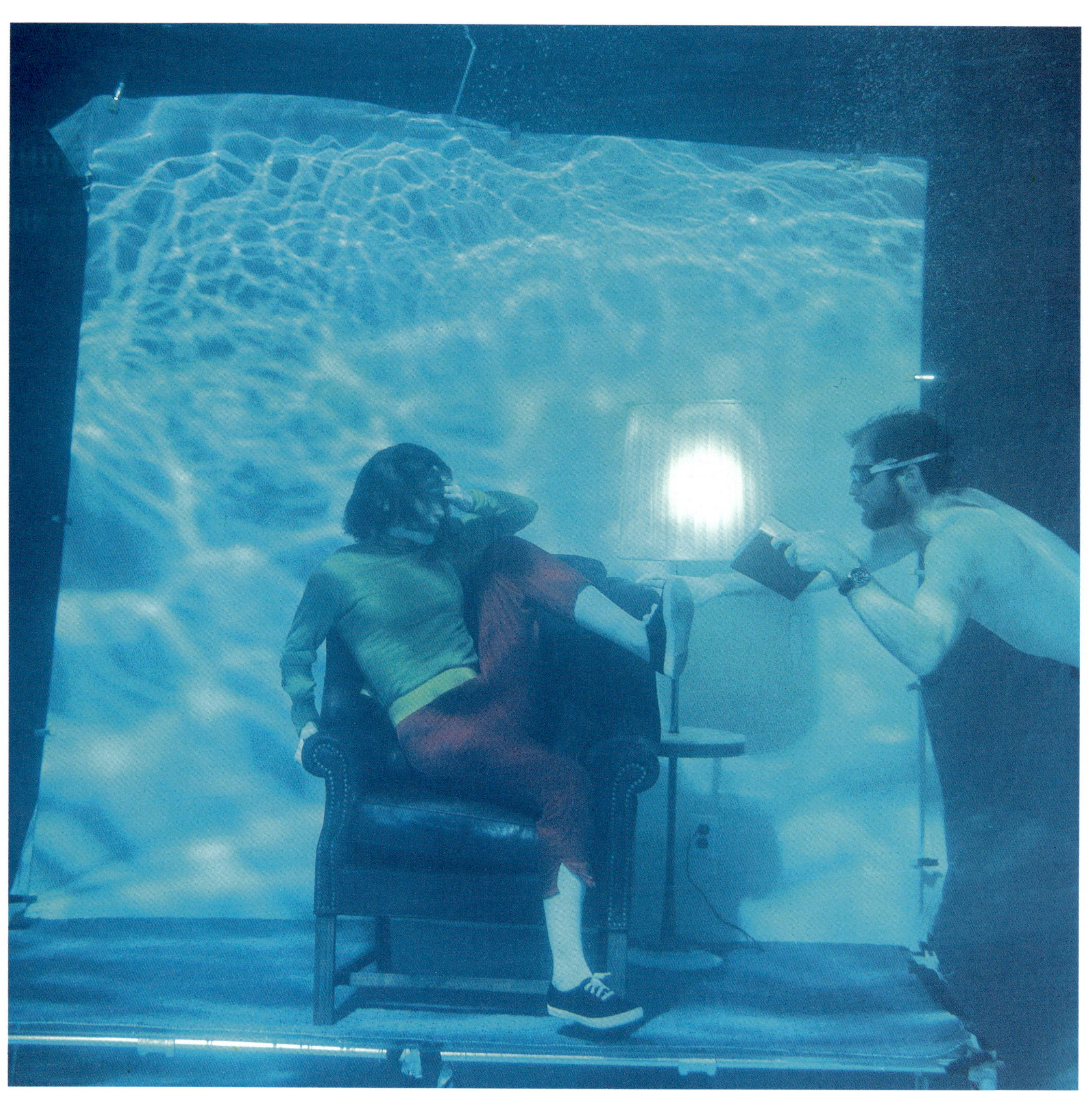

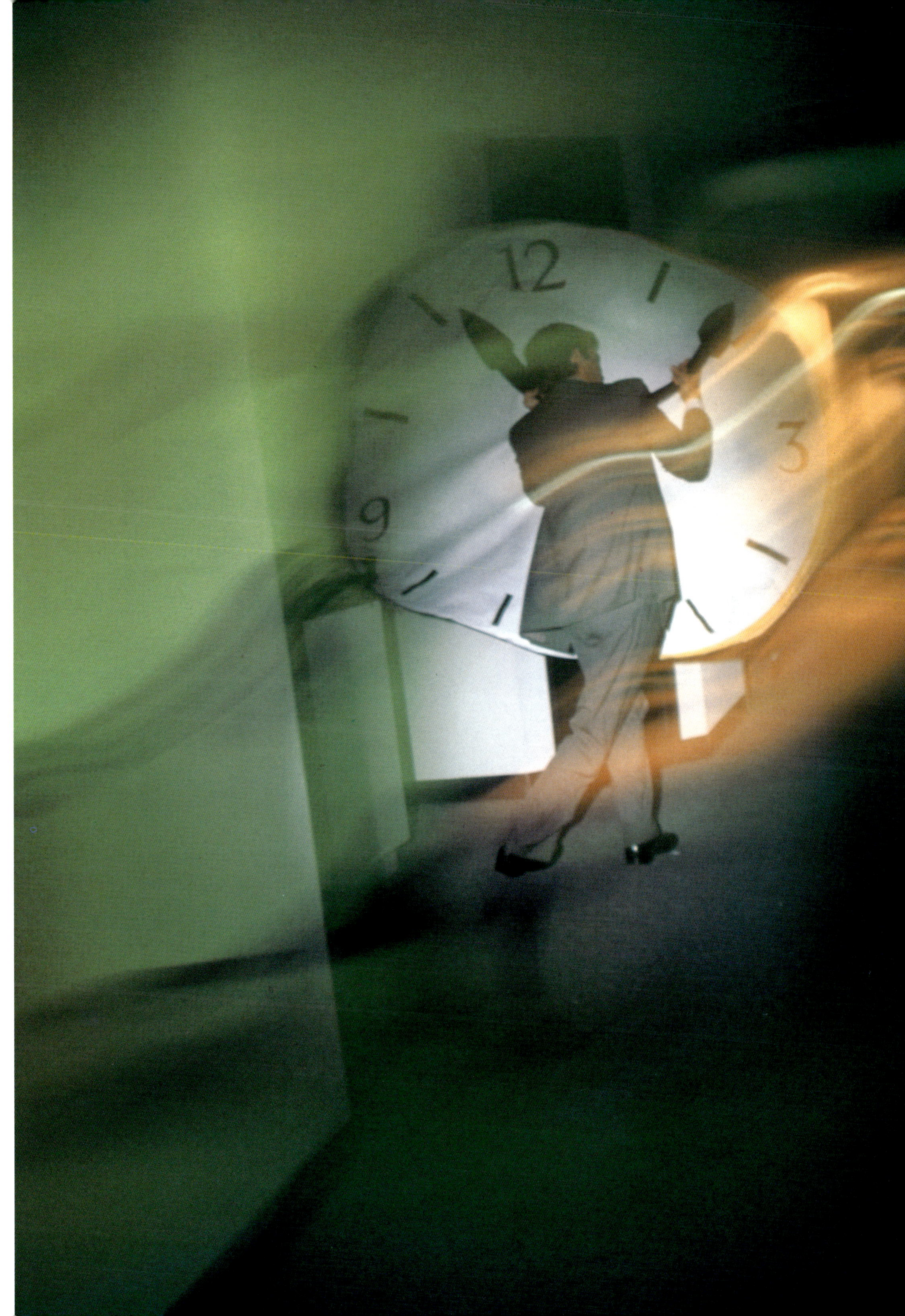

CHRIS CALLIS 91 FIFTH AVENUE NY, NY 10003 REPRESENTED BY KERRY O'BRIEN (212) 243-0231

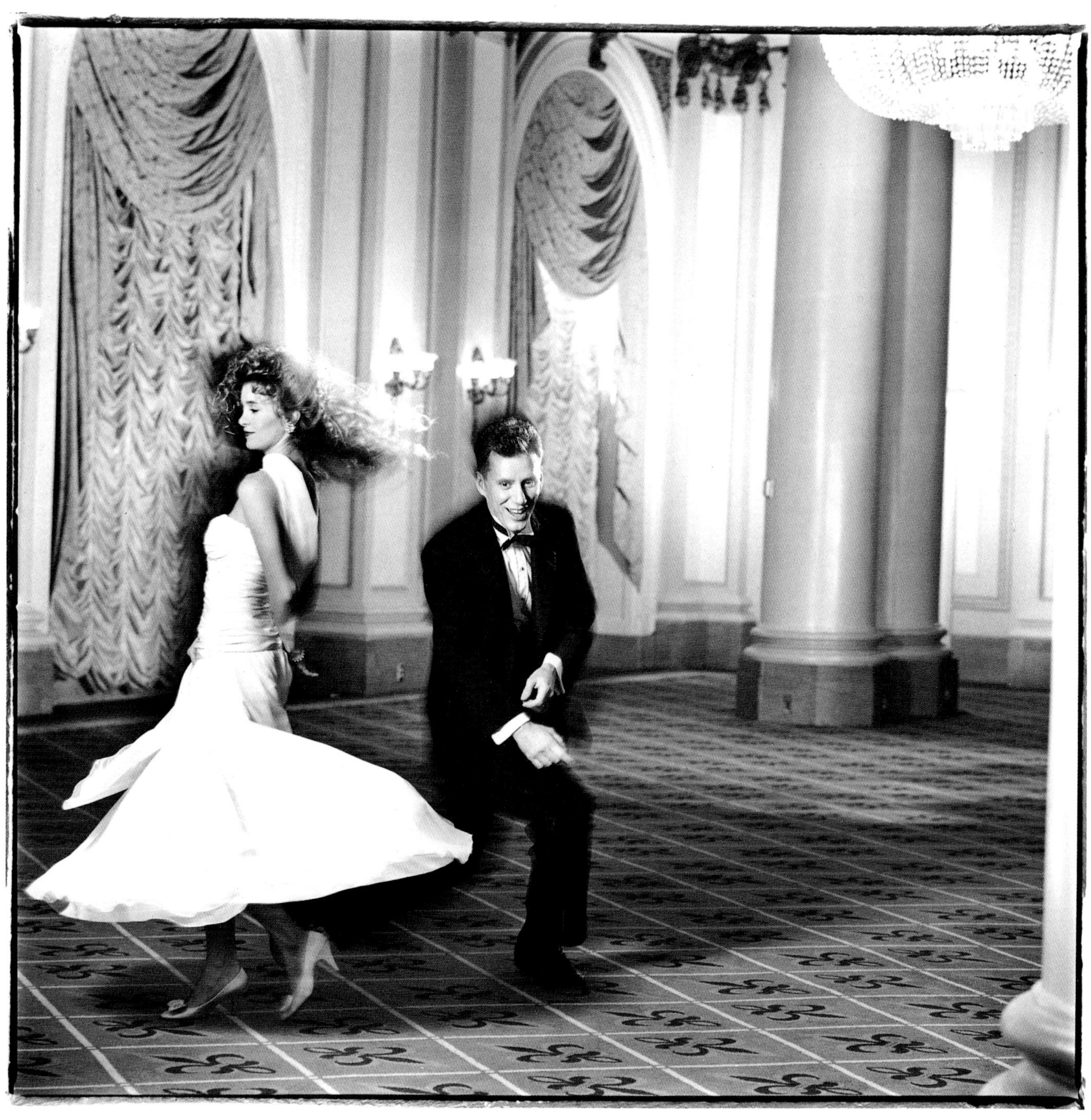

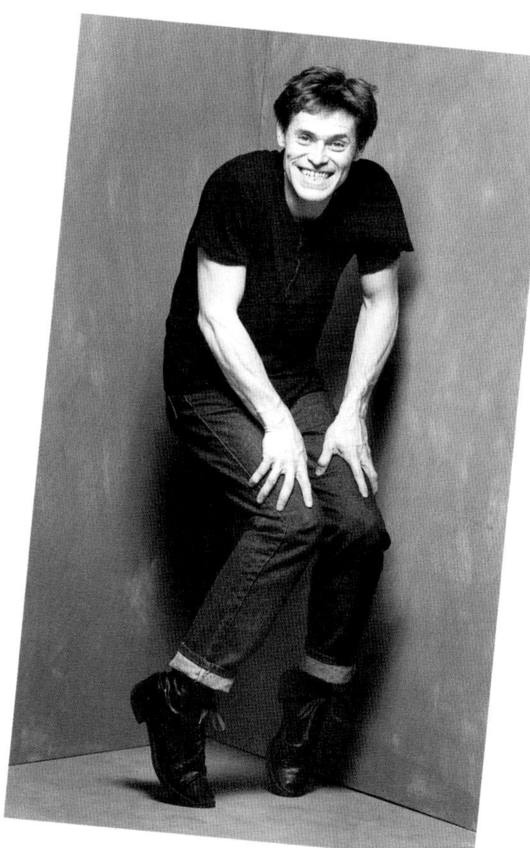

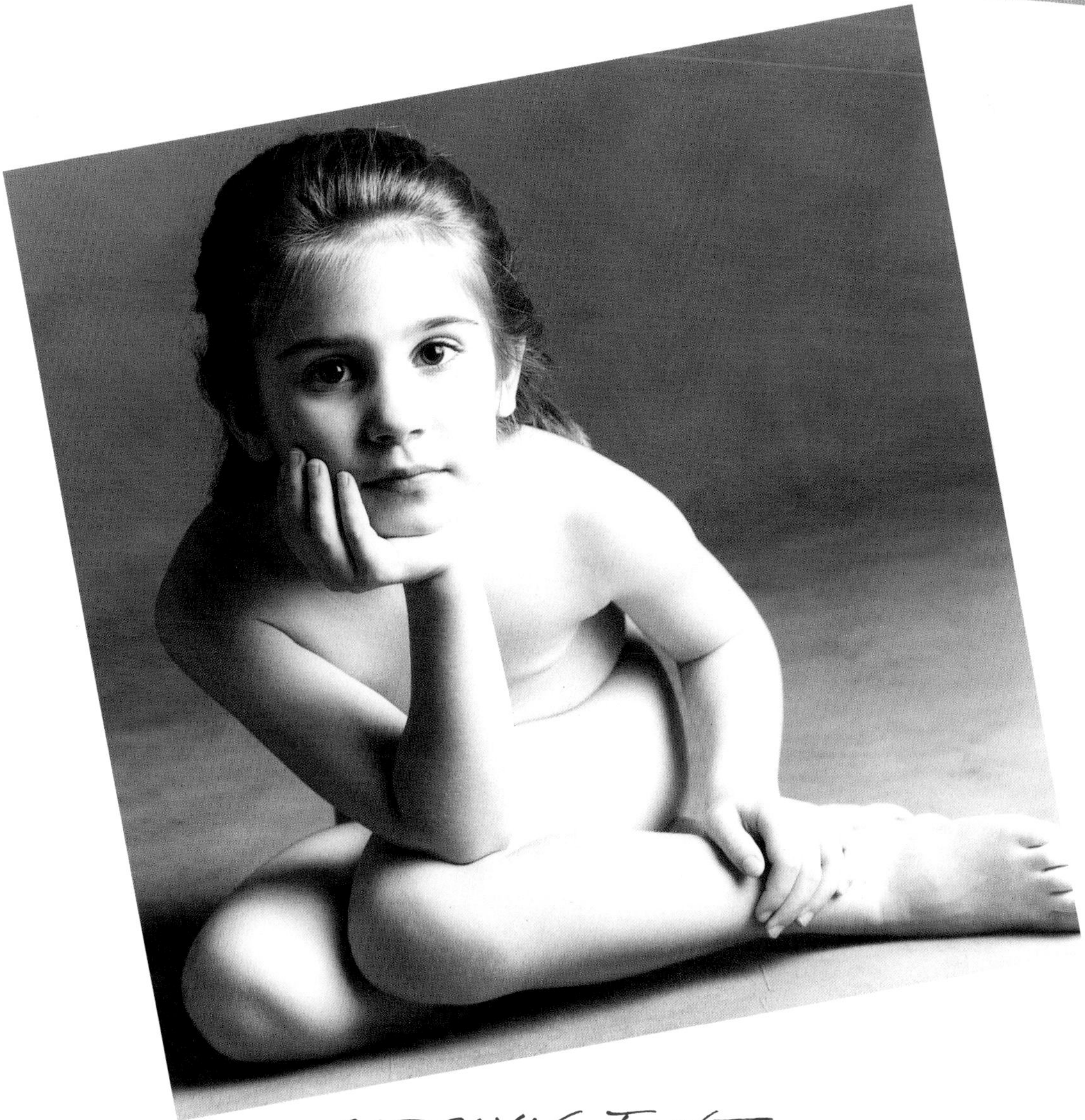

CAROLYN JONES

REPRESENTED BY GEORGIA GOODROW 167 SPRING ST. (212) 431 9696

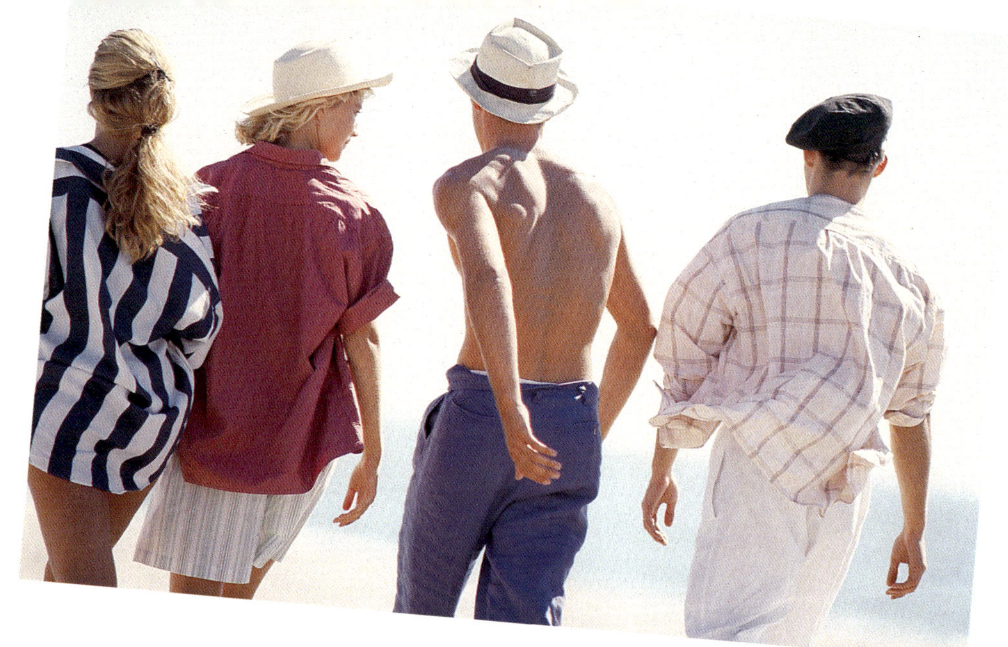

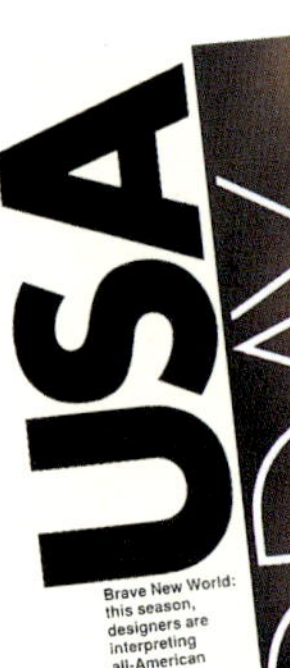

USA TODAY

Brave New World: this season, designers are interpreting all-American idioms–like this pair of flag-strewn sweaters–in new and unexpected ways. Blue turtleneck sweater, Ralph Lauren Roughwear, $425. At Polo/Ralph Lauren, NYC, Pittsburgh. White crewneck sweater, Polo by Ralph Lauren, $275. For details, see Retail Guide. Hair, Bruno Weppe for Jean Louis David; makeup, Giorgio for Suga Salon, NYC; stylist, Jane Hsiang.

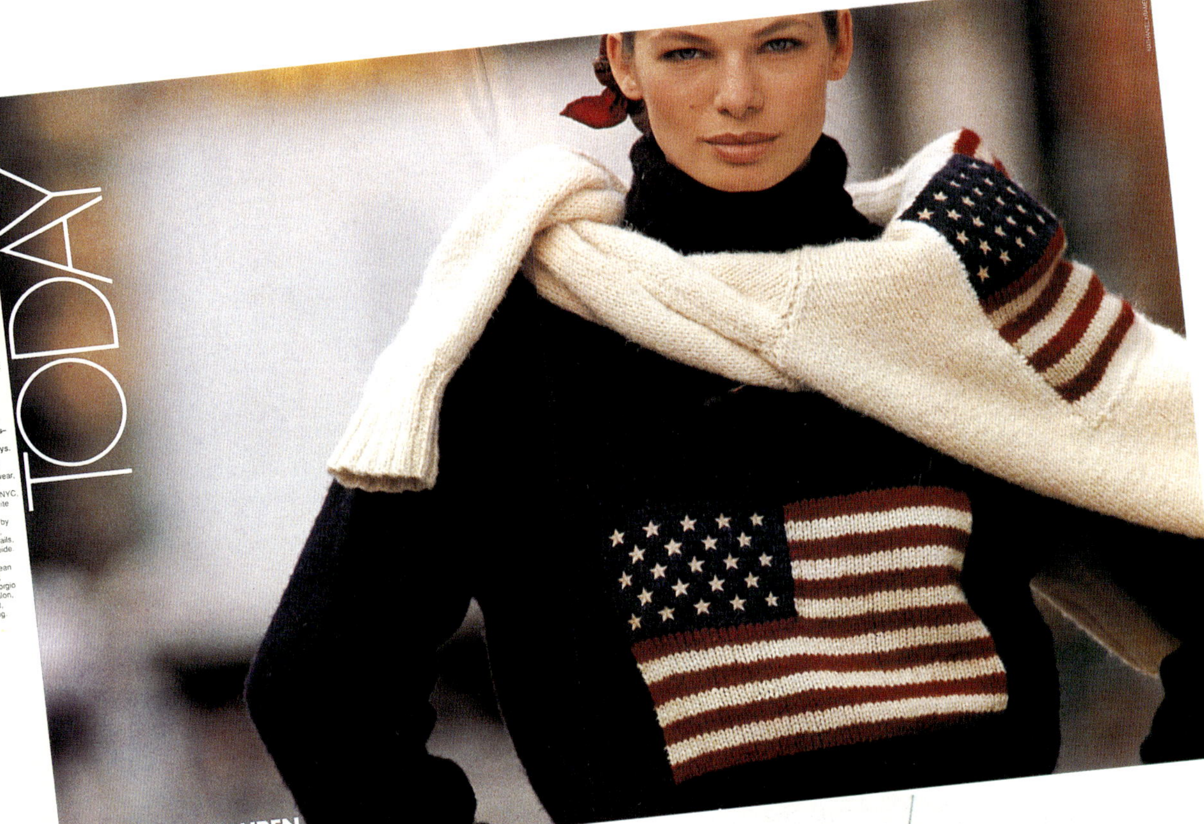

RALPH LAUREN

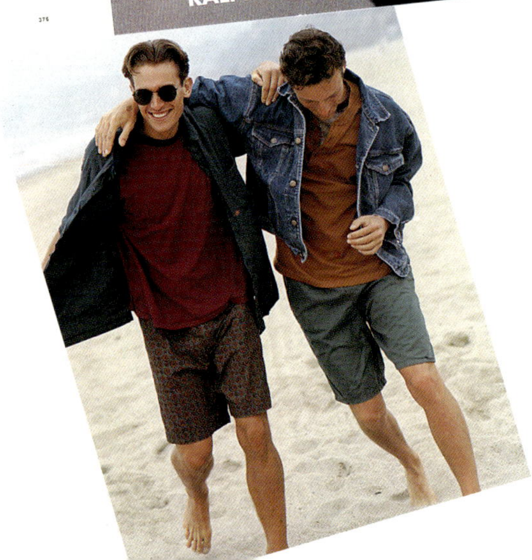

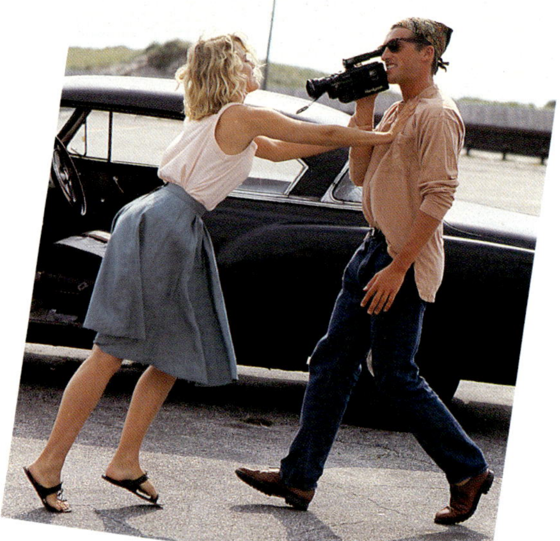

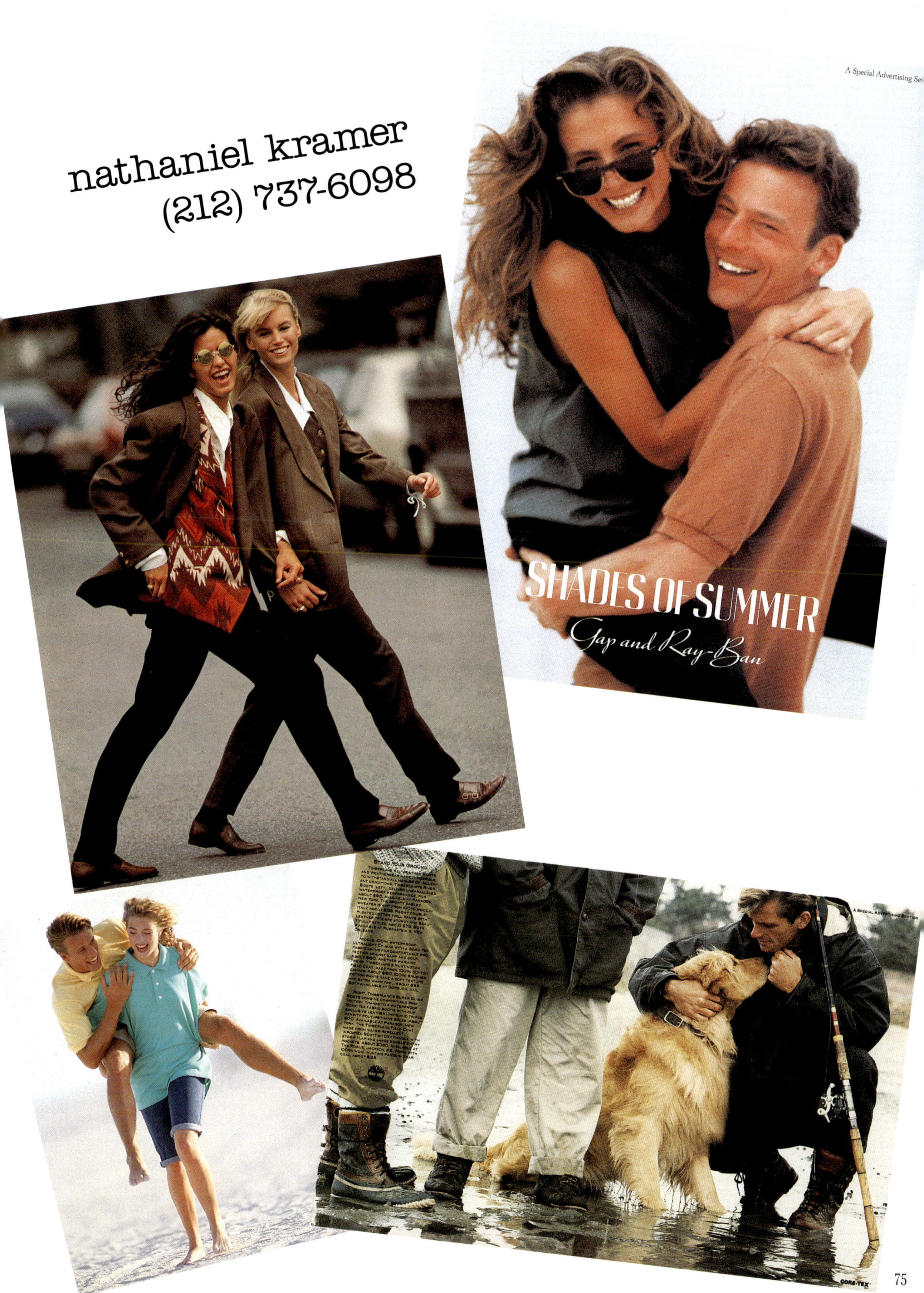
nathaniel kramer
(212) 737-6098
A Special Advertising Se
SHADES OF SUMMER
Gap and Ray-Ban
GORE-TEX

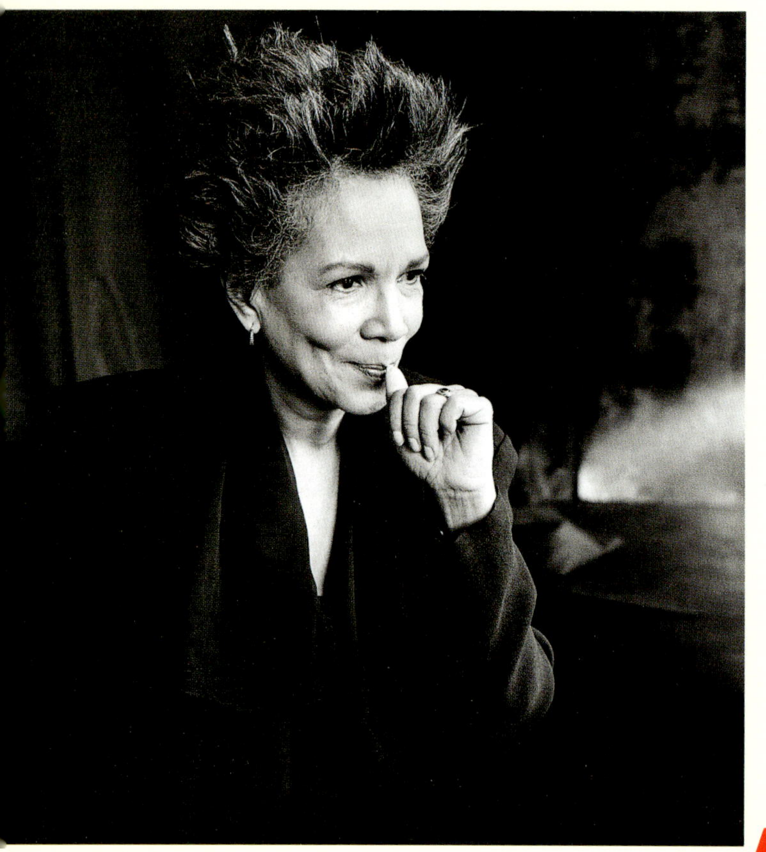

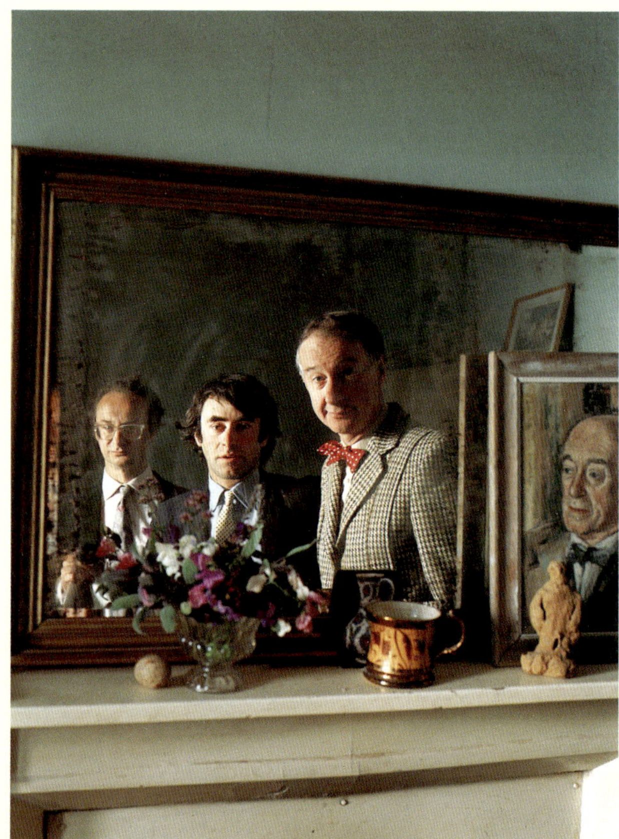

Alen MacWeeney

Represented by Robert Feldman (212) 243-7319.

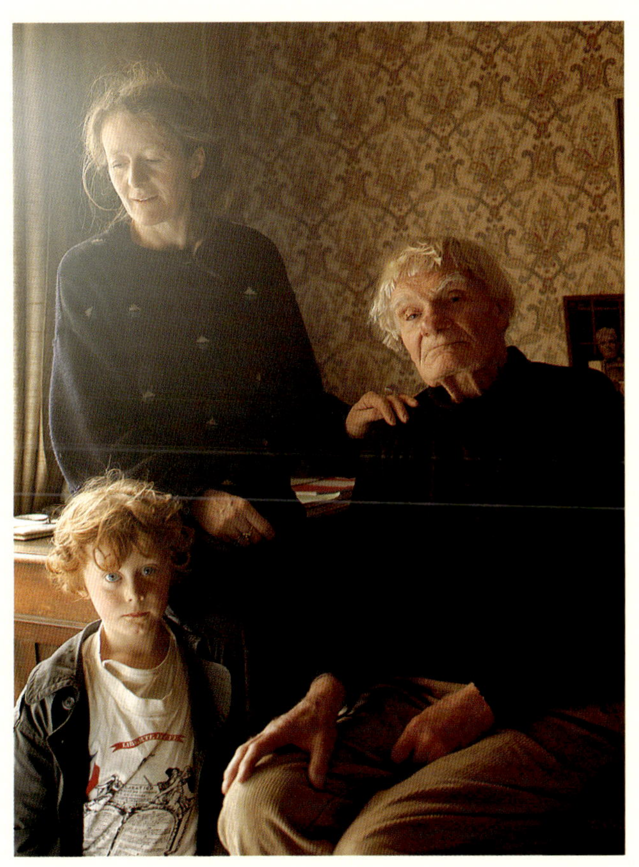

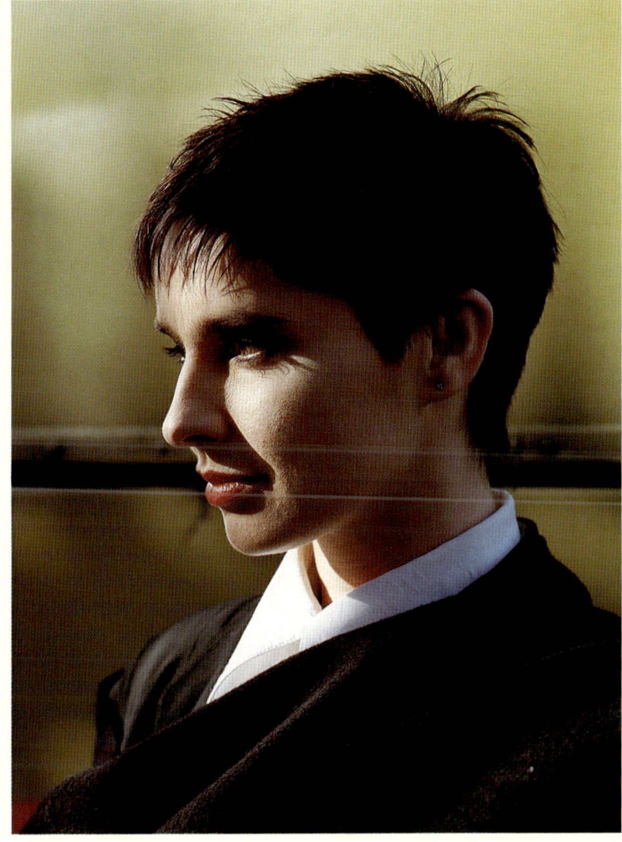

Alen MacWeeney Inc. 171 First Avenue, New York, NY 10003 (212) 473-2500 Fax (212) 473-2250.

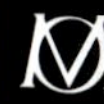

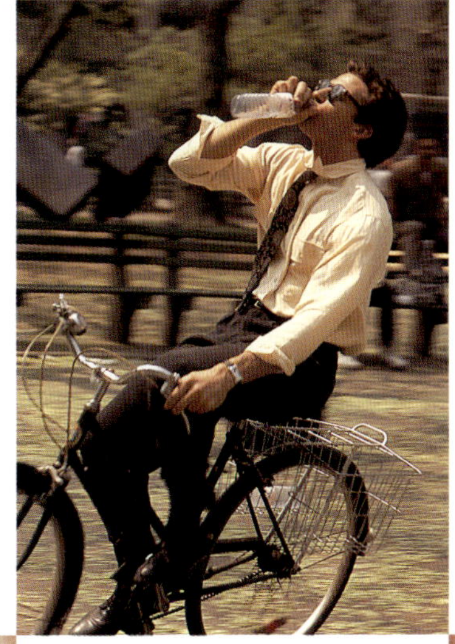

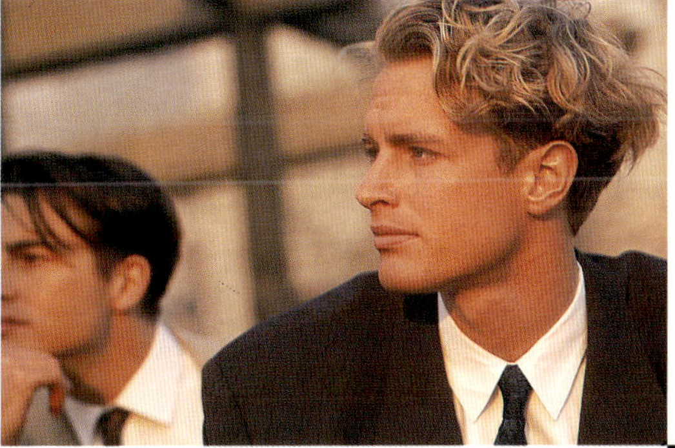

OSKAR
MARTINEZ
STUDIO

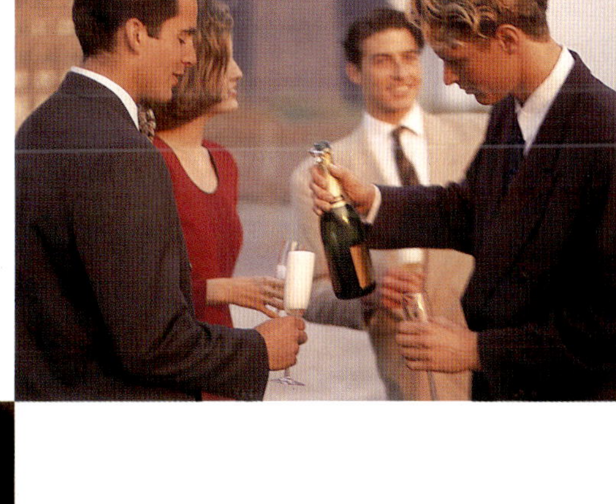

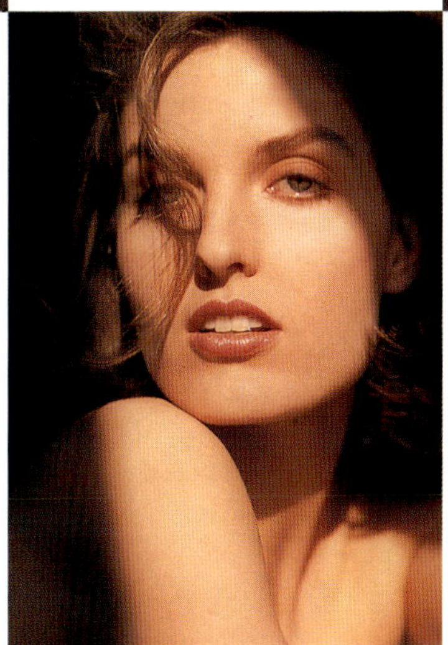

303 Park Avenue South, Suite 408, New York, New York 10010 212-673-0932

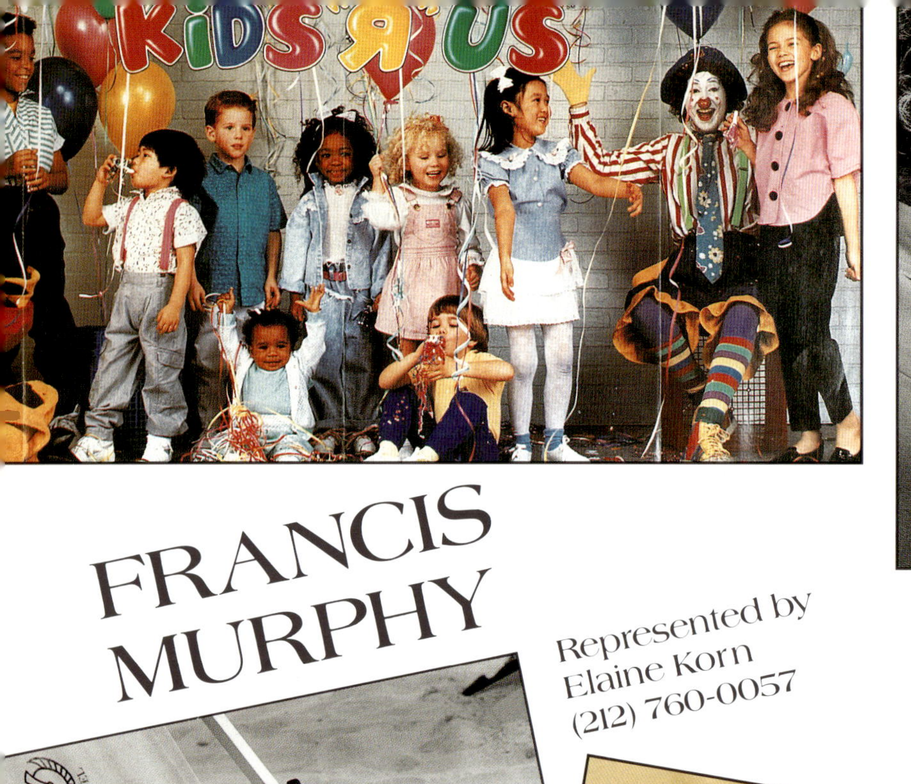

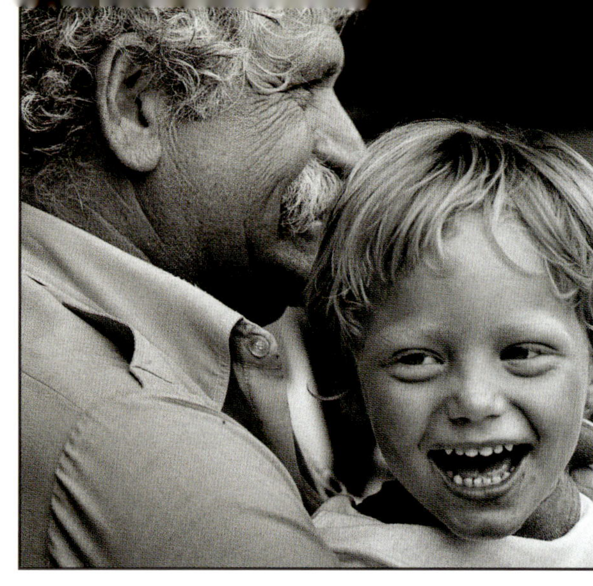

FRANCIS MURPHY

Represented by
Elaine Korn
(212) 760-0057

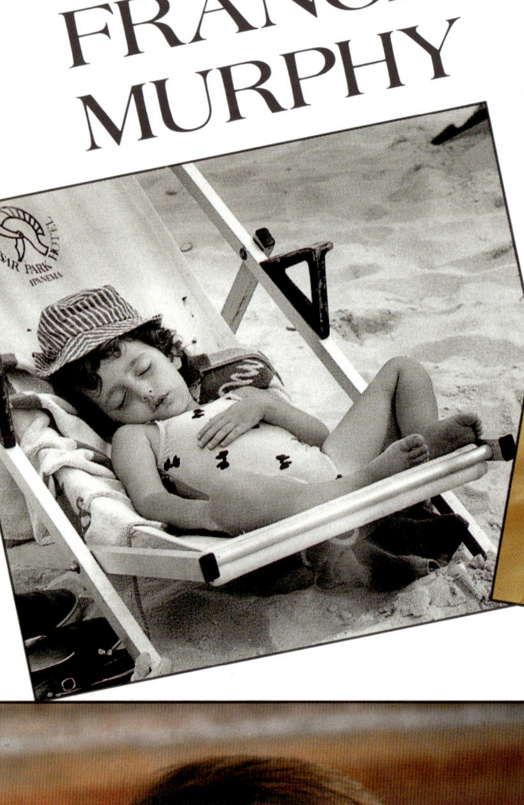

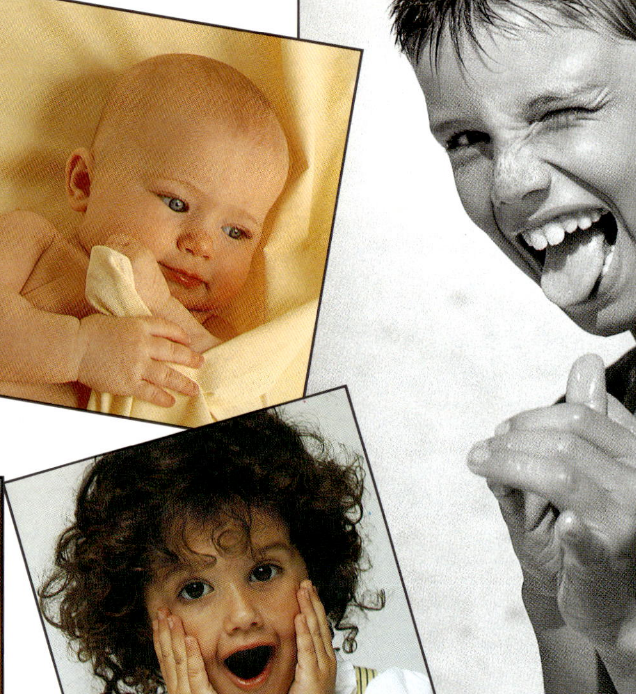

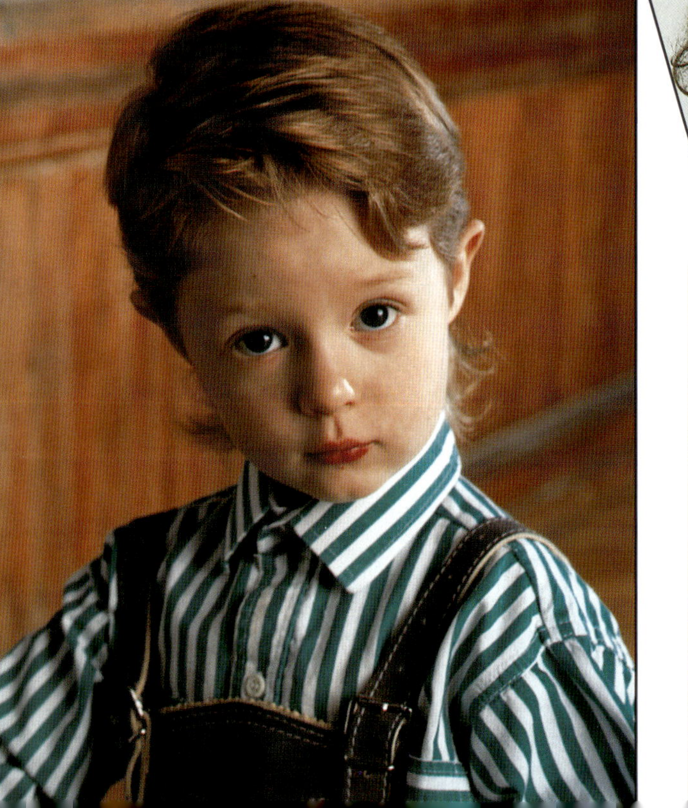

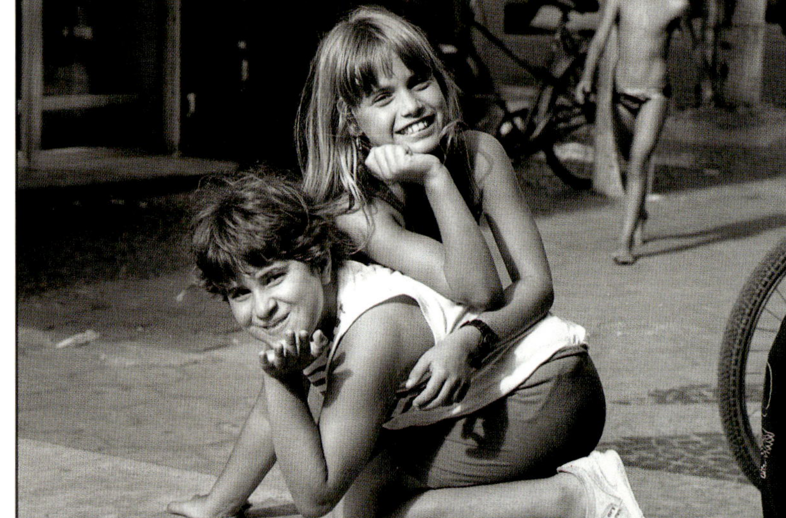

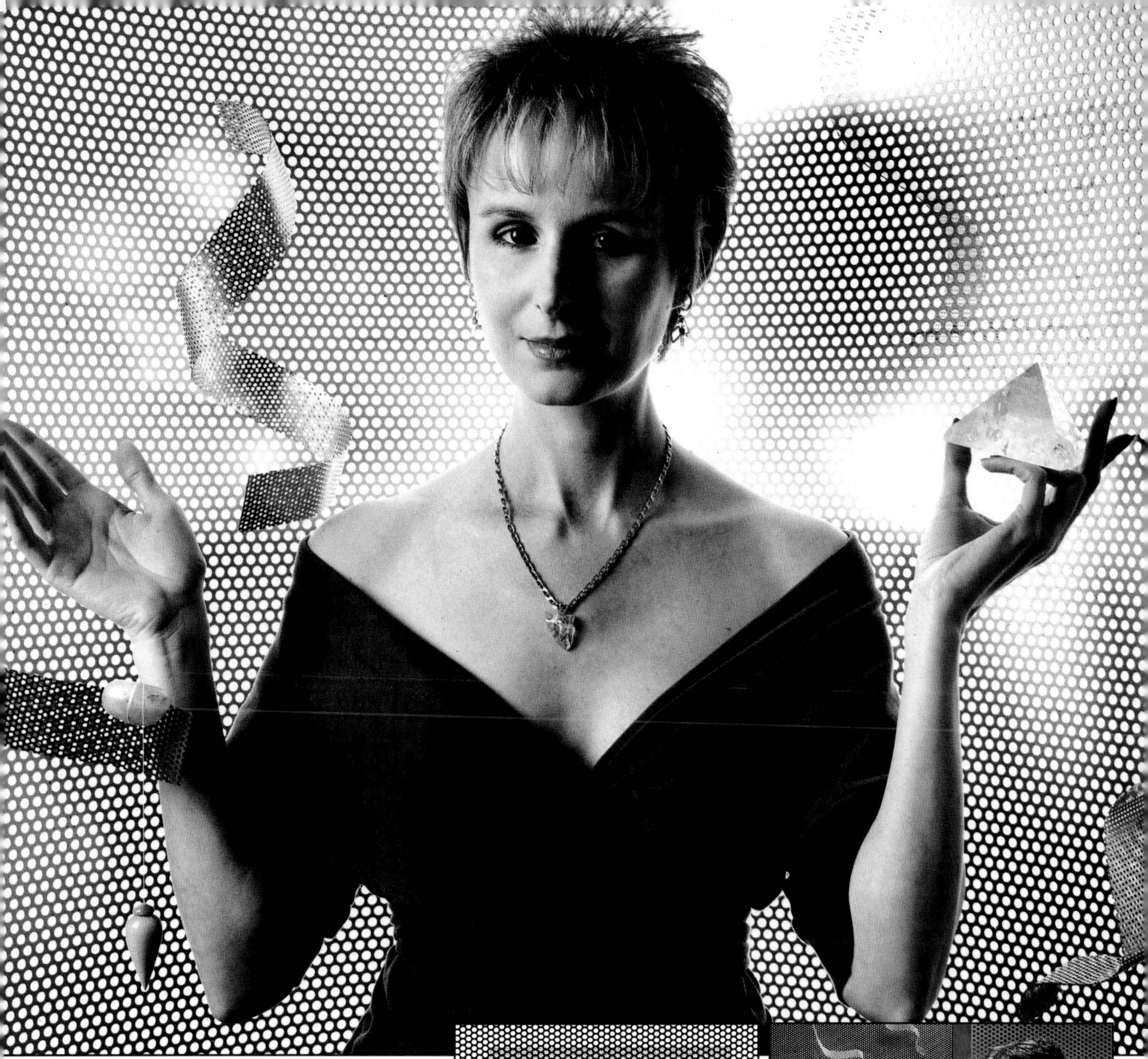

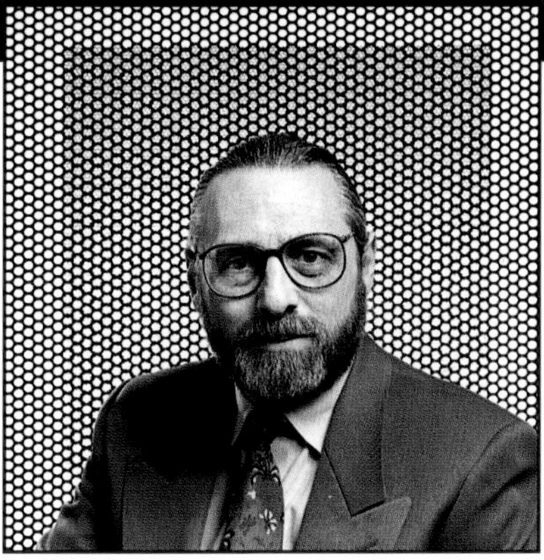

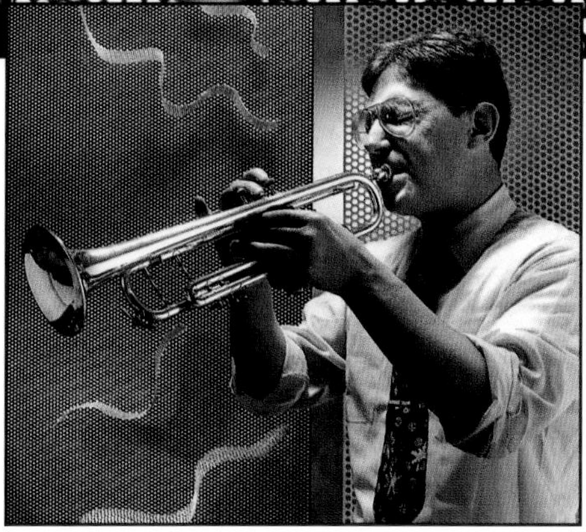

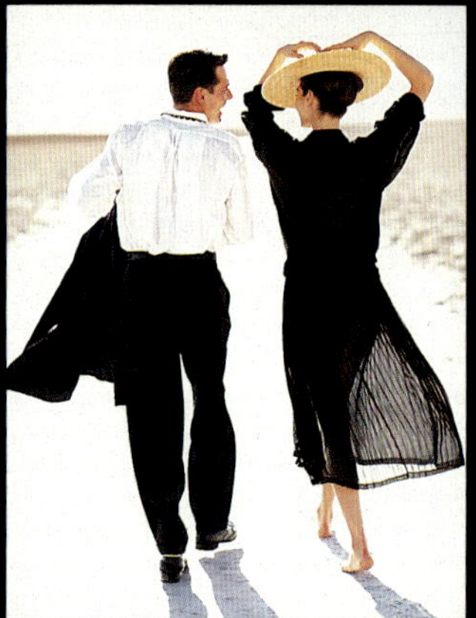
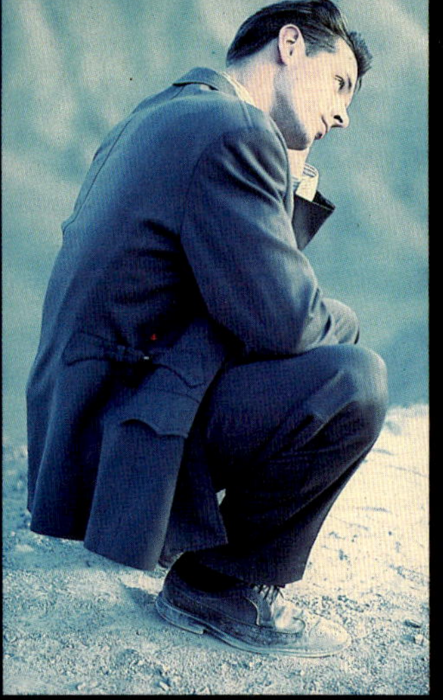
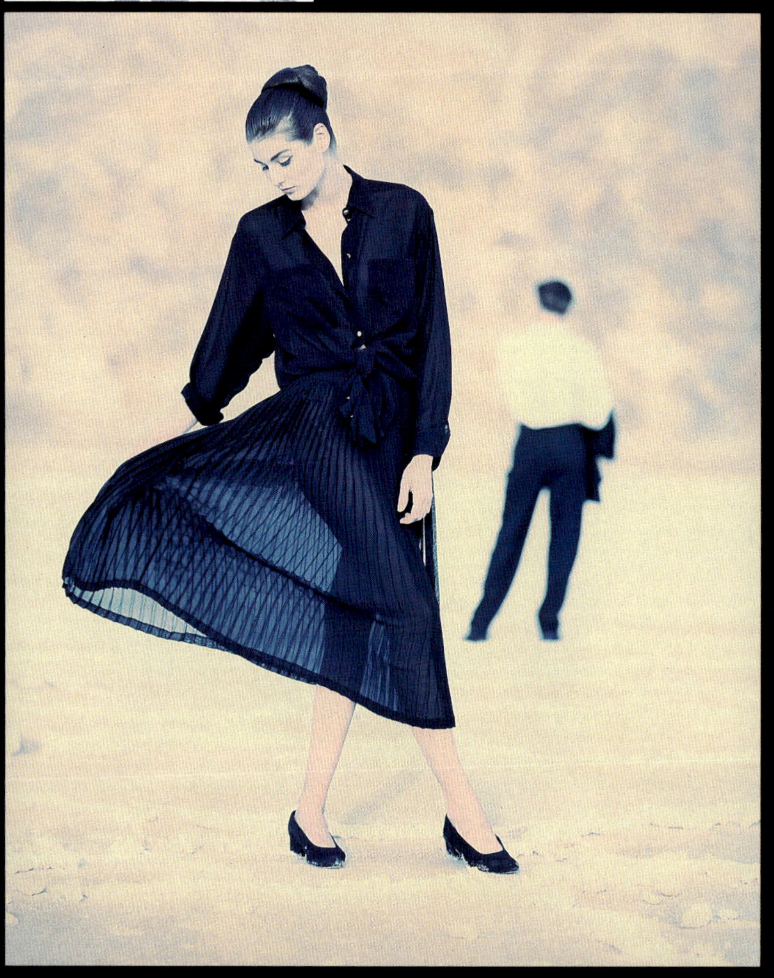
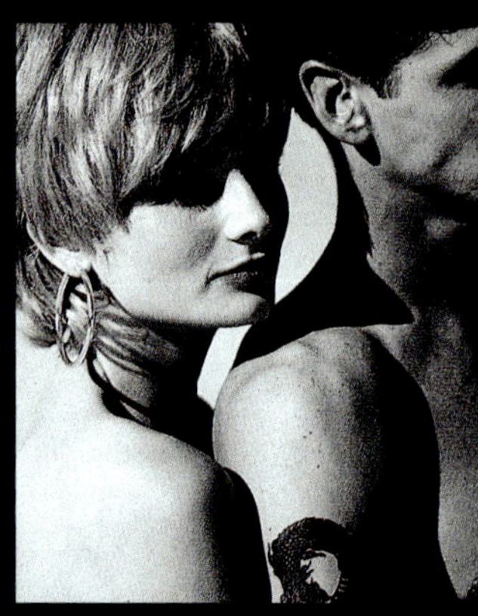

kip meyer represented by Pat Herron·212·683·9039 Nob Hovde Associates·212·753·0462

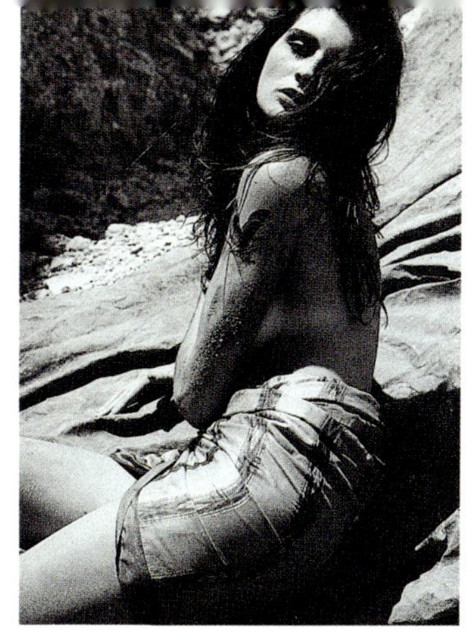

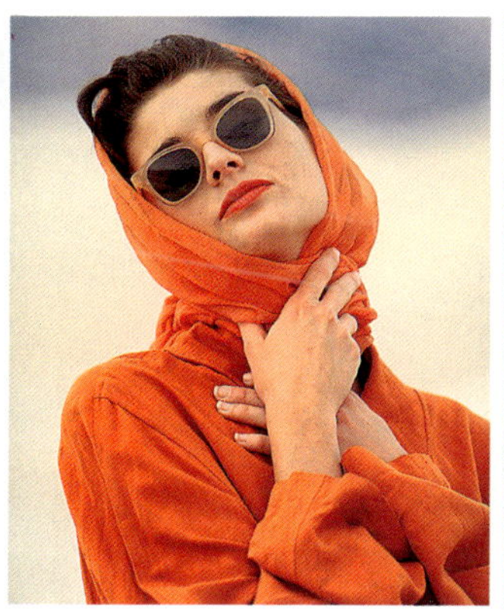

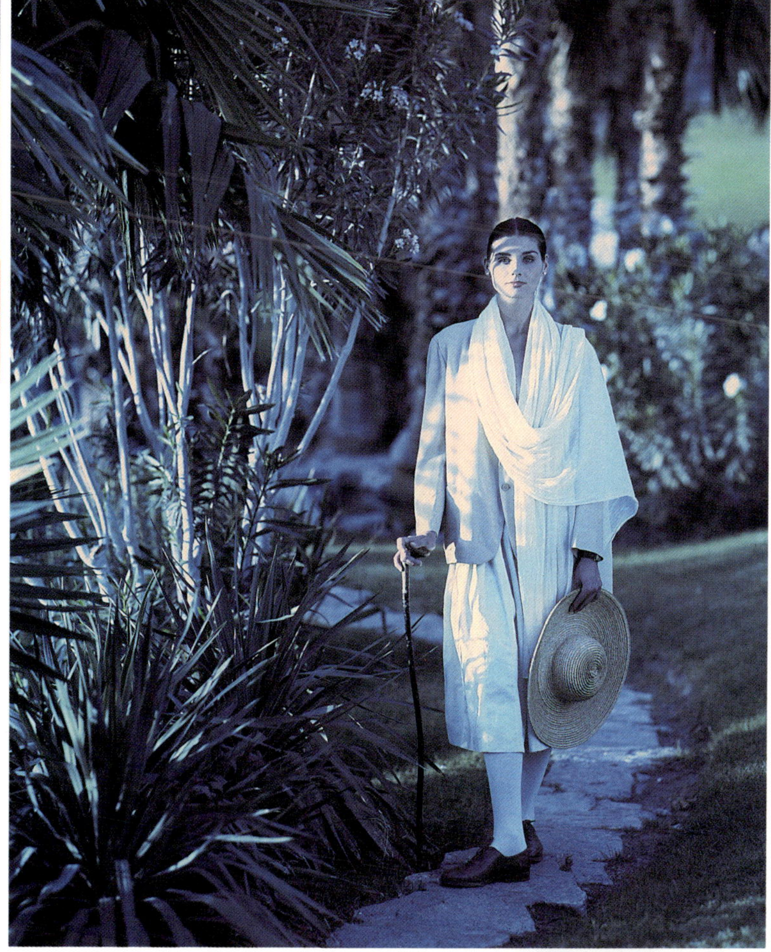

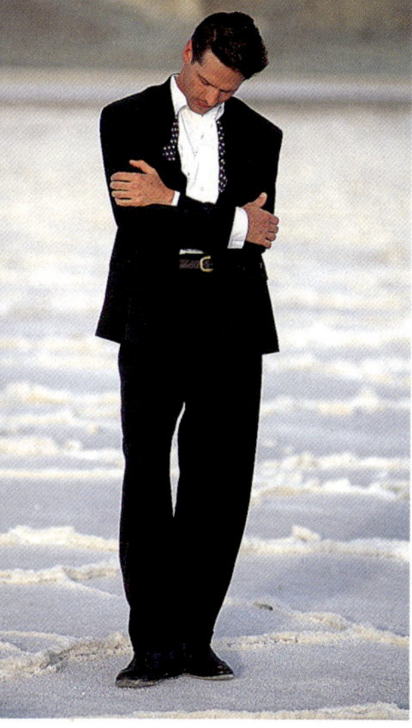

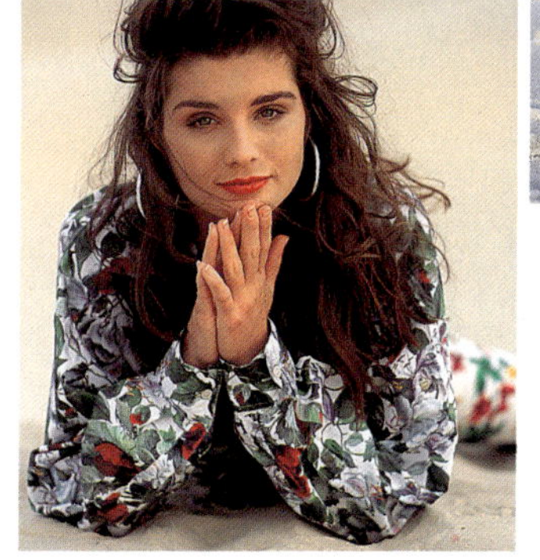

kip meyer represented by Pat Herron·212·683·9039 Nob Hovde Associates·212·753·0462

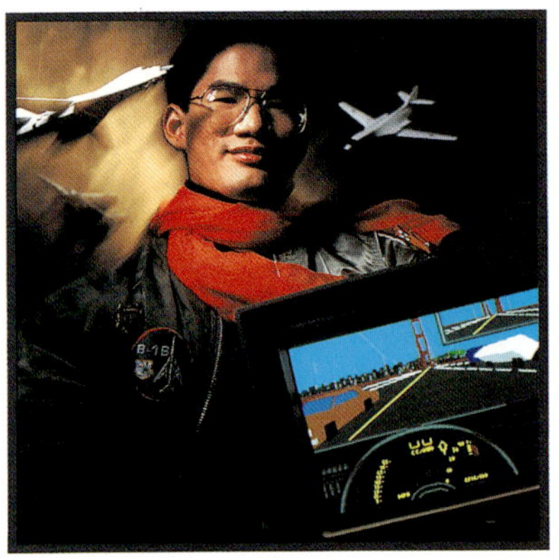

Gilman Louie
Flight Simulator Designer For Pentagon
Amiga/Commodore Computers

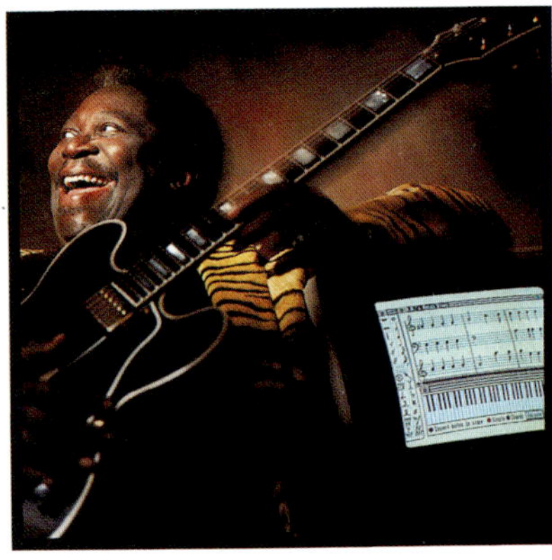

B. B. King
Amiga/Commodore Computers

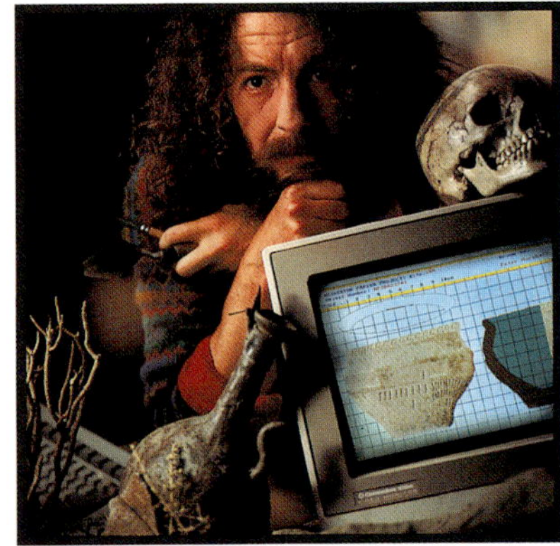

Dominic Powlesland
Archaeologist
Amiga/Commodore Computers

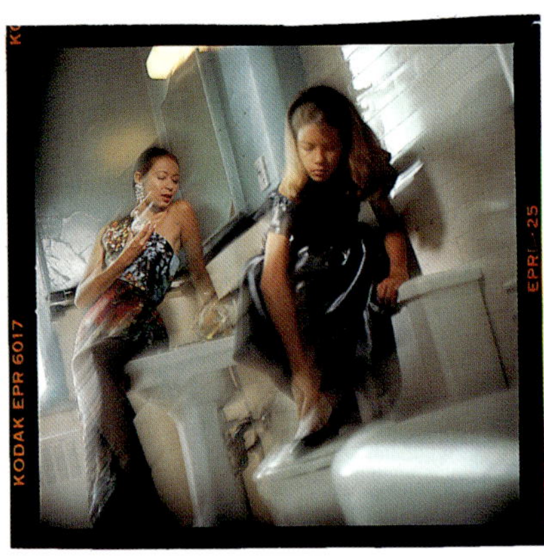

Lears Magazine

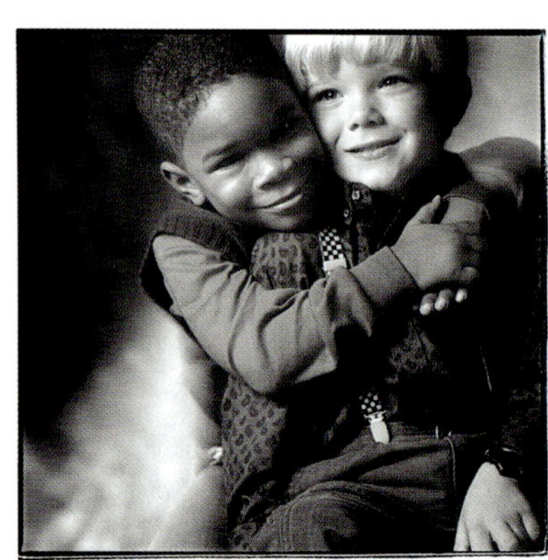

Nobody's Born A Bigot
Anti-Racism Campaign
NCCJ

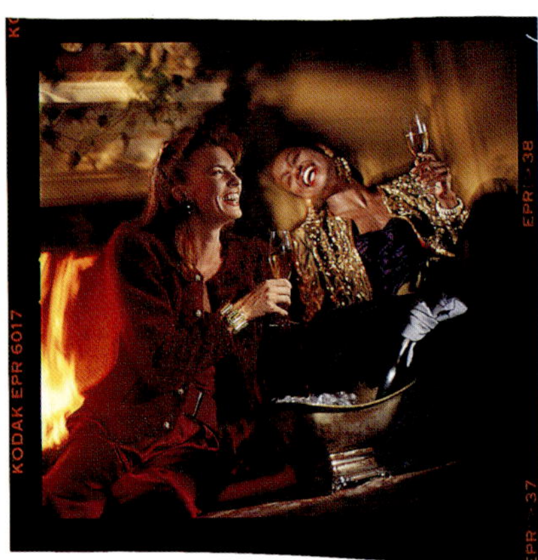

Lears Magazine

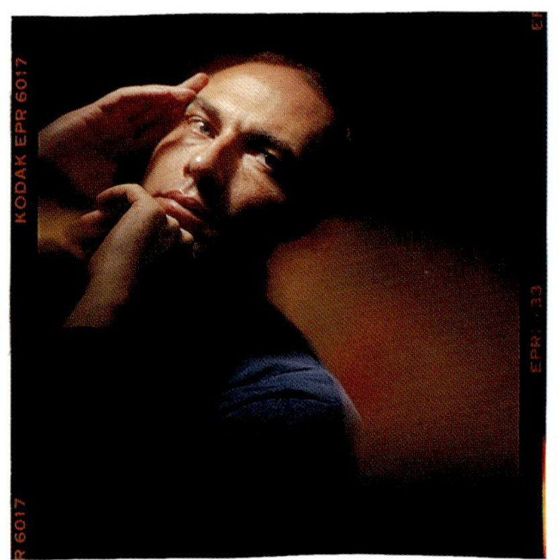

Ron Vawter
Actor: *sex, lies, and videotape*
Premiere Magazine

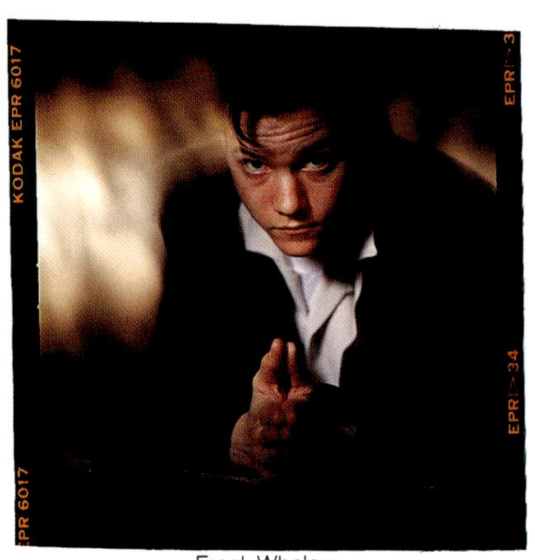

Frank Whaley
Actor: *Born on the 4th of July*
Premiere Magazine

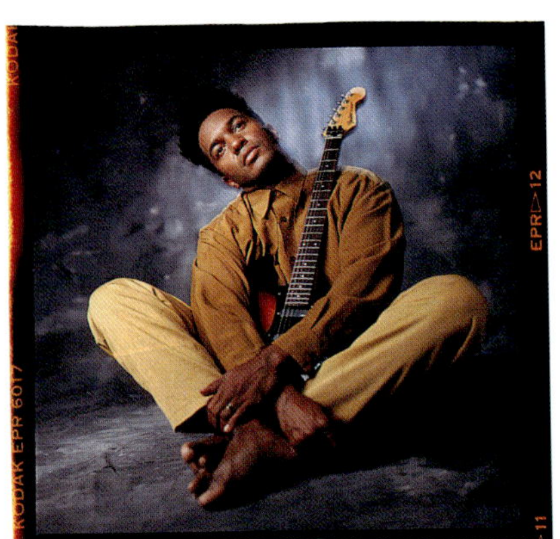

Dwight Sills
CBS Records

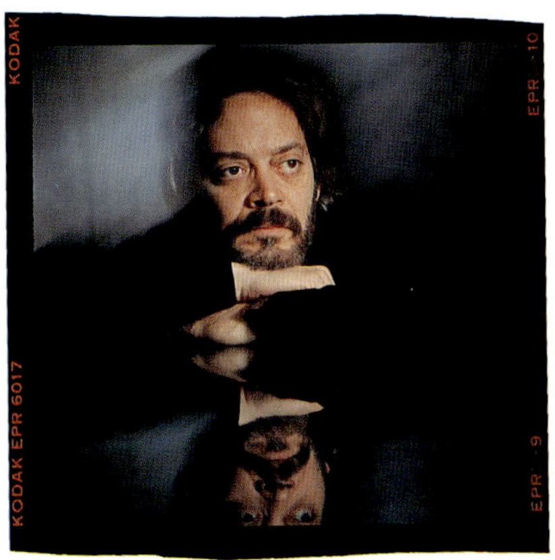

Raul Julia
USA TODAY

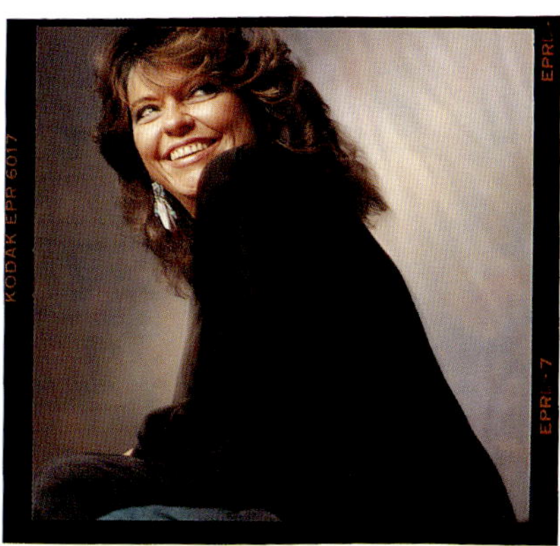

Linda Ellerbee
Savvy Magazine

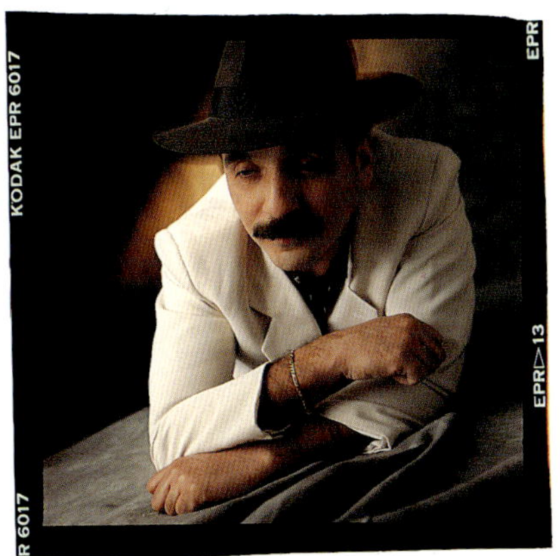

Willie Colon
Musician
Rolling Stone Magazine

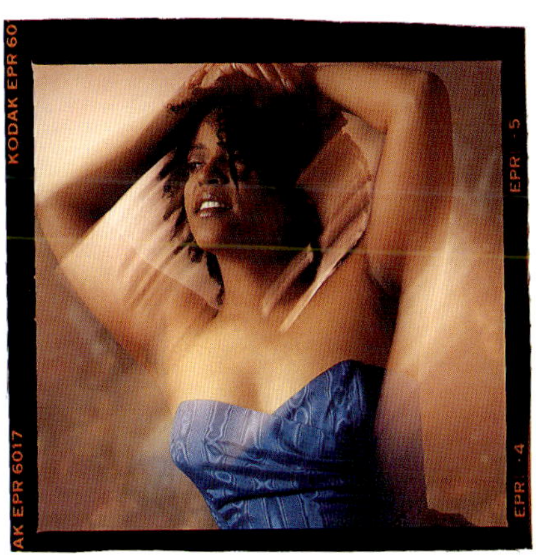

Cassandra Wilson
Polygram Records

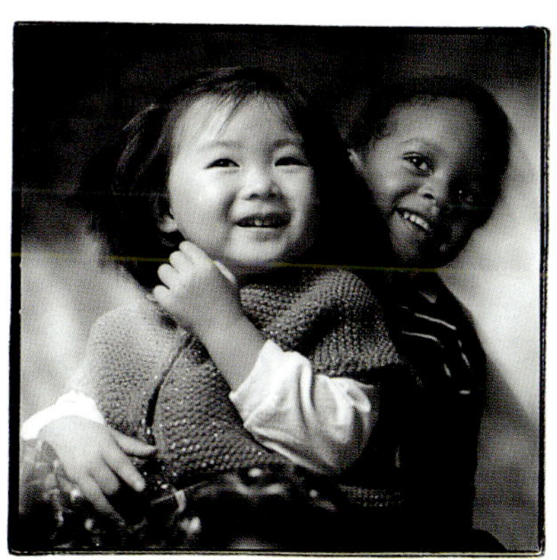

To End Racism Start Small
Anti-Racism Campaign
NCCJ

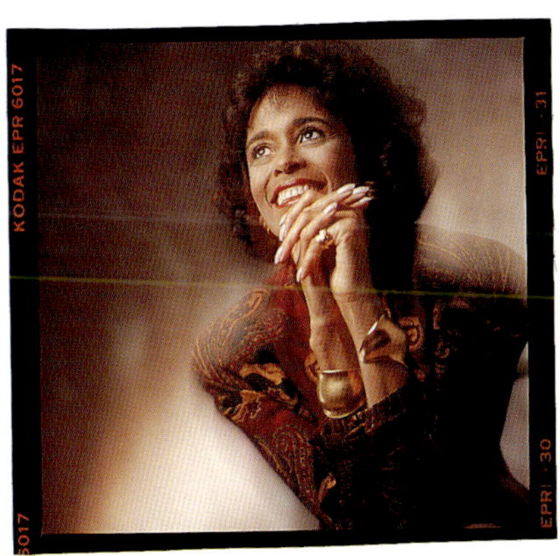

Faye Wattleton
President of Planned Parenthood
Ms. Magazine Cover

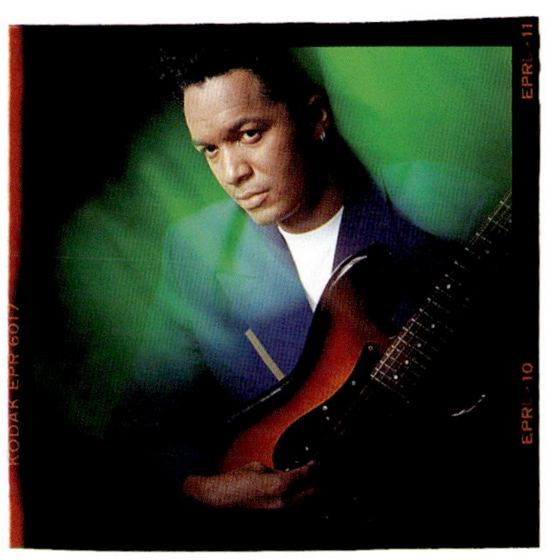

Dwight Sills
CBS Records

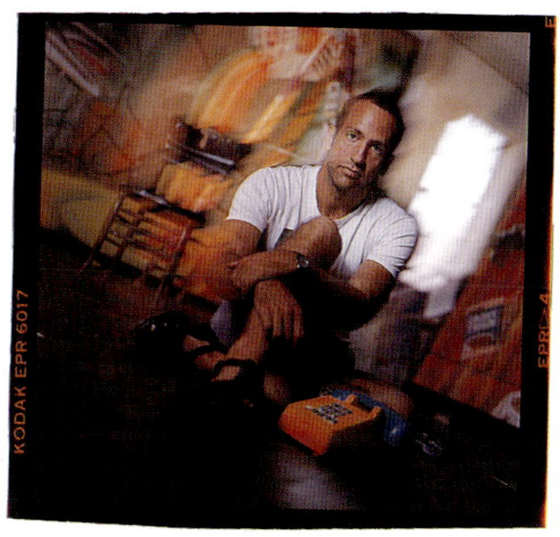

Kenny Scharf
Artist
Save the Rain Forest Promotion

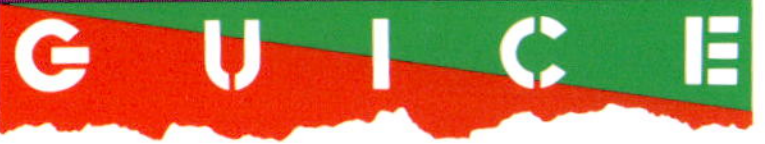

Brad Guice Photography

Phone (212) 206-0966

Represented by Janice Moses
Phone (212) 779-7929

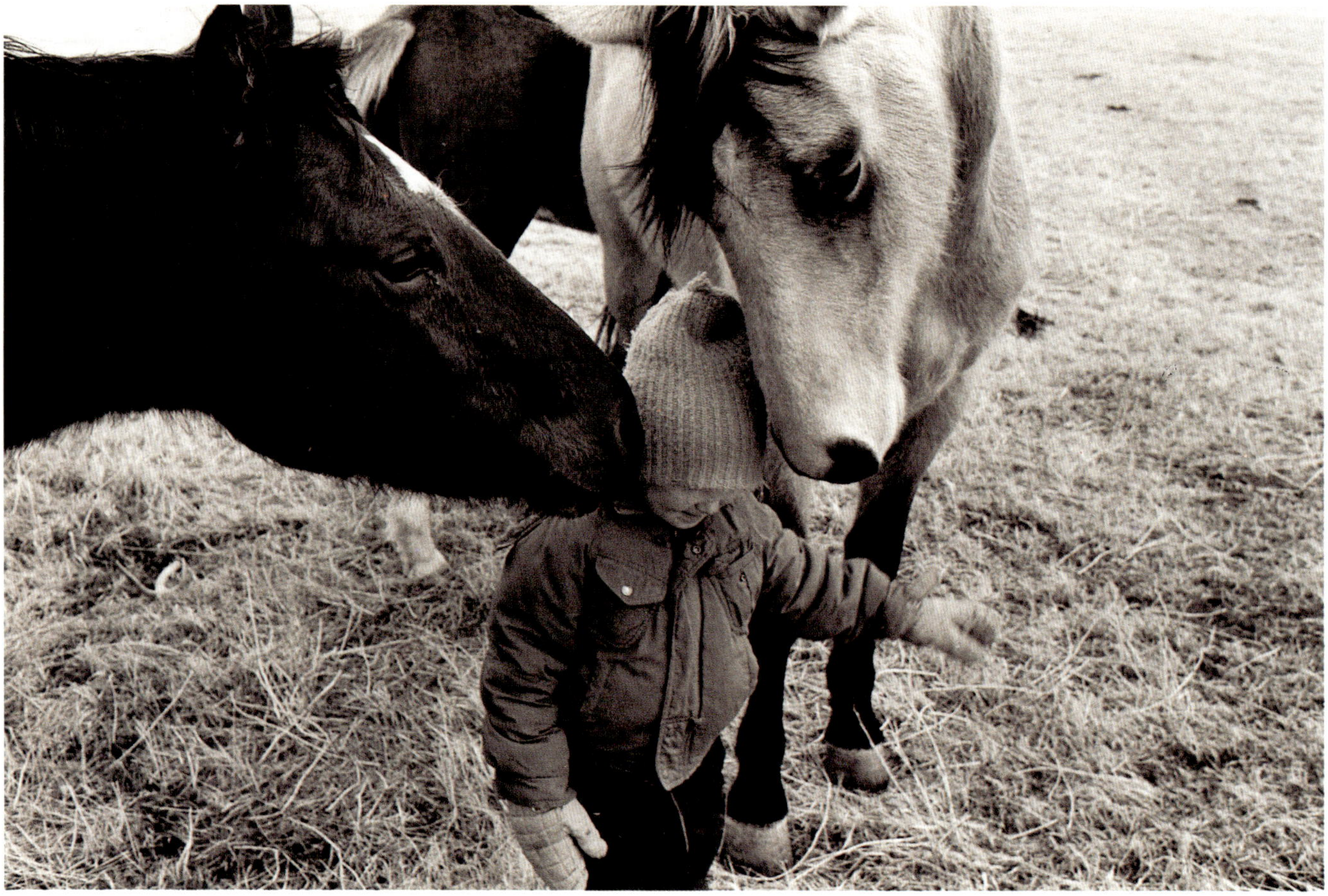

DANA BUCKLEY

156 Waverly Place
New York 10014
212/206/1807

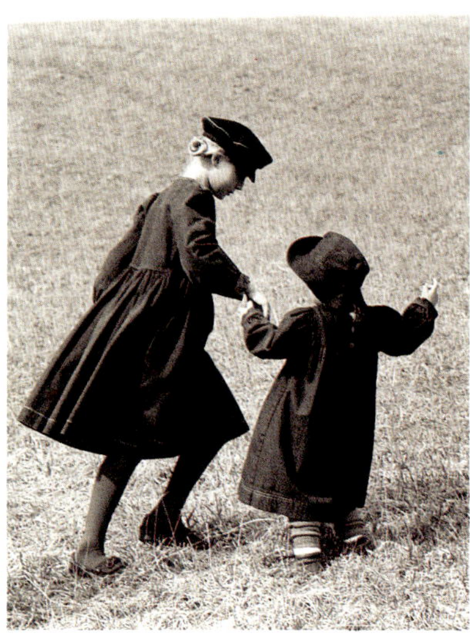

Represented by Korman + Company 212/633/8407

Studio Portfolio Available—CLIENTS INCLUDE, CBS Records, Epic Records, Young Fashions, Koos Van Den Akker, Alain Mikli, Schwab, Self, Cosmopolitan, Redbook, Ladies Home Journal

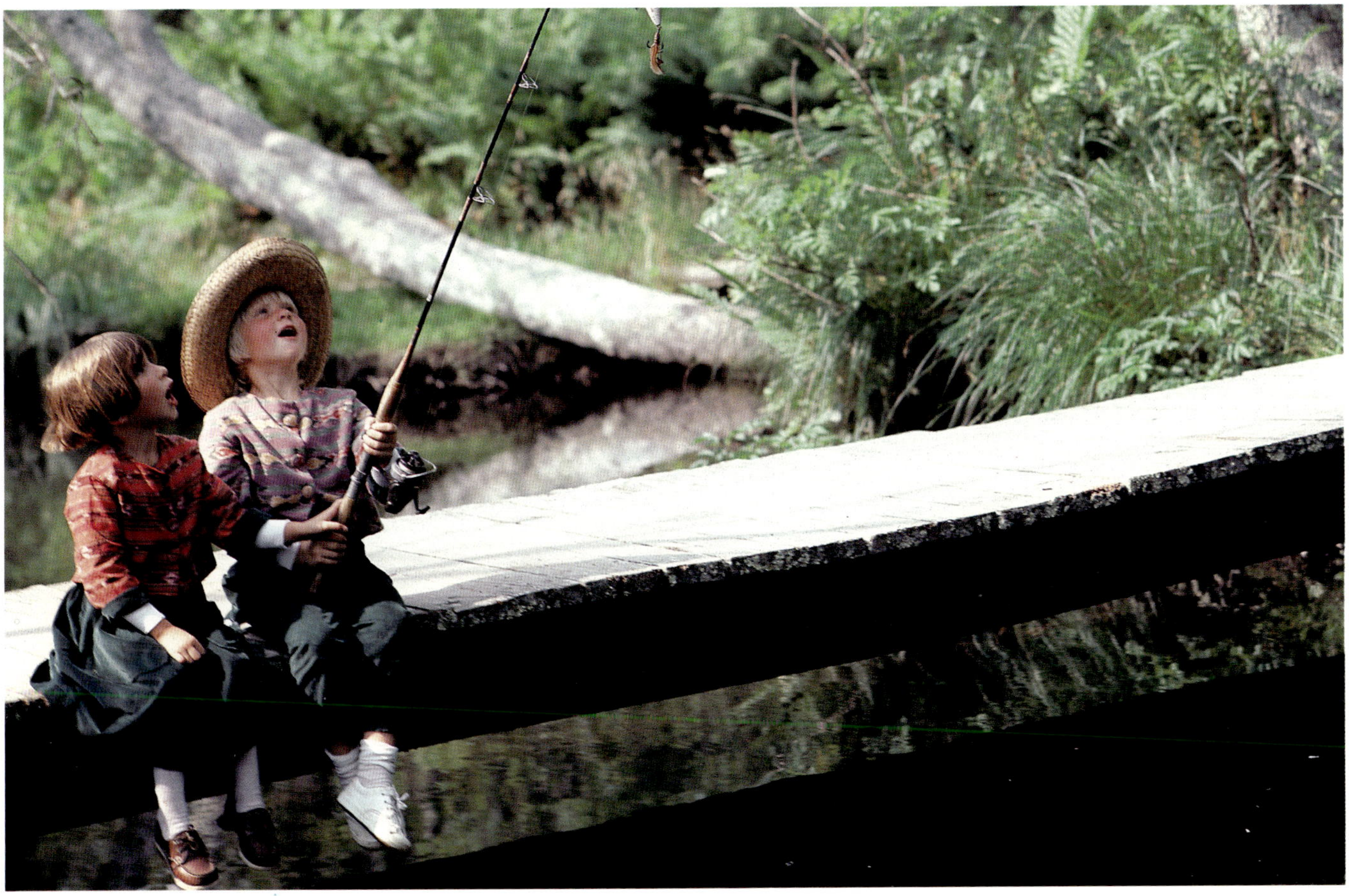

DANA BUCKLEY

156 Waverly Place
New York 10014
212/206/1807

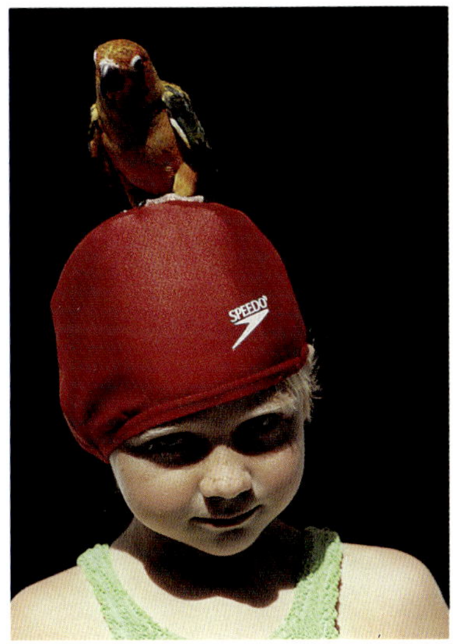

Represented by Korman + Company 212/633/8407

Studio Portfolio Available—CLIENTS INCLUDE, CBS Records, Epic Records, Young Fashions, Koos Van Den Akker, Alain Mikli, Schwab, Self, Cosmopolitan, Redbook, Ladies Home Journal

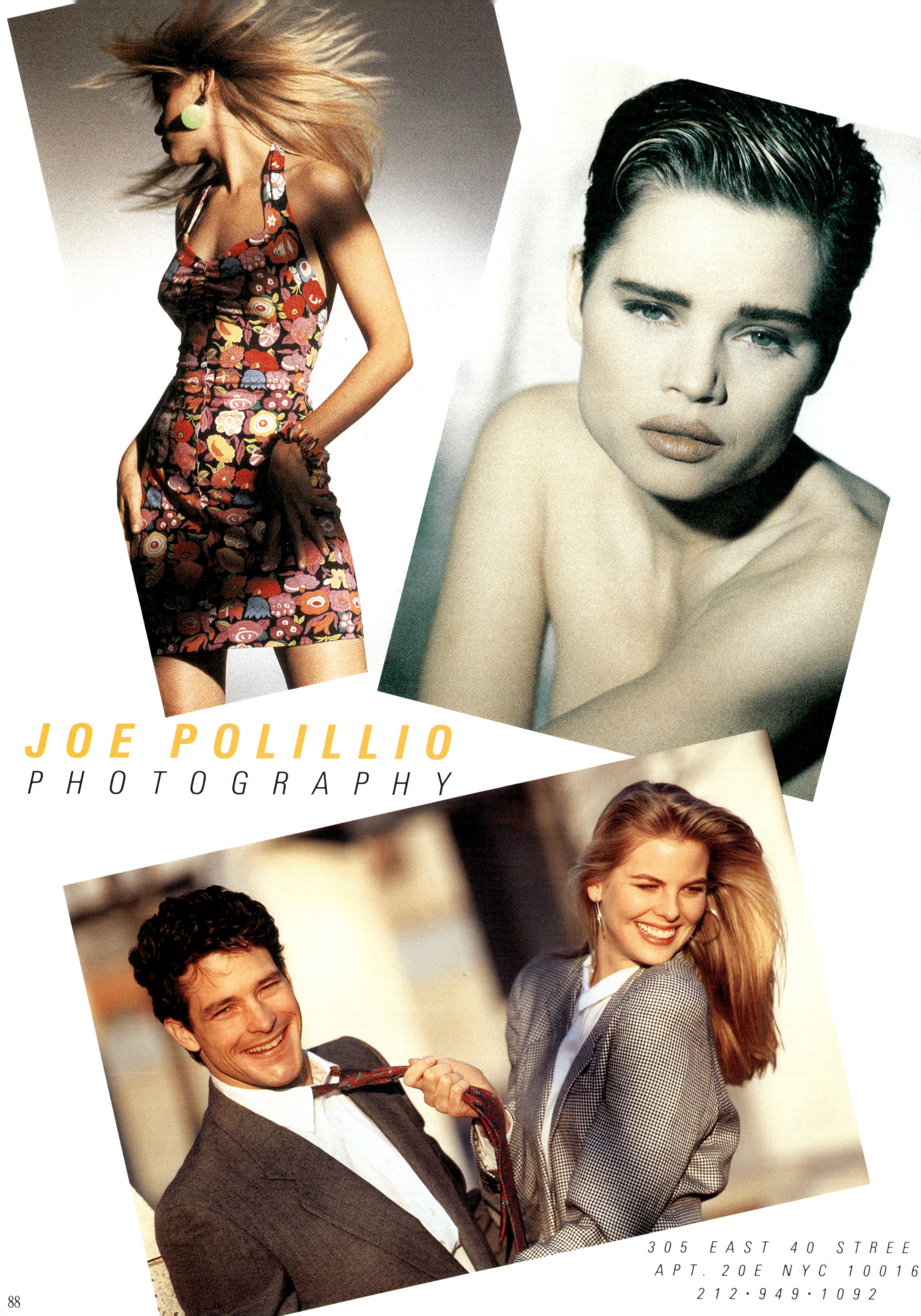

JOE POLILLIO

PHOTOGRAPHY

305 EAST 40 STREE
APT. 20E NYC 10016
212·949·1092

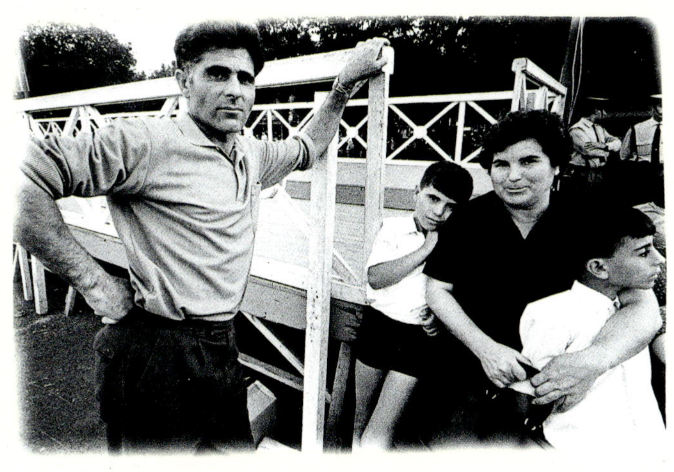

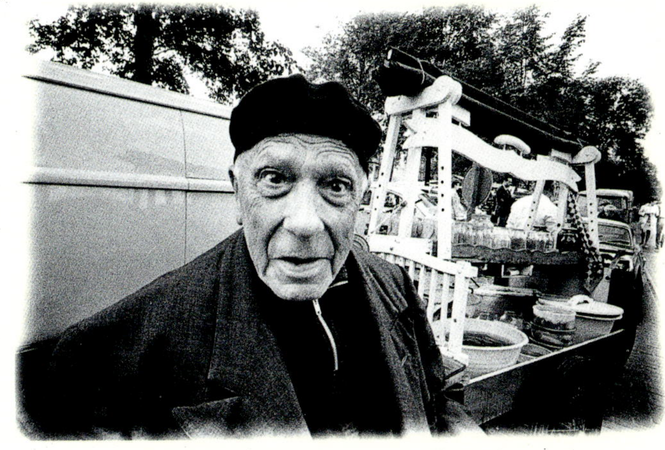

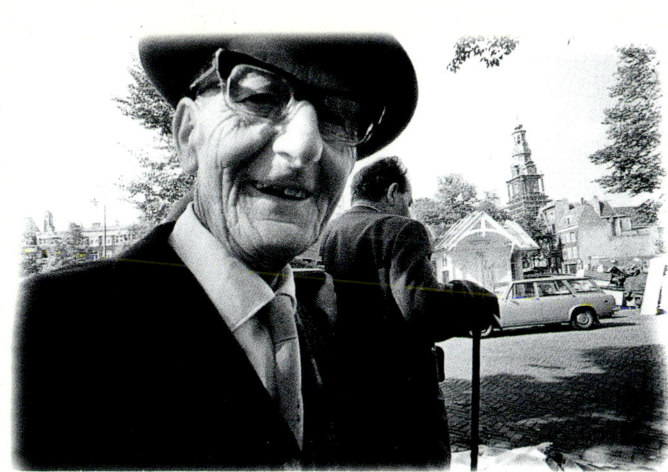

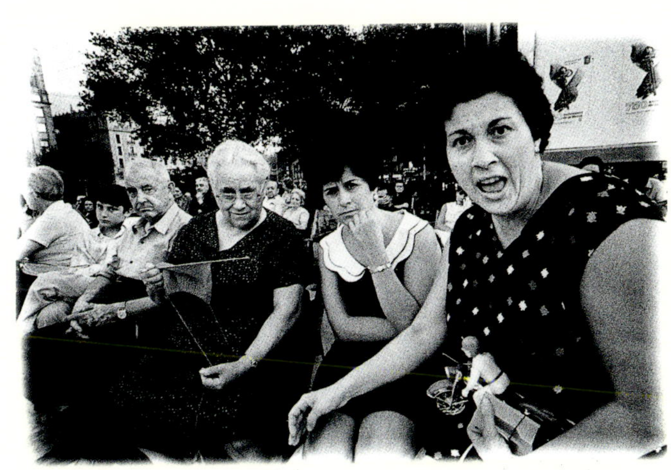

photographs by;

Michael Raab

831 Braoadway N.Y.C. 10003 (212) 533 0030

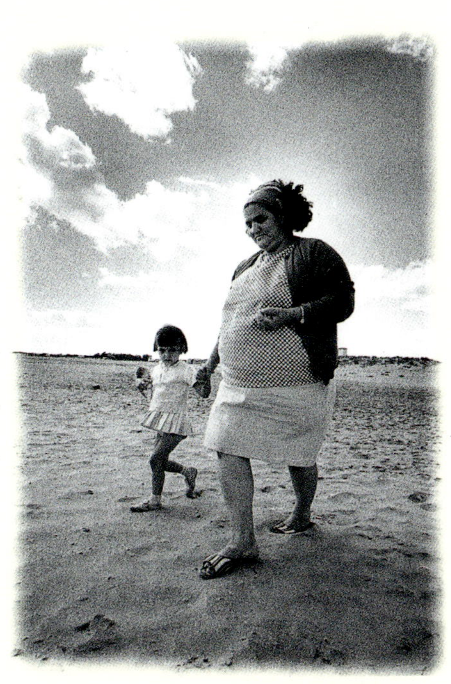

JACK DEUTSCH PHOTOGRAPHY

48 West 21st Street
New York, New York 10010
212-633-1424

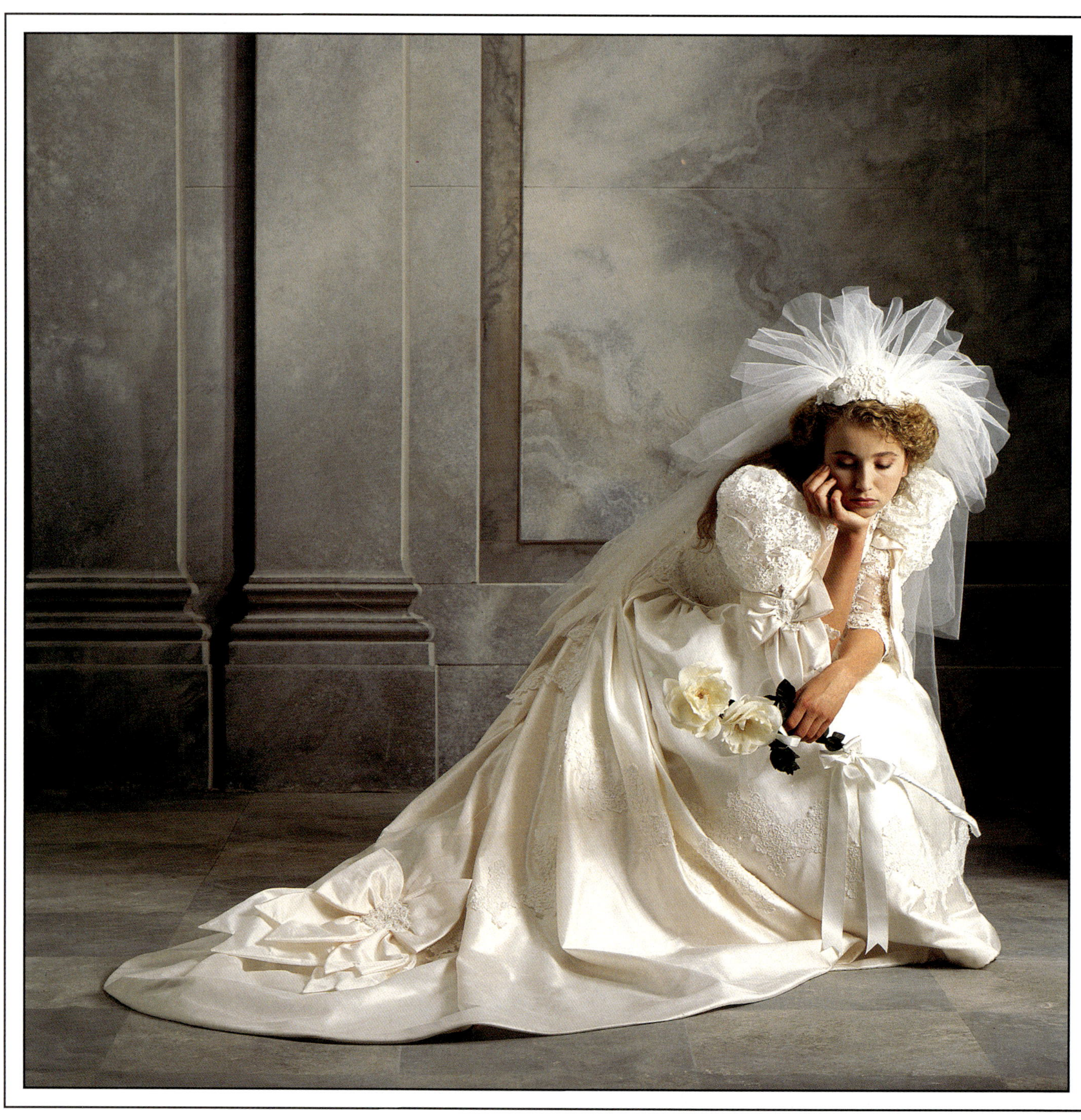

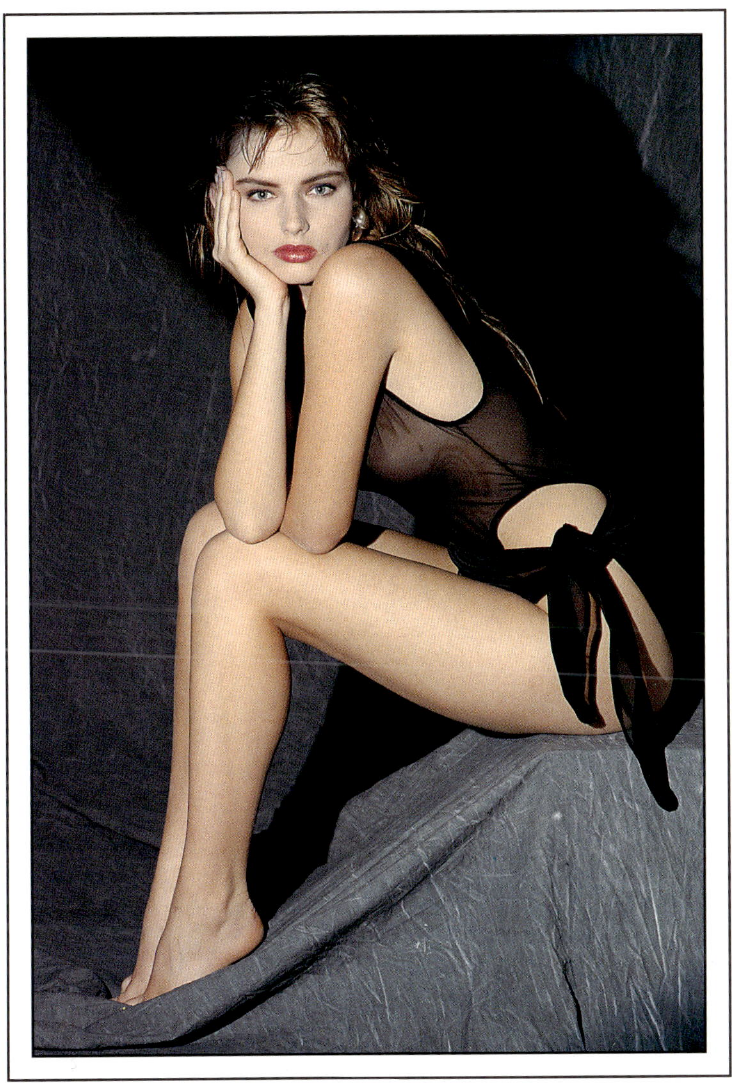

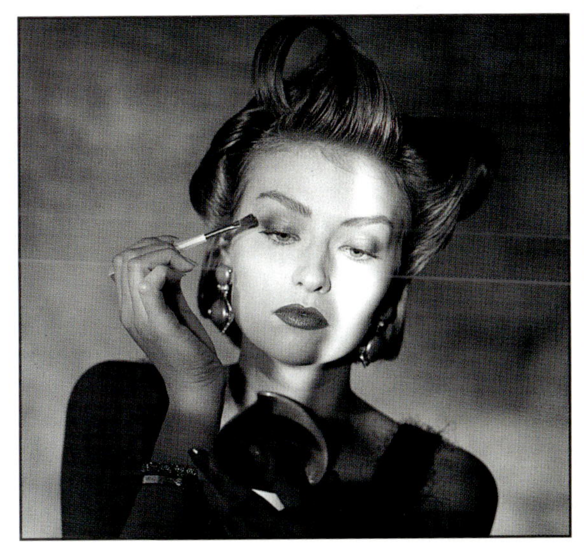

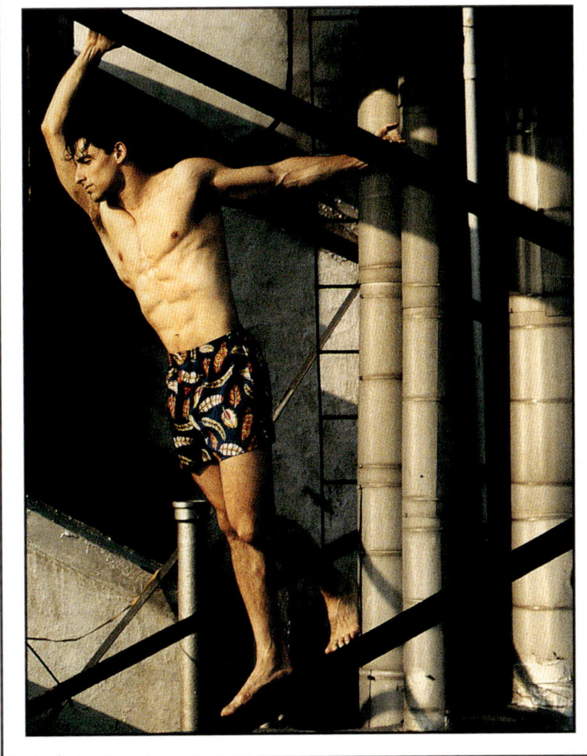

JACK DEUTSCH PHOTOGRAPHY

48 West 21st Street
New York, New York 10010
212-633-1424

MICHAEL PATEMAN

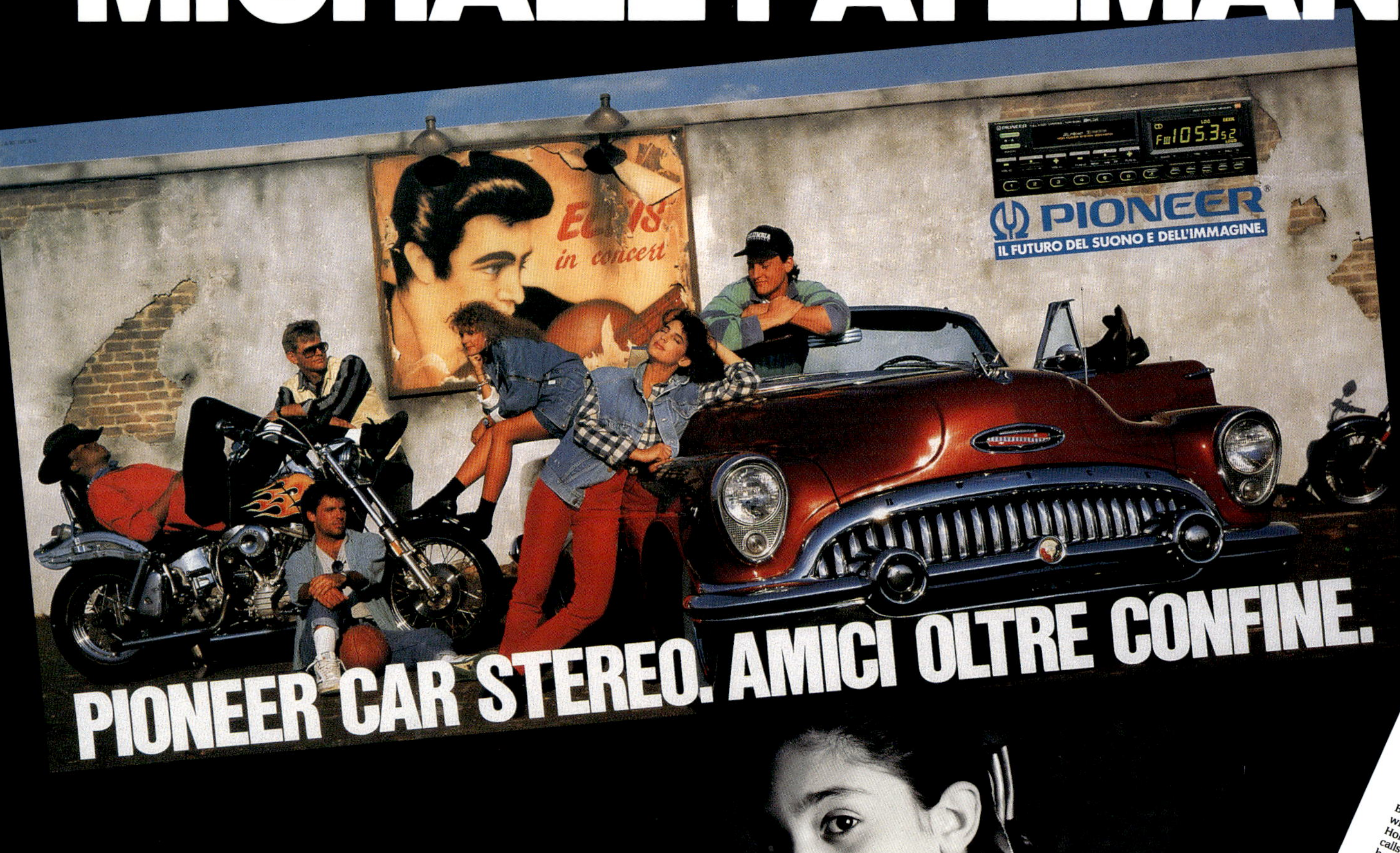

Her 14 year old sister is pregnant.
How do we keep it from happening to her?

Adolescent pregnancy affects more people than just the teenage mother and her child. Whole families are touched by this situation, yet are usually neglected when it comes to counseling and support.

That's why when Family Service America, a health and human service organization, requested a grant for a program to provide advice and counsel to pregnant teens, The Prudential Foundation went one step further. They took the initiative to join the forces of FSA and Bank Street College of Education, which had done extensive research on family counseling.

With FSA's desire to implement a program and Bank Street's research, the result of this collaboration is a program that treats the entire family. By involving parents, siblings and partners in the counsel... service is now aimed at strengthening the support for pregnant teens and their families.

The Prudential stands ready to provide a wide range of assistance. Whether it ... or the active participation of Prudential people.

Whatever it takes, The Prudential is committed to helping in ...

For more information, contact: The Prudential Founda... Newark, N.J. 07101

The**Prudential**
Foundation

Contro... Waiting...

Because when Hollywood calls you do... be interrupte... Uncle Bob.

You got the part! And ... Bob got a busy signal. Sure, he's your favorite u... But you have Totalphone — ... who wants to be interrupted ... the Call Waiting signal when th... big break is at hand? That's why today's Totalphone℠ service from

℠Servicemark registered in Connecticut. *Check ... †Plus CT sales tax. Totalphone costs $6.58 a month ... and the monthly rate will be charged from the begin...

IF DAIRY FARMING WERE STILL A HANDS-ON OPERATION, YOU WOULDN'T NEED OLIN CHEMICALS.

But stool and pail were put out to pasture years ago. Today, dairies are mechanized. And like the rest of the food processing industry, they use equipment that must be kept clean and germ-free at all times.

To help formulators make compounds that clean and sanitize, Olin has a range of vital chemicals.

For hard surface cleaning, our new *Poly-Tergent®* surfactant families of polycarboxylates and disulfonates offer stability in strong acid or alkaline solutions. Our phosphates offer excellent detergent building properties. And for sanitizing and bleaching, there's nothing better than *CDB®* chlorinated isocyanurates and calcium hypochlorite.

So no matter what kind of cleaner you're formulating — liquid or powder, industrial or institutional — when you have questions, farm them out to Olin. We have answers. Write, or call (203) 356-2000.

Olin
120 Long Ridge Road, Stamford, CT 06904

... business and already you're

... four humble lines.

SHE: *But now there's something new called 800 FlexLine℠ from Southern New England Telephone. With 800 FlexLine, calls to our 800 number would come in on one of our regular business lines. No new equipment. Very simple. Very inexpensive. Great SNET service.*

HE: Shall we convene the Board of Directors?

SHE: *I move we look into 800 FlexLine.*

HE: Motion carried.

(LATER)

SHE: *Just look at this nine-month statement! Sales over the last three months are up 38 percent! And we're getting orders from all over the state.*

HE: I told you 800 FlexLine was the answer.

SHE: *You told — !*

HE: ...Or was it your idea?

SHE: *Very funny.*

”

800 FlexLine: To find out about it, call your SNET sales representative or 1-800-272-SNET.

SNET
We go beyond the call

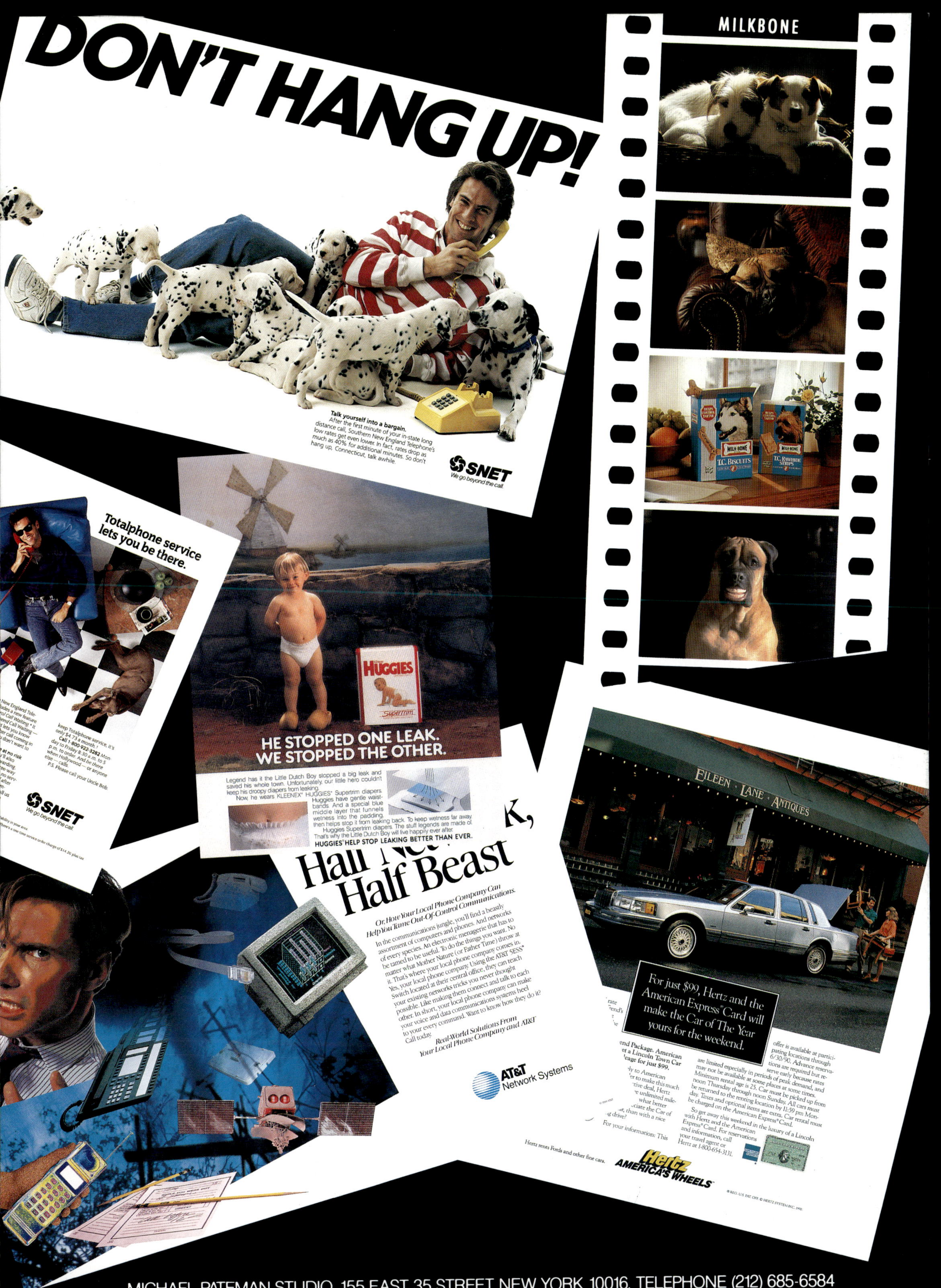

MICHAEL PATEMAN STUDIO, 155 EAST 35 STREET, NEW YORK 10016, TELEPHONE (212) 685-6584
REPRESENTED BY NORA DAVIES, TELEPHONE (212) 628-6657, REEL ON REQUEST

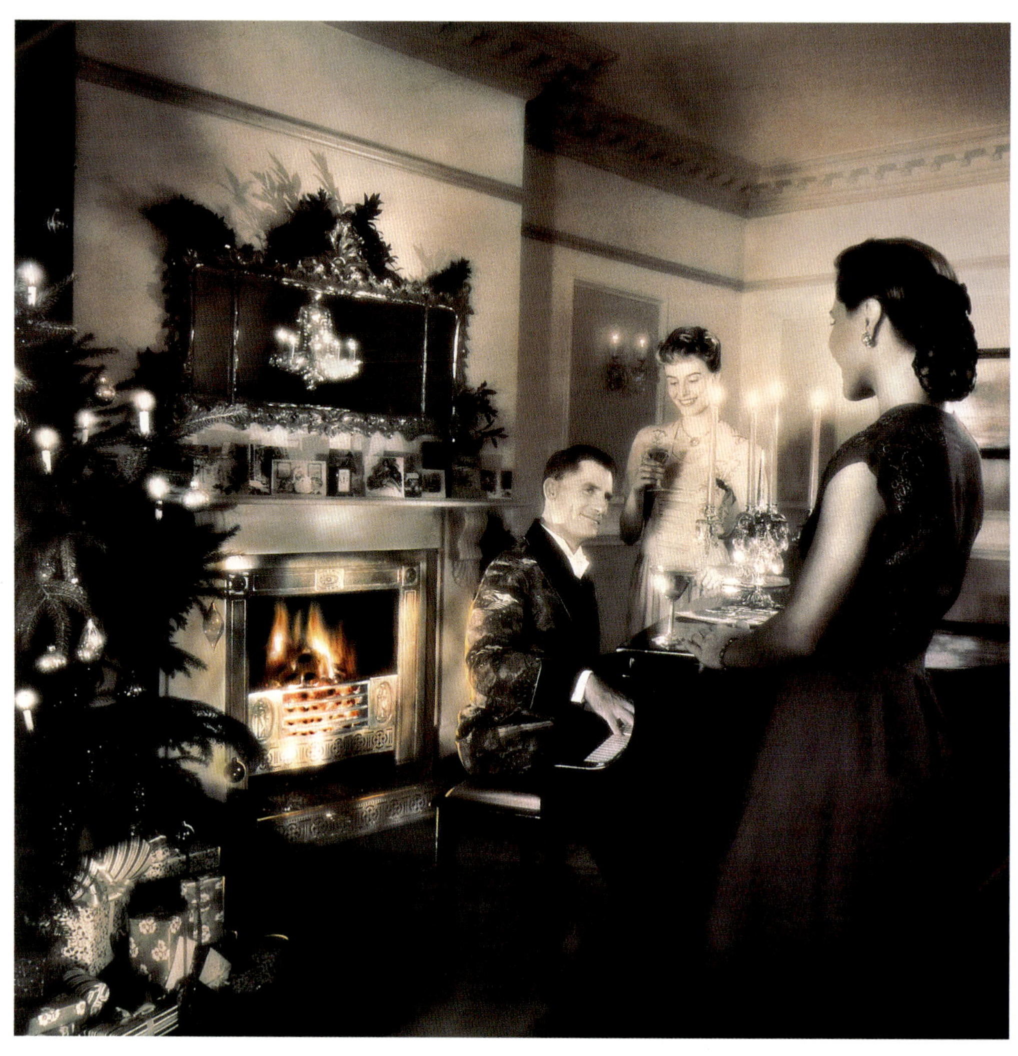

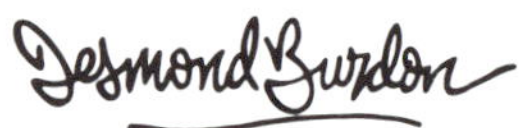

DESMOND BURDON ~ REPRESENTED BY SUSAN MILLER ON ~ 212 905 8400
FAX 212 427 7777

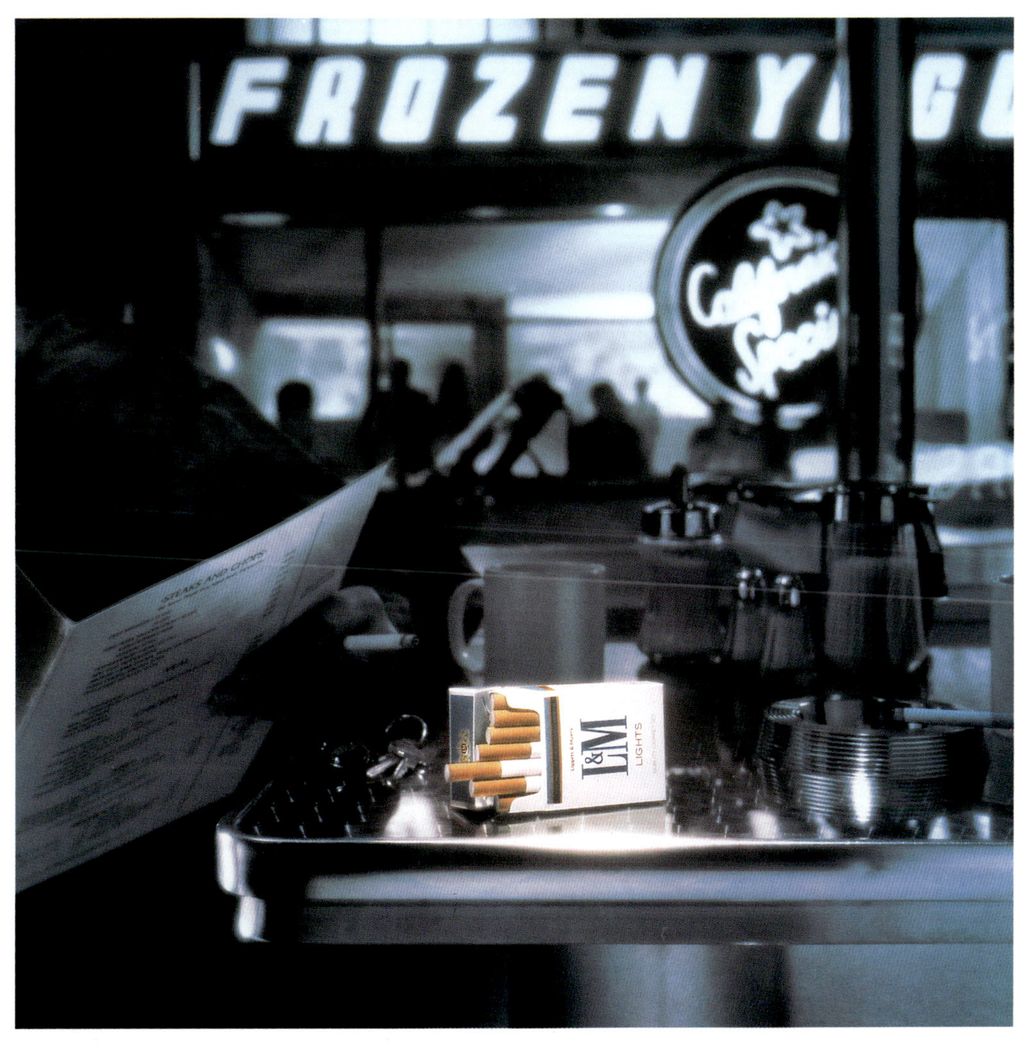

Desmond Burdon

DESMOND BURDON ~ REPRESENTED BY SUSAN MILLER ON ~ 212 905 8400
FAX 212 427 7777

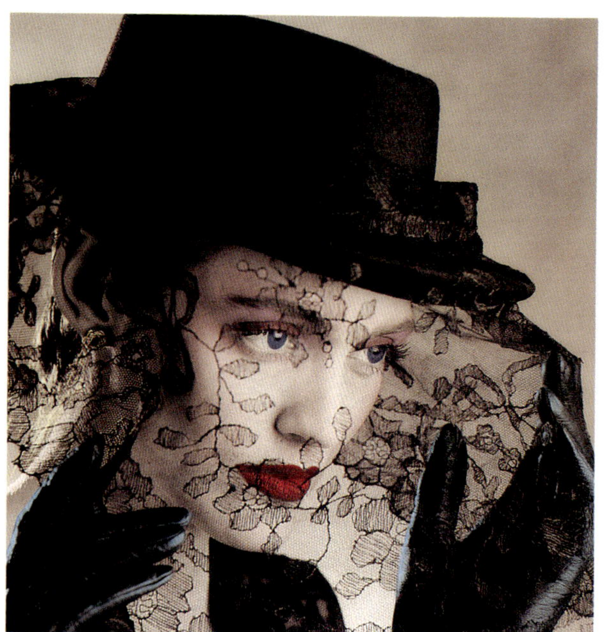

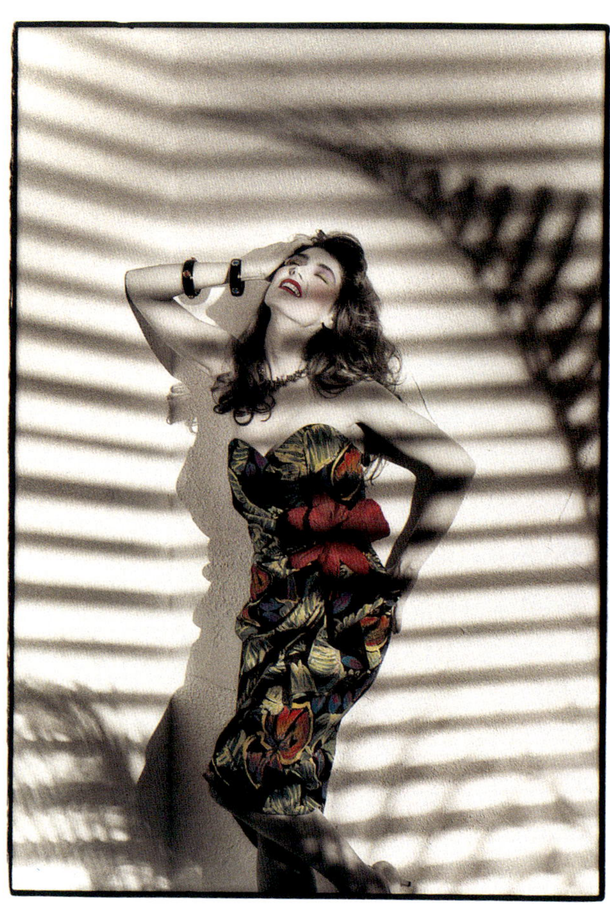

William D. King

PHOTOGRAPHY 718/9988351

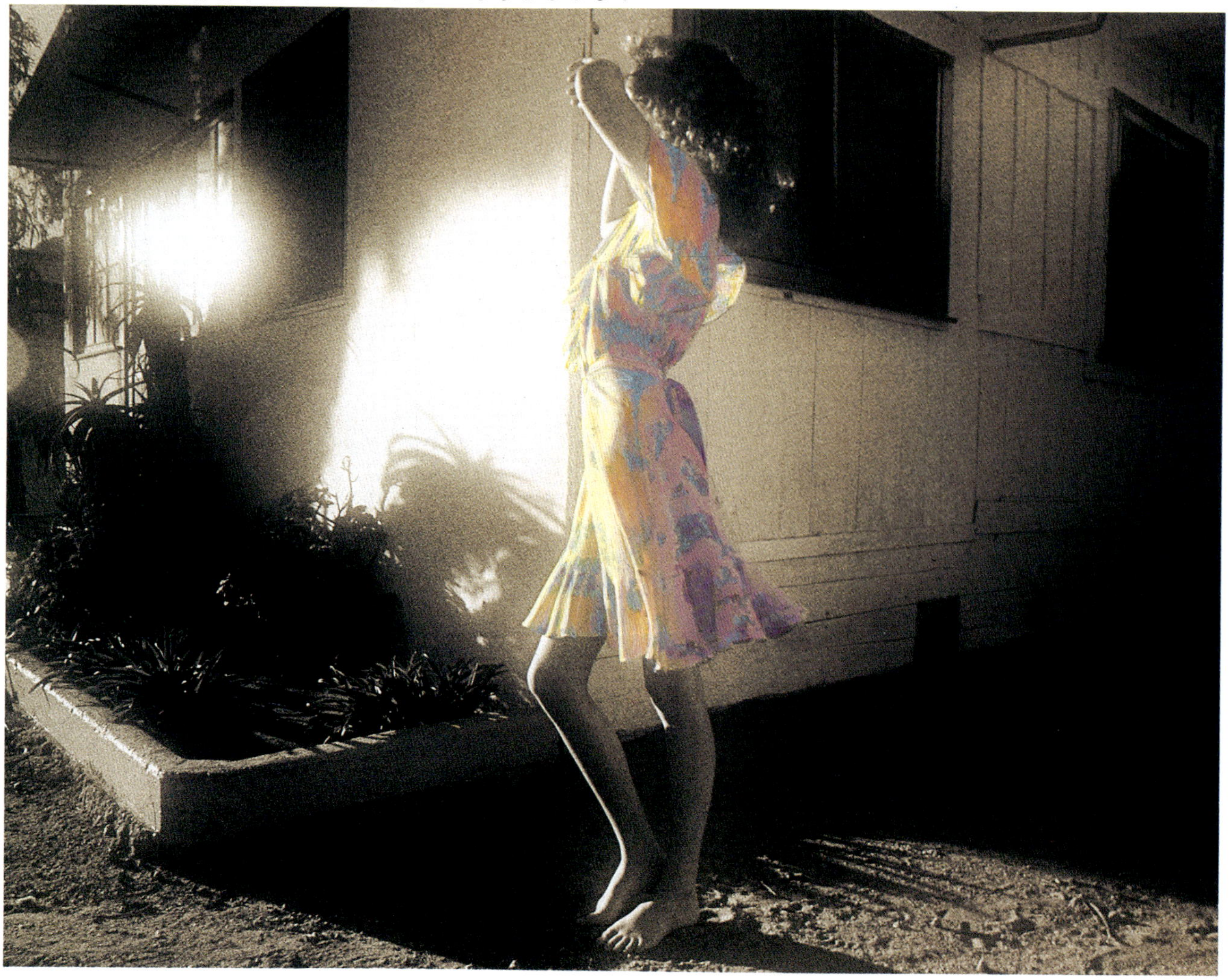

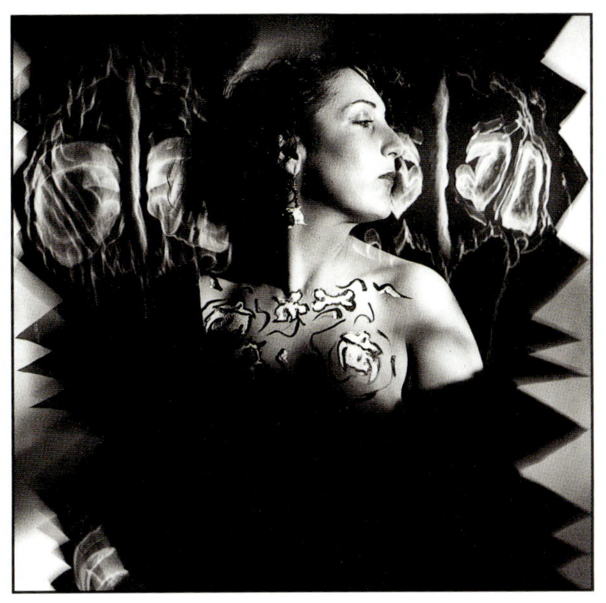

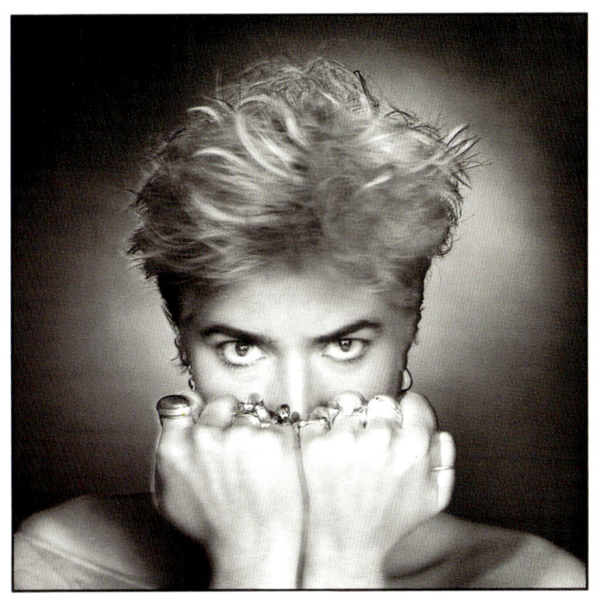

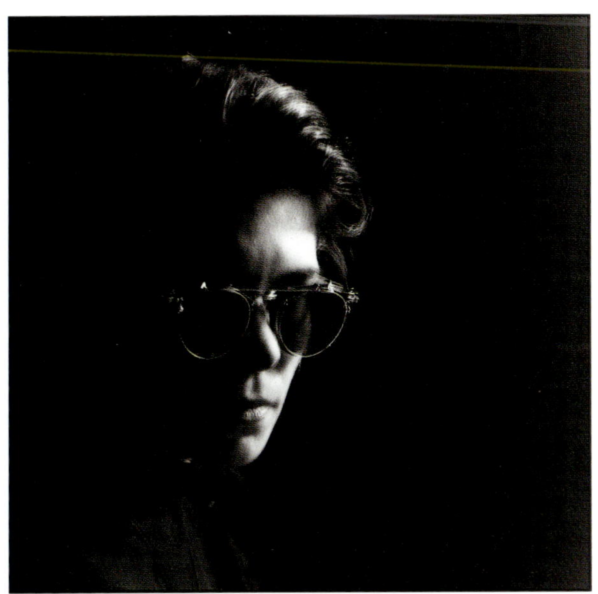

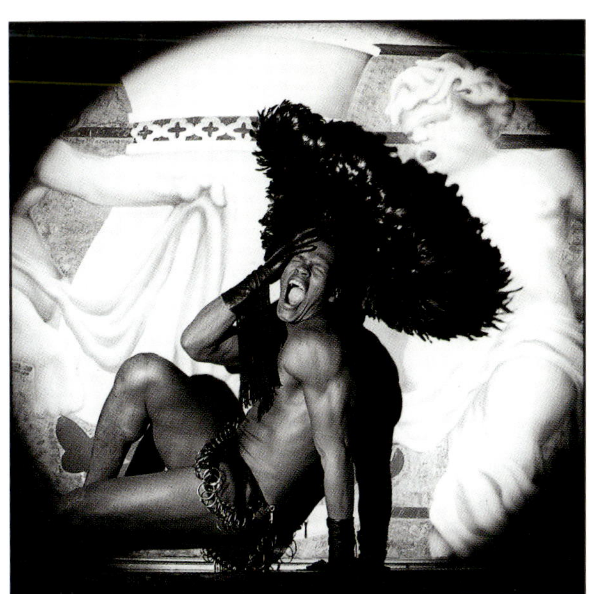

CHARLIE PIZZARELLO PHOTOGRAPHER 15 WEST 18TH STREET NEW YORK NY 10011 212.243.8441

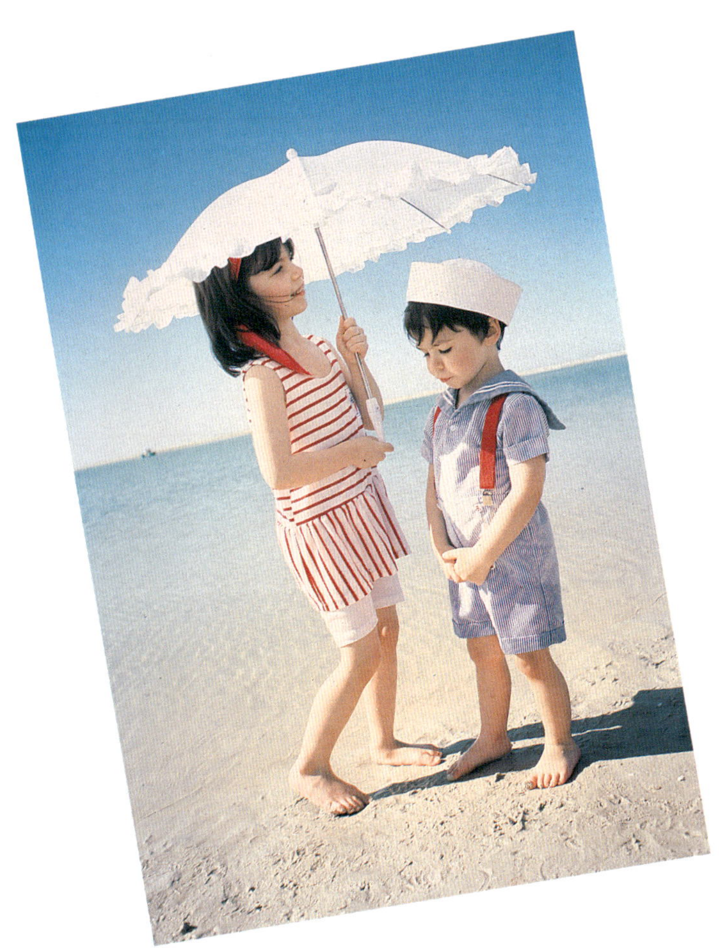

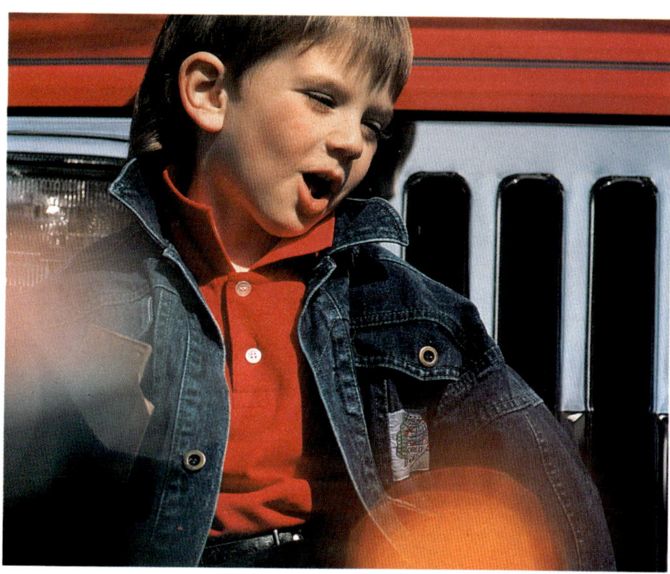

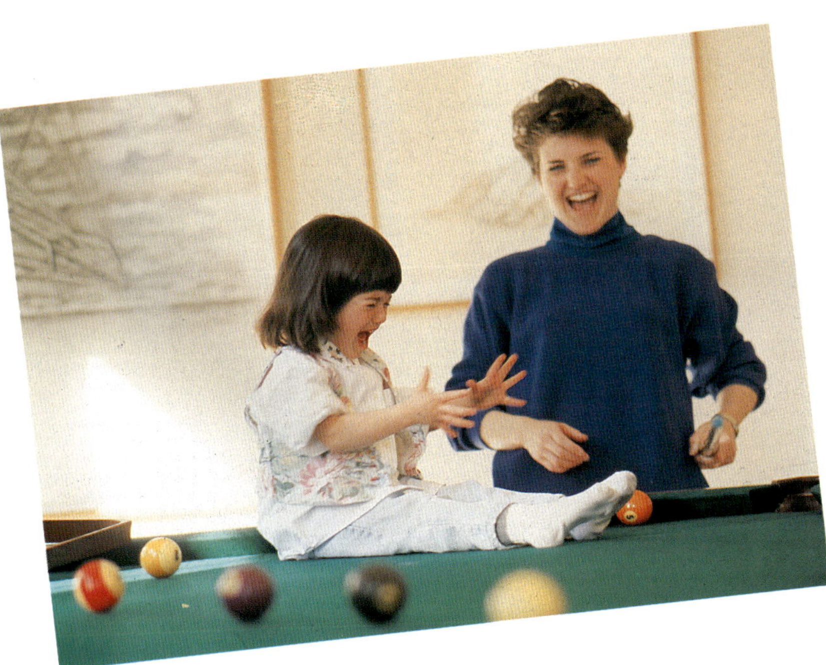

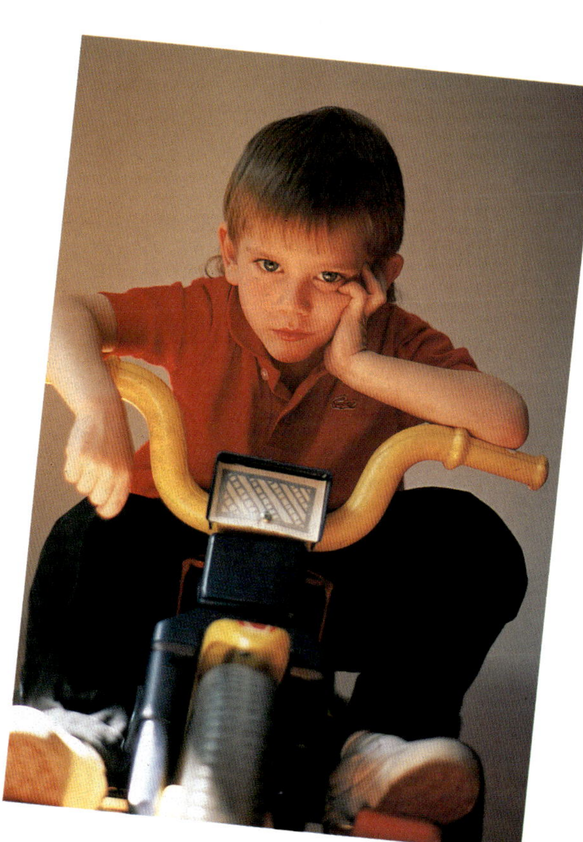

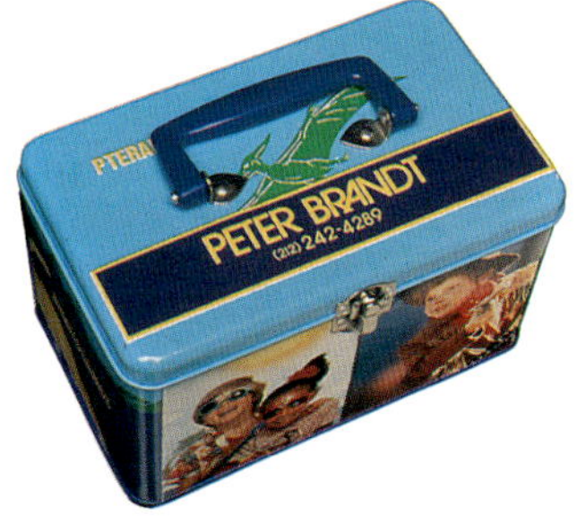

stock available

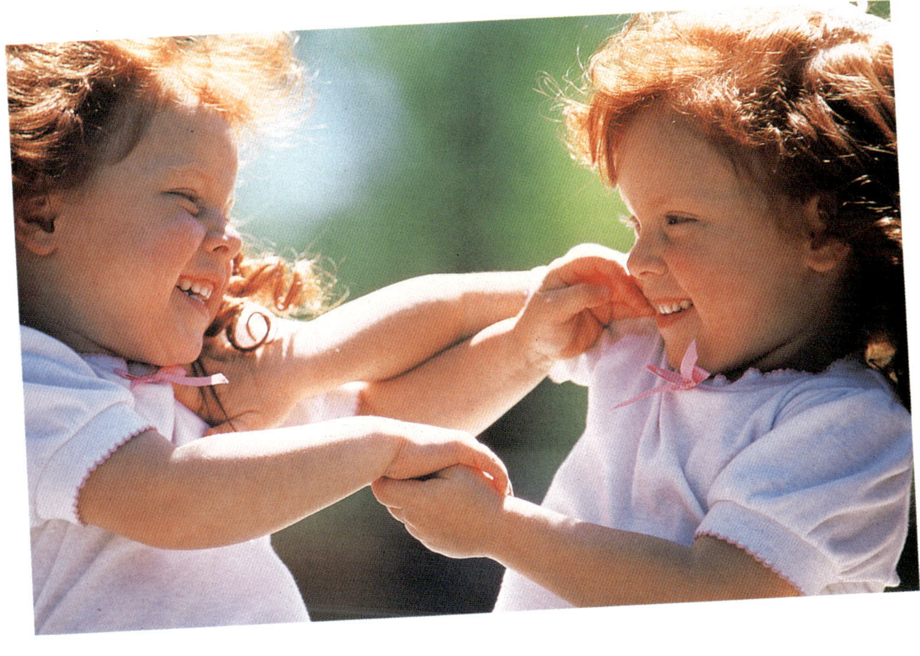

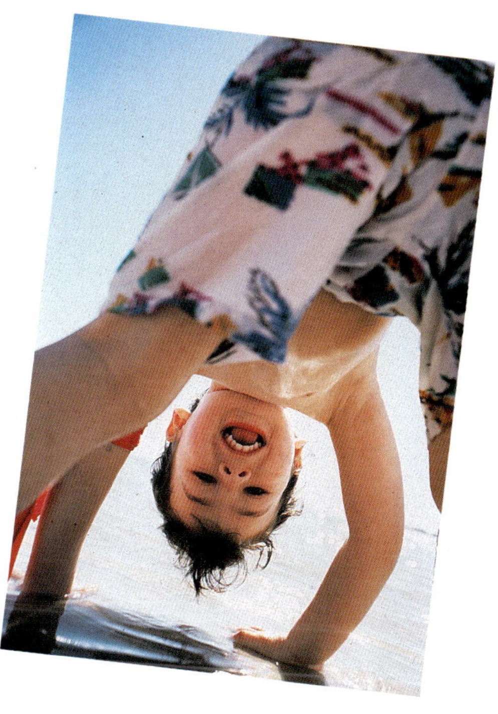

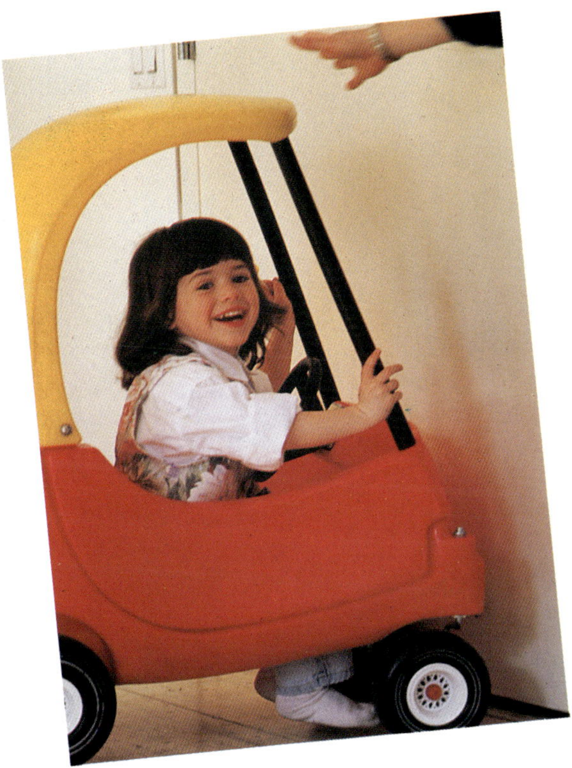

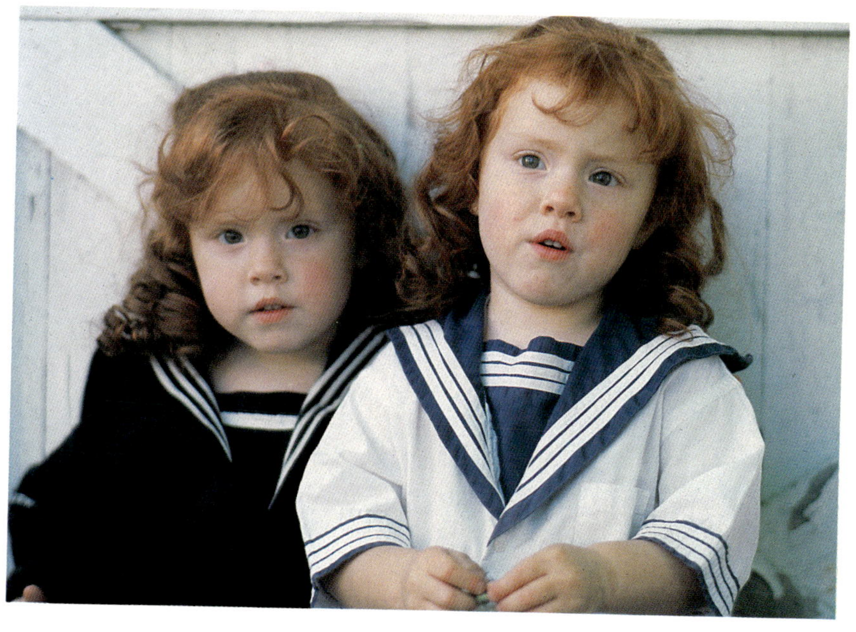

PETER BRANDT

73 Fifth Ave., New York N.Y. 10003

(212) 242-4289

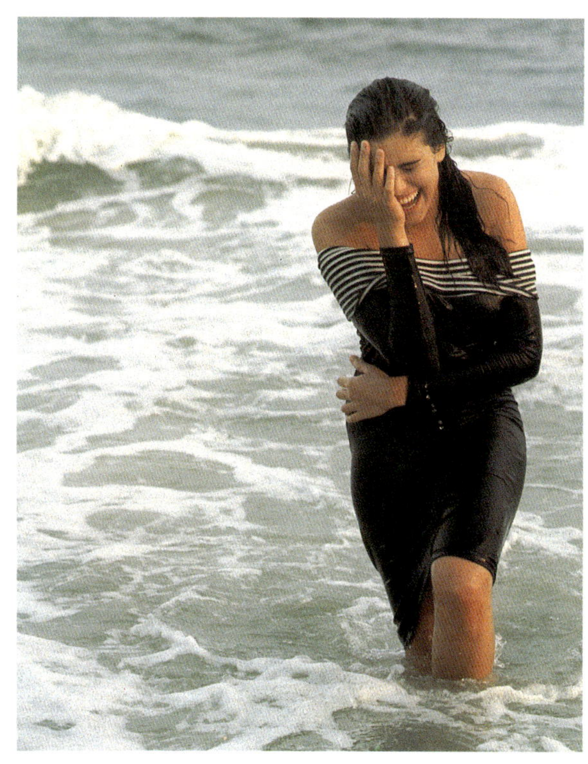

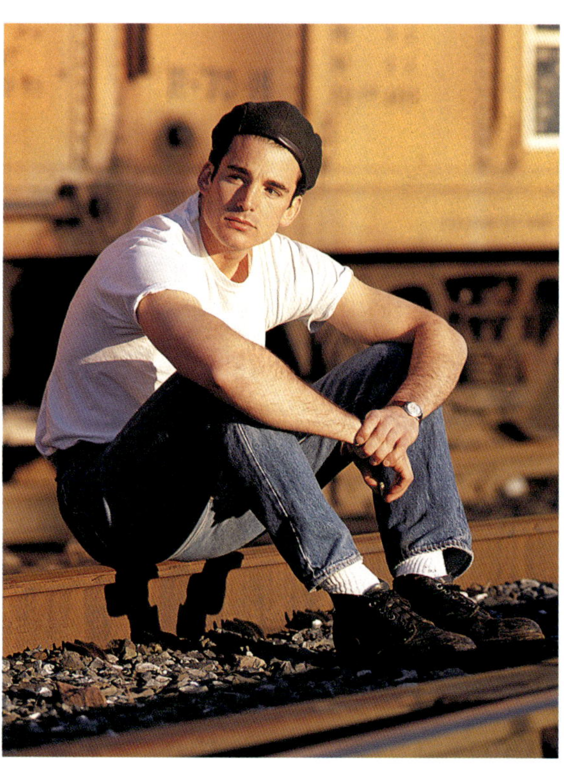

ROB LANG PHOTOGRAPHY STUDIO 212-595-2217

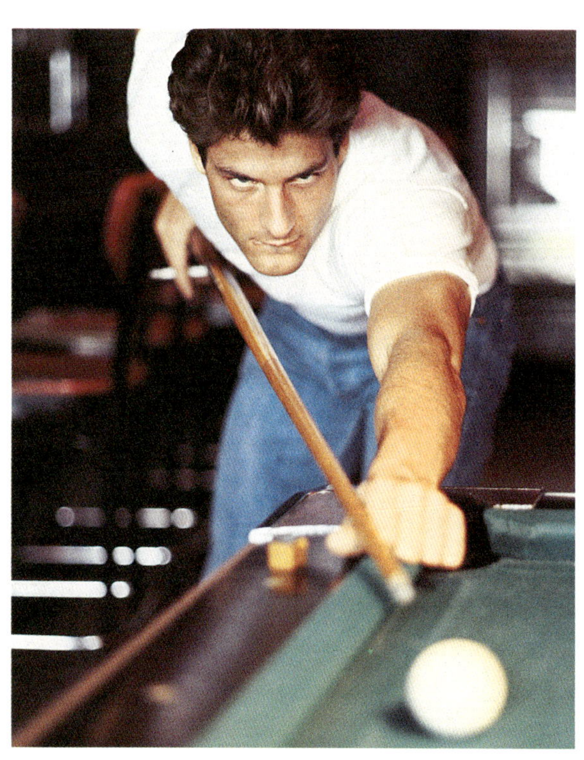

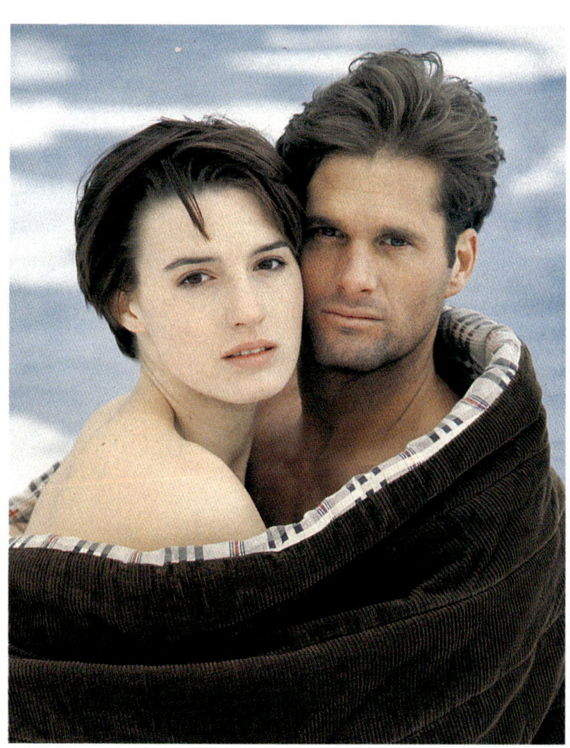

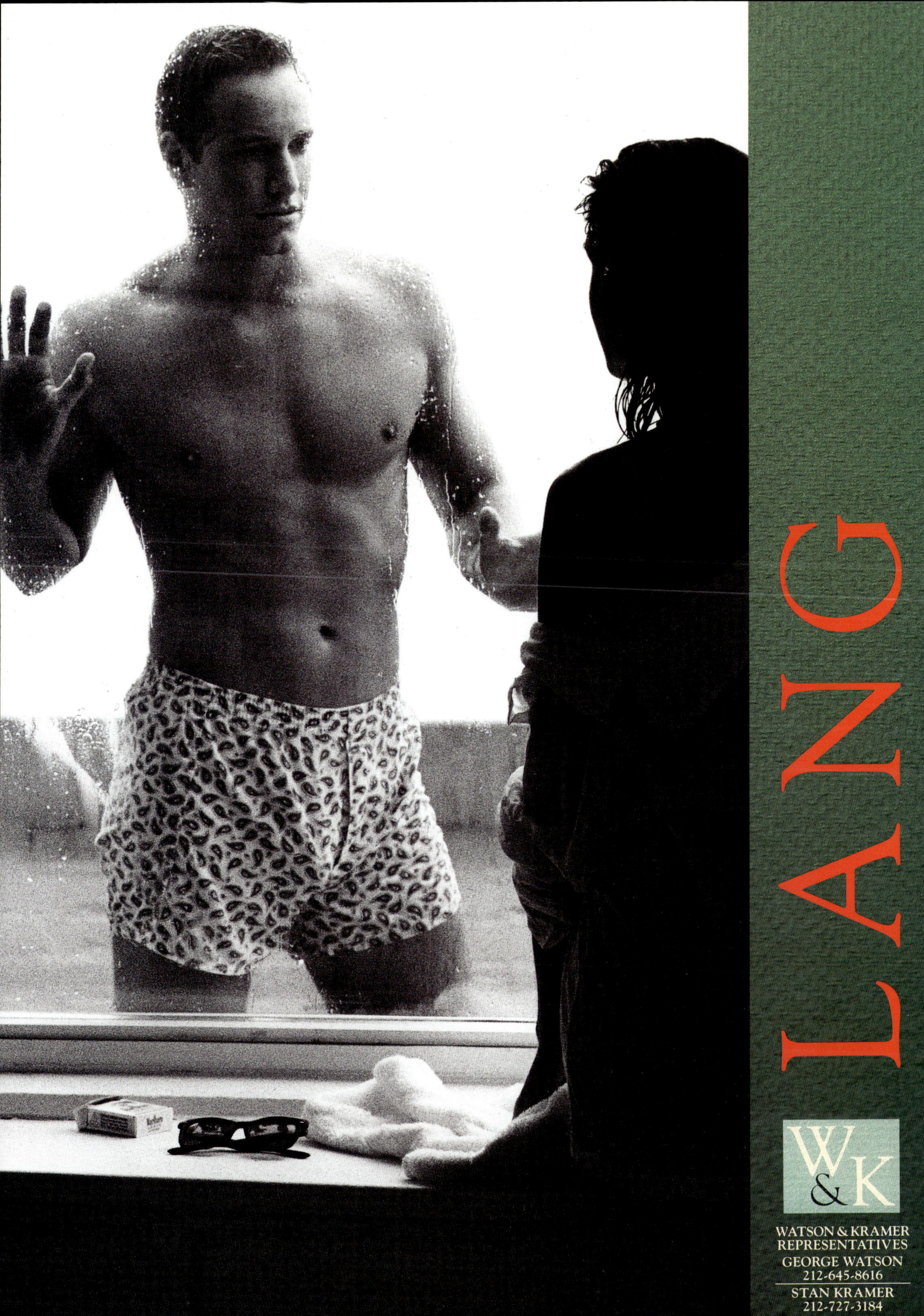
LANG
W&K
WATSON & KRAMER
REPRESENTATIVES
GEORGE WATSON
212-645-8616
STAN KRAMER
212-727-3184

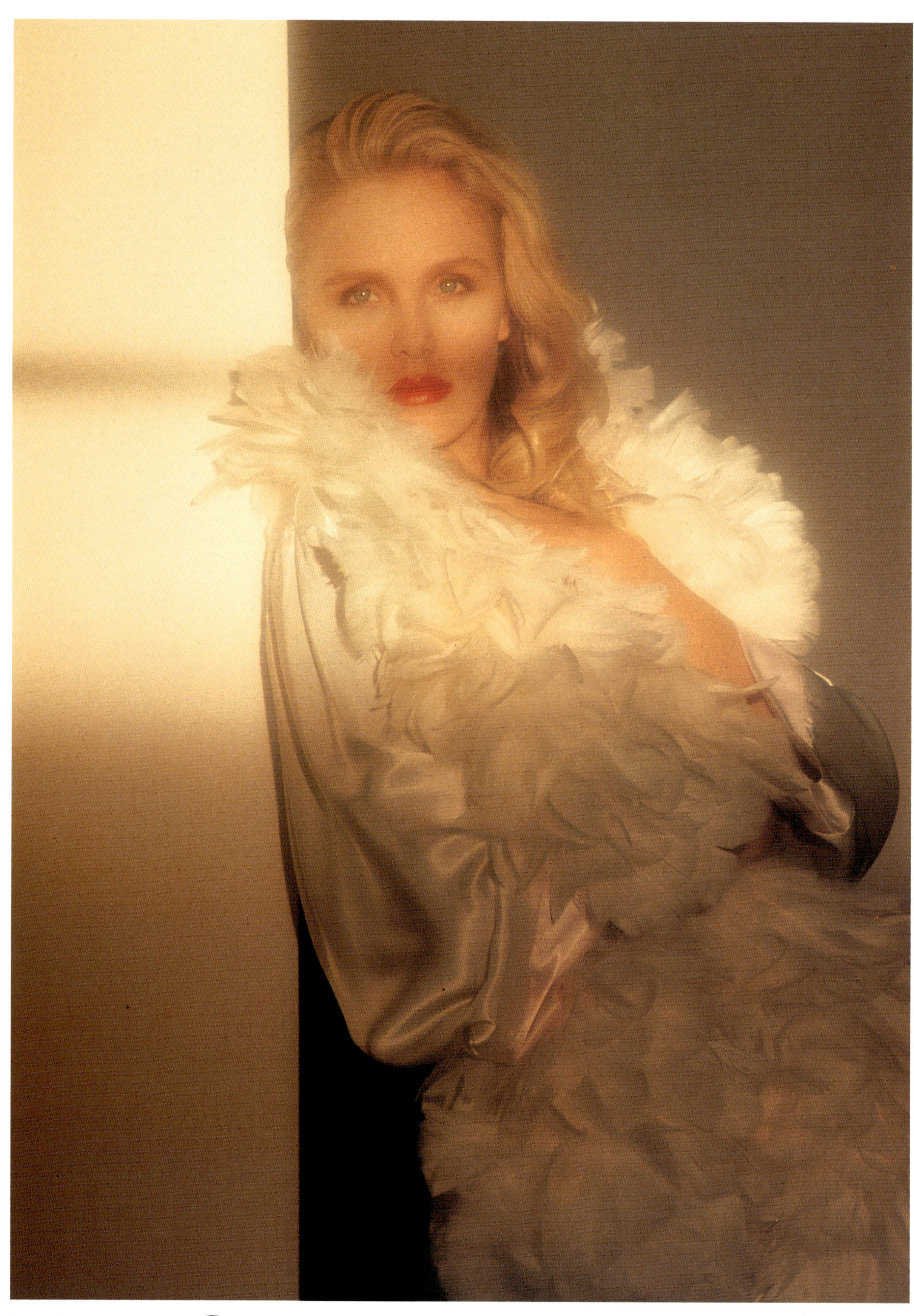

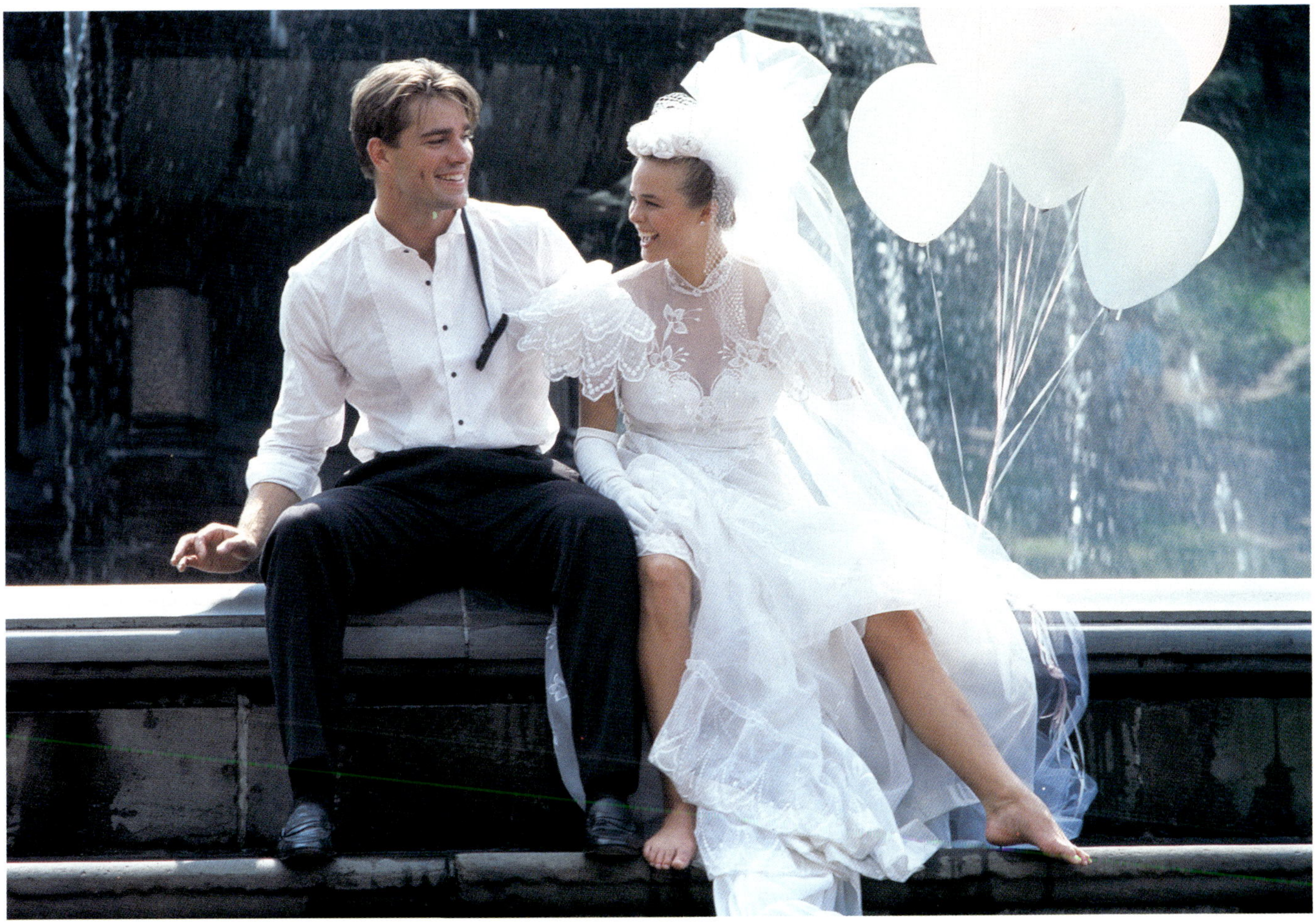

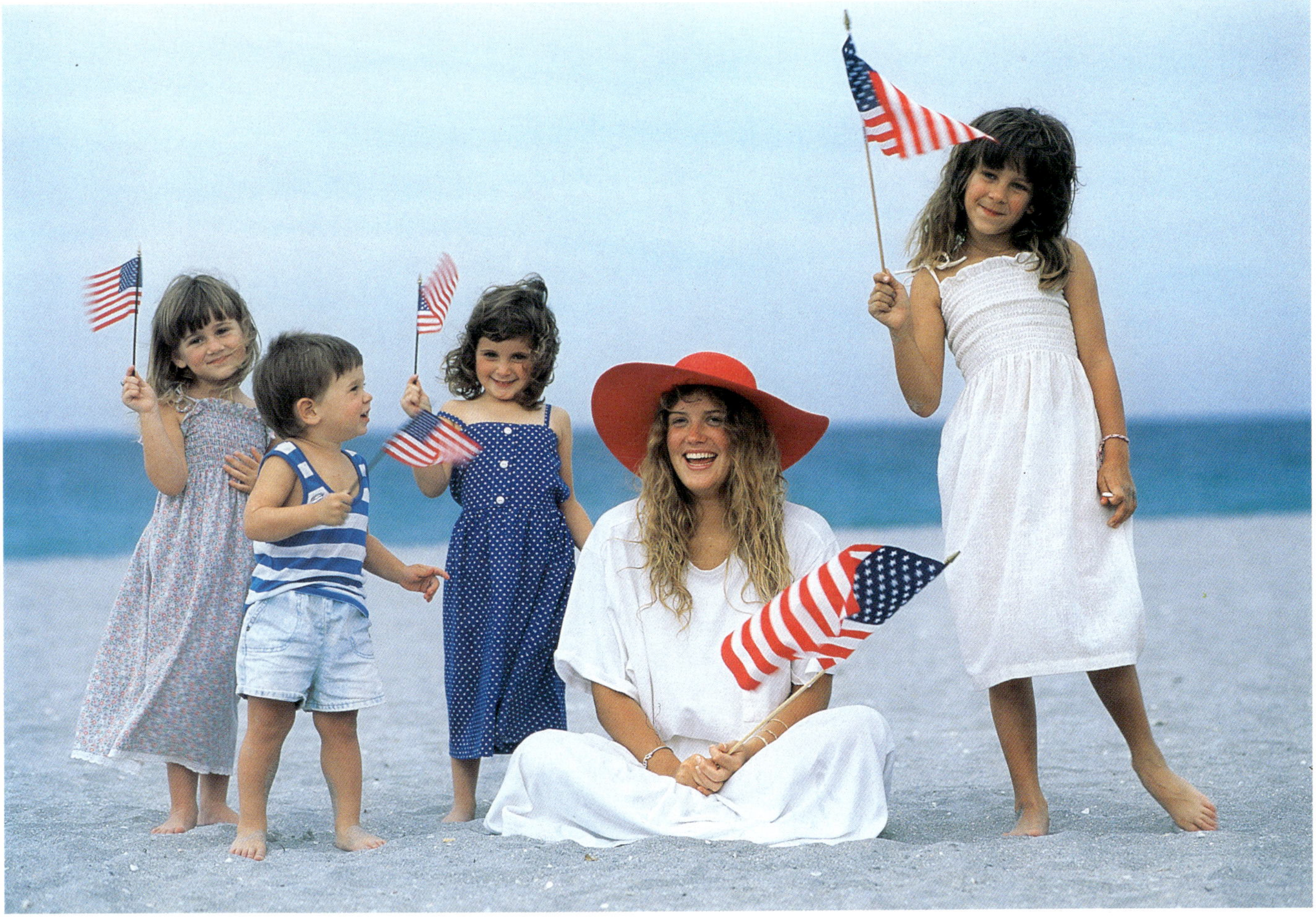

NANCY BROWN

6 W. 20 ST., NY, NY 10011
(212) 924-9105 • FAX: (212) 633-0911
ASMP APA STOCK: IMAGE BANK
SEE MORE WORK IN '91 BLACK BOOK

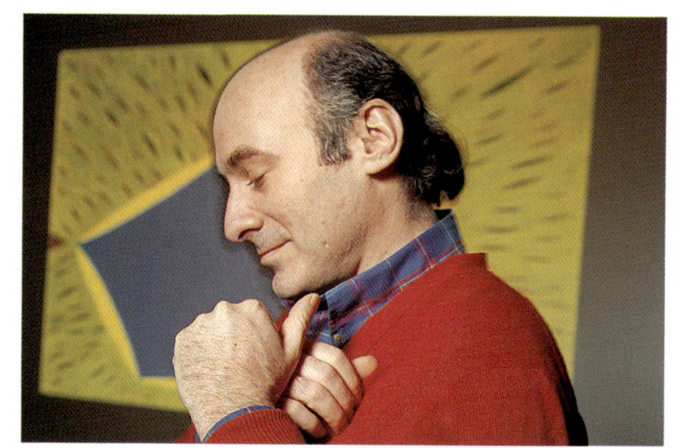

JOHN STUART

photography

212-966-6783

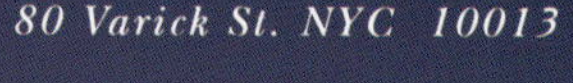

80 Varick St. NYC 10013

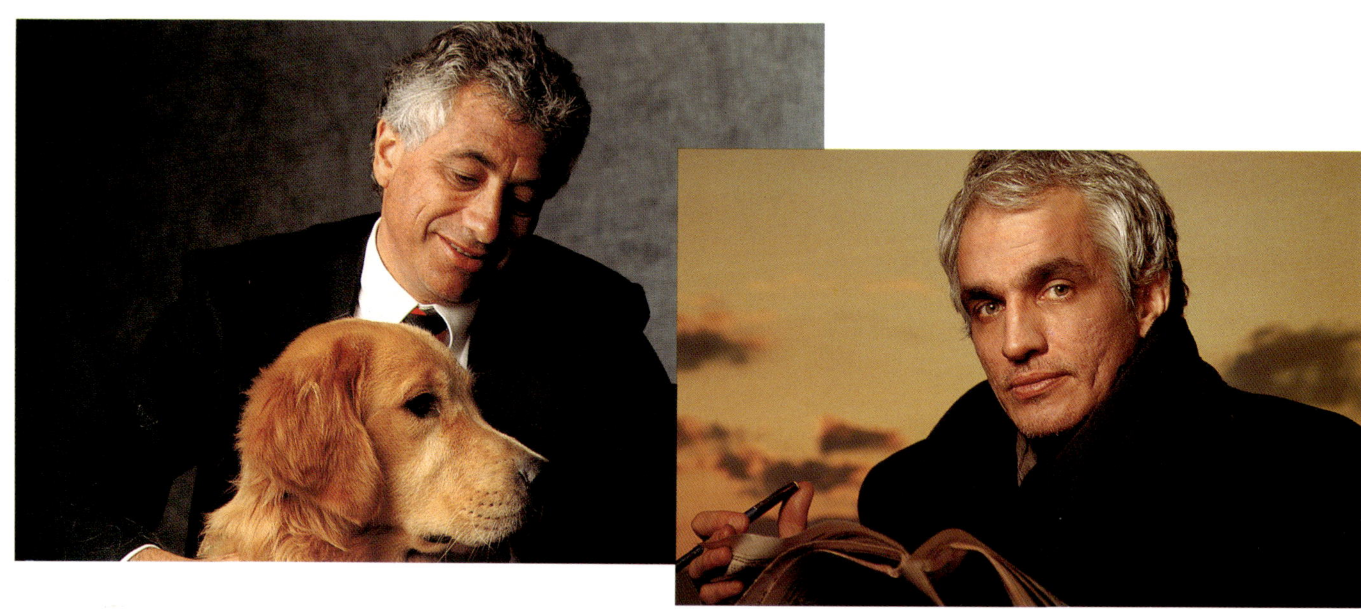

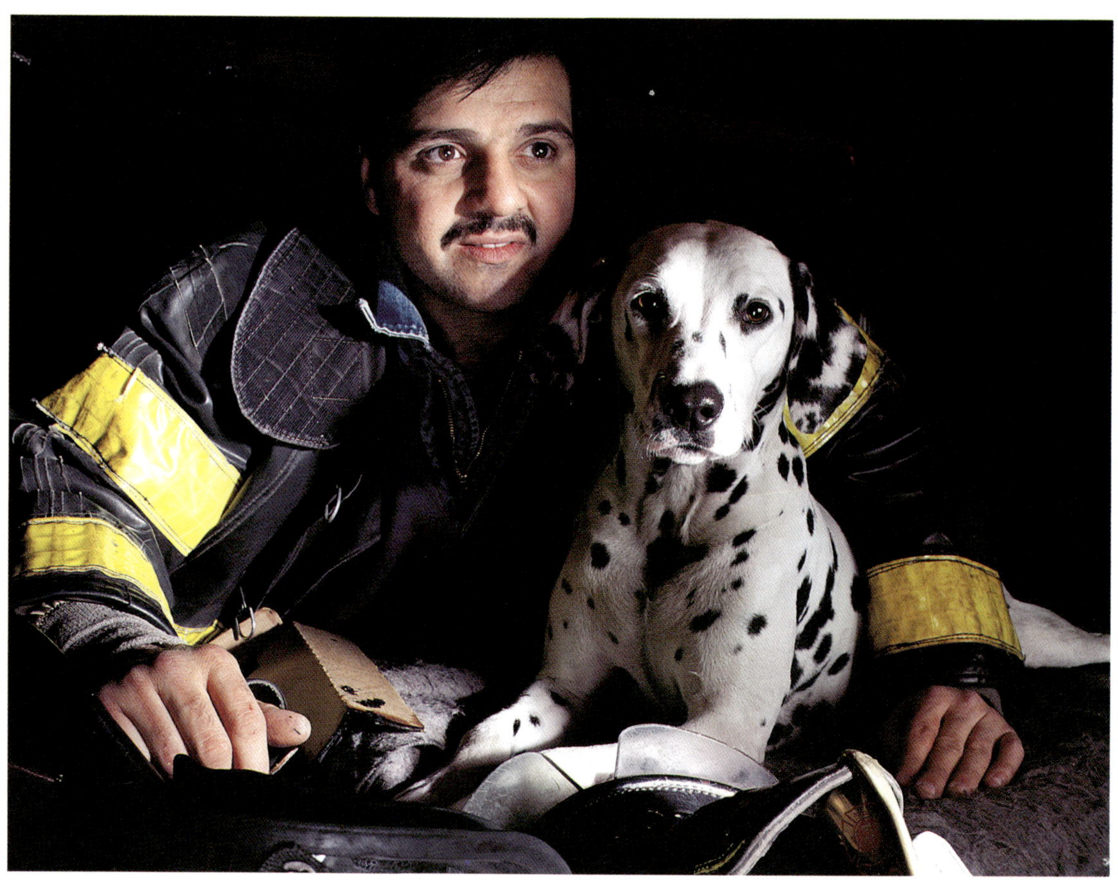

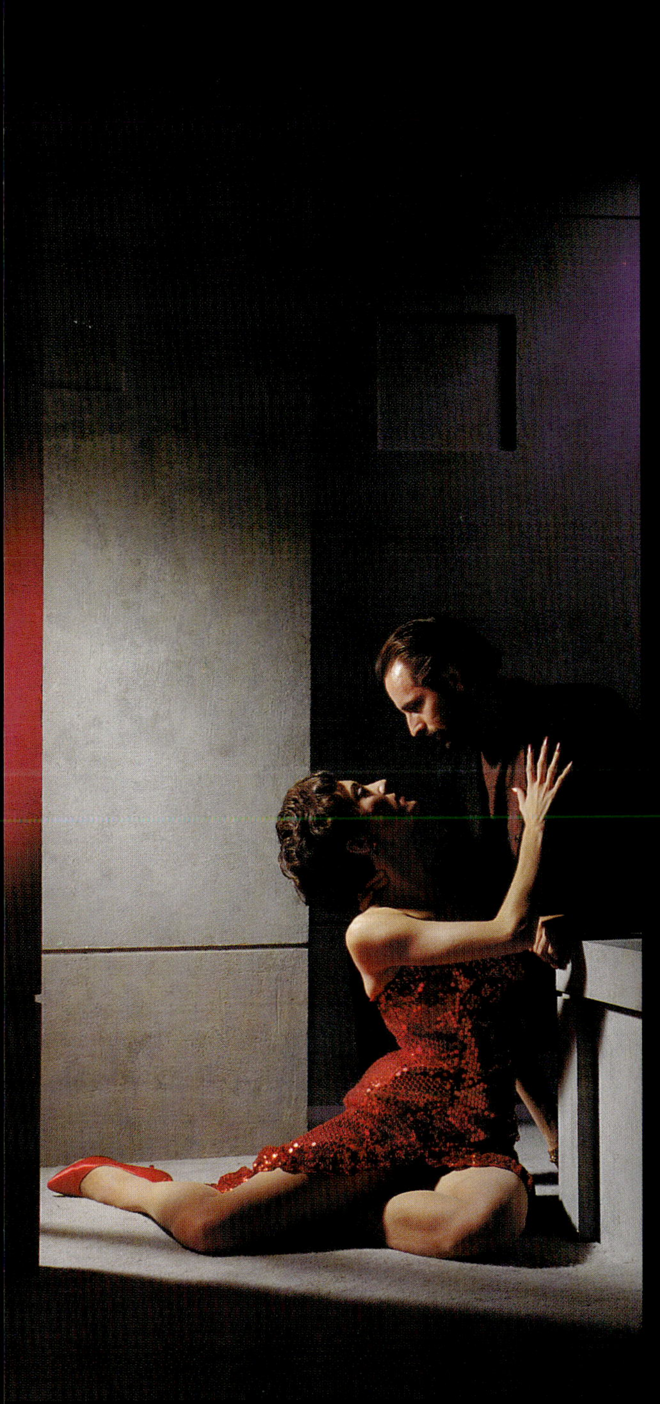

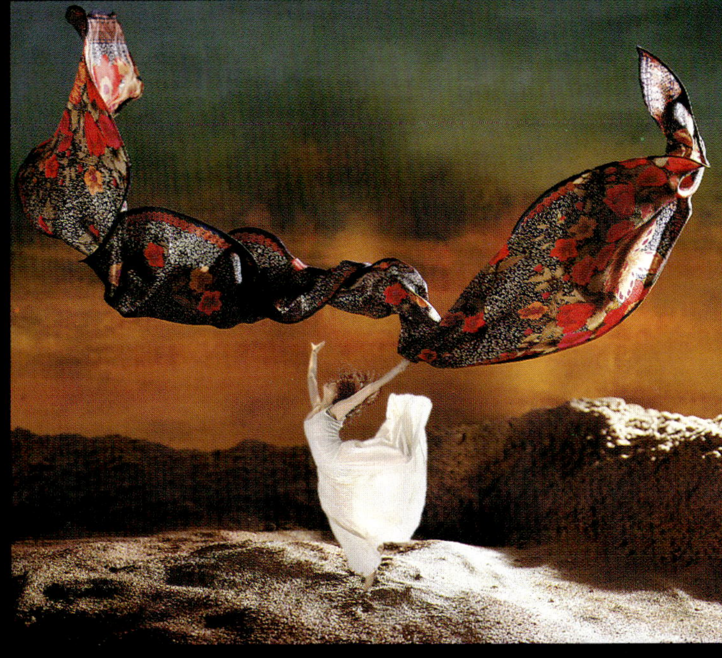

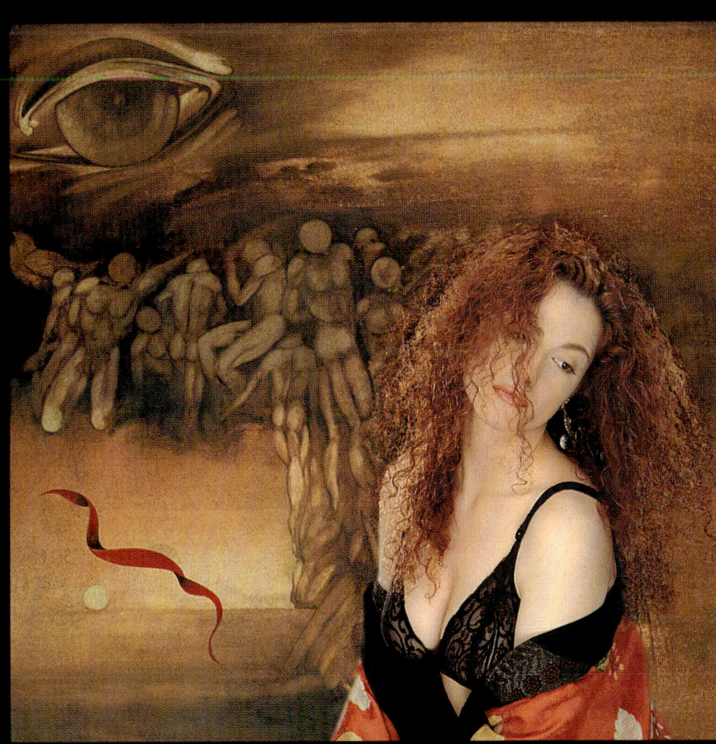

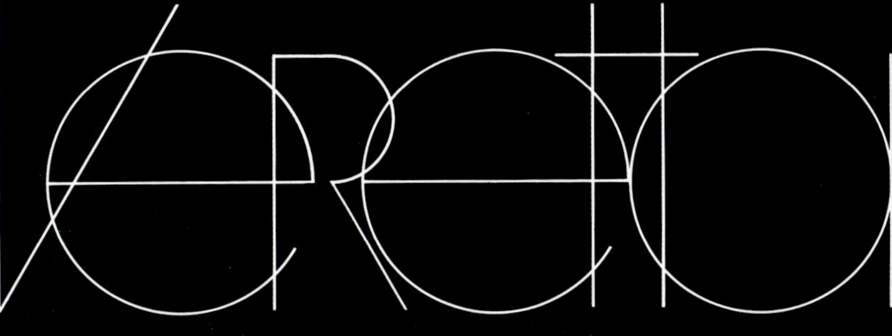
Véretta

ZAN/BEAUTY

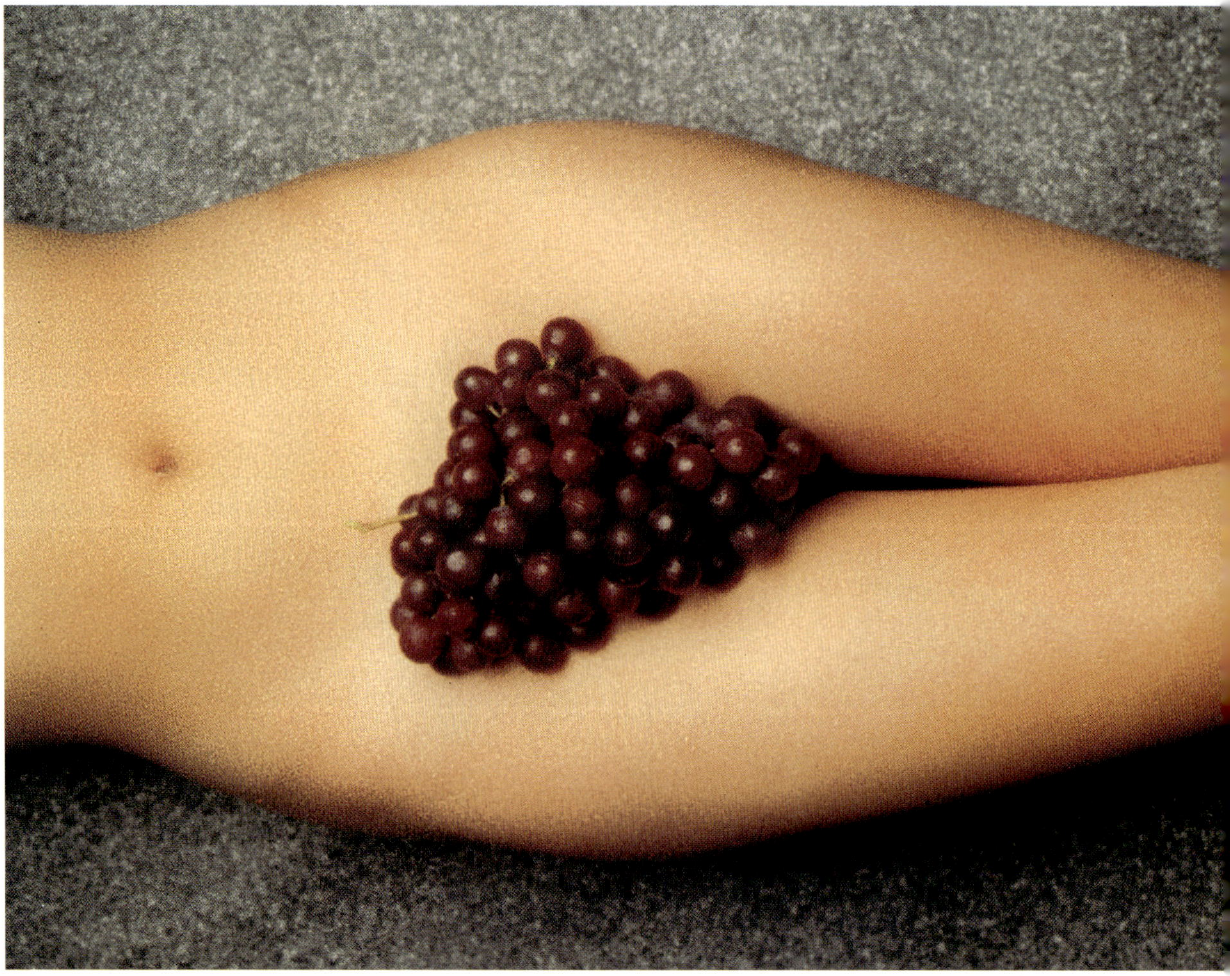

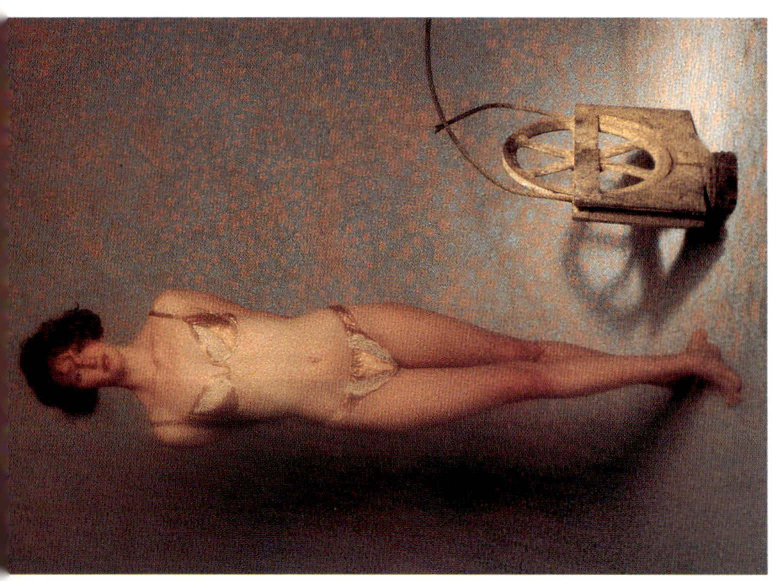

ZAN PRODUCTIONS/35 E 20 STREET/NYC 10003/REPRESENTATIVE—RICK WEISBROT

ZAN

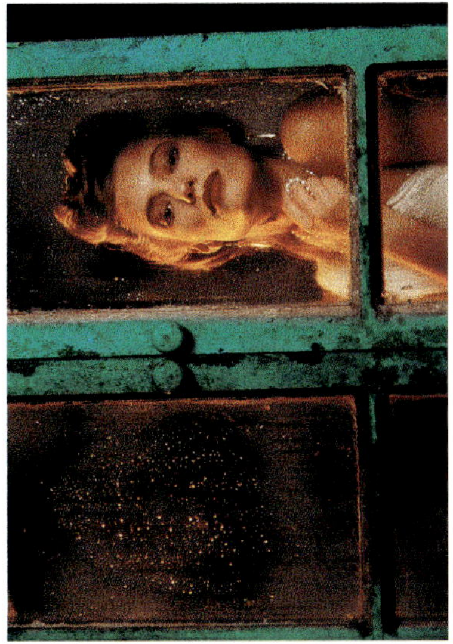

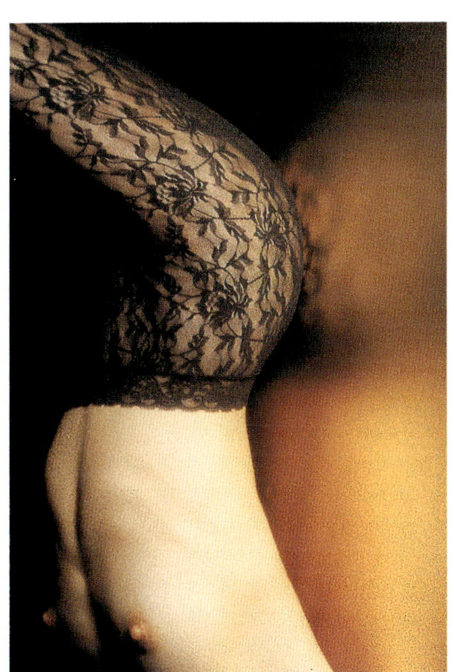

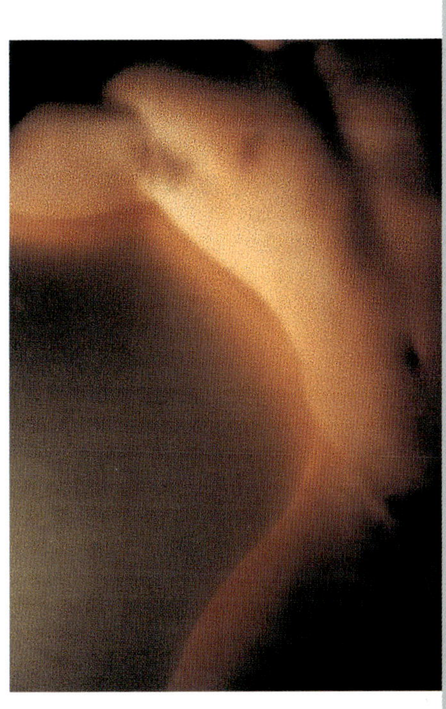

212-477-3333 / FAX-212-477-3337

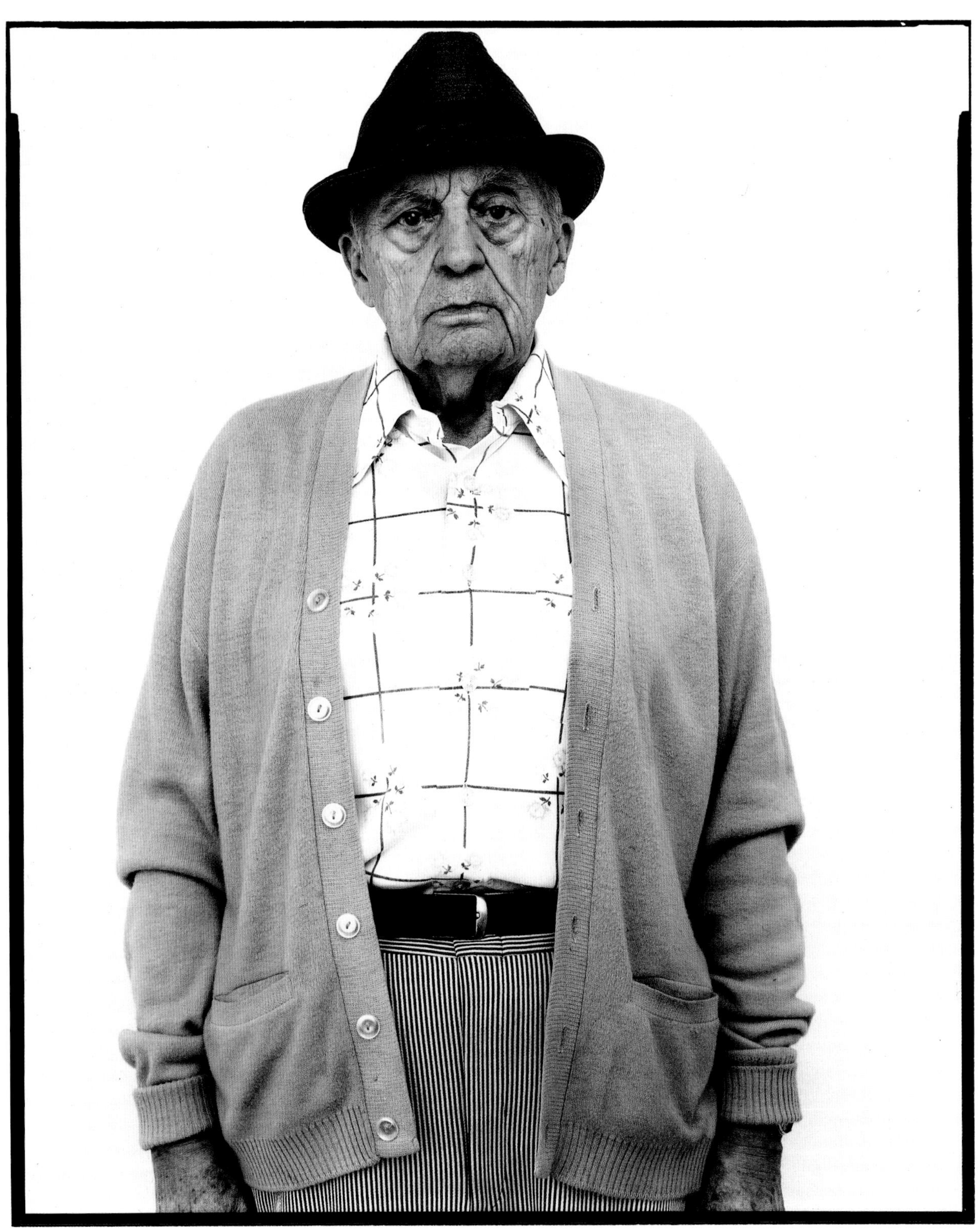

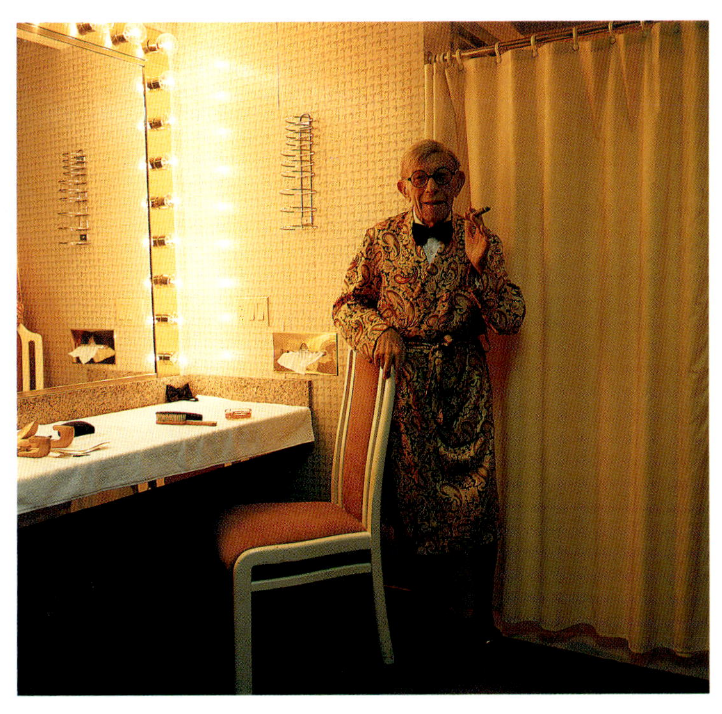

James Salzano Photography 212-242-4820
Represented by Marty Boghosian 212-353-1313

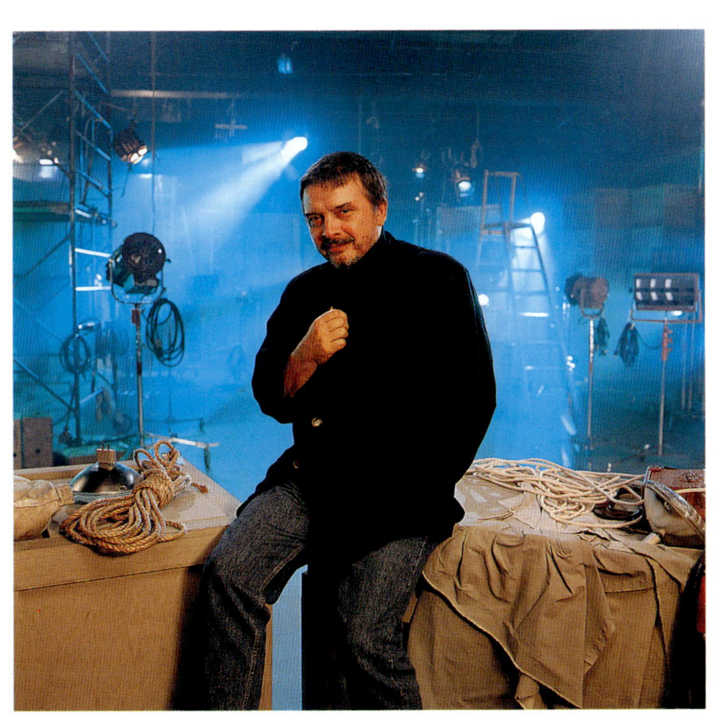

ARIEL SKELLEY

80 VARICK ST. 8F
NYC 10013
226-4091

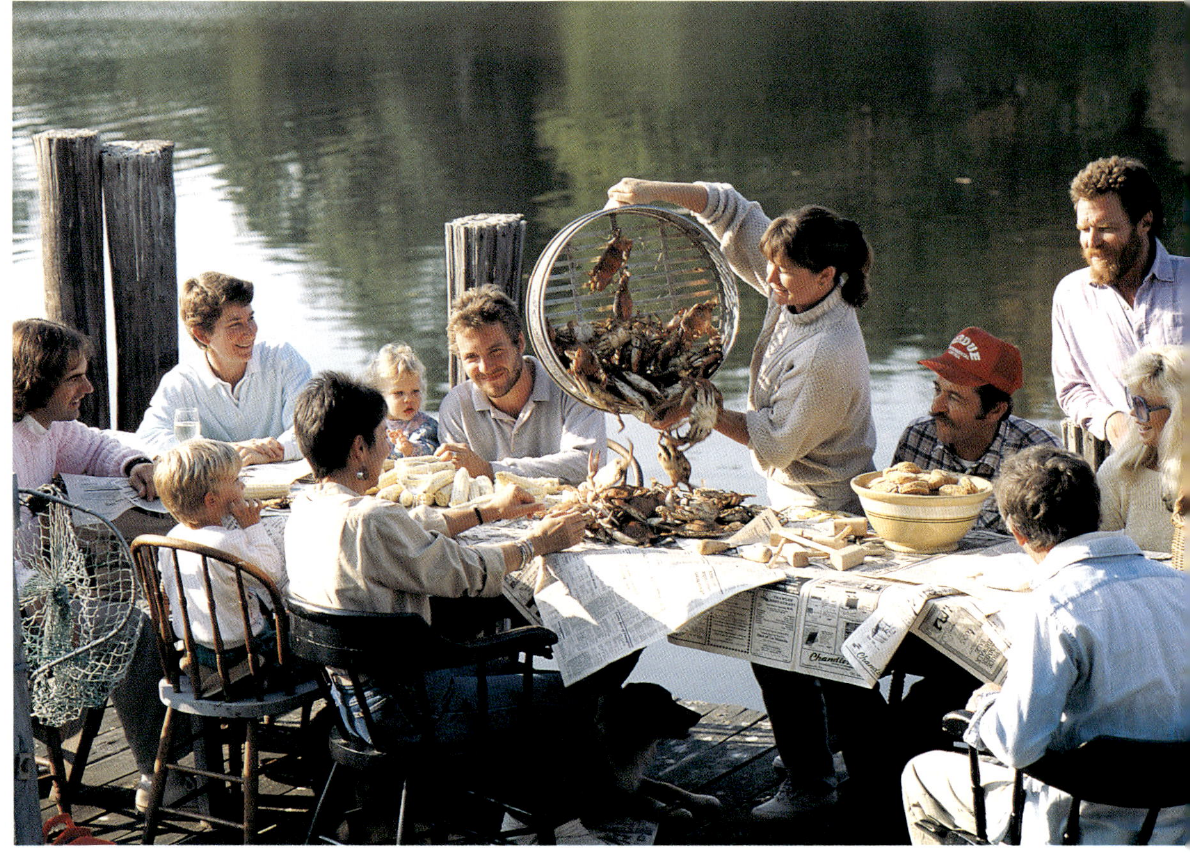

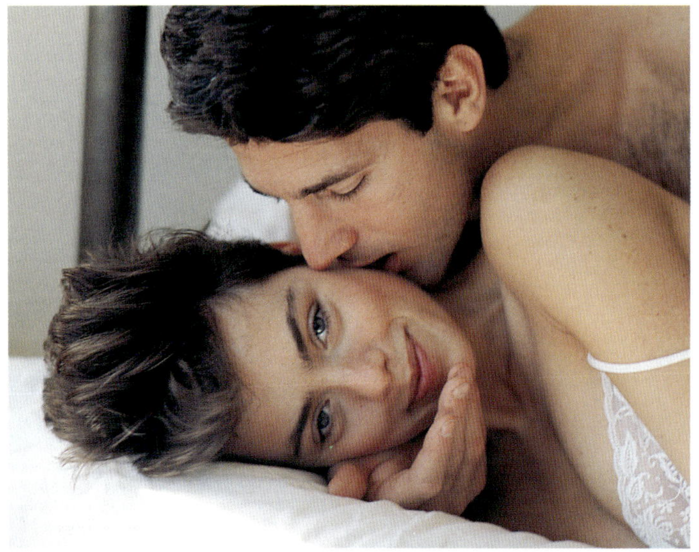

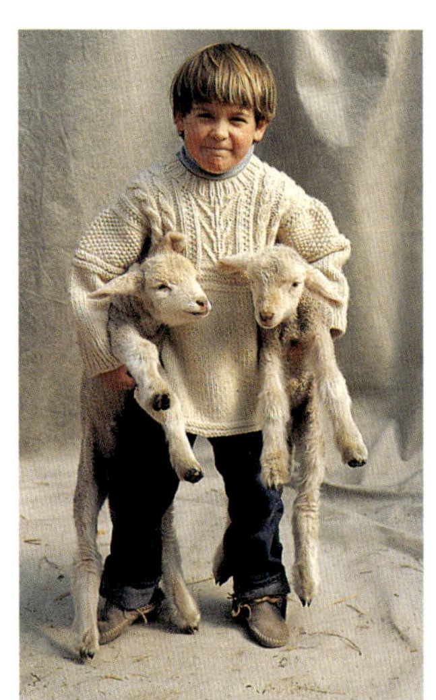

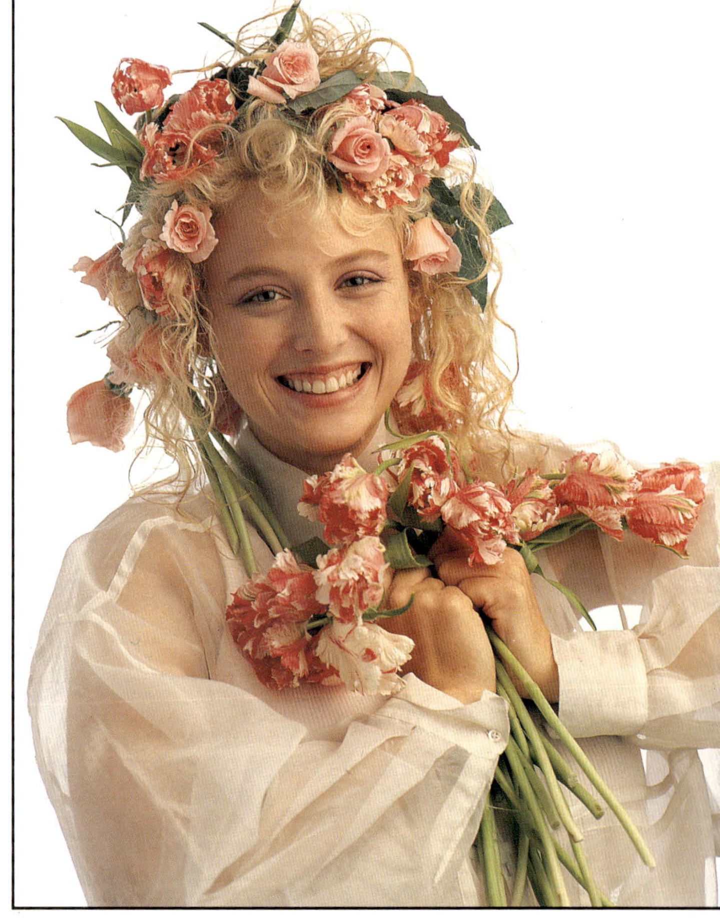

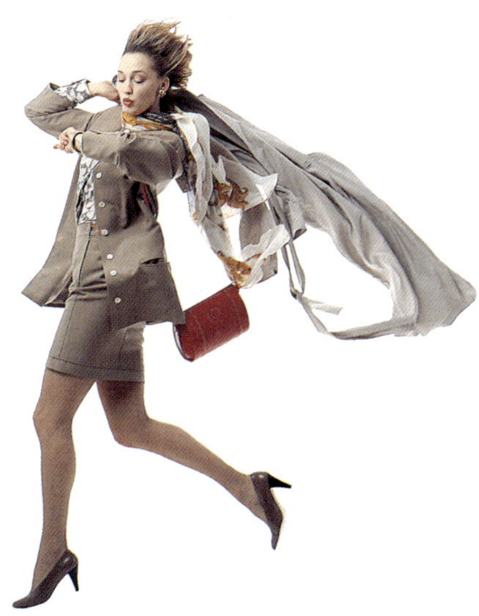

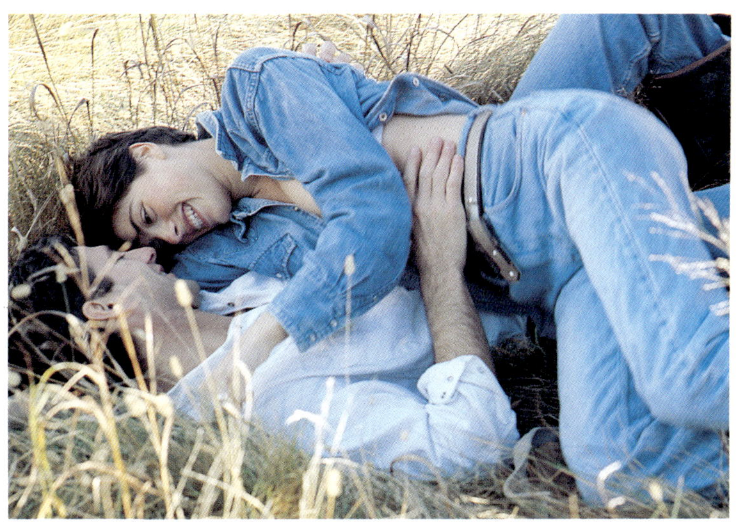

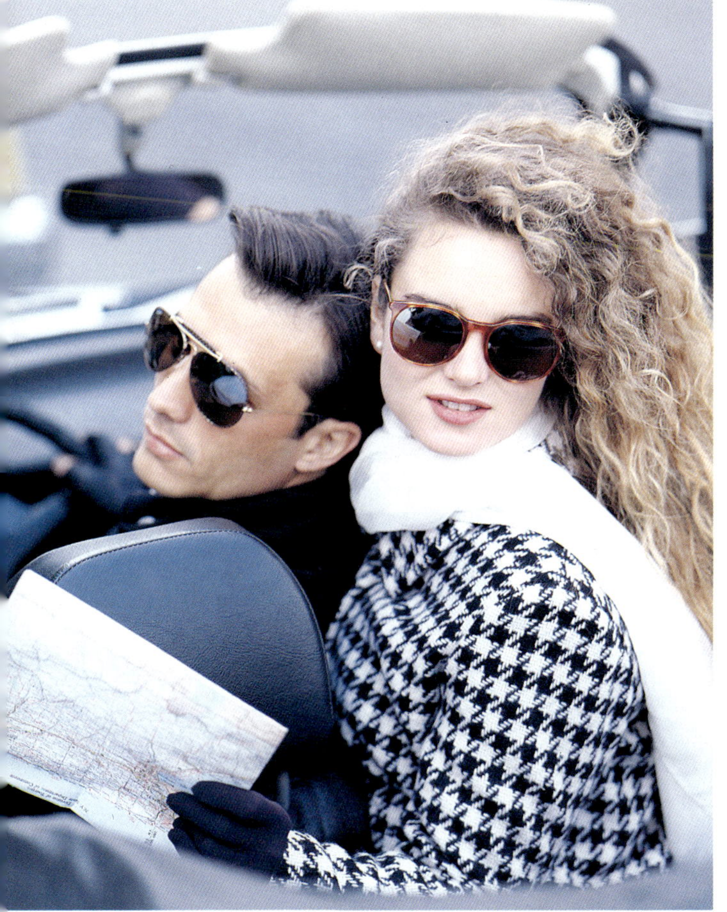

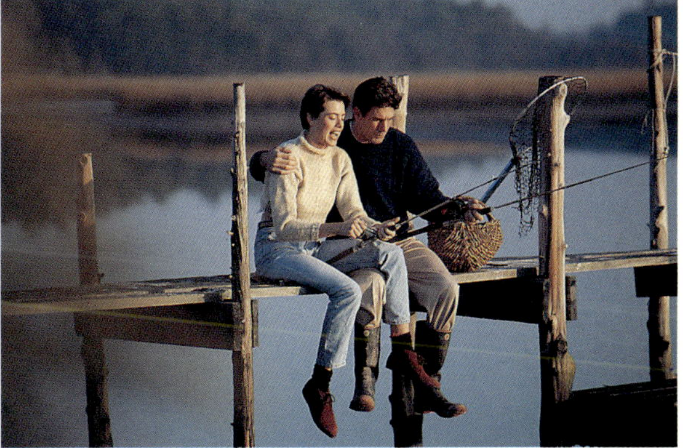

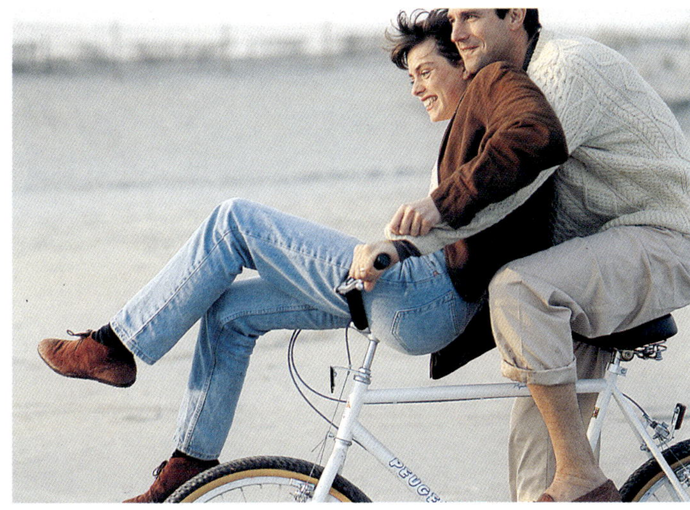

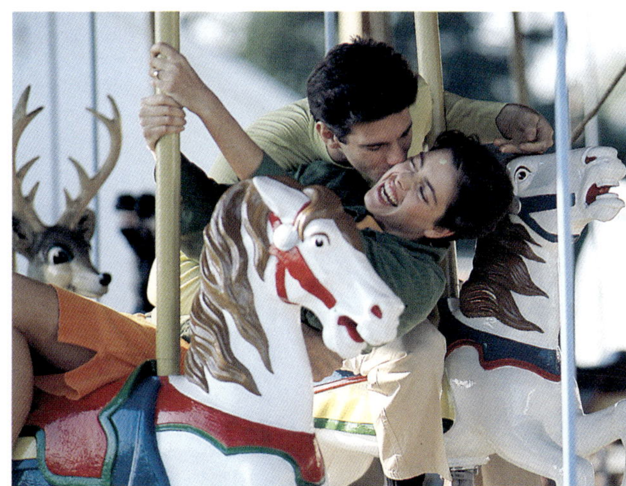

ARIEL SKELLEY

80 VARICK ST. 8F
NYC 10013
226-4091

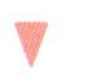

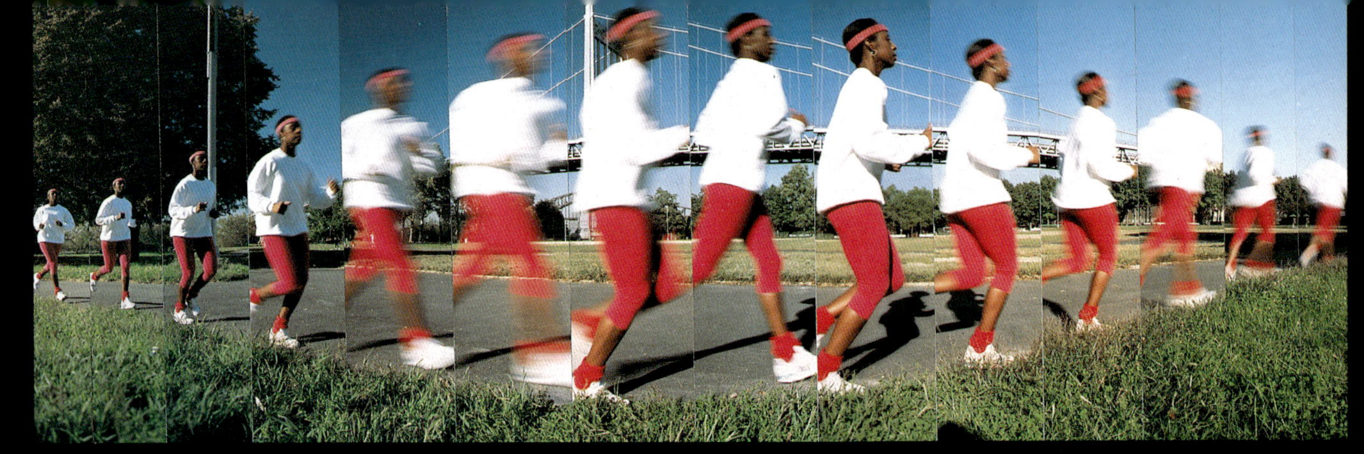

DAVID McGLYNN

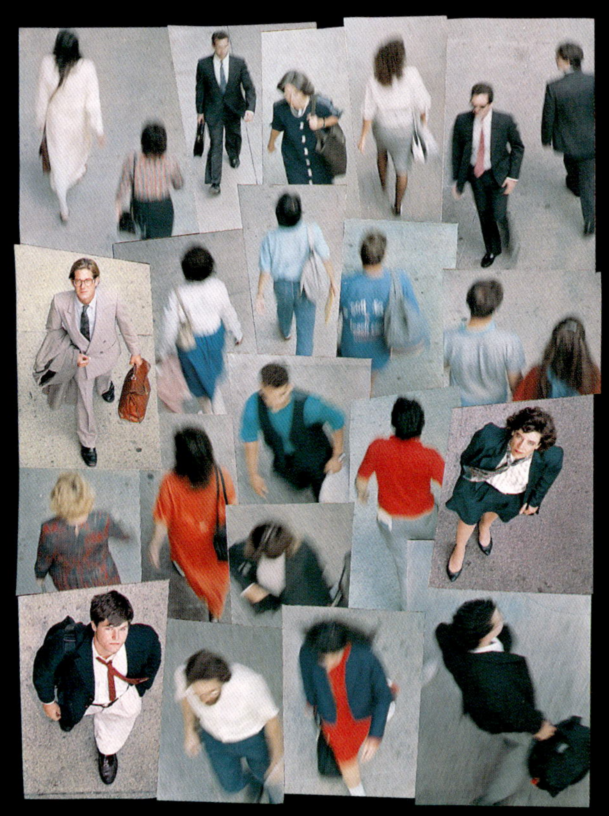

718.626.9427

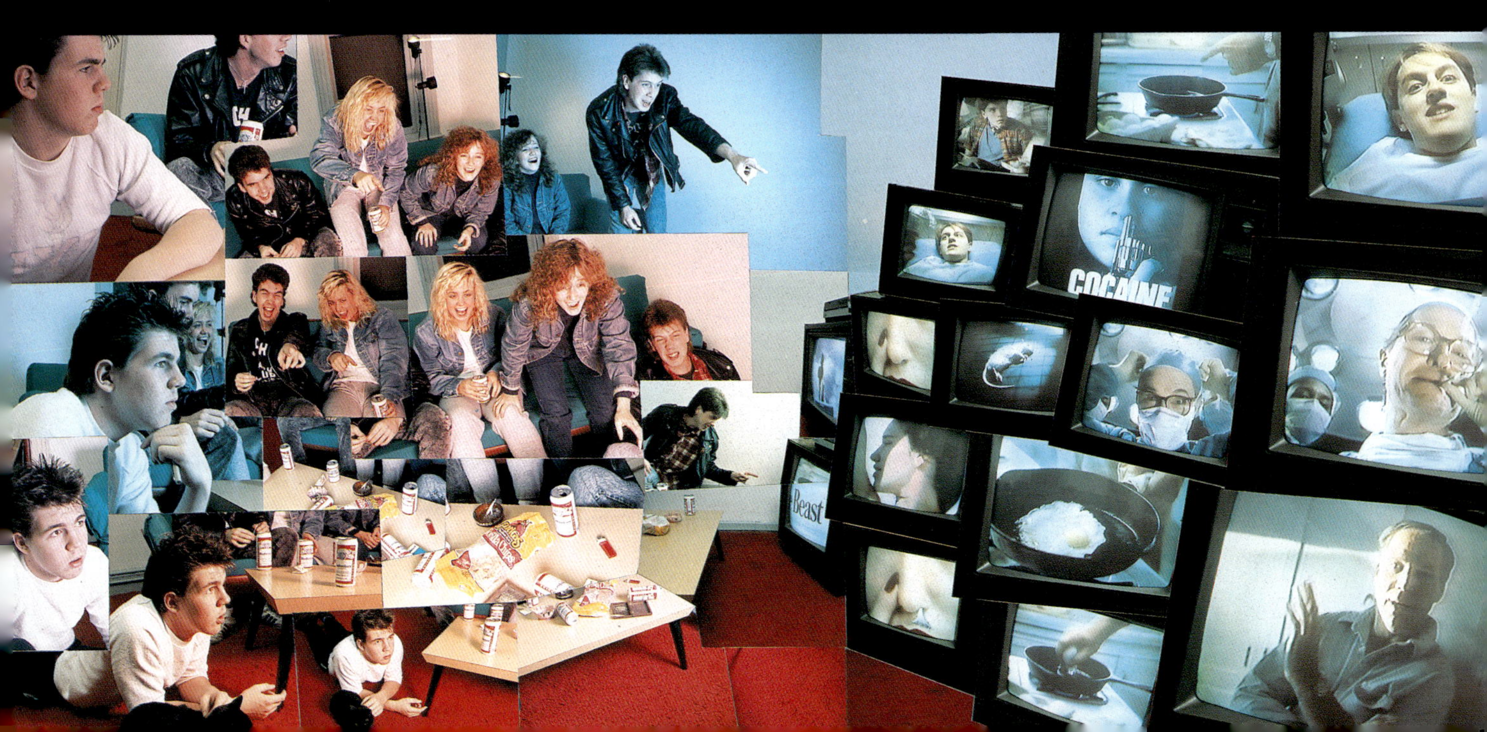

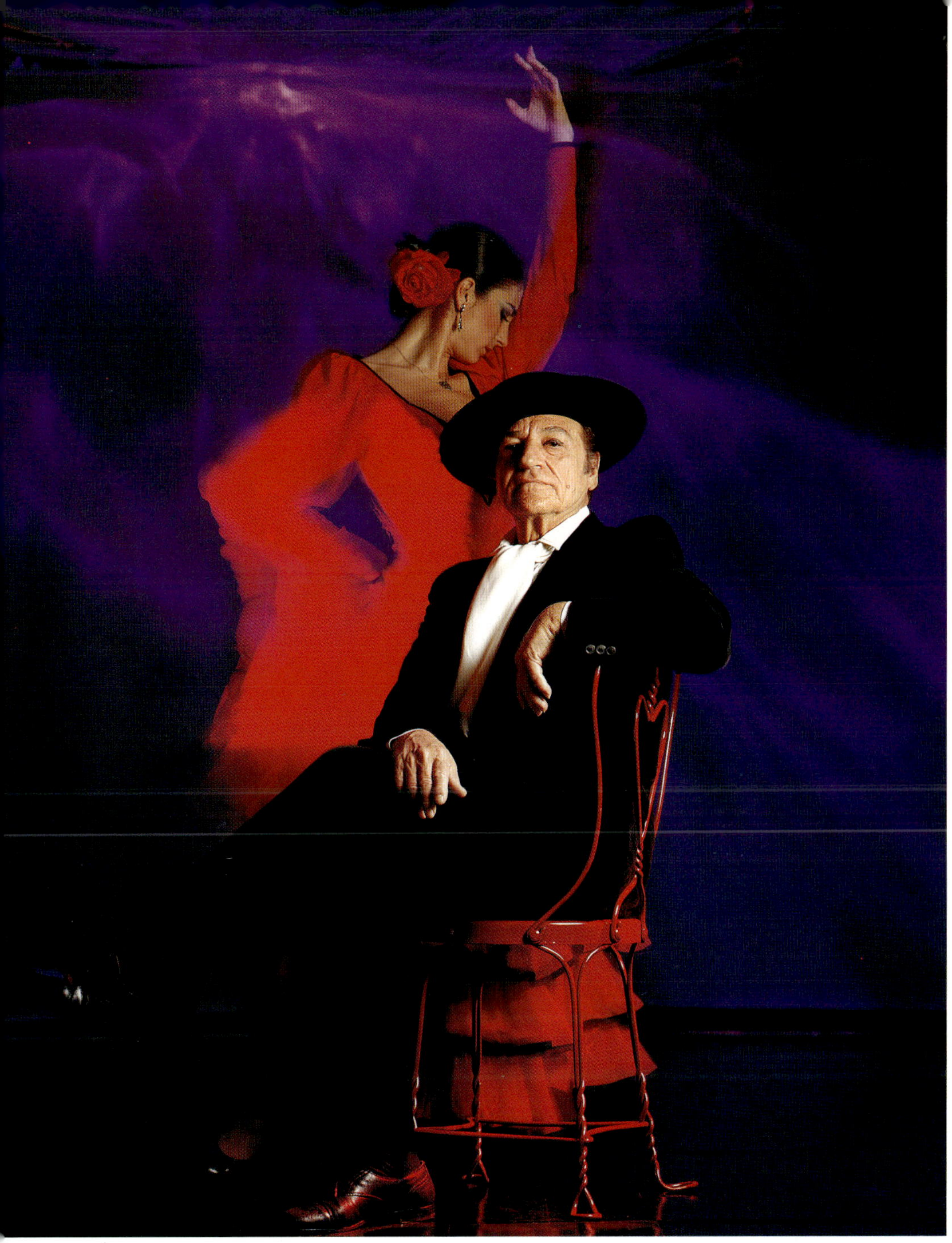

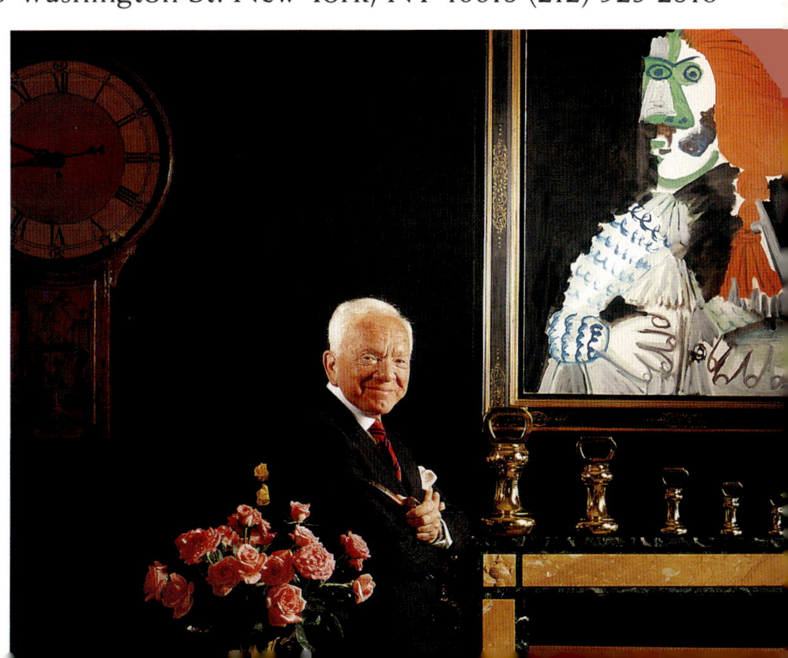

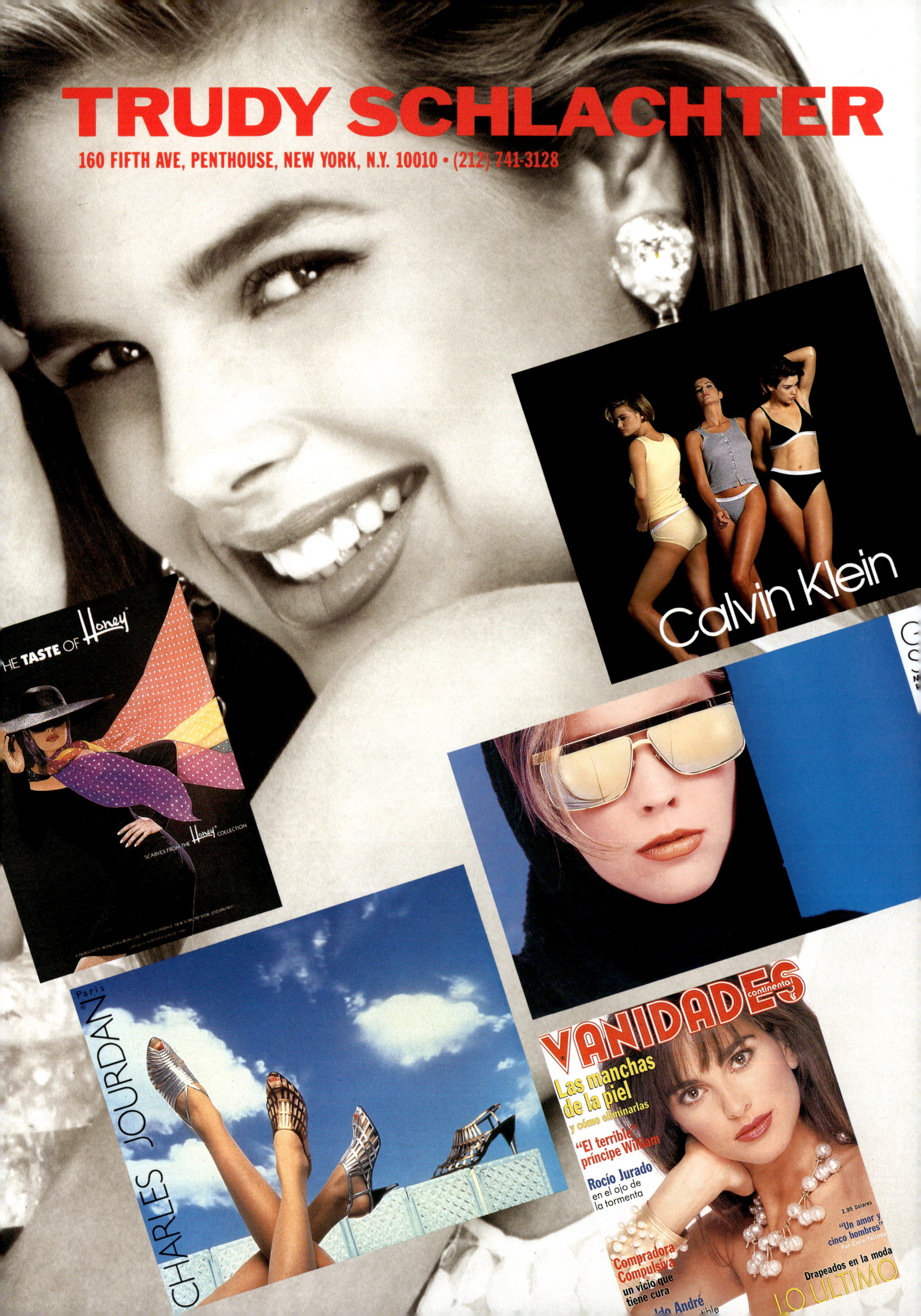
TRUDY SCHLACHTER
160 FIFTH AVE, PENTHOUSE, NEW YORK, N.Y. 10010 • (212) 741-3128
Calvin Klein
HE TASTE OF Honey
SCARVES FROM THE Honey COLLECTION
CHARLES JOURDAN Paris
VANIDADES continental
Las manchas de la piel
y cómo eliminarlas
"El terrible" príncipe William
Rocío Jurado
en el ojo de la tormenta
2.95 Dólares
"Un amor y cinco hombres"
Compradora Compulsiva
un vicio que tiene cura
Drapeados en la moda
LO ULTIMO

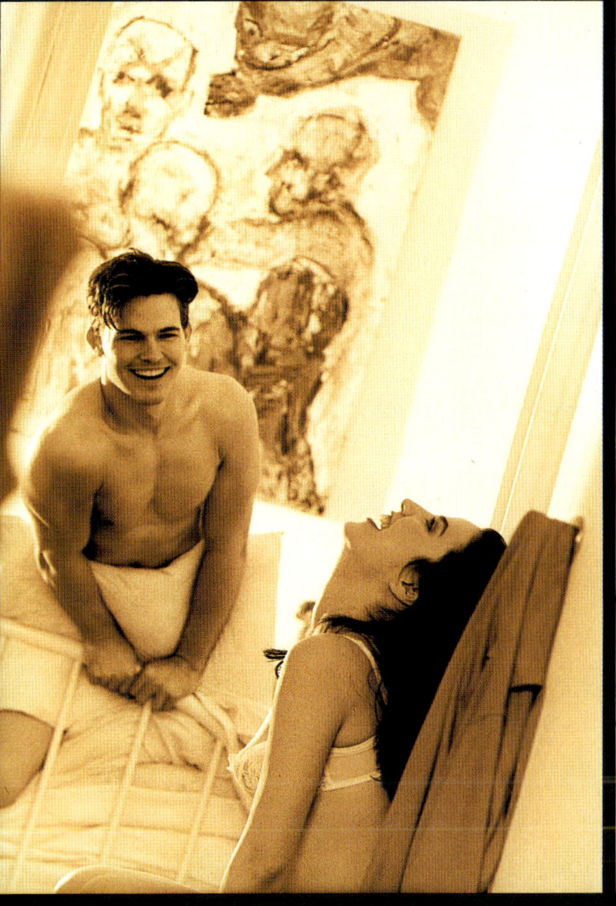

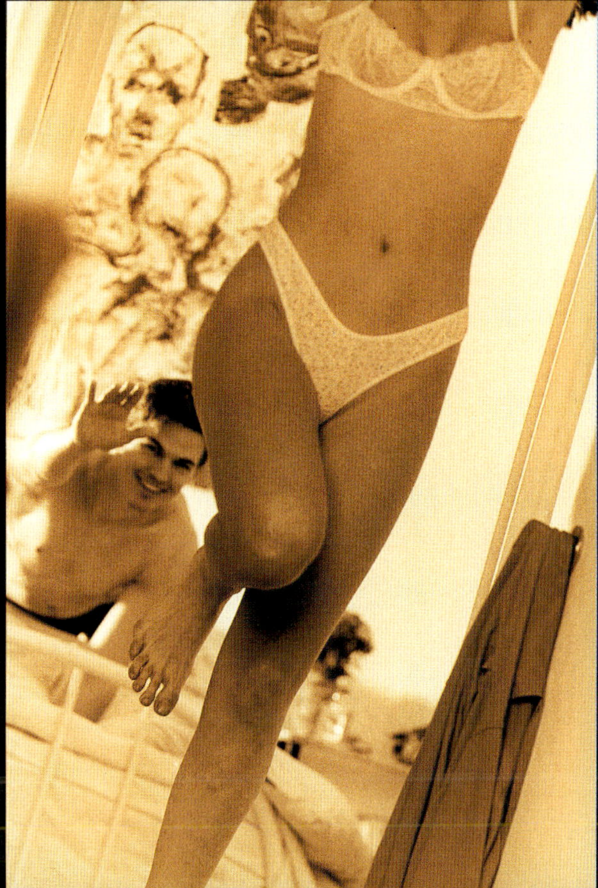

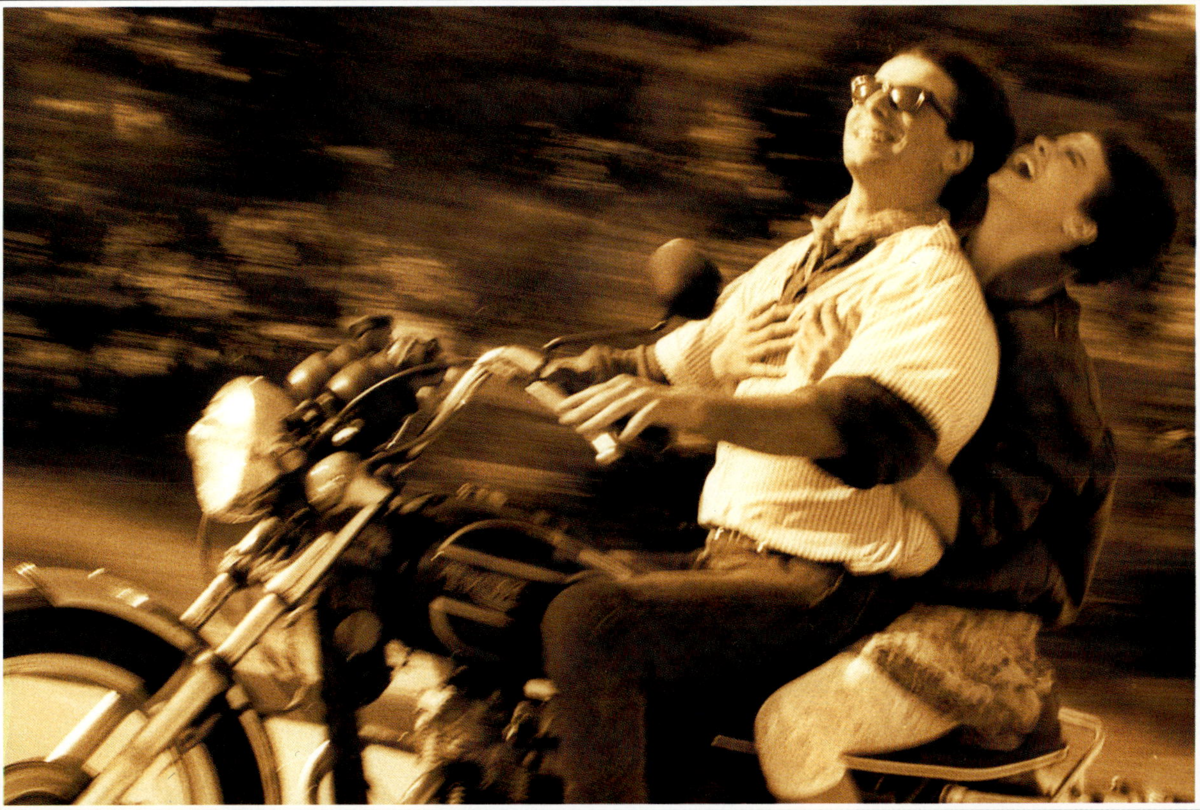

ROB GOLDMAN

212 557-1510

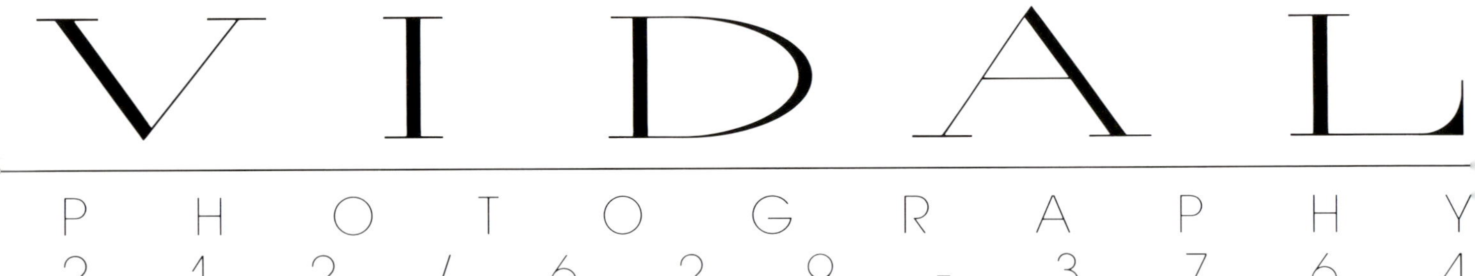

PHOTOGRAPHY
212/629-3764

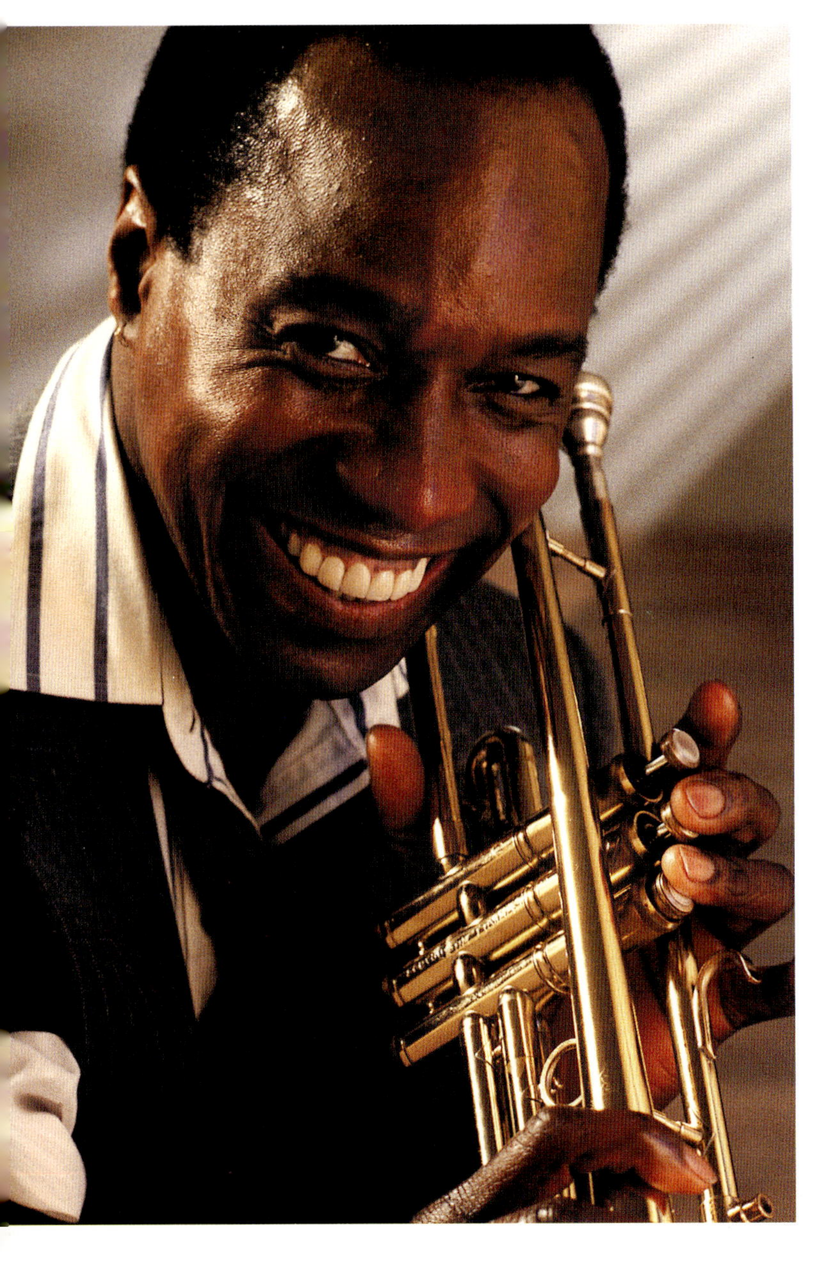

REEL AVAILABLE
FAX/629-3874

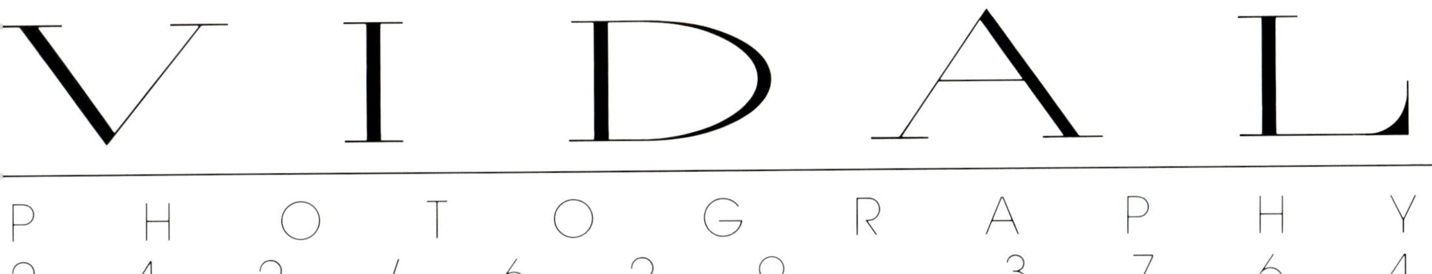

PHOTOGRAPHY
212/629-3764

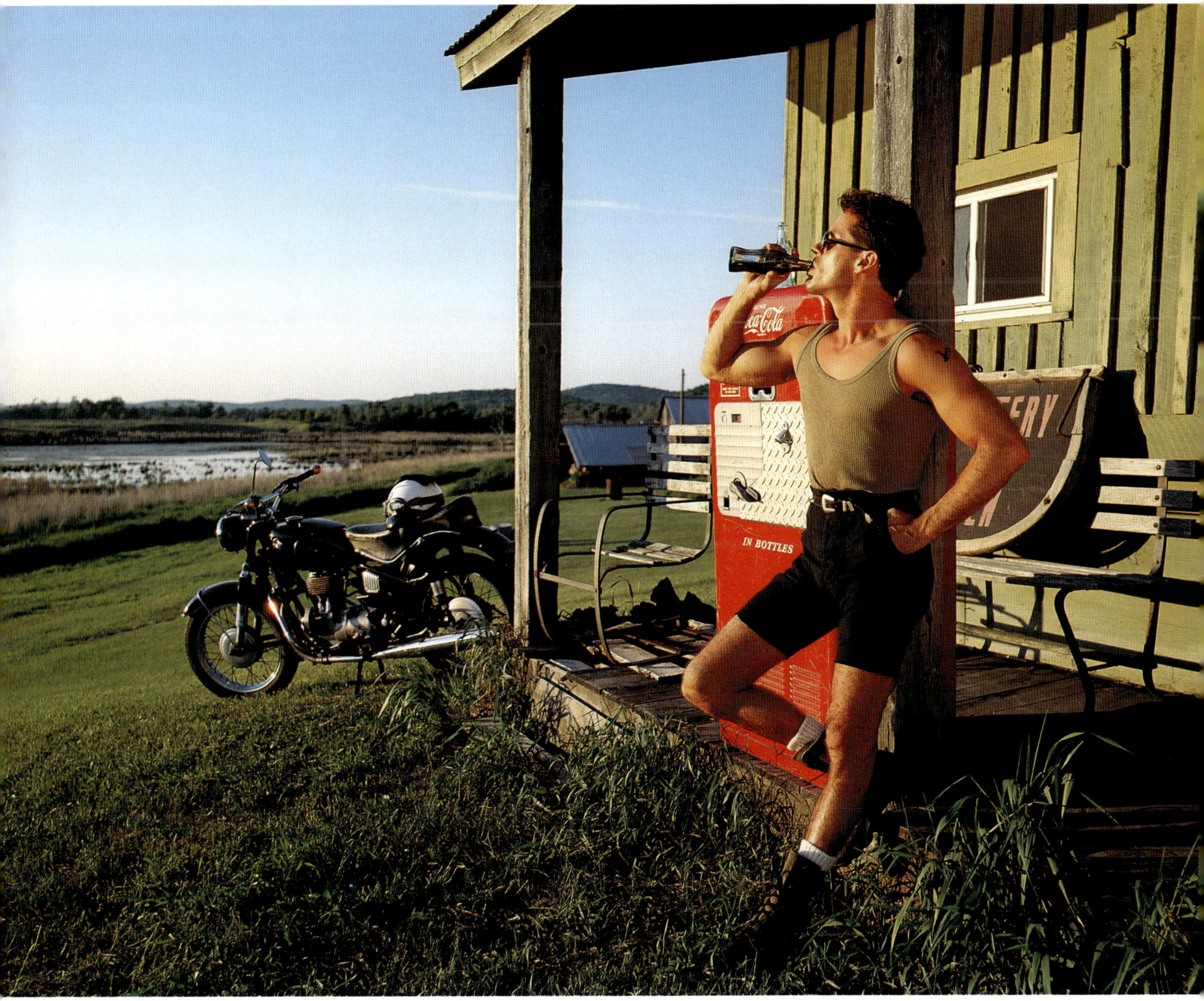

REEL AVAILABLE
FAX/629-3874

M c L o u

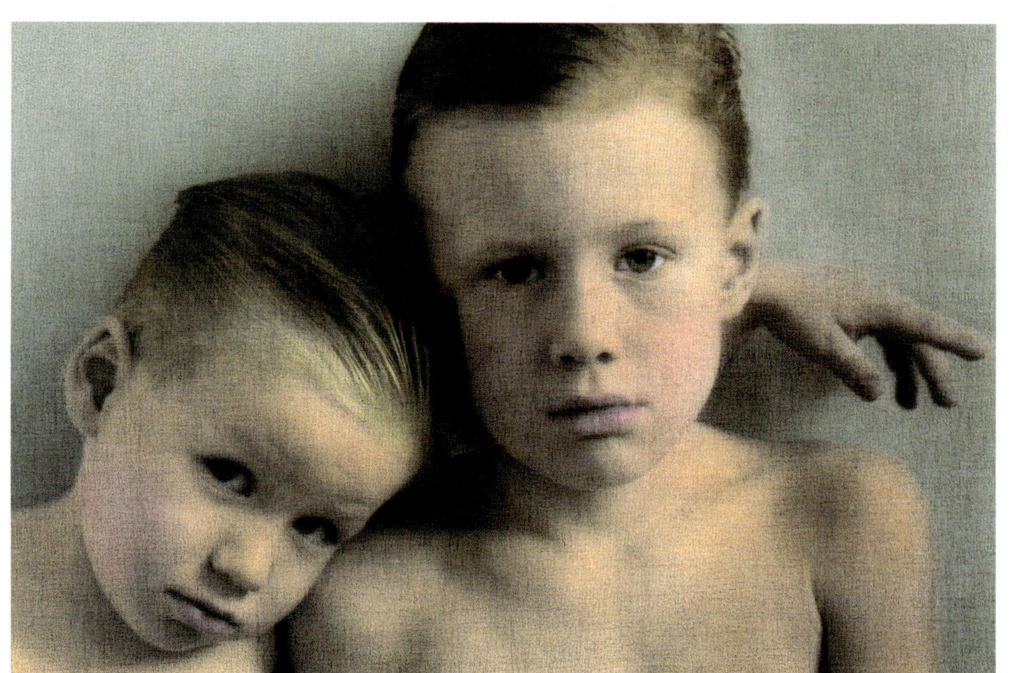

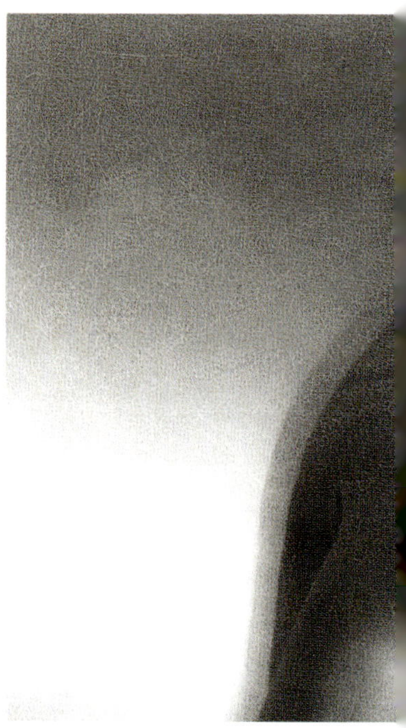

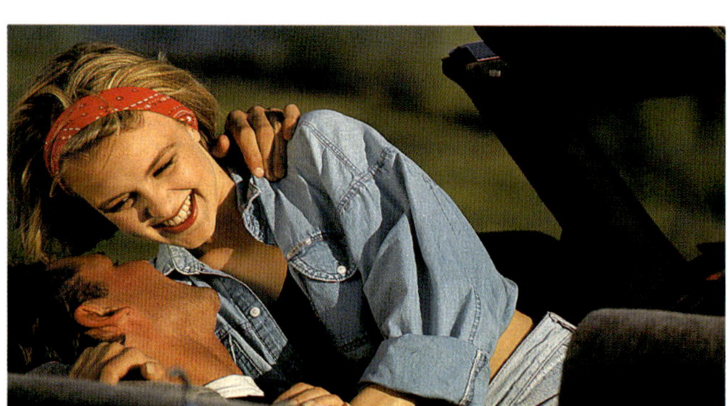

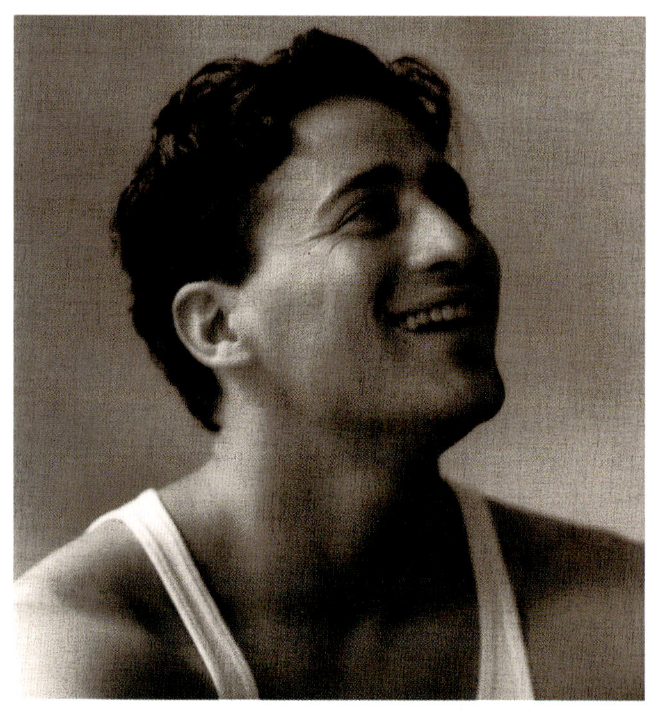

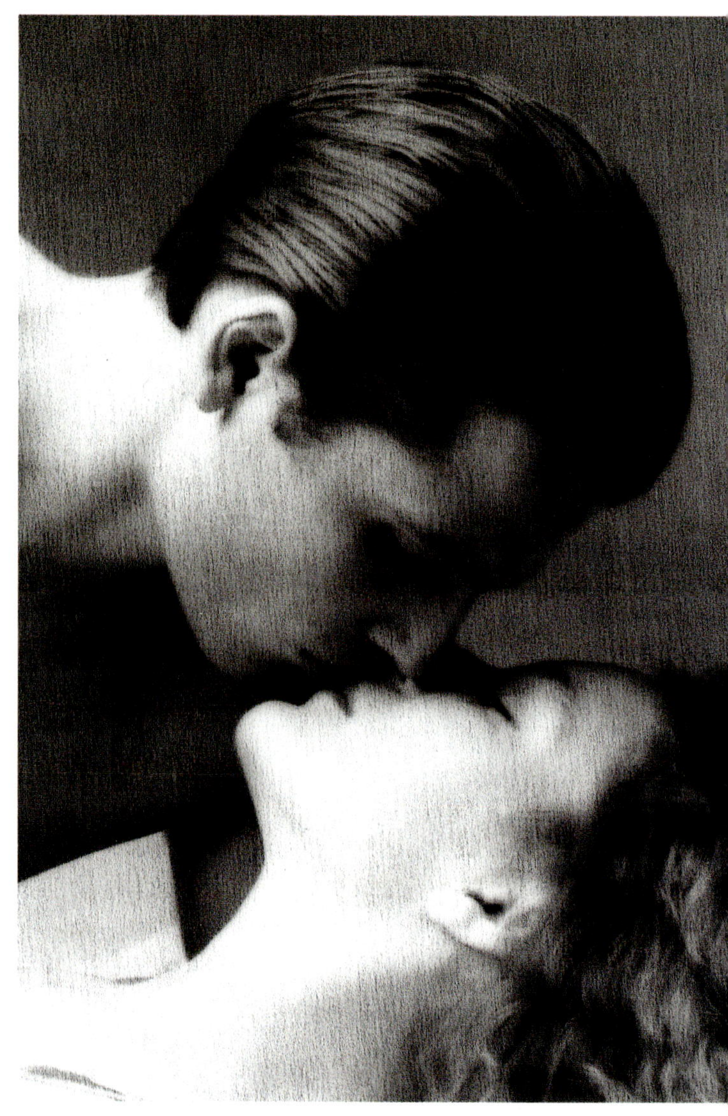

Additional work: • Creative Black Book • Workbook • Select Magazine • Single Imag

g h l i n

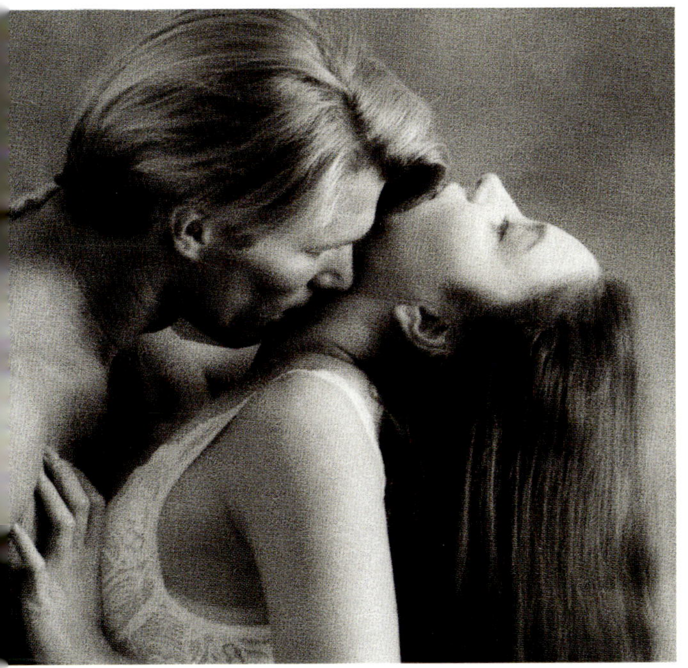

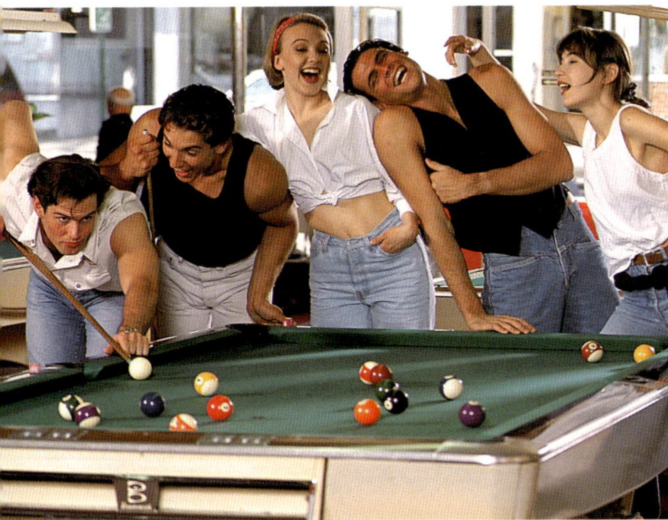

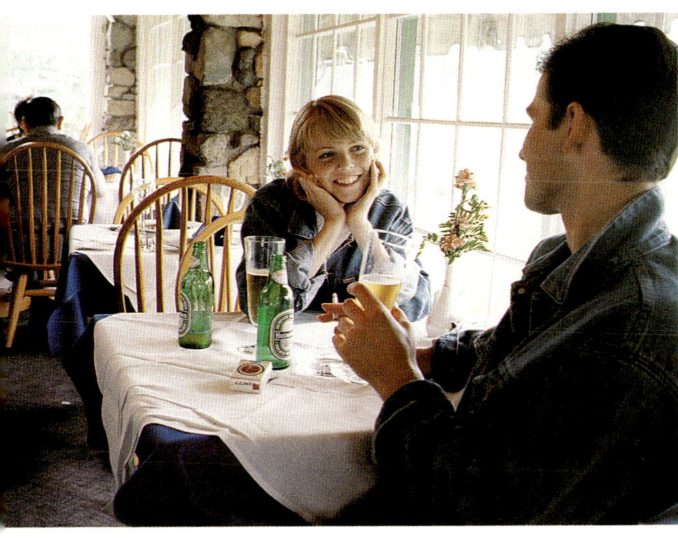

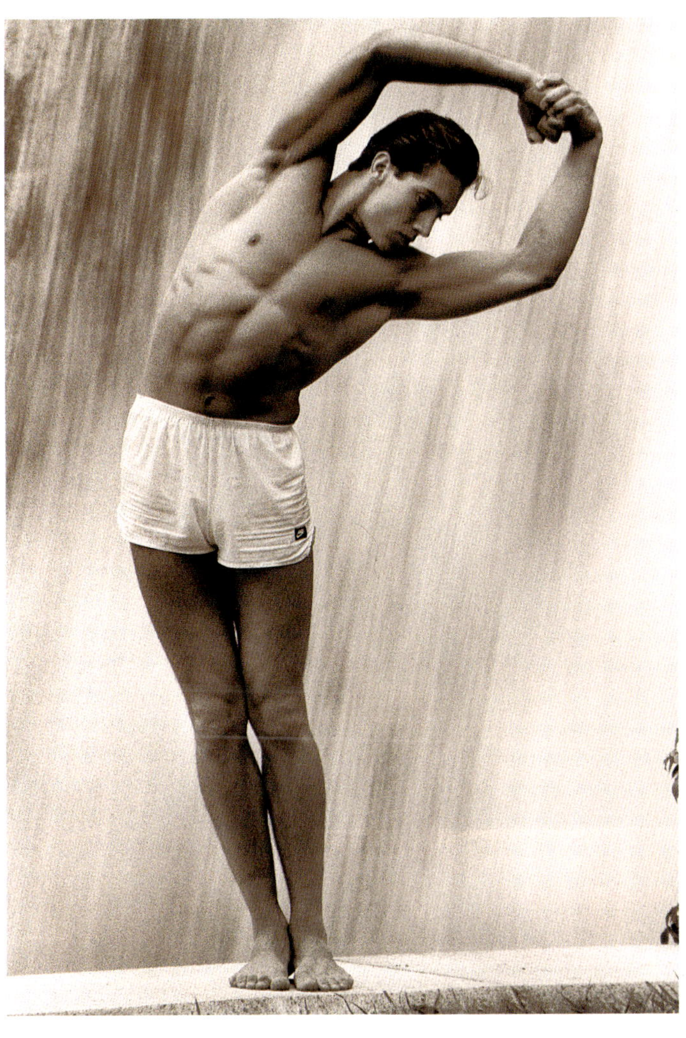

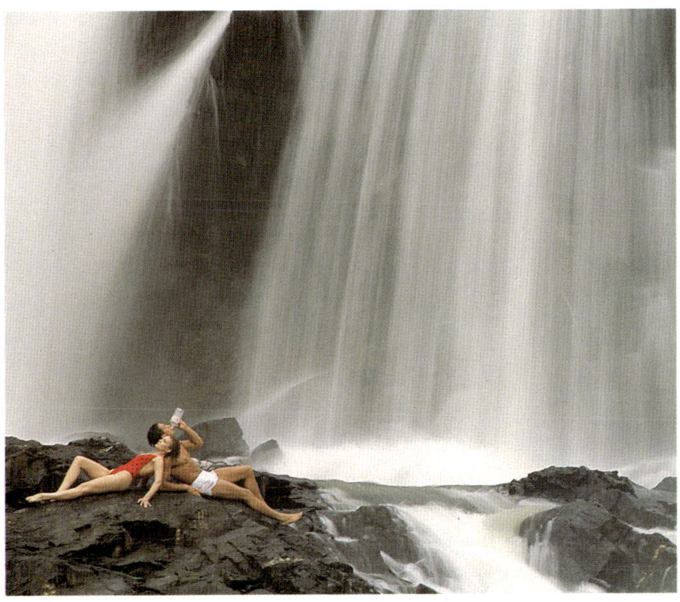

James McLoughlin Photography

New York City

Tel. 212.206.8207 Fax 212.206.9339

Peter Gregoire

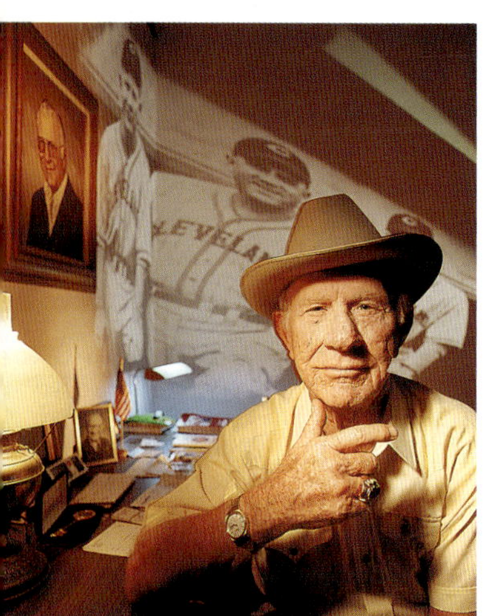

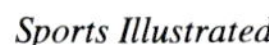

Sports Illustrated

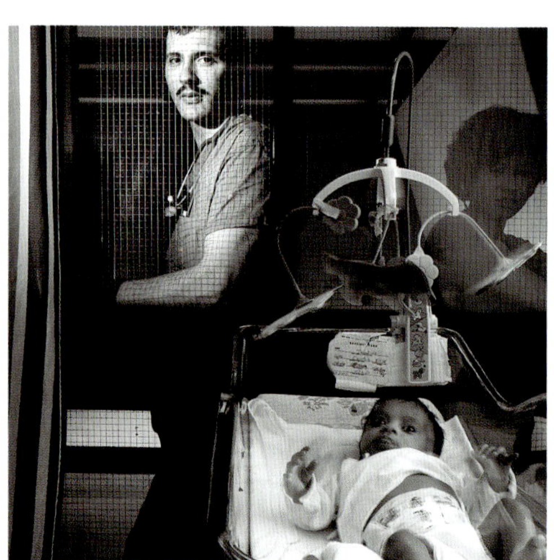

N.Y.C.H.H. Corporation

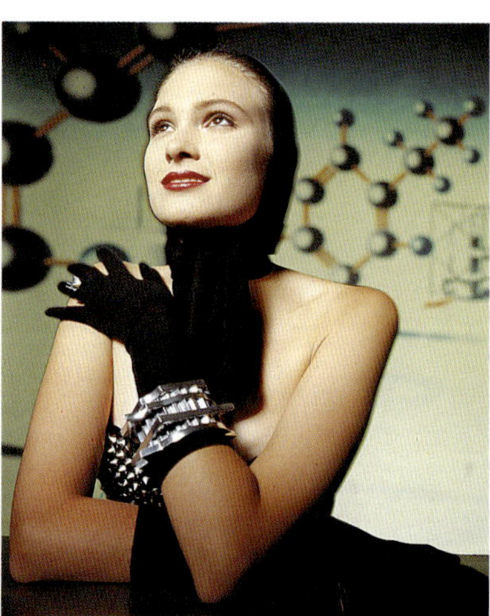

My Science Project

448 West

37 Street

12C

New York

NY 10018

212 967 4969

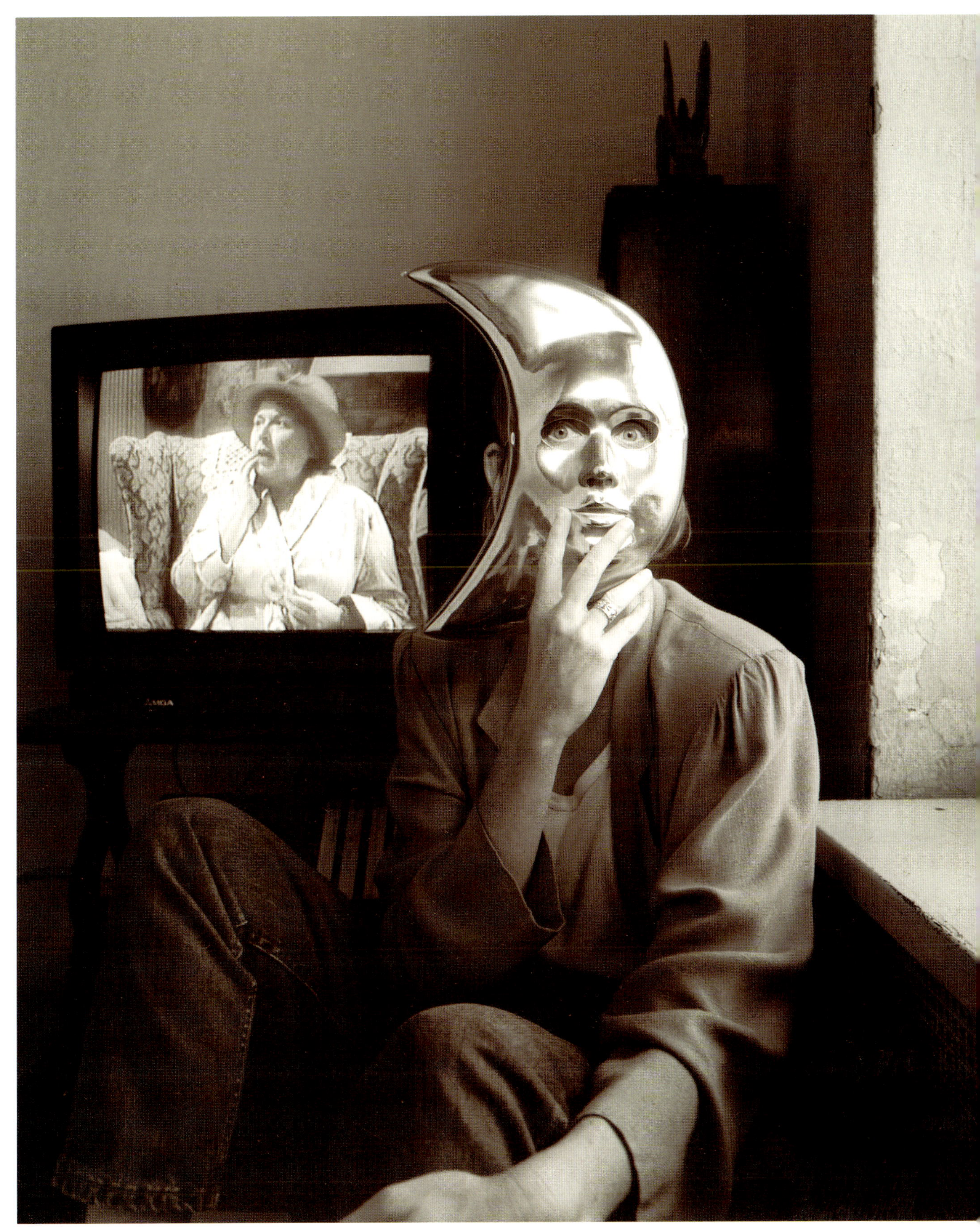

Tina Howe, Playwright

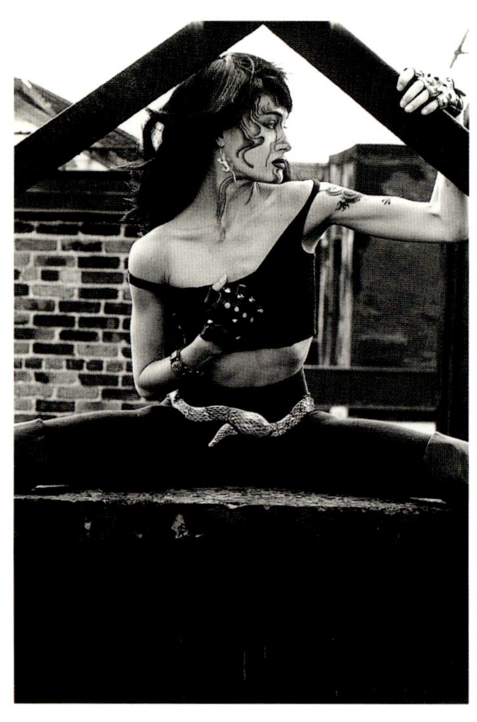

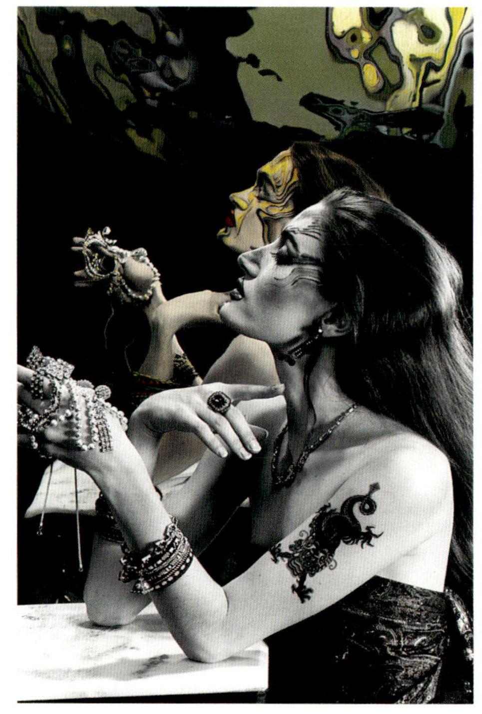

BARBARA E. LEVEN

PHOTOGRAPHER

48 WEST 21ST ST.

12TH FL., NEW YORK

NEW YORK 10010

TEL. (212) 645-4828

FAX (212) 675-1259

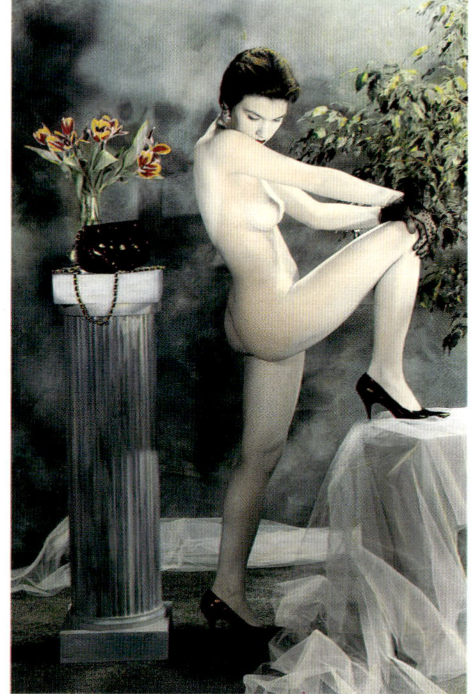

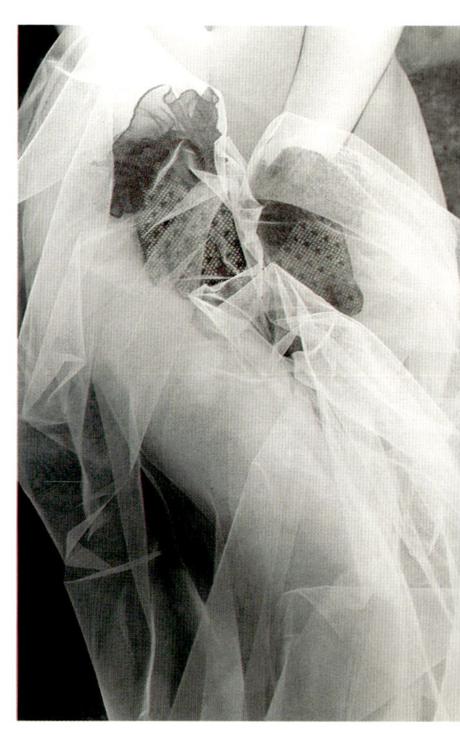

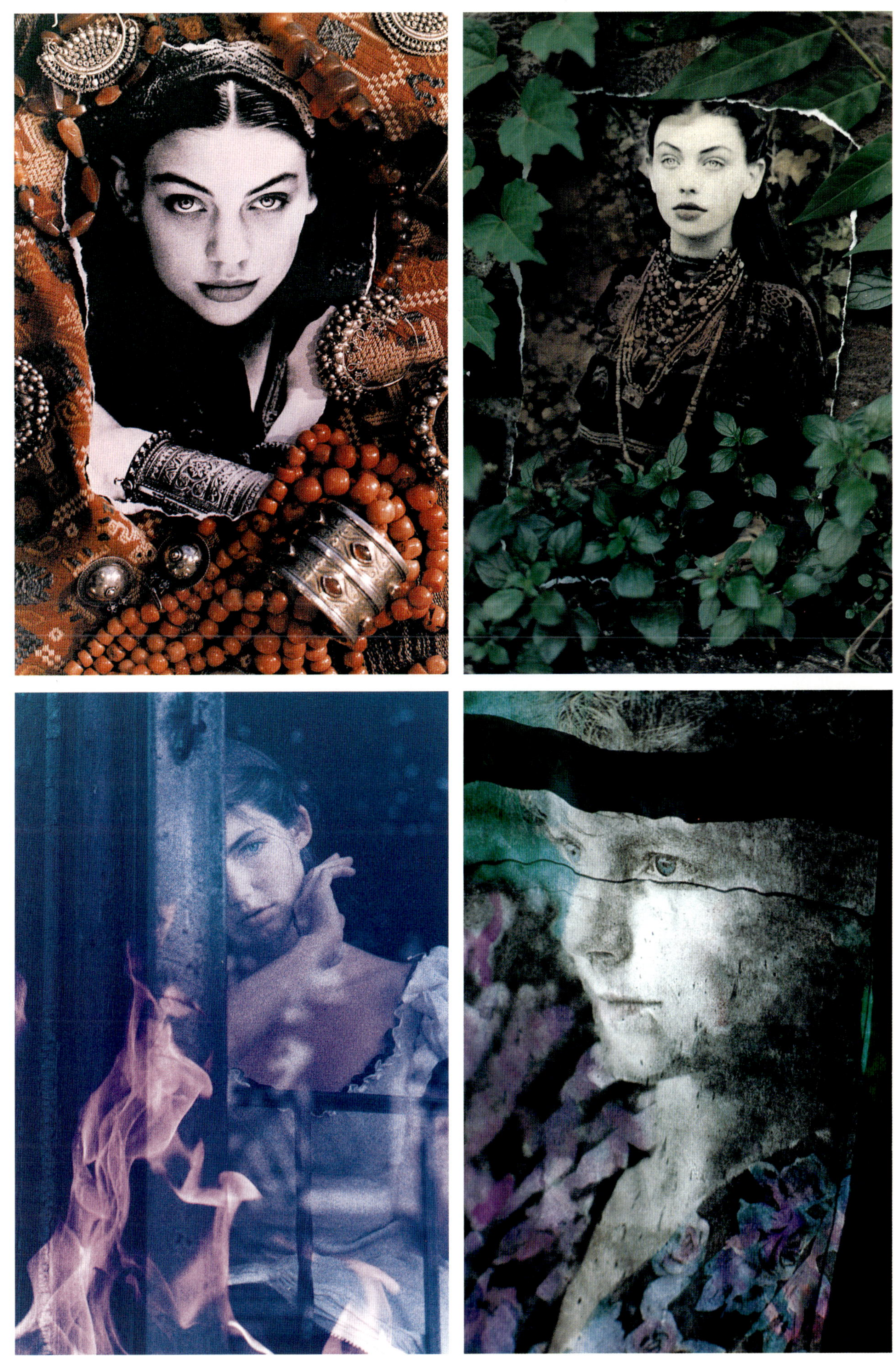

NICHOLAS ROZSA [212] 734 · 5629

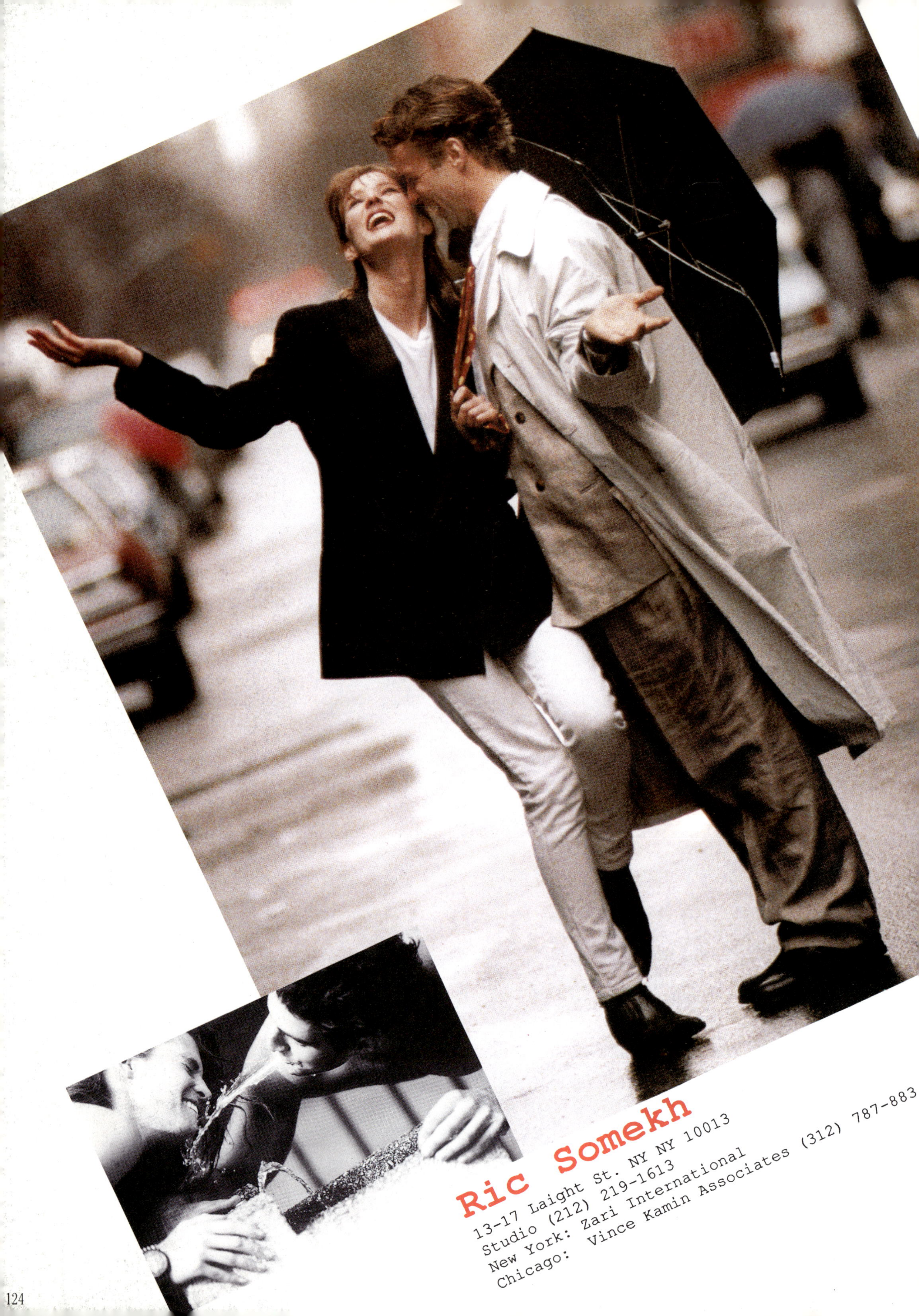

Ric Somekh

13-17 Laight St. NY NY 10013
Studio (212) 219-1613
New York: Zari International
Chicago: Vince Kamin Associates (312) 787-883